D1756130

Social Innovation

Social Innovation

Blurring Boundaries to Reconfigure Markets

Edited by

Alex Nicholls

and

Alex Murdock

First published 2012 by
PALGRAVE MACMILLAN

Palgrave Macmillan in the UK is an imprint of Macmillan Publishers Limited, registered in England, company number 785998, of Houndmills, Basingstoke, Hampshire RG21 6XS.

Palgrave Macmillan in the US is a division of St Martin's Press LLC, 175 Fifth Avenue, New York, NY 10010.

Palgrave Macmillan is the global academic imprint of the above companies and has companies and representatives throughout the world.

Palgrave® and Macmillan® are registered trademarks in the United States, the United Kingdom, Europe and other countries.

ISBN 978–0–230–28017–5

This book is printed on paper suitable for recycling and made from fully managed and sustained forest sources. Logging, pulping and manufacturing processes are expected to conform to the environmental regulations of the country of origin.

A catalogue record for this book is available from the British Library.
A catalog record for this book is available from the Library of Congress.

10   9   8   7   6   5   4   3   2   1
21   20   19   18   17   16   15   14   13   12

Printed and bound in Great Britain by
CPI Antony Rowe, Chippenham and Eastbourne

For J.R.N with love

Contents

List of Tables and Figures

Tables

Figures

Preface

We should like to acknowledge and thank all those who helped in the development and production of this collection. First, our thanks go to the staff of the Skoll Centre, University of Oxford – particularly Pippa Hichens – who were instrumental in organizing the first International Social Innovation Conference that provided many of the papers published here. We also thank the editorial and commissioning team at Palgrave Macmillan for their support and patience in the assembling of this book. A special mention here goes to Virginia Thorp. The production and copy editing team also deserve our gratitude for their professionalism and attention to detail. We also thank and acknowledge all those who offered contributions to this book. Unfortunately it was not possible to include all the submissions received.

This book is dedicated to the memory of Professor Anthony Hopwood.

About the Editors

Alex Murdock is Professor of Not for Profit Management and Leadership and Head of Centre for Government and Charity Management at London South Bank University. The Centre is part of the Social Enterprise Cluster of the Third Sector Research Centre (funded by the Economic and Social Research Council, UK). His research focused on the intersection of the public, private, and third sectors. He is on the Editorial Board of the *Social Enterprise Journal* and has published in the areas of public management and social enterprise. He is actively involved in charities and social enterprises as a trustee and board member. He has worked at The University of Paris (Sorbonne), Copenhagen Business School, and Brunel University and is a Visiting Professor at two Norwegian Universities. He has degrees from the University of London, University of Maryland (USA), and London Business School. Murdock qualified as a Probation Officer at the University of Newcastle and previously worked in Social Work.

Alex Nicholls is the first tenured lecturer in social entrepreneurship appointed at the University of Oxford. He has published more than forty papers in a wide range of peer-reviewed journals and books, including five papers in Financial Times Top 30 journals. His 2009 paper on social investment won the Best Paper Award (Entrepreneurship) at the British Academy of Management. In 2010, Nicholls edited a Special Edition of *Entrepreneurship, Theory and Practice* on social entrepreneurship – the first time a top-tier management journal had recognized the topic in this way. He is the General Editor of the Skoll Working Papers series and the Editor of the *Journal of Social Entrepreneurship*. Nicholls is also the co-author of a major research book on Fair Trade (with Charlotte Opal, Sage, 2005) and the editor of a collection of key papers on social entrepreneurship (Oxford University Press, 2008). Both represent the best selling and most cited academic books on their subjects globally. He has held lectureships at a wide variety of academic institutions including University of Toronto, Canada; Leeds Metropolitan University; University of Surrey; and Aston Business School.

About the Contributors

Randy M. Ataide is a Professor of Entrepreneurship and Executive Director of the Fermanian Business and Economic Institute at Point Loma Nazarene University in San Diego, CA. He provides primary leadership for the Institute's mission, is the Executive Editor of its publications, and speaks frequently on a variety of topics. He teaches the undergraduate and MBA entrepreneurship and negotiation courses, and was named one of San Diego's Top 50 Influentials for 2010. Peer-reviewed research has been presented at many conferences and conventions and/or published in various academic journals or conference proceedings. Ataide holds a B.A. degree in Speech Communication (*Magna Cum Laude*), a M.A. in Theology, and a J.D.

Heather Cameron is an Assistant Professor of Education at the Freie Universität Berlin and an Associate Professor Extraordinarius at the University of the Western Cape in South Africa. She did her M.A. and her Ph.D. in Social and Political Thought at the York University in Vancouver, Canada. Cameron was post-doctoral fellow at the Centre for Technology and Society of the TU Berlin and a guest professor at the School of Communications of the Simon Fraser University in Vancouver. In 2010 she became an Ashoka Fellow with her international girls' empowerment NGO Boxgirls.

Benedetto Cannatelli is a Ph.D. student in Management at the Università Cattolica del Sacro Cuore in Milan, Italy. He is also actively involved as researcher at ALTIS, the Postgraduate School of Business and Society at the same University. His main research interests are Social Entrepreneurship and Small Business Management. In 2009 he was visiting scholar at the Lester Center for Entrepreneurship and Innovation at HAAS School of Business, UC Berkeley. In 2010 he was international visiting scholar at the Center for Social Entrepreneurship at Farmer School of Business, Miami University.

Victor Galaz, Ph.D., is a researcher and a research theme leader at the Stockholm Resilience Centre (Stockholm University). His current research and teaching focuses on adaptive governance and global governance of complex environmental risks such as pandemics and planetary boundaries.

Kai Hockerts is an Associate Professor at the Copenhagen Business School (CBS) where he coordinates the Minor in Social Entrepreneurship. His research has been published in the *Journal of Business Venturing*, the *International Review of Entrepreneurship*, the *Journal of Business Ethics, Business Strategy and the Environment*, and *Greener Management International*. He has also written a number of award-winning case studies. Hockerts was a co-convener of the International Social Entrepreneurship Research (ISERC) Conference series held in Barcelona in 2005, in New York in 2006, in Copenhagen in 2007. From 1991 to 1997 he was co-founder and Managing Director of a non-profit start-up, the Bayreuther Initiative für Wirtschaftsökologie. Hockerts holds a Ph.D. from the University of St. Gallen (CH).

Carin Holroyd is an Associate Professor of Political Science and a member of Social Innovation Generation in the School of Environment, Enterprise and Development at the University of Waterloo. She works on government policy and social innovation, the promotion of environmental innovation, and national innovation policies in Asia. She is the author of *Government, International Trade and Laissez-Faire Capitalism: Canada, Australia and New Zealand's Relations with Japan* and co-author of two books on science and technology in Japan.

Janelle A. Kerlin is an Assistant Professor in the Department of Public Management and Policy at Georgia State University where she conducts research on non-profit development and operation often from an international perspective. Her present interests include social enterprise and international nonprofits. Kerlin has published articles in the *Nonprofit and Voluntary Sector Quarterly, Voluntas, Nonprofit Management and Leadership*, and the *American Review of Public Administration* and authored several book chapters. She edited the book, *Social Enterprise: A Global Comparison* and authored, *Social Service Reform in the Postcommunist State*. She holds an M.Sc. from Columbia University and a Ph.D. in political science from Syracuse University.

Fergus Lyon is a Professor of Enterprise and Organisations in the Centre for Enterprise and Economic Development Research, Middlesex University, UK. His research interests include social and community enterprises, provision of public services by social enterprises, collaboration and trust amongst enterprises, and enterprise support policy. He is the Associate Director (Social enterprise) of the Third Sector Research Centre funded over five years by Economic and Social Research Council and Office for Civil Society. Previously he has carried out research in

Ghana, Nigeria, India, Pakistan, and Nepal. He is also a founder and director of a social enterprise preschool.

Michel Marée is senior researcher at the Centre for Social Economy (HEC – Management School of the University of Liège) where he conducts statistical work on social enterprises and where he studies the performance of social enterprises. He holds a master's degree in Economics (University of Liège) and a master's degree in Public Economics (University of Paris I – Panthéon – Sorbonne).

Antonio G. Masi is a research fellow – mainly interested in social entrepreneurship implementation in developing countries – in ALTIS (Postgraduate School Business & Society) at the Università Cattolica del Sacro Cuore of Milan, where he has recently gained a Ph.D. in Management. He received *cum laude*, from the University of Bari (Italy), a master's degree in Economics in 2002, and a master's degree in Business Administration in 2006. He has been an official from the Italian Ministry of Welfare since 2006, after working as an inspector of the Italian Revenue Guard Corps from 1997 to 2006.

Sybille Mertens is an Associate Professor at HEC – Management School of the University of Liège. She is the holder of the Cera Chair in Social Entrepreneurship and is a member of the Research Centre for Social Economy. Within this research centre, she carries out research activities in the domains of social entrepreneurship, management of social enterprises, educating social entrepreneurs, and evaluation of social enterprises. She holds a Ph.D. in Economics from the University of Liège.

Mario Molteni is full Professor of Business Administration and Corporate Strategy at the Università Cattolica del Sacro Cuore of Milan. He is Founder and Director of ALTIS, the Postgraduate School of Business & Society at the same university, an international research and education institute for the study of entrepreneurship and corporate sustainability. He is founder of Borsa Progetti Sociali (Social Projects Exchange), a non-profit organization created to develop partnerships between profit and non-profit sectors. He is the author of numerous books and scientific articles on corporate strategy, entrepreneurship, corporate social responsibility, and social entrepreneurship.

Michele-Lee Moore is a Ph.D. candidate in Global Governance in a joint program between Wilfrid Laurier University and the University of Waterloo in Canada. She currently holds a McConnell Fellowship with SiG@Waterloo where her research has primarily focused on the role of networks in enabling social innovation, the cross-scale interactions between global and local governance, and national public policy efforts aimed at fostering social innovation and improving socio-ecological resilience. Previously, Moore served as a water strategy advisor for the British Columbia Ministry of Environment.

Geoff Mulgan is the Chief Executive of NESTA, the UK's National Endowment for Science, Technology and the Arts. From 2005 to 2011 he was the Director of the Young Foundation, a leading centre for social innovation, combining research, venture funds, local projects, and a global network. Prior to this, Mulgan had various roles in the UK government including Director of the Government's Strategy Unit, Head of Policy in the Prime Minister's Office, and Director of the Performance and Innovation Unit. He was also a Founder and Director of the think-tank Demos. Mulgan is a Visiting Professor at London School of Economics, University College London, and Melbourne University, China Executive Leadership Academy and a Visiting Fellow at the Australia–New Zealand School of Government and the UK National School of Government. Mulgan has published five books, many newspaper articles and opinion pieces, and numerous pamphlets including two on innovation with the Center for American Progress and one on social innovation for the President of the European Commission.

Per Olsson, Ph.D., is a researcher and a research theme leader at the Stockholm Resilience Centre (Stockholm University). His primary research interest is in linked socio-ecological system dynamics and resilience and he uses a complexity perspective on social change and innovation. His current research and teaching focuses on sustainability transformations and shifts towards more flexible and integrated approaches for governing and managing natural resources and ecosystem services.

David Robinson is Chair of the Department of Economics, and Director of the Institute for Northern Ontario Research and Development at Laurentian University. A leading expert on Northern Ontario economic development, he has had significant impact on regional policy. He is currently studying linkages between arts communities and the value-added sector in Boreal Shield towns and cities. He teaches game theory and Regional Economics. Recent publications include a book on 2x2 games and several papers analysing issues in the Northern Ontario economic development.

Kirsten Robinson began in philosophy at Laurentian before transferring to Systems Design Engineering at the University of Waterloo. She has since worked on creating ethanol from waste cellulose, reducing pain from pressure on neurofibromas, and on building underwater robots, adjustable high-heeled shoes, operating systems for Blackberries, and energy models. She is interested in policy and technology. Her current research, designing distributed mechanisms for responsive architectural membranes, uses evolutionary and agent-based models that mirror those used to understand systems ranging from cells to societies. Robinson is interested in the role of agent-based systems, social change, and complexity in stopping species loss and supporting the development of caring communities.

Ola Tjörnbo is a Ph.D. student in Global Governance at the Balsillie School of International Affairs and Wilfrid Laurier University. He is also a Balsillie fellow and a McConnell fellow. Tjörnbo's research is focused on the role of social media in governing complex problems. In particular, his Ph.D. thesis looks at the importance of virtual social networks as sites of problem solving and governance. His other research interests include focusing on the dynamics of power and agency in complex systems transformations.

Frances R. Westley is the JW McConnell Chair in Social Innovation at the University of Waterloo and leads the Waterloo Institute for Social Innovation and Resilience. In this capacity, she is one of the principle leads in a Canada wide initiative in social innovation, SiG (Social Innovation Generation), a cross-sectoral partnership to build capacity for social innovation in Canada funded by the JW McConnell Family Foundation, University of Waterloo, and the Ontario government. Frances leads a research team dedicated to understanding social innovation, and has designed both graduate and undergraduate curricula in social innovation. Previously held positions include: Director, Nelson Institute for Environmental Studies (2005–2007) at the University of Wisconsin, Madison, James McGill Professor of Strategy at McGill University's Faculty of Management, Director of the McGill-Dupont Initiative on Social Innovation, and Director of the McGill-McConnell Masters program for National Voluntary Sector leaders – an innovative executive masters customized for the leaders of voluntary organizations across Canada.

Rolf Wüstenhagen holds the Good Energies Chair for the Management of Renewable Energies at the University of St. Gallen and is a Director of the Institute for Economy and the Environment (IWÖ-HSG). With a background in Management Science and Engineering (TU Berlin) and a

Ph.D. in Business, he finished his post-doctoral research thesis in 2007 on Venturing for Sustainable Energy. In 2005 and 2008, respectively, Wüstenhagen was a Visiting Professor at University of British Columbia, Vancouver, and Copenhagen Business School. His research focuses on decision-making under uncertainty by energy investors, consumers, and entrepreneurs, and has been published in leading entrepreneurship, energy policy, and environmental management journals.

The Nature of Social Innovation

Alex Nicholls and Alex Murdock

> *O, wonder!*
> *How many goodly creatures are there here!*
> *How beauteous mankind is! O brave new world,*
> *That has such people in't!*
> (*The Tempest*: Act V, Scene 1)

Catch a wave and you're sitting on top of the world[1]

Historical analyses of macro-level innovation across the developed economies often identify a series of waves of technological change, typically starting with the Industrial Revolution in the eighteenth century (Kondratiev, 1998; Alexander, 2001; Moulaert, 2009). Each wave is usually presented as distinct from what came before, but also as sharing particular economic and social outcomes. Broadly speaking, five waves – or 'ages'[2] – of modern macro-innovation have been discerned, each associated with a disruptive technology in the Schumpeterian (1934) sense:

- The Industrial Revolution (1771–1829)
- The Age of Steam and Railways (1829–75)
- The Age of Steel, Electricity and Heavy Engineering (1875–1908)
- The Age of Oil, the Automobile and Mass Production (1908–71)
- The Age of Information and Telecommunications (1971–).

While such analyses can differ in some details, the majority share a set of critical analytic variables that are clustered around evidence of step-changes in the financial sector (especially wider credit availability and the growth of equity), productivity growth, urbanization,

1

mass-production, knowledge intensity and transfer, and per capita income growth. Much of this research has, therefore, identified *economic* factors (or, at least, political economy issues; e.g. Berry, 1991) and effects as of primary importance in explaining and defining such waves of innovation, acknowledging social or societal factors only as being subsidiary or external to the central drivers and rationales for wide-scale change.

However, despite challenges to these somewhat monological approaches to macro-level innovation (Hobsbawm, 1989, 1999), it is only fairly recently that work focussed specifically on *social* innovation has emerged. The drivers behind the appearance of such literature are various, but – as is discussed further below – such research gives analytic primacy, on the one hand, to systems and processes of change in social relations and, on the other, to innovation around the conceptualization, design, and production of goods and services that address social and environmental needs and market failures (e.g. Goldenburg et al., 2009).[3]

This book concerns itself with social innovation as a 'sixth wave' of macro-level change and suggests that it has the potential to be as disruptive and influential as the technological-economic waves that went before. However, rather than simply providing disruption within existing systems, it is proposed here that social innovation often goes further and attempts to disrupt and reconfigure systems themselves via changes to their internal institutional logics, norms, and traditions (see parallels in Schockley and Frank, 2010). This is often in reaction to the negative externalities of such extant systems or as an institutional critique of their inherent inability to deliver social and environmental outcomes. Such responses are enacted via processes of, at one extreme, opposition and resistance and, at the other, co-option and co-operation and are often characterized by acts of institutional entrepreneurship that blur the boundary between structure and agency in ways akin to models of structuration elsewhere in sociology (Lawrence and Phillips, 2004; Nicholls and Cho, 2006;). Social innovation is, thus, simultaneously the production of new ideas and new structures (Scott, 2007) *and* a process of recontextualization within socially (re)constructed norms of the public good, justice, and equity. Such innovation demonstrates a contingent construction of societal change that gives primacy to 'the knowledge and cultural assets of communities and which foregrounds the creative reconfiguration of social relations' (MacCallum et al., 2009, p. 2).

Social innovation cuts across all sectors of society. Indeed, as is discussed further below, it can often be defined by its unique combinations of the conventionally disparate logics of the private, public, and civil society sectors. For the private sector this is reified in two dimensions of social innovation for firms: first, the recognition that technological innovations fail if they are not integrated with changes in social relations within the organization (Porter and Kramer, 2011); second, as a new agenda for the role of business in society (Elkington, 1997). For the state, social innovation connects with an established tradition of welfare reform based upon notions of increased efficiency and effectiveness under conditions of financial (supply-side) scarcity and almost limitless demand (see LeGrand and Bartlett, 1993). It also represents a challenge to the governance status quo in societies by aiming to transform the power structures across social relations that allocate goods and services ineffectively or unequally (see Moulaert, 2009, p. 12). For civil society, social innovation encompasses both internal processes of organizational change (e.g. new legal forms and collaborations) and novelty in external outputs and outcomes (e.g. new products and services). However, despite evidence that all sectors of society are embracing innovation in social relations and the production of social goods ever more readily (see Bornstein, 2004; Nicholls, 2006; Light, 2008; Elkington and Hartigan, 2008), epistemological and definitional problems remain. The next section considers the boundaries of social innovation in theory and practice, and addresses some of the definitional debates and arguments that characterize the field.

What's in a name?

Social innovation suffers from not one, but two potential crises of definition. First, there is the question of what is actually meant by 'innovation'. A passing knowledge of Latin suggests that this term requires evidence of something new, a novelty, or even, in some definitions, something strange to us. Innovation may also contain a sense of renewal. Although scholars and public thinkers from a range of disciplines have explored the nature and scope of innovation in various settings, much ambiguity persists. Novelty typically demands a context and contexts are subject themselves to change and multiple interpretations and perspectives. Furthermore, within the study of innovation there is typically a distinction made between processes of invention (i.e. generating new ideas) and implementation (i.e. creating successful practice) which define novelty in different ways. In financial terms, this bifurcation represents the difference between turning resources into ideas (investment) or ideas into resources (income).

Drawing on the cognate social entrepreneurship literature suggests a further important insight into the nature of social innovation;

namely, that systems-level change demands a variety of types and levels of – often interrelated – innovation across time. Put another way, for the disequilibria of unjust social structures to be rebalanced requires multiple changes, interventions, disruptions and oppositions (Martin and Osberg, 2007). In this sense, social innovation is never neutral but always political and socially constructed. Three levels of social innovation can be identified (see Table I.1). First, there is incremental innovation in goods and services to address social need more effectively or efficiently. This is the objective of many successful charities and not-for-profits, as well as some of the so-called 'Bottom of the Pyramid' commercial firms (Prahalad, 2005). From this perspective, social innovation may be a good business opportunity. Second, there is institutional innovation that aims to harness or retool existing social and economic structures to generate new social value and outcomes. This level of social innovation is often – but not always – driven by experts repositioning new technology or intellectual capital to social rather than purely economic ends. However, while social in focus, such innovation should not be divorced from economic issues: indeed, institutional social innovation is often a response to problematic patterns of economic change across sectors

Table I.1 Levels of social innovation

Level	Objective	Focus	Example Organization (Sector)
Incremental	To address identified market failures more effectively: e.g. negative externalities and institutional voids	Products and services	Kickstart (low-cost irrigation foot pump) Aurolab (low-cost intraocular lenses) Afghan Institute of Learning (female education)
Institutional	To reconfigure existing market structures and patterns to create new social value	Markets	MPESA (mobile banking) Institute for One World Health ('orphan' drugs) Cafédirect (Fair Trade)
Disruptive	To change the cognitive frames of reference around markets and issues to alter social systems and structures	Politics (social movements)	Greenpeace (environmental change) BRAC (micro-finance) Tostan (human rights)

or societies (Hamalainen and Heiskala, 2007). Finally, disruptive social innovation aims squarely at systems change from the start. This is the realm of social movements and self-consciously 'political' actors, groups, and networks aiming to change power-relations, alter social hierarchies, and reframe issues to the benefit of otherwise disenfranchised groups. It can also be driven from within state structures by policy entrepreneurs and revisionist ideology (Hall, 1992, 1993). Disruptive social innovation can be characterized by structured mass-participation in political parties or formal membership schemes of social movements, on the one hand, or loose coalitions of individuals and interests united by an evanescent issue or technology, such as social media, on the other. Social innovation, as systems change, can be violent and rapid – as in the revolutions of the Arab Spring of 2011 – or (mostly) peaceful and gradual – as in the empowering developments in gender roles in the workplace over the past 30 years.

It should also be acknowledged that social innovation is not, in and of itself, a socially positive thing. Social innovation may have a 'dark side'. This could be evidenced in several ways:

- with socially divisive or destructive objectives and intentions (e.g. secret societies or extreme political parties)
- by deviant or unintended consequences that achieve negative social effects (e.g. by excluding some groups from the focus of social goods, services, or change)[4]
- in cases of operational failure, mission drift, or strategic co-option by an external party (e.g. Tracey and Jarvis, 2006).

Phills et al. (2008, p. 36) appeared to recognize the potential for a dark side of social innovation in a definition that emphasized *improvement* rather than *change* as a central feature:

A novel solution to a social problem that is more effective, efficient, sustainable, or just than existing solutions and for which the value created accrues primarily to society as a whole rather than private individuals.

Moreover, this conceptualization also highlights a potential bifurcation of value creation and value appropriation within social innovation that renders the interests of the individual (social) innovator secondary to wider social value creation (see Nicholls, 2010a for a similar argument in the context of social investment).

Another set of problematic issues for social innovation concerns the societal legitimacy of all innovations in their institutional contexts – the so-called liability of newness (Stinchcombe, 1968). From a neo-institutionalist perspective, all sectoral or organizational change is constrained by existing social norms as the status quo attempts to maintain stasis by means of various processes of isomorphism (DiMaggio and Powell, 1983). In this context, innovation is a problem at the organizational level as it undermines perceptions of legitimacy at normative, pragmatic, and cognitive levels with potentially fatal consequences in terms of resource acquisition and retention (Suchman, 1995). Yet, for all the complexity surrounding innovation as a socially constructed and contingent set of variables, it is argued here that the term is sufficiently well understood in scholarly and practical terms to be resilient and comprehensible when combined with the 'social'. However, this combination – innovative in itself – demands further careful analysis of its qualifying adjective.

So what can be meant by the 'social' in social innovation? Sociologists, economists, anthropologists, and political scientists (among others) have addressed this question for over a century, but – again – ambiguities remain (Cantor et al., 1992). For sociologists, the 'social' is the realm of all human activity, for anthropologists it is specifically located in community settings, rituals, and interactions. For many economists, it is best understood in terms of the externalities generated by market activity or as a contingent factor in an individual's utility curve. For political scientists, 'the social' is often framed as the realm of public goods interpreted by Bethamnite, utilitarian, policy objectives and framed by cost-benefit analyses.

Moreover, from some perspectives, all innovations can been seen as social. One argument suggests that since all new products and services have an impact on people's lives, all innovation has a social dimension. Those products and services that specifically enable improved human well-being can be seen as a sub-set of this larger group in that they have demonstrably *positive* social effects. Another argument reminds us that even innovations that do not have such effects typically require social participation in their production and diffusion which may be novel or transformative (e.g. Latour, 2005). These debates suggest that the differences in the positioning of the 'social' in social innovation are primarily sociological issues and that, as a consequence, they can be somewhat resolved by careful attention to the actors involved in instigating and experiencing the innovation itself. These actors can be analysed at micro, mezzo, and macro levels, namely in the individual, organization/

network, or systems context. Combine these levels with the two types of social innovation impacts noted above – process and outcome – and a framework for interpreting the wide range of expressions of social innovation presents itself (see Table I.2). This analytic framework focusses on the actor within social innovation but also incorporates contextual issues.

However, it is not the intention of this introduction to revisit the manifold – and sometimes sterile – definitional discussions already present in the social entrepreneurship literature (see Dacin et al., 2010), but rather to note that all qualifying uses of the term 'social' create interpretive challenges for which the only (partial) resolution is a statement of clarity in context. In this spirit, social innovation is defined here as varying levels of deliberative change that aim to address suboptimal issues in the production, availability, and consumption of public goods defined as that which is broadly of societal benefit within a particular normative and culturally contingent context.

What is abundantly clear is that social innovation is complex and multi-faceted. This volume cannot promise to resolve every aspect of the difficult epistemology of social innovation, but by presenting a cross-section of new research in the field it hopes to offer greater clarity in terms of the boundaries, activities, and key determinants of this field of action. Moreover, this introduction aims to offer both a context for the range of research that is subsequently presented here and a road-map for the logic and ambitions of this collection as a whole. Next, the contexts and responses defining the sixth wave of *social* innovation are considered.

Table I.2   Dimensions of social innovation

	Social Process (Example)	Social Outcome (Example)
Individual	Co-production (Southwark Circle)	Lost-cost healthcare (Aravind Eye Hospital)
Organization	Wiki-production (Wikipedia)	Work integration social enterprise (Greyston Bakery)
Network/Movement	Open source technology (Linux)	Non-traditional training and education (Barefoot College)
System	Micro-finance (Grameen Bank)	Mobile banking (MPESA)

Contexts and responses

One account of the increased focus on social innovation in recent years casts it as a response to an acceleration of global crises and so-called wicked problems characterized by multiple, contradictory analyses and diagnoses (Rayner, 2006; Murray et al., 2010). Examples include: the failure of modern state welfare systems (Leadbeater, 1997; Mulgan, 2006b); the impacts of mass urbanization (Moulaert et al., 2007); the failure of conventional market capitalism (Murray, 2009); increasingly urgent global resource constraints (Moody and Nogrady, 2010); the impacts of climate change; increased social breakdown; rising life expectancy and associated health and social care costs; growing cultural diversity within and across countries; growing inequality; rising incidences of chronic long-term conditions and pandemics; behavioural problems associated with the 'challenge of affluence' (Offer, 2006); difficult transitions to adulthood; and endemic reductions in individual happiness and indices of well-being (Mulgan et al., 2007, p. 9). In this context, intractable problems are seen as highlighting the failure of conventional solutions and established paradigms entrenched in intractable institutional settings across all three conventional sectors of society: private sector market failures; public sector, siloed thinking; a lack of scale in, and fragmentation across, civil society.

An important sub-set of these 'wicked problems' concerns public sector welfare reform. After the Second World War, a new model of welfare provision emerged across many developed economies with the state delivering universal public services largely free at the point of access, funded by taxation and compulsory individual 'national' insurance. The centrepiece of many welfare states has been the development of powerful public healthcare systems. However, demographic and societal changes combined with the economic realities of rising welfare costs and worsening public finances have led to radical innovation in the provision of welfare goods and services in recent years (Leadbeater, 1997). In many cases this has involved a retreat from centralized state-led provision and an engagement with new 'partnership' models involving both the private and civil society sectors. A key objective has been increased economic efficiency, but there has also been a realization that innovation and reform offer the opportunity to improve the effectiveness of services too. For example, in both the UK and elsewhere there has been a clear move in public policy towards enabling greater 'choice' and control for the recipient of welfare services (DaRoit et al., 2007; Pavolini and Ranci, 2008; Bartlett, 2009a). Indeed, policy reform offers an important mechanism by which social innovation can be both incubated and enacted as a part of 'reinventing government' (Osborne and Gaebler, 1992).

In a different reading of the rising interest in social innovation, such action is seen as a necessary (but not always automatic) companion to rapid technological change and economic innovation (Heiskala and Hamalainen, 2007). This conceptualization links to notions of social innovation as a process of reshaping social relations to maximize productivity and economic development, often framed by the optimistic assumption that the benefits of these changes will be shared equally. Such a setting also connects to work that suggests that social entrepreneurship represents the reconciliation of an historical division between private and public sector mechanisms of productivity growth with 'everyone a changemaker' (Drayton, 2002). Both approaches share a view of globalization as a set of interlinked activities that blend flows of goods and services, labour, communications, and finance in new combinations that drive innovation but also create problematic outcomes (Clegg, 2010). This is a systems level of analysis that relates most clearly to the disruptive form of innovation mentioned above, but that can also encompass changes at the product and market levels.

Common to all three contexts is a series of complex and multifaceted issues that drive innovation not only in processes and outcomes but also, increasingly, as boundary blurring activity across the conventional sectors of society. As Murray et al. (2010, p. 3) noted:

> Social innovation doesn't have fixed boundaries: it happens in all sectors, public, non-profit and private. Indeed, much of the most creative action is happening at the boundaries between sectors.

Furthermore, social innovation can often be the product of contradictions and tensions across fields of action and at the individual, cognitive level. Each of the three sectors of society – civil society, public, and private – has its own internal logics of action and defining features. These include specific ownership structures, different key beneficiaries, distinctive accountability regimes and reporting systems, bespoke resource acquisition and retention strategies, and dominant organizational forms (see Table I.3).

Taken together, these three ideal-type sectors can be conceptualized as a Triad represented in stability as a triangle. Between each of the three ideal-type points lies a range of institutional and organizational hybridities that represent sites for social innovation as boundary blurring

Table I.3   Institutional logics across sectors

	Civil Society	Private Sector	Public Sector
Institutional logic	Public benefit	Profit maximization	Collective democracy
Ownership	Mutual	Private	Collective
Key beneficiaries	Clients	Owners	General public
Strategic focus	Social value creation	Financial value creation	Public service
Accountability	Stakeholder voice	Published accounts, stock performance	Ballot box
Resource strategy	Donations, grants, earned income, volunteers, tax breaks	Debt, equity, earned income	Taxes
Dominant organizational structure	Charity, co-operative	Private company	Departmentalized bureaucracy

activities (see Figure I.1). Thus, between the civil society sector and the private sector there lies a variety of social enterprises that combine business logics and models with social objectives and ownership structures (such as mutual societies and co-operatives; see Alter, 2006). Some examples will be closer to the logic of business (i.e. businesses with a social purpose; see also Corporate Social Innovation, Kanter, 1999) and some to that of civil society (i.e. not-for-profits that have an earned income stream). Between the private and public sector ideal types are hybrid innovations such as the public–private partnerships mentioned above that provide new models of welfare provision outside of, but often in tandem with, the state (Bovaird, 2006; Osborne, 2010). Finally, between the state and civil society there are variations of a 'shadow state' in which community organizations, as well as larger charities and non-governmental organizations, function as a surrogate state in terms of the functions of an elected government. Good examples of this are the roles played by BRAC and the network of Grameen organizations in Bangladesh as providers of education, healthcare, employment, and financial services across the country in and around institutional voids at the policy and market levels (Mair and Marti, 2009).

The value of social innovation across sector boundaries has also been demonstrated in practice by the emergence of social innovation 'hubs',

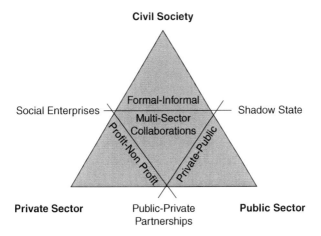

Figure 1.1 Social innovation as boundary blurring across institutional logics

incubators, and networks such as the Social Innovation Exchange (SIX) that aim to bring together disparate players from across institutional fields to spark new thinking and modelling.[5] The value of clustering organizations working across boundaries in a larger innovation eco-system is also behind the notion of 'Social Silicon Valleys' (Mulgan, 2006a). Clearly, there is already a good deal of conceptual thinking behind the analysis of the drivers of social innovation and the subse-quent responses. The next section will categorize more fully the schol-arly work on this subject to date.

Theoretical traditions

The topic of innovation – like entrepreneurship – has been of interest to scholars for many years. Schumpeter's work in the first half of the twentieth century provided much of the foundational thinking for sub-sequent innovation research, particularly within an economic context. Of particular influence have been Schumpeter's reimagining of Marxian notions of 'creative destruction' (1942) caused by systemic innovation and his typology of 'five dimensions' of innovation (1934). The latter provided a conceptual classification used in much of the subsequent analysis of innovation:

1. The introduction of a new product or an improved version of an existing product
2. The introduction of an improved method of production

3. The development of a new market (or entry into an existing market for a new player)
4. The development of a new source of supply or supply chain
5. The more efficient or effective organization of any industry or sector.

Schumpeter's work was also significant in that it introduced the construct of the entrepreneur as endogenous to economic systems in contrast to conventional economic analyses that had largely cast the change-agent actor as exogenous. This change of focus transformed the study of innovation, but has also been problematic in that it has led to the rise of an 'heroic entrepreneur' focus of analysis that can obscure the critical operational role of collaborations, networks, and groups.[6]

The next significant contribution to innovation theory came from rural sociology with Rogers's (1962) analysis of the processes behind the diffusion of innovation in this context. This research established categories of adopters of innovation – 'innovators, early adopters, early majority, late majority, laggards' – that are still used today. Faced with a series of industrial crises, stagflation, and increasing overseas competition, a second wave of modern innovation research emerged from the 1970s onwards focussing on the effects of new technologies on economic productivity. For example, Nelson and Winter (1977) examined comparative industrial productivity in the context of public policy, Freeman (1982, 1984) explored the economic effects of innovation – particularly in industrial contexts – while Khan and Manopichetwattana (1989) produced comparative work on small-firm innovation.

In tandem with a range of new theorizing concerning the competitive strategy of firms (cf. Porter, 1980), the 1980s saw the emergence of innovation studies based firmly within the management discipline and pioneered by Drucker (1985) and von Hippel, E. (1988, 2005); see also Utterback and Suarez, 1993). This work led to important subsequent contributions by Christensen (1997, 2002) and Chesbrough (2003). Fagerberg (2004) captured much of this new thinking in a seminal collection of papers. In the past ten years, there has been a plethora of more generalist management books on aspects of innovation (e.g. Tuomi, 2002; Luecke and Katz, 2003; Hitcher, 2006; Sarkar, 2007; McKeown, 2008), as well as specific studies looking at a single aspect of innovation and its effects. For example: Miles (2000) looked at innovation in services; Davila et al. (2006) focussed on measurement and performance issues in the context of the economic value (profitability) of innovation; and Baregheh et al. (2009) took a multi-disciplinary approach to defining innovation at a more holistic level.

As part of this proliferation of work on innovation, a specific social innovation literature began to emerge, most notably with attempts by Drucker (1987) and Moss Kanter (1999) to blend commercial and social innovation theory together within a hybrid construct of 'business in society'.[7] However, the distinctiveness of – as well as overlaps between – these two streams of work have been the subject of specific work only in the past ten or so years. As noted above and building upon the analysis of the existing social innovation literature set out by Pol and Ville (2009), two broad research conceptualizations of social innovation can be identified: innovation in social relations (that typically reflects process changes); innovation to address social market failures (that typically reflects outcome changes).

Innovation in social relations

The largest and most well-developed category of social innovation research focusses on innovation that addresses various dimensions of changes in social relations. Mumford (2002) summarized this research as exploring a continuum of activities from – at one extreme – the founding of new social institutions, innovating existing public institutions, or forming new social movements to – at the other – more modest action that aims to create new processes of collaborative or flexible work or instigate new organizational practices. As he noted:

> Social innovation ... refers to the generation and implementation of new ideas about how people should organize interpersonal activities, or social interactions, to meet one or more common goals.
>
> (2002, p. 253)

This literature can be subdivided into five categories of scholarship, as set out below.

Research design challenges

Early work on social innovation developed from within behavioural science with a particular interest in devising 'social change' approaches to tackle key, contemporary social problems, often at a community level (Fairweather, 1967). This work included reflections on how best to structure action research methodologies to empower and engage research subjects (Taylor, 1970) as well as research into the evaluation of government social programmes in a public administration context (Shipman, 1971) that concluded that capturing the performance of social interventions as innovation is complex and problematic and requires careful and iterative experimental design.

Changes in social structures

Simms (2006) considered social innovation in the context of human history, evolution, and, specifically, with respect to living systems theory. The author pointed out that – unlike other life forms – humans have developed the capacity to innovate within their environment at both technological and social levels. He also considered the technological and social determinants of human behaviour as they relate to living systems science.

Hamalainen and Heiskala (2007) provided a substantial analysis of the implications and effects of dramatic economic and technological change on social structures, arguing that it is social innovation processes which ultimately determine the economic and social performance of nations, regions, and industrial sectors and organizations. They stated:

> Social innovations are changes in the cultural, normative or regulative structures ... of society which enhance its collective power resources and improve its economic and social performance.
>
> (2007, p. 59)

Elsewhere, Nunez Jover et al. (2008), working within the Science and Technology Studies (STS) field, explored the development of STS within Cuba and concluded that this process constituted social innovation. Their argument was based around an analysis of the political framing of social need in this communist country with respect to an overtly ideological conceptualization of the role of science and technology in ameliorating such needs.

Changes in patterns of work

Holt (1971) focussed on social innovation within organizations, conceived of as new social patterns of employee interaction. This work was echoed in the activities of the Netherlands Centre for Social Innovation 30 years later (see Pot and Vaas, 2008).

In contrast to work that explored the economic effects of technological innovation on society, Gershuny (1982) used a sociological analysis to explore new modes of provision of (domestic) services as determinants of wider social and sectoral structures seen as social innovation. Expanding on these themes, his 1983 book suggested that for innovations to diffuse across society, new technologies required receptive social structures; and that when the two were aligned, social innovation followed. His work specifically explored changes in patterns of work (unpaid versus paid), time usage in domestic settings, and the balance of industrial and occupational employment as constituting indicators and drivers of such social innovations. For Gershuny, the term 'social innovation' provided a common analytic space for economists and sociologists to discuss economic growth as a set of societal changes in terms of patterns of employment and the balance between leisure and work.

Later, McElroy (2002) considered the importance to firm performance of 'social innovation capital', characterized as the 'collective capacity of a firm to innovate'. This conceptual extension of the more familiar construct of intellectual capital is defined by its collective context at the social systems level – namely how 'firms organize themselves ... around the production and integration of new knowledge' (ibid., p. 32).

In the context of the increasing obsolescence of the 'standard employment contract', Regalia (2006) examined a range of case material demonstrating innovations in local-level co-operation around the regulation of more flexible patterns of employment. Her edited book presented a detailed analysis of various changes in employer and union practices and strategies, particularly with regard to the governance of transient employment relationships. These inter-organizational developments within a radically changing employment market were presented as social innovation.

Diffusion of social change

From within sociology, there are analyses of the micro-level structures of innovation and diffusion that affect society – for example, how medical innovations spread across groups of clinicians – that have been classed as social innovation (Burt, 1987). In a different context, Westley (1991) provided a detailed analysis of the relationship between 'visionary leadership' and global social innovation using the case of the Live Aid concert in 1985 and its attendant objectives and effects. Of special significance in this study was a strategic use of the affective impact of music to bypass more conventional, rationalist responses to generating social innovation in the face of a terrible human disaster. Henderson (1993) was also interested in the relationship between social innovation and political change in terms of diffusion processes. He explored how citizen movements catalyze social innovation – conceptualized as distinct from dominant cultural norms – from fluid positions outside of conventional societal structures.

Urban studies

There is a significant cluster of work within Urban Studies exploring innovative responses to social exclusion as social innovation under the heading of Integrated Area Development. Much of this work centres on innovation within social relations in urban contexts, and as a body of work it explores the potential of public, private, and civil society models, interventions, and interactions. Perhaps the first example of this work came in the early 1970s, when Rosenbloom and Marris (1972) produced a collection of papers exploring how enterprise could be used as an engine of community development and social innovation. Interestingly, this prefigured the substantive social enterprise literature of the past decade by many years (cf. Alter, 2006). Twenty years later, Moulaert et al. (2005) identified three dimensions of social innovation in the context of tackling urban social exclusion:

- content dimension: the satisfaction of human needs
- process dimension: changes in social relations, particularly with respect to governance
- empowerment dimension: increases in the socio-political capabilities of particular disenfranchised groups, often by creating new access routes to resources.

Drawing on the work of Moulaert et al. (2005), Novy and Leubolt (2005) explored the relationships between the state and civil society in the context of experimentation around new structures of local politics in Brazil. Social innovation was identified in this work as occurring at the interface of state and civil society within new modes of participatory budgeting as part of urban development. Gerometta et al. (2005) suggested that civil society organizations had an important role to play in developing new governance relations – recognized here as social innovation – to address social exclusion in urban settings.

In 2007, a special edition of *the European Journal of Urban and Regional Studies* was dedicated to social innovation and governance in European cities. The purpose of the special edition was to build on previous work and to clarify the distinctive localism of a social innovation approach to social exclusion in contrast to other neo-liberal models (Moulaert et al., 2007). Such social innovation was characterized as 'a polymorphic constellation of counter-hegemonic movements and initiatives' (ibid., p. 196) engaged in active processes of social struggle and change. Papers in the special edition variously addressed issues of citizen participation, community resistance, and bottom-up action in diverse urban sites and political contexts. For example, Christiaens et al. (2007) presented a detailed historical analysis of a particular case example of a neighbourhood development association in Antwerp to highlight shifts in normative economic and policy frameworks around social exclusion over time. The study suggested that the social innovation model developed by Moulaert and others had been subject to multiple interpretive contexts – some supportive, some hostile – over time, reflecting changes in the dominant ideological and economic norms.

More recently, a range of research in this school of Urban Studies was presented in an important edited collection (MacCallum et al., 2009) that aimed to analyse the social innovation construct as an alternative perspective on development and territorial transformation that paid particular attention to social relations. The volume presented different aspects of social innovation as a set of alternative development options that highlight solidarity, co-operation, cultural-artistic action, and communitarian diversity. The collection as a whole provided a variety of critiques of normative, neo-liberal approaches to urban deprivation and social exclusion.

Innovation to address social market failures

In contrast to the stream of research that conceptualizes social innovation as changes in social relations, a more recent and less well-developed strand of research focusses on social innovation as the answer to social market failures. This perspective is supported by the OECD (2011, p. 1) definition:

> Social innovation is distinct from economic innovation because it is not about introducing new types of production or exploiting new markets in itself but is about satisfying new needs not provided by the market (even if markets intervene later) or creating new, more satisfactory ways of insertion in terms of giving people a place and a role in production.

This definition relates to the outcome-driven model of social innovation already discussed above and focusses on innovation as the means by which new products and services can be provided to underserved market segments. At the macro level this includes the mechanisms by which new markets are created in weak institutional spaces or to address market failures. The latter is conceived of as not only encompassing failures in commercial markets, but also in public sector 'markets', where the state fails to provide public goods, and civil society 'markets', where charities, not-for-profits and non-governmental organizations fail to provide effective goods and services to their beneficiaries. Such failures typically provide innovation opportunities, but can also provide challenges in terms of reconciling potentially competing institutional logics and legitimacies.

In one of the earliest examples of this type of analysis, Ornetzeder (2001) examined the socio-economic drivers behind the successful adoption of a new, renewable energy technology (solar water heaters) in Austria. The paper identified specific, local, market variables as accounting for the fact that such heaters were much more popular in Austria than in other European countries. The two key factors were a well-established do-it-yourself tradition and an atypical group of early adopters based in rural regions, who were interested in solar heaters from the perspective of enhancing their own personal comfort. Crucially, both these factors could be connected and exploited by commercial firms to diffuse the new technology as a social/environmental innovation.

In a different academic tradition, Morelli (2007) provided a synthesis of design thinking to reassess the role of conventional processes of industrialization around innovation with respect to new agendas aimed at creating systems of co-production in welfare and other public goods. She argued that industrial logics could be applied to social innovation in terms of generating organizational structures, codifying knowledge and building economies of scope. However, the author made it clear that to be successful such logics must draw upon the cultural history of industrial districts and socially embedded clusters, rather than Fordist notions of mass-production.

Recognizing the centrality of hybrid logics to much of social innovation in practice, Gardner et al. (2007) addressed the pressing issue of healthcare innovation in developing countries by suggesting that local innovation can best be nurtured and diffused by a combination of global public–private product development partnerships and a focus on systemic solutions in health policy and research. This is exemplified in the paper by an analysis of public–private research and development partnerships, implementation research, and the effects of individual leadership in specific programmes. Social and adaptive innovation are identified as being equally – or even more – important than technological innovation. Elsewhere, Le Ber and Branzei (2010) also examined the relational processes that underpinned social innovation in several cross-sector partnerships between not-for-profit and for-profit organizations. Social innovation was conceived of here as novel approaches to social or environmental problems. Using a rich, longitudinal case method, the authors identified role (re)calibration as being a key indicator of success, by which was meant the ability to identify a partner's needs and respond flexibly to them to strengthen relational ties. However, the paper also acknowledged negative aspects of building relational intensity such as the increased potential for partner complacency and disillusionment.

Two other papers in this stream of work took a more ethnographic approach. First, Yasushi et al. (2007) examined social innovation in the context of community renewable energy in Japan using an Actor Network Theory approach. Specifically they considered the socio-economic dynamics around community ownership that changed the rules of risk–benefit distribution, the roles of social actors, and the social acceptance of renewable energy as a concept. Their empirical study highlighted the complex networks, multiple interest groups, and participation structures that enabled the project to succeed. In a similar study, Tapsell and Woods (2008) examined social innovation within indigenous communities. In particular, they considered entrepreneurial activity in Maori communities where innovation arose through the interaction of the young entrepreneur and the elders. Their work drew upon a neo-Schumpeterian understanding of innovation as self-organization within indigenous entrepreneurship at the intersection of social and economic entrepreneurship. Here, Maori entrepreneurship was presented as a complex adaptive system that combines opportunity recognition and cultural heritage.

This analysis of the academic work to date on social innovation demonstrates that there is already a rich tradition of theoretical and empirical research in this field ranging across multiple disciplines and empirical settings. The next section gives an overview of the work in this collection that aims to build on and complement these prior traditions.

Structure and purpose of the book

This book is divided into three parts. Part one sets the scene for the book as a whole and frames the more focussed chapters that follow. Thus, the first part considers the context of modern social innovation in several comparative settings and also provides some macro-level theoretical models by which social innovation can be analysed. In the first chapter, Mulgan expands on some of the theoretical material already highlighted here to set out a broad sweep of theoretical traditions and trajectories of relevance for a deeper analytical understanding of social innovation. He suggests that social innovation shares an intellectual heritage with the study of technological and commercial/business innovation, but that it also demands a new set of approaches. Of particular importance with respect to the latter is a re-evaluation of the pragmatist school of social philosophy. Mulgan goes on to connect the study of social innovation with current concerns about individual well-being and happiness. The chapter ends by offering some observations on key research gaps and opportunities in the field going forward.

The second chapter changes the focus to a cross-country comparison of the forms and contexts of social innovation, particularly with respect to one of its most important organizational forms – social enterprise. Based upon previous research, Kerlin establishes four country-level types of context for social innovation and then explores each in more detail via an organizational case study. The four countries used for analysis are: Zimbabwe; Argentina; Italy; and the United States. The chapter concludes by making some further comparative observations suggesting that different forms of social innovation become institutionalized over time partially in response to specific socio-economic and cultural contexts. This insight is particularly useful with respect to developing strategies for the successful transfer and replication of social innovation ideas across countries. Kerlin acknowledges some limitations to her analysis, specifically with respect to regions outside of her study, notably China.

In the next contribution, Moore et al. use resilience theory to frame an analysis of the relationship between public policy and social innovation. Resilience theory derives from work in ecology in the 1970s and suggests that, to be resilient, an ecosystem must move through an 'adaptive cycle' rather than remain in a fixed equilibrium. The adaptive cycle is shown here to have four distinct phases: release; reorganization; exploitation; and conservation. The authors use this cycle as an analytic device to suggest that different policy interventions suit different phases of the adaptive evolution of social innovation. The chapter goes on to explore each of these four phases with case studies of the interrelation of policy and successful social innovation outcomes. This leads to the development of a series of propositions with respect to the relevance of resilience theory to social innovation. Finally, the full social innovation cycle is explored through an examination of the policies that promoted economic development for the Inuit people of Arctic Canada in the 1950s. The chapter ends by summarizing its overall contribution and going on to set out a further research agenda.

Part I concludes with Marée and Mertens's discussion of the theory and practice of social innovation impact measurement. Their approach is to critique the techniques already well established in economics in the context of social innovation. From this perspective, the authors are particularly interested in the so-called 'non-market' or 'social' value created by social innovation that is typically not captured by economic performance measurement systems. The chapter falls into two broad sections: in the first, the various methods used to measure the non-market dimensions of production are set out; in the second, the authors develop an integrated framework for understanding the advantages and disadvantages of these various methods, by focussing on the notion of the economic value of non-market goods. Central to this chapter is a critical analysis of three types of performance measurement system: accounting measures of production, based on the resources used; measurements of performance through the use of indicators, according to the principles of cost-efficiency analysis (CEA); the monetary valuation of production based upon cost-benefit analysis (CBA). The chapter concludes by asserting the use-value of evaluations based mainly on non-monetary indicators and on multi-criteria analysis rather than on a single monetary or economic measure.

Following the macro-level, theoretical frameworks offered in Part I, Part II of this collection captures a series of more micro-level perspectives on social innovation strategies and institutional logics. Lyon opens it with an exploration of the role of collaborative, inter-organisational relationships in the enactment of social innovation. Specifically, he examines partnerships with the state in new models for the delivery of public services and presents a framework for understanding how collaboration is built and maintained in this context. The chapter suggests that the emergence of 'quasi markets' and competition for the delivery of public services provide new challenges and opportunities for organisations in the creation of collaborative relationships with the state. This work, therefore, is centrally interested in social innovation as changes in social – here, inter-organizational – relations. The chapter is structured in three sections: first, it examines various types of inter-organisational relationships and explores building trust as a key success factor; next, it sets out the various processes used to build co-operation, reflecting further on issues of trust and power; finally, the chapter considers the conflicting norms of behaviour that underpin inter organisational relationships and participation by socially innovative actors in competitive markets for public service delivery. The chapter ends by identifying further the theoretical and policy implications of its analysis.

In the next chapter, Robinson et al. address the challenges of modelling agency in social innovation. Their specific focus is on the features of the 'projective agent' that are useful in developing formal models of social innovation as a process. The authors' central argument is that the agent in social innovation differs in a fundamental way from the agent as it is usually modelled in the social sciences particularly in structuralist accounts of society. In the latter, the agent is typically presented as constrained by the system's institutions, rules, and structures, and this presents theoretical problems in analysing agents that consciously promote change by shaping the rules and structures of the system itself. The authors go on to argue that such innovative agents must themselves model the system they are attempting to change and of which they are a part. The challenge for modelling change in this context is, therefore, how to 'put the model of the system' into the model of the agent and, then, how to put the agent back into the model of the system. This chapter uses theoretical analysis to explore this issue and then applies the resultant thinking to a short case study to test its implications and draw some conclusions.

Following this, Ataide draws upon an emergent strand of scholarship concerning the connection between religious faith and institutions and social innovation to argue for a new category of innovator, the 'socio-religious entrepreneur'. The chapter begins by exploring definitions of entrepreneurship and innovation, and notes how they have been extended beyond purely commercial settings over recent years. Next it considers work on entrepreneurship in religious or faith-based settings and suggests that the existing literature lacks categorizations appropriate to empirical reality. As a response to this lacuna, Ataide sets out a definition of socio-religious entrepreneurs as people 'who by virtue of their personal and shared religious values and ideology are compelled to create social enterprises with the primary goal of achieving non-religious social purposes'. Having established a working definition based on theoretical synthesis, the second half of the chapter uses three short case studies to test and explore the neologism. The chapter ends with an exhortation to include socio-religious entrepreneurship within the analysis of social innovation more generally not by virtue of its moral or ethical positioning but simply as an under-researched topic.

Part II of this collection concludes with Cameron's investigation of how social entrepreneurs emerge and position themselves regarding the social innovation ecosystem, specifically within universities. Theoretically, this chapter draws upon Foucauldian analysis to contrast the logics of the social innovator with his model of the 'specific intellectual' in four respects: function; methods; risks; and position in relation to the university. Having set out its theoretical argument in terms of the nature of social innovation ecosystems and the role within them of the specific intellectual, the chapter goes on to analyse data collected from 41 semi-structured interviews in a particular ecosystem setting: the annual Skoll World Forum on Social Entrepreneurship at the University of Oxford in 2009. This data analysis reveals three clusters of issues for social innovators that are then explored in turn: the dangers of moral heroism; the challenges of system change from within; the lack of institutional support for growing social innovation. The chapter concludes with recommendations about how to foster a greater critical awareness of the tensions and risks of social entrepreneurship and how the university can provide an enabling environment from within which social innovators may emerge.

The third and final part of this collection contains three contributions that address sustainability and environmental innovation as an important sub-set of social innovation. In the first chapter, Olsson and Galaz argue for greater levels of innovation to drive creative solutions to deal with the problems of global environmental change. Echoing some of the theoretical material discussed by Moore et al. in Chapter 3, the authors suggest that there is a pressing need to develop models that can create dynamic feedback loops in which humans both influence and are influenced by ecosystem processes to build higher levels of environmental resilience in natural systems. They note that the resilience literature generally uses the term 'social-ecological systems' to highlight the interconnectedness and co-evolution of human-environmental systems and human dependence on the capacity of ecosystems to generate essential services; and that humans should, therefore, be seen as a part of ecosystems and, ultimately, dependent on their capacity to support human life. Olsson and Galaz draw on this literature to set out a framework for applying social innovation and entrepreneurship research to sustainability issues. The chapter ends by suggesting that a step-change in social and environmental innovation is urgently required in order to improve human well-being without degrading the biosphere and its life support systems in the process.

Next, Cannatelli et al. explore opportunity recognition for sustainable technologies in developing-country contexts. The authors draw on research concerning the behavioural theory of the firm to build a business model design process for this context. Empirical material is provided by a case analysis of Greentecno S. A., a Switzerland based, for-profit, green technology firm. The case suggests that there may be potential conflicts between opportunities identified according to different social, economic, and environmental logics but that these can be managed by designing innovative business models. The discussion concludes by setting out the benefits that can arise from including environmental sustainability criteria in business planning more generally.

The final chapter also explores the processes by which sustainable innovation and environmental entrepreneurship can thrive at the firm level to achieve an ideal-type trajectory of 'green growth'. In this context, Hockerts and Wüstenhagen contrast models of sustainable entrepreneurship between large and small firms to identify which setting may provide the best opportunity for accelerated growth and impact. Specifically, the chapter aims to clarify the role of these two different settings of sustainable entrepreneurship as 'Greening Goliaths' versus 'Emerging Davids' and to develop an evolutionary model of how their combined impact may promote the sustainable transformation of industries. The chapter employs a Schumpeterian notion of entrepreneurship as an innovative process of creating market disequilibria which, in turn, lead to imitation. Using this theoretical lens the authors identify three phases in a dynamic view of industry transformation: the initial phase is characterized by the sustainability initiatives of idealistic 'Davids'; the second by some pioneering 'Goliaths' mimicking David initiatives and bringing them into the mainstream; and a final stage of development where 'Emerging David' firms find ways to scale up their sustainable innovations without compromising their sustainability ambitions, and 'Greening Goliaths' simultaneously take on the challenge of building sustainability into their mainstream businesses. The chapter ends by arguing that the sustainable transformation of industries is not going to be brought about by either Davids or Goliaths alone, but instead that their interaction is essential.

Taken as a whole, this collection aims to move the research agenda on social innovation forward in three ways. First, these chapters demonstrate that this is a topic with sufficient theoretical and empirical distinctiveness to be worthy of further analysis as a field of action in itself. This book includes theoretical analyses drawing on multiple disciplines including economics, sociology, business strategy, organizational theory, ecology, and philosophy. However, there remains plenty of scope for other theoretical approaches to social innovation including cross-disciplinary work, as set out here by Mulgan and others. The empirical material presented in this volume is largely qualitative and case study-based, but there is also a clear opportunity for more quantitative work on social innovation, particularly in policy or industry-level analyses. Key research topics that are ripe for further work include: the measurement of innovation impacts; the governance and accountability mechanisms for organizations in change processes or systems in flux; the challenges of the 'liability of newness' in terms of funding mechanisms and wider resource strategies for social innovation.

Second, social innovation offers a compelling set of examples of hybrid logics and organizational models that offer both micro-level novelty and the potential for macro-level systems-change influence. These models provide useful templates to understand how innovation and change can be operationalized in other settings, as well as generating a range of interesting research questions concerning how to go to scale and the development of ecosystems models of social and environmental change. The need for more fluidity across the ideal-type sectors of the Triad model is increasingly recognized by policymakers, private sector leaders and civil society actors. This book has offered a range of examples of such new hybridities.

Finally, the study of social innovation offers the opportunity to grapple with the central real-world challenges of our time. Indeed, rather than conceptualizing social innovation as a sub-set of technological-economic innovation, it may be the case that the reverse now makes a more compelling case. As this volume underlines, social innovation offers potential solutions to climate change, the crisis of the welfare state, health pandemics and failures, social dislocation and inequality, and educational failure. The need to address – if not solve – these 'wicked problems' presents us with global challenges that will become increasingly evident in all our everyday lives. It is, therefore, the ultimate purpose of this book to suggest that a focus on the sixth wave of *social* innovation represents not only a scholarly opportunity but a global imperative.

Notes

1. Brian Wilson and Mike Love (1963).
2. Interestingly, these have parallels with the financial cycles marked by the stock-market crises of 1797, 1847, 1893, 1929, 2008; see Mulgan in this collection.
3. In the first edition of the *Stanford Social Innovation Review*, the Editor aimed, to some extent, to encompass both dimensions in his definition of social innovation as, 'the process of inventing, securing support for, and implementing novel solutions to social needs and problems' (Barley (2003), p. 1).
4. For example, Froud et al. (2010) critiqued the framing of the poor's increased access to debt products as a positive social innovation characterized by some as 'emancipatory' or 'empowering'. The authors suggested, instead, that the opening up of 'subprime' markets was a 'privately-led' social innovation designed only to benefit rent-seeking financial institutions – an innovation that did not increase the asset ownership of the poor, but rather accelerated the growth of their levels of overall indebtedness.
5. http://socialinnovationexchange.org.
6. This has also been the case in social entrepreneurship research; see Nicholls (2010b).
7. Moss Kanter (1999) developed a model of corporate social innovation that suggested that cross-sector partnerships between not-for-profits and business offered valuable opportunities for innovation as a setting for 'beta-testing' new ideas and processes. These pioneering ideas around 'new paradigm partnerships'

led directly to subsequent work in 'corporate social entrepreneurship' by Austin et al. (2006) and 'creating shared value' by Porter and Kramer (2011). See also Collins's (2005) reflections on the similarities between his analysis of 'great' businesses and successful social sector organizations.

References

Alexander, M. (2001), *The Kondratiev Cycle: A Generational Interpretation*, iUniverse Press.

Alter, K. (2006), Social Enterprise Models and their Mission and Money Relationships', in A. Nicholls (ed.) *Social Entrepreneurship: New Models of Sustainable Social Change*, Oxford University Press, pp. 205–32.

Austin, J., Leonard, H., Reficco, E. and Wei-Skillern, J. (2006), 'Social Entrepreneurship: It is for Corporations, Too', in A. Nicholls, (ed.), *Social Entrepreneurship: New Models of Sustainable Social Change*, Oxford University Press, pp. 169–80.

Baregheh A, Rowley, J. and Sambrook S. (2009), 'Towards a Multidisciplinary Definition of Innovation, *Management Decision*, 47 (8), pp. 1323–39.

Barley, S. (2003), 'Editor's Note', *Stanford Social Innovation Review*, Spring, pp. 1–2.

Bartlett, J. (2009a), *At Your Service: Navigating the Future Market in Health and Social Care*, Demos.

Bartlett, J. (2009b), *Getting More for Less: Efficiency in the Public Sector*, Demos.

Berry, B. (1991), *Long-Wave Rhythms in Economic Development and Political Behavior*, The Johns Hopkins University Press.

Bornstein, D. (2004), *How To Change The World: Social Entrepreneurs and the Power of New Ideas*, Oxford: Oxford University Press.

Bovaird, T. (2006), 'Developing New Forms of Partnership with the 'Market' in Procurement of Public Services', *Public Administration*, 84 (1), pp. 81–102.

Burt, R. (1987), 'Social Contagion and Innovation: Cohesion versus Structural Equivalence', *The American Journal of Sociology*, 92 (6), pp. 1287–335.

Cantor, R., Henry, S. and Rayner, S. (1992), *Making Markets: An Interdisciplinary Perspective on Economic Exchange*, Westport CT: Westport, CT Greenwood Press.

Chesbrough, H. (2003), *Open Innovation: The New Imperative for Creating and Profiting from Technology*, Boston, MA: Harvard Business School Press.

Christensen, C. (1997), *The Innovator's Dilemma*, Boston, MA: Harvard Business School Press.

Christensen, C. (2002), 'The Rules of Innovation', *Technology Review*, 105 (5), pp. 32–38.

Christiaens, E., Moulaert, F., and Bosmans, B. (2007), 'The End of Social Innovation in Urban Development Strategies?', *European Urban and Regional Studies*, 14 (3), pp. 238–51.

Clegg, S. (2010), 'The Four Flows of Globalizing', paper presented at the 26th European Group for Organization Studies (EGOS) Colloquium in Lisbon, July, 2010

Collins, J. (2005), *Good to Great and the Social Sectors: Why Business Thinking Is Not the Answer*, Boulder, CO.

Dacin, P., Dacin, T. and Matear, M. (2010), 'Social Entrepreneurship: Why We Don't Need a New Theory and How We Move Forward From Here', *Academy of Management Perspectives*, 24 (3), pp. 37–57.

Da Roit, B., Le Bihan, B. and Österle, A. (2007), 'Long-Term Care Policies in Italy, Austria and France: Variations in Cash-For-Care Schemes', *Social Policy & Administration*, 41 (6) pp. 653–71.

Davila, T., Epstein, M. and Shelton, R. (2006), *Making Innovation Work: How to Manage It, Measure It, and Profit from It*, Upper Saddle River: Wharton School Publishing.

DiMaggio, P. and Powell, W. (1983), '"The Iron Cage Revisited", Institutional Isomorphism and Collective Rationality in Organizational Fields', *American Sociological Review*, 48 (1983), pp. 147–60.

Drayton, W. (2002), 'The Citizen Sector: Becoming as Entrepreneurial and Competitive as Business', *California Management Review*, 44 (3), pp.120–32.

Drucker, P. (1985), *Innovation and Entrepreneurship Practice and Principles*, University of Illinois.

Drucker, P. (1987), 'Social Innovation – Management's New Dimension', *Long Range Planning*, 20 (6), pp. 29–34.

Elkington, J. (1997), *Cannibals with Forks: The Triple Bottom Line of 21st Century Business*, London: Capstone.

Elkington, J. and Hartigan, P. (2008), *The Power of Unreasonable People*, Harvard Business School Press.

Fagerberg, J. (2004), 'Innovation: A Guide to the Literature', in J. Fagerberg, D. Mowery and R. Nelson, *The Oxford Handbook of Innovation*, Oxford University Press, pp. 1–26.

Fairweather, G. (1967), *Methods for Experimental Social Innovation*, Hoboken, NJ: John Wiley.

Freeman, C. (1982), *The Economics of Industrial Innovation*, London: Frances Pinter.

Freeman, C. (1984), 'Prometheus Unbound', *Futures*, 16 (5), pp. 494–507.

Gardner, C., Acharya, T. and Yach, D. (2007), 'Technological and Social Innovation: A Unifying New Paradigm for Global Health', *Health Affairs*, 26 (4), pp. 1052–61.

Gerometta, J., Haeussermann, H. and Longo, G. (2005), 'Social Innovation and Civil Society in Urban Governance: Strategies for an Inclusive City', *Urban Studies*, 42 (11), pp. 2007–21.

Gershuny, J. (1982), 'Social Innovation. Change in the Mode of Provision of Services', *Futures*, December, pp. 496–516.

Gershuny, J. (1983), *Social Innovation and the Division of Labour*, Oxford University Press.

Goldenburg, M., Kamoji, W., Orton, L. and Williamson, M. (2009), *Social Innovation in Canada: An Update*, CPRN Research Report.

Hall, P. (1992), 'The Movement from Keynesianism to Monetarism: Institutional Analysis and British Economic Policy in the 1970s', in S. Steinmo, K. Thelen and F. Longstreth (eds) (1992), *Structuring Politics: Historical Institutionalism in Comparative Perspective*, Cambridge University Press, pp. 90–113.

Hall, P. (1993), 'Policy Paradigms, Social Learning, and the State: The Case of Economic Policy Making in Britain', *Comparative Politics*, 25 (3), pp. 275–96.

Hamalainen, T. and Heiskala, R. (eds) (2007), *Social Innovations, Institutional Change and Economic Performance: Making Sense of Structural Adjustment Processes in Industrial Sectors, Regions and Societies*, SITRA: Edward Elgar.

Henderson, H. (1993), 'Social Innovation and Citizen Movements', *Futures*, April, pp. 322–38.

Hitcher, W. (2006), *Innovation Paradigm Replaced*, Hoboken, NJ: Wiley.

Hobsbawm, E. (1989), *The Age of Empire, 1875–1914*, London: Abacus Press.

Hobsbawm, E. (1999), *The Age of Extremes: The Short Twentieth Century 1914–1991*, London: Abacus Press.

Holt, K. (1971), 'Social Innovations in Organizations', *International Studies of Management and Organization*, 1 (3), pp. 235–52.

Khan, A. and Manopichetwattana, V. (1989), 'Innovative and Non-Innovative Small Firms: Types and Characteristics', *Management Science*, 35 (5), pp. 597–606.

Kondratiev, N. (1998), *The Works of Nikolai D. Kondratiev*, Samuels, W., Makasheva. N. and Wilson, S. (eds) Pickering Masters, London: Pickering & Chatto.

Latour, B. (2005), *Reassembling the Social: An Introduction to Actor Network Theory*, Oxford University Press.

Lawrence, T. and Phillips, N. (2004), 'From Moby Dick to Free Willy: Macrocultural Discourse and Institutional Entrepreneurship in Emerging Institutional Fields, *Organization*, 11 (5), pp. 689–711.

Le Ber, M. J. and Branzei, O. (2010), '(Re)Forming Strategic Cross-Sector Partnerships: Relational Processes of Social Innovation', *Business & Society*, 49 (1), pp. 140–72.

Leadbeater, C. (1997), *The Rise of the Social Entrepreneur*, London: Demos.

LeGrand, J. and Bartlett, W. (eds) (1993), *Quasi-Markets and Social Policy*, Basingstoke: Palgrave Macmillan.

Light, P. (2008), *The Search For Social Entrepreneurship*, Brookings Institution Press.

Luecke, R. and Katz, R. (2003), *Managing Creativity and Innovation*, Boston, MA: Harvard Business School Press.

MacCallum, D., Moulaert, F., Hillier, J. and Haddock, S. (eds) (2009), *Social Innovation and Territorial Development*, Farnham: Ashgate.

Mair, J. and Marti, I. (2009), 'Entrepreneurship in and around Institutional Voids: A Case Study from Bangladesh', *Journal of Business Venturing*, 24 (5), pp. 419–35.

Martin, R. and Osberg, S. (2007), 'Social Entrepreneurship: the Case for Definition', *Stanford Social Innovation Review*, Spring, pp. 28–39.

McElroy, M. (2002), 'Social Innovation Capital', *Journal of Intellectual Capital*, 3 (1), pp. 30–9.

McKeown, M. (2008), *The Truth About Innovation*, London, UK: Prentice Hall.

Miles, I. (2000), 'Services Innovation: Coming of Age in the Knowledge Based Economy', *International Journal of Innovation Management*, 14 (4), pp. 371–89.

Moody, J. B. and Nogrady, B. (2010), *The Sixth Wave: How to Succeed in a Resource-Limited World*, New York: Random House.

Moss Kanter, R. (1999), 'From Spare Change to Real Change: The Social Sector as Beta Site for Business Innovation', *Harvard Business Review*, May–June, pp. 122–32.

Moulaert, F. (2009), 'Social Innovation: Institutionally Embedded, Territorially (Re)Produced', in D. MacCallum, F. Moulaert, J. Hillier, S. Haddock (eds) (2009), *Social Innovation and Territorial Development*, Ashgate, pp. 11–23.

Moulaert, F., Martinelli, F., Gonzalez, S., and Swyngedouw, E. (2007), 'Introduction: Social Innovation and Governance in European Cities', *European Urban and Regional Studies*, 14 (3), pp. 195–209.

Moulaert, F., Martinelli, F., Swyngedouw, E. and Gonzalez, S. (2005), 'Towards Alternative Model(s) of Local Innovation', *Urban Studies*, 42 (11), pp. 1969–90.

Morelli, N. (2007), 'Social Innovation and New Industrial Contexts: Can Designers "Industrialize" Socially Responsible Solutions?', *Design Issues*, 23 (4), pp. 3–21.

Mulgan, G. (2006a), *Social Silicon Valleys: A Manifesto for Social Innovation*, London: Young Foundation.

Mulgan, G. (2006b), 'The Process of Social Innovation', *Innovations: Technology, Governance, Globalization*, 1 (2), pp. 145–62.

Mulgan, G., Tucker, S., Ali, R. and Sanders, B. (2007), *Social Innovation: What It Is, Why It Matters and How It Can Be Accelerated*, Oxford: Skoll Centre for Social Entrepreneurship Working Paper.

Mumford, M. (2002), 'Social Innovation: Ten Cases from Benjamin Franklin', *Creativity Research Journal*, 14 (2), pp. 253–66.

Murray, R. (2009), *Danger and Opportunity: Crisis and the New Social Economy*, London: Young Foundation/NESTA.

Nelson, R. and Winter, S. (1977), 'In Search of a Useful Theory of Innovation', *Research Policy*, 6 (1), pp. 36–76.

Nicholls, A. (ed.) (2006), *Social Entrepreneurship: New Models of Sustainable Social Change*, Oxford University Press.

Nicholls, A. (2010a), 'The Institutionalization of Social Investment: The Interplay of Investment Logics and Investor Rationalities', *Journal of Social Entrepreneurship*, 1 (1), pp. 70–100.

Nicholls, A. (2010b), 'The Legitimacy of Social Entrepreneurship: Reflexive Isomorphism in a Pre-Paradigmatic Field', *Entrepreneurship Theory and Practice*, 34 (4), pp. 611–33.

Nicholls, A. and Cho, A. (2006), 'Social Entrepreneurship: The Structuration of a Field', in Nicholls, A. (ed), *Social Entrepreneurship: New Models of Sustainable Social Change*, Oxford University Press, pp. 99–118.

Nunez Jover, J. and Lopez Cerezo, J. (2008), 'Technological Innovation and Social Innovation: Science, Technology and the Rise of STS Studies in Cuba', *Science, Technology and Human Values*, 33 (6), pp. 707–29.

Novy, A. and Leubolt, B. (2005), 'Participatory Budgeting in Porto Alegre: Social Innovation and the Dialectical Relationship of State and Civil Society', *Urban Studies*, 42 (11), pp. 2023–36.

OECD (2011), *LEED Forum on Social Innovations*, available at: http://www.oecd.org/document/22/0,3746,fr_2649_34417_39263221_1_1_1_1,00.html. Accessed: 10 July 2011.

Ornetzeder, M. (2001), 'Old Technology and Social Innovations. Inside the Austrian Success Story on Solar Water Heaters', *Technology Analysis and Strategic Management*, 13 (1), pp. 105–15.

Osborne, S. (2010), 'Delivering Public Services: Time for a New Theory?', *Public Management Review*, 12 (1), pp. 1–10.

Osborne, D. and Gaebler, T. (1992), *Reinventing Government: How the Entrepreneurial Spirit is Transforming the Public Sector*, Boston, MA: Addison-Wesley.

Offer, A. (2006), *The Challenge of Affluence*, Oxford University Press.

Pavolini, E. and Ranci, C. (2008), 'Restructuring the Welfare State: Reforms in Long-Term Care in Western European Countries', *Journal of European Social Policy*, 18 (3), pp. 246–59.

Phills, J., Deiglmeier, K. and Miller, D. (2009), 'Rediscovering Social Innovation', *Stanford Social Innovation Review*, Fall, 34–43.

Pol, E. and Ville, S. (2009), 'Social Innovation: Buzz Word or enduring Term', *The Journal of Socio-Economics*, 38, pp. 878–85.

Porter, M. (1980), *Competitive Strategy*, New York: Free Press.–February, 89 (1/2), pp. 62–77.

Pot, F. and Vaas, F. (2008), 'Social Innovation, the New Challenge for Europe', *International Journal of Productivity and Performance Management*, 57 (6), pp. 468–73.

Prahalad, C. K. (2005), *The Fortune At The Bottom of The Pyramid*, Chicago: Wharton Publishing.

Rayner, S. (2006), *Wicked Problems: Clumsy Solutions – Diagnoses and Prescriptions for Environmental Ills*, Jack Beale Memorial Lecture on Global Environment, available at: http://www.sbs.ox.ac.uk/research/Documents/Steve%20Rayner/ Steve%20Rayner,%20Jack%20Beale%20Lecture%20Wicked%20Problems.pdf. Accessed: 7 March 2011.

Regalia, I. (ed.) (2006), *Regulating New Forms of Employment: Local Experiments and Social Innovation in Europe*, London: Routledge.

Rogers, E. (1962), *Diffusion of Innovation*, New York, NY: Free Press.

Rosenbloom, R. and Marris, R. (1972), *Social Innovation in the City: New Enterprises for Community Development*, New York.

Sarkar, S. (2007), *Innovation, Market Archetypes and Outcome – An Integrated Framework*, New York: Springer.

Schumpeter, J. (1934), *The Theory of Economic Development*, Cambridge, MA: Harvard University Press.

Schumpeter, J. (1942), *Capitalism, Socialism and Democracy*, Cambridge, MA: Harper and Row: New York.

Shipman, G. (1971), 'The Evaluation of Social Innovation', *Public Administration Review*, 31 (2), pp. 198–200.

Shockley, G. and Frank, P. (2010), 'Schumpeter, Kirzner, and the Field of Social Entrepreneurship', *Journal of Social Entrepreneurship*, 2 (1), pp. 6–26.

Simms, J. (2006), 'Technical and Social Innovation Determinants of Behaviour', *Systems Research and Behavioral Science*, 23 (3), pp. 383–93.

Stinchcombe, A. (1968), *Constructing Social Theories*, Chicago University Press.

Suchman, M. (1995), 'Managing Legitimacy: Strategic and Institutional Approaches', *Academy of Management Review*, 20 (3), pp. 571–610.

Tapsell, P. and Woods, C. (2008), 'A Spiral of Innovation Framework for Social Entrepreneurship: Social Innovation at the Generational Divide in an Indigenous Context', *Emergence, Complexity and Organization*, 10 (3), pp. 25–34.

Taylor, J. (1970), 'Introducing Social Innovation', *Journal of Applied Behavioral Science*, 6 (1), pp. 69–77.

Tracey, P. and Jarvis, O. (2006), 'An Enterprising Failure – Why a Promising Social. Franchise Collapsed', *Stanford Social Innovation Review*, Spring, pp. 66–70.

Tuomi, I. (2002), *Networks of Innovation*, Oxford University Press.

Utterback, J. and Suarez, F. (1993), 'Innovation, Competition and Industry Structure', *Research Policy*, 22 (1), pp. 1–21.

von Hippel, E. (1988), *The Sources of Innovation*, Oxford University Press.

von Hippel, E. (2005), *Democratizing Innovation*, Boston: MIT Press.

Westley, F. (1991), 'Bob Geldof and Live Aid: The Affective Side of Global Social Innovation', *Human Relations*, 44 (10), pp. 1011–36.

Yasushi, M., Nishikido, M. and Tetsunari, L. (2007), 'The Rise of Community Wind Power in Japan: Enhanced Acceptance Through Social Innovation', *Energy Policy*, 35 (5), pp. 2761–9.

Part I
Context and Frameworks

1
The Theoretical Foundations of Social Innovation

Geoff Mulgan

Introduction

The field of social innovation has grown up primarily as a field of practice, made up of people doing things and then, sometimes, reflecting on what they do. There has been relatively little attention to theory, or to history, and although there has been much promising research work in recent years, there are no clearly defined schools of thought, no continuing theoretical arguments, and few major research programmes to test theories against the evidence.

But to mature as a field, social innovation needs to shore up its theoretical foundations, the frames with which it thinks and makes sense of the world. Sharper theory will help to clarify what is and is not known, the points of argument as well as agreement. It will help in the generation of testable hypotheses and in guiding answers to questions: How much is social change driven by entrepreneurial individuals, by movements, teams or networks, or for that matter by political parties and governments? Why do some ideas travel well and others poorly? Should we expect any common patterns as to where the most influential ideas come from? Can the experimental methods of natural science be transplanted to social change? Do social innovations scale in the same way as business innovations? Is it possible to measure the innovative capacity of an organization or a nation?

Above all, sharper theory may help to guide practice. Social theories, unlike theories in fields like physics, are inseparable from their purposes and their uses. Not all innovations are good, and nor are all social innovations. So theory needs, ideally, to fuse three things: rigorous and objective analysis of patterns, causes, and dynamics; normative analysis of social change (including the use of concepts such as 'social value' or 'capabilities' to bridge the worlds of analysis and ethics, of 'is' and 'ought'); and guidance to help the practitioners of social innovation do better in improving well-being, alleviating poverty, or widening distributions of power.

Here I map some of the main theoretical currents that have flowed into the broad river of social innovation and that have useful insights to offer. Some are theories to interpret the world, concerned with description and analysis; others are theories to change the world, more deliberately designed to encourage and advocate.

I also suggest how some of these may be synthesized; and the contribution that other fields may make. To summarize, I suggest that together these theories show that:

- Social innovations tend to originate in contradictions, tensions, and dissatisfactions that are caused by new knowledge, new demands, and new needs that make the transition from being personal to being recognized as social in their causes and solutions. The philosophical roots lie in a view of societies as plastic, and a view of humans as impelled to 'resist the present'.
- Ideas then take shape through trial and error, often as hybrids, novel combinations of existing elements. Just as technologies originate in observation of natural phenomena which they try to mimic or amplify, so too do social innovations often originate in observation of social phenomena (such as trust, tacit knowledge, and problem solving).
- They then depend on a wide array of actors, including social entrepreneurs, movements, governments, foundations, teams, networks, businesses, and political organizations, each with different ways of working, motivations, and capacities.
- Innovations gain traction only when they can attract vital resources, that include money, time, attention, and power (the diversity of these resources explains why particular disciplines, from economics to political science, have struggled to generate useful theories).
- The processes whereby innovations develop have strong analogies with a much wider family of evolutionary processes, that multiply options, select and then grow those best suited to changing environments; However, it is misleading to focus on the invention and adoption of single innovations: instead they evolve in interdependent groups, and one set of innovations makes possible new ones (while closing off the space for others).
- Innovations gain impact through being formalized, as pilots, ventures and programmes, and through dynamic processes of externalization

and internalization (that may often leave their creators redundant and alienated).

- Innovations gain resonance and wider impact when they achieve a fit with wider patterns of historical change, including techno-economic paradigms and situations of political hegemony.
- The fundamental goals of social innovation include the creation of socially recognized value, the promotion of greater well-being, and the cultivation of capabilities, and these provide increasingly rigorous tests to judge what works and what does not.
- Most of the knowledge created through social innovation is historically and spatially contextual, specific, and liable to decay. But it is also pulled by the future, and by imagination of possible worlds.

This is very much a preliminary sketch and needs to be built on. The promise is that understanding these intellectual traditions can help in the devising of new tools, new practices, and new methods of communication. To that end I draw out a series of conclusions and suggest some of the fields where there is an urgent need for more rigorous theoretical work.

Definitions: The boundaries of the field

Social innovation, like social entrepreneurship, has struggled with definitions and boundaries (Dees and Anderson, 2006). Some feel anxious talking about anything without a precise definition; others fear that excessive rigidity obscures more than it reveals. This is not the place for a detailed discussion of definitions (The Young Foundation, 2010). There are many, often lengthy definitions of social innovation in circulation (from sources including Stanford University, the OECD, and NESTA), all describing the field of social innovation as concerned with ideas, products, services, that are for the public good.

My preference is simple and short and defines the field as concerned with 'innovations that are social both in their ends and in their means'. In other words it covers new ideas (products, services, and models) that simultaneously meet socially recognized social needs (more effectively than alternatives) *and* create new social relationships or collaborations, that are both good for society *and* enhance society's capacity to act. This definition helps to capture the dual quality of both the practice, which is usually concerned with means as well as ends, and of much of the theoretical literature on which the field has drawn, which is concerned with notions of value as well as the values that are expressed in the pursuit of value, and with capacities as well as products and services. The definition also internalizes within itself the conflict that is inevitable in the use of the word 'social': what counts as good, or a socially recognized need, is constantly contested, and this very contest provides some of the dynamic energy that drives the field.

This definition hopefully clarifies what social innovation is not as well as what it is. It is not just a sub-set of technological or economic innovation. It is not the same as, or a substitute for, larger-scale political programmes for structural or systemic change, or programmes to extend rights, though there are clear complementarities between such programmes and the field of social innovation. If social innovation has any ideological bias it is towards deeper democracy and empowerment of society – but does not of itself imply any view as to whether particular functions or services are best provided by public, private, or non-profit organizations.

Plasticity and progress

In everyday life, social innovation is often prompted by unhappiness, disappointment, or anger: the gap between what is and what could be. Some of the theoretical roots of social innovation also lie in a radical view of social plasticity. The premise of any social innovation is that the world is imperfect; that our knowledge of the world is incomplete; that creative innovation can achieve improvement; and that the best way to discover improvements lies in experiment, rather than revelation or deduction. These premises may seem obvious. But right from the start they set social innovation at odds with many other traditions. They imply a view of society as engaged in its own self-creation. They see the invention of the future as a natural part of human action, and extend the enlightenment belief that the world is malleable, plastic, and amenable to reform.

In all of these senses, social innovation is a progressive approach (in the widest sense), clearly at odds with what Albert Hirschman called the 'rhetorics of reaction' (Hirschman, 1991), the theories and arguments that present all attempts at conscious social progress as liable to futility (they simply will not work), jeopardy (if they have any effect at all it will be to destroy something we value), and perversity (the claim that if any attempts at improvement had effects these would not be the ones intended, so that, for example, wars on poverty leave behind a dependent underclass). Social innovation tends to ally itself, by contrast, with the mirror rhetorics of progress (Mulgan, 2009): rhetorics of justice – the arguments for righting wrongs and meeting needs, whether these are for pensions or affordable housing, which draw on fundamental moral senses of fairness. Its practitioners draw on rhetorics of progress, the idea that change is cumulative and dynamic: new reforms are needed to reinforce old ones, or to prevent backsliding. So, for example, new rights to maternity leave are essential to make a reality of past laws outlawing gender discrimination. And they use rhetorics of tractability: the claims that social action works, and that whether the problem is unemployment or climate change, the right mix of actions can solve it.

These optimistic views about the potential for change, and their related claim that the future can be found in the present, in embryo, are highly political stances that are largely inconceivable outside the contexts of active democracy and civil society. They connect social innovation to a deep democratic belief in the virtue of empowering society to shape society; a view that the more broadly power is spread, the greater the capacity for good to prevail; and an enlightenment belief in the possibility of cumulative growth of knowledge and insight. Such ideas also connect to the world view of science and technology, conceived of as progressive in nature, and in impact, with technology having its own logics of evolution as one invention leads to another.

This progressive instinct is central to the liberal democratic view of the world, but alien to many strands of conservatism, rigid Marxism-Leninism, theocracy, and belief in autocratic rule. It also runs counter to many of the claims of the Austrian school of philosophy and economics which, as I show later, has contributed important insights to social innovation, but whose fundamental stance was much closer to the rhetorics of reaction than to those of progress.

One of the most interesting contemporary exponents of the connection between social innovation and progress is the Brazilian theorist, professor of law at Harvard, and former minister, Roberto Mangabeira Unger, who in a series of works analysed the 'plasticity' of the world, and the role of law in processes of social change. His recent book *The Self Awakened* (Mangabeira Unger, 2007) presents a bold attempt to provide a philosophical foundation for social innovation. In it, Unger argues that individuals and communities are not contained by their present circumstance: 'the habitual settings for action and thought, especially as organised by the institutions of society and the conventions of culture, are incapable of containing us ... this transcendence of self over its formative circumstances occurs in every department of human experience'. From this, Unger deduces a more fundamental argument about the potential for systemic change: 'we can do more than innovate in the content of our social and cultural contexts: we can innovate as well in the character of our relation to them: we can change the extent to which they imprison us' (ibid., p. 56). Unger draws on the pragmatist traditions of Peirce and Dewey (which I discuss later), but gives them a modern, political edge, advancing their arguments to advocate systematic experimentation, a model of social change as self-aware but also cautious about the hubris of grand plans and reforms. Its core is a belief in people as struggling with constraint and contingency, but able to create entirely new ideas and things; a belief in permanent innovation so that 'we rethink and redesign our productive tasks in the course of executing them', using 'the smaller variations that are at hand to produce the bigger variations that do not yet exist' (ibid., p. 43); and a practical commitment to making change internal to social and political institutions, through permanent experimentation. In this, co-operation and innovation are seen as twins, but also in tension with each other since innovation will tend to disrupt.

The social sciences could play a central role in this story but instead are 'dominated by ... rationalisation, humanisation and escapism' which together 'disarm the transcending imagination' (ibid., p. 110). His view is echoed by many practitioners: social science looks backwards and lacks the tools to look forwards. And so although we need evidence, we also need not to be imprisoned by it.

Stephen Goldsmith – a rare combination of politician, entrepreneur, and academic – made parallel comments on 'the scourge of experts': 'programme, legislative, and regulatory professionals' who 'inadvertently limit civic entrepreneurship by asserting a technical definition of "the right approach"' so that credentials and prescribed approaches matter more than results (Goldsmith, 2010).

The solution, according to Unger, is to see the problem-solving mind as the bridge of 'is' and 'ought'. We become human 'only by resisting the constraints of all the established structures ... of life, organisation, thought and character'. That means teaching children from an early age with the 'means to resist the present' (2007, p. 206) and not to see it as fixed, law-like and immutable. It also leads Unger to advocate systematic experimentation – a vision of society and government constantly trying new things, sometimes failing, and sometimes succeeding, but with experiment as the only reliable path to progress.

This view of life accords with the implicit views of many innovators, restlessly resisting the present, and struggling to avoid being weighed down by the common sense of everyday reality, while also avoiding the risk of floating off into fantasy.

It chimes with many of the most interesting innovations in innovation: the widespread experiment in new tools for crowd-sourcing, the mobilization of mass social entrepreneurship, or of users as shapers of innovation and design.

It also leads to a strong commitment to pluralism. This is the view, contrary to the claims of Marxism and the more assertive strands of modern economics, that societies are singular, indivisible, and organized according to a single coherent logic. Instead, Unger and others argue that even if everything connects they do so only loosely. Attempts to fit all things into a single frame of logic lead to pathologies and errors. This is the pluralism explored by figures such as Daniel Bell, who showed how advanced capitalist societies are made up of spheres with very different logics, languages, and rhythms of change, and by Jane Jacobs, who showed how healthy societies contain within themselves often contradictory moral syndromes (and whose work on cities, as I show later, provided some of the mental frameworks for innovators). Bruno Latour's development of actor-network theory is also a very useful corrective to the notion that there is a coherent entity called a society which has views and interests (Latour, 2005). In short, the foundation of social innovation is a belief in people's capacity to create, to shape and experiment, in tension with the present, but also with a bias against both over-confident top down control or planning, and the fatalistic view that nothing works.

Life and forms and the dialectics of change

The next set of theories amplify this exploration of plasticity. The philosopher and sociologist Georg Simmel provided a particularly compelling account that resonates with the experience of innovators themselves. After writing some of the definitive works of modern sociology, Simmel became increasingly interested in fundamental questions about the nature of life and its processes (Simmel, 2010). Life, he wrote, involves flux, freedom, and the creative exploration of new combinations, yet it constantly creates forms and it is through forms that action is organized. So genetic mutations lead to the form of the body and the cell; musical experiment leads to forms like the symphony or the three-minute pop song; and social action leads to the creation of new institutions. Yet it is the nature of forms that they are almost opposite to life: they are fixed, permanent, limited by rules. And so forms both express life and also stand against it.

Simmel used this insight to develop a remarkable set of ideas that went on to influence leading thinkers from Martin Heidegger to Jurgen

Habermas. But his account also echoes the common experience of innovators themselves. Out of engagement with the world they come up with ideas, usually through messy processes of trial and error, 'kneading the dough' again and again until it takes the right form. Then ideas become formalized, codified, and defined. Then in time they become new organizations and practices. But having become forms of this kind they also begin to become new orthodoxies. The greatest aspiration of the innovator is in this sense, paradoxically, to stop innovation, so that their idea can be scaled or mainstreamed. Not surprisingly, many innovators experience ambivalence when they see their ideas translated into formal organizations. Some fall out with their creations; and some have to be moved to one side by their organization as the necessary condition for it to grow (since growth usually involves further formalization).

Philosophy also points to other similarly dialectical features of innovation in practice. In Hegel's account of change, like Simmel's, change is described as taking place through processes of differentiation: by becoming different from what exists, or even negating it, we create the new and define our own identity. These processes of dialectical change are sometimes summarized in the famous triad – thesis, antithesis and synthesis – which can be a rough description of some of the history of social innovation with its common patterns of inversion in which peasants become bankers or patients become doctors or readers become editors of encyclopedias, usually on the way to new syntheses which combine elements of the old as well as the new. Dialectics can also (more accurately) be understood as a method for finding unity in opposites, ideas, and practices that hold in balance apparently divergent forces, like the pressure to be simultaneously commercial and social.

But even more relevant to the experience of social innovation is Hegel's account of the dynamics of externalization and internalization (Pines, M. and Hopper, E. 2003 92). Often ideas have to be extracted from daily life, taken from tacit knowledge and turned into formal shape before they can become powerful. In this externalized form they can then be processed and adapted – for example, defined as a business model or a business plan. But they only become useful if they are then reinserted into the practice of everyday life and internalized into the thinking of providers or citizens. Hegel's apparently abstract ideas were used to guide innovation in Japanese firms, notably through the theories of Nonaka, who paid particular attention to the need for processes that drew out the insights of tacit knowledge among shopfloor workers, and then made them formal (Nonaka and Takeuchi, 1995).

They also fit with what we know about the processes of scaling and growth of social innovations. These are sometimes portrayed simply as diffusion or spread, or in terms of the growth of enterprises. But without exception, social innovations with the greatest impact achieve their effects by changing how people think and how they see the world: in other words the are reinternalized.

Evolution and complexity: Frames for thinking about the processes of innovation

The next set of sources are present, if only implicitly, in any contemporary discussion of social change: the ideas of Charles Darwin and a century-and-a-half of thinking about the nature of evolution. Innovation is in large part a process of evolution that has direct parallels in the natural world. Evolutionary theory in particular helps us to focus on the three stages that are present in any process of innovation. One involves mutation – in evolutionary theory the random mutation of DNA that creates the potential for adaptation. Most mutations contribute little; and those that do contribute significant change generally fail. Sex is one of the devices which ensures a constant supply of new variants. Then comes selection – in evolutionary theory the focus is on fitness for environments: occasional mutations outperform their predecessors and thus allow new types of organism to flourish. Finally there is replication – those mutations that pass the tests of selection will grow, displacing others and replicating their genes. Only the fit survive. Within evolutionary theory there are a huge range of sub-theories and metaphors that can be useful: such as the theories of predator–prey relationships and the many claims of evolutionary psychology which provide some insights into why certain kinds of innovation arise and then spread. The metaphor of the 'meme', the cultural equivalent of genes, has also proved influential, though so far less useful for analysis.

In the social field, today's interest is not in social Darwinism (the various late nineteenth-century attempts to directly transplant evolutionary ideas into society petered out in failure). Instead the interest lies in an inverted Darwinism of conscious action to advance evolution for human ends. By its nature, social change cannot be comprehensively planned: but it can be pushed, nudged. and guided. Where Darwinism focuses on how different organisms cope with changes to the environment, the inverted Darwinism of social innovation attends to how action can change the environment as well as the actors within it (so social innovators, for example, work to influence demand for their ideas as well as their supply) (Ali, Mulgan et al., 2008). It leads to interest in how societies can institutionalize some of the features of evolutionary processes (e.g. through crowd-sourcing ideas, rapid prototyping, and so on). While evolution in nature evolves through mutations of individual elements in the genome, social innovation tends to involve more conscious hybrids, combinations, and adaptations.

Evolutionary theory provides some very direct concepts for innovators. But there are also many other perspectives on social change which are essentially evolutionary in nature and which have shaped the practice of the field. Jane Jacobs, influenced by the work of Michael Young and others, used a variant of evolutionary thinking about cities as an antidote to the excesses of top-down planning. She favoured organic development, trial, and error; dispersed power, and in later writings extended this to a world view of how economies and societies should be run. More recently the open data and open source movement have advocated self-organizing systems which use multiple horizontal links and complexity to solve problems.

In some of these fields there is growing attention to the importance of co-evolution. Biologists now emphasize the co-evolution of genes and cultures, making it meaningless to claim that a particular trait is x per cent caused by genes and y per cent by culture. We know much more about the co-evolution of institutions and behaviours too – whether at the large scale of democracy and welfare states, or at the more granular level of public health programmes. Some of the difficulties experienced in spreading social innovations – such as Grameen's micro-credit model or the public health models of Finland – can best be explained through this lens.

Evolutionary theory itself has c-evolved with complexity theory, which has been much drawn on by people involved in social innovation (Westley et al., 2006). Complexity theory is neither a single theory, nor wholly coherent and consistent. Rather, it is a family of concepts and insights that have been applied in many fields, sometimes extending the earlier insights of systems thinking and sometimes pointing in different directions. Its key concepts include: the role of feedback loops (or, more broadly, feedback processes) to understand why change sometimes accelerates and more often is inhibited; the idea of 'strange attractors', and of social change as the shift from one to another; the idea that societies are made up of both tightly and loosely coupled systems which respond very differently to shocks; the idea of organizations operating at 'the edge of chaos'; the idea of emergence, of complex structures and institutions emerging from very simple principles; and the idea of non-linearity, that many social processes do not follow linear relationships.

The insights of figures such as Ilya Prigogine, Brian Arthur, Stuart Kauffman – and others coming from very different backgrounds such as Niklas Luhmann, Humberto Maturana, and Donald Schon – have made this a rich and stimulating field. It has certainly provided a useful antidote to the more simplistic currents of social innovation; anyone who has engaged with complexity theory is unlikely to talk glibly about 'solving social problems' or 'scaling' solutions. Instead they are more likely to recognize that the majority of issues that motivate innovation are complex, messy, interconnected, and not amenable to one-dimensional solutions. Complexity theory tends to force attention to the connections between things, to feedback and feedforward processes; to path dependence and to the many ways in which initial conditions can radically change outcomes. It implies that policy should create generative rules rather than detailed top-down prescription; that it should allow evolution and adaptation to local conditions; and that it should encourage the maximum feedback. In recent years these perspectives have been helped by improvements in modelling techniques which have made it easier to map and simulate social dynamics, or the patterns of linkages between social enterprises.

So far these theories have mainly been useful for providing a rich menu of metaphors, and a mindset. Complexity theory has suffered from the weakness of all attempts to transplant theories from the natural sciences to social sciences: the inability to take account of reflexivity, the awareness of the people within systems. The same has been true in economics. Figures like Benoit Mandelbrot successfully used complexity theory to demolish the hubristic claims of financial forecasters – but offered little to replace them (Mandelbrot and Hudson, 2008). A good example of both the strengths and weaknesses is the case of the hugely successful campaign to cut AIDS in Uganda. The ABC campaign (abstain, be faithful, use condoms) has been described as an example of complexity theory in practice: ABC provided a few simple principles that could then be extended and adapted in many different ways. Yet the relative failure of attempts to replicate the ABC model confirms that complexity theory is rarely useful for prediction, or for shaping actions except at the most general level. As Gareth Morgan suggested nearly 30 years ago in his classic work on 'images of organisation', these ideas may be useful mainly as ideas and frames rather than as tools which can directly guide action (Morgan, 1997: 222).

Innovation studies

Innovation was not a central concern for the classical and neo-classical economists. Innovations were seen as exogenous; or as a black box that did not need to be explained. But since the 1950s, as the importance of innovation has become ever more obvious, a field of innovation studies has slowly taken shape that has had some influence on social innovation.

One strand of innovation studies tried to make innovation more endogenous to economics – this was the central theme of the work of Robert Solow (who attempted to analyse the contribution of new knowledge and innovation to economic growth and argued that, in the long run, growth in per capita output depends *only* on the rate of technological progress resulting from improvements in outputs or the efficiency with which inputs are transformed into outputs, and of the endogenous growth theory associated with Paul Romer. William Baumol described capitalism as an innovation machine, as well as showing how the 'cost disease' associated with labour-intensive activities like teaching and nursing can become a prompt for innovation (Baumol, 2003). Everett Rogers pioneered the study of diffusion patterns, both in business and beyond, (Rogers, 2003) and was followed by an impressive school of successors (Stoneman and Diederen, 1994) studying the cognitive, economic, as well as organizational barriers to diffusion, and the importance of new kinds of behaviour (what Bart Nooteboom calls 'scripts') in business and social innovation.

Various other disciplines have also offered their insights, including the sociology of innovation (e.g. Michael Piore's work on the decisive role played by interpretation). Historians of innovation have shown how many innovations have long roots, and countered the idea that innovation is a modern innovation. Arnold Pacey studied the roles of institutions as varied as monasteries and the military in innovation, and suggested that the most creative societies may have been those 'in which many types of institutions were active and in dialogue with each other', cutting across the different sectors and professions (see Stoneman and Diederen, 1994: 19). Richard Nelson's work focused on the transformational impact of some technologies, with obvious relevance to social innovation (Nelson, 1982). He too has been a pioneer of the analysis of innovation systems, and there is now a lively body of work underway looking at the dynamics of systems within nations or sectors, with some theorists connecting innovation patterns to broader changes in political economy and the global division of labour, and others extending the innovation systems approach to the social field and public services.

The parallel study of scientific innovation has cross-fertilized with the economics of innovation, for example through the work of Nathan Rosenberg on the ways in which the end uses of innovations can be very different from the ones originally envisaged (a pattern which is certainly common in social innovation). Brian Arthur's recent work on technology is a particularly impressive attempt to provide a more structured analysis of technological change with clear implications for social innovation. Technology often starts with observation of natural phenomena – such as light, heat, and motion in the case of physical technologies, and social interactions in the case of social ones. It then seeks to replicate or otherwise mimic these in ways that amplify their power. It is organized in architectures that include sub-systems and components, each of which can evolve in tandem. And it has its own logic of evolution, as advances in one field prompt advances in another, or as an entirely new domain of knowledge is brought to bear on a particular problem. Arthur highlights the importance of domains, and domain knowledge; the mix of formal and informal insight that allows technologists to assemble new combinations. Social innovation arguably still lacks both the formal knowledge and the depth of experience that characterize more mature fields of innovation.

The most visible strand of innovation studies has been within business studies. Figures such as Rosabeth Moss Kanter, Gary Hamel, and Clayton Christensen have tried to understand some of the common patterns of innovation, such as the role of disruption or the relatively poor performance of very successful innovations in their early phases of competition with more mature, and more optimized, incumbents. There has also been a recent surge of interest in open innovation (Henry Chesbrough, 2006) and user-driven innovation (Eric von Hippel, 1988), both of which are interesting examples of ideas with a long history in the social field being adapted to business.

The field of social innovation has drawn many useful insights from these literatures, and many have used the basic concepts of innovation studies: the distinctions between incremental and radical innovation; first mover and second mover advantage; the importance of absorptive capacity; and the ways in which innovation diffusion involve innovation too, since adopters will succeed best if they further enhance the innovations they adopt. In a later section I discuss the implications of one of the most impressive strands of innovation studies – the work undertaken over many years by Christopher Freeman, Giovanni Dosi,

Luc Soete, and Ian Miles – which combine rigorous empirical analysis with theoretical creativity in mapping the larger 'techno-economic paradigms' within which innovation takes place.

The field of innovation studies has also raised fundamental questions which are relevant to the social field. A major issue is whether innovation is slowing down, either because the pool of possible innovation is being exhausted, or because of greater complexity requiring more skills, more interdisciplinary teams and longer time periods to bring any specific idea to fruition. The evidence in some sectors seems to confirm this view – but it is entirely possible that new technological breakthroughs could suddenly accelerate the pace of innovation, as has happened repeatedly in IT. Other important issues include the links between market structures and innovation. Some research suggests that sectors with oligopolistic cores and competitive edges may be more innovative than either monopolies or sectors made up of small competitors. But little serious analysis has been done of how much this is applicable to social fields. The same is true of analyses of the role of the state in driving innovation. This is obviously true in countries such as Japan, Taiwan, Israel, and France. In the US, although the sums invested by government (primarily through the Pentagon) are much greater than anywhere else, this has been in some respects a 'hidden developmental state' that has coexisted with an ideological aversion to state involvement and has made the scale of engagement invisible even to many leading practitioners and commentators. Again, this has made it harder to judge what kinds of developmental state might work best for social innovation.

Another example is the lack of any definitive view in the literature on whether businesses and other organizations benefit most from specialist innovation teams, funds, and labs, or from making innovation pervasive across the whole organization. There has been much analysis of the boundary between public returns and private returns in R&D, but this has proven hard to extend to the social field. Nor is there much clarity on how relevant intellectual property (IP) is. Clearly it is vital to innovation in technology. But it is fairly rare for IP to be easily protectable in the social field.

Much of the research on business innovation has been broadly descriptive rather than offering testable theses, and some of the business literature has been discredited by eulogizing companies for their innovative genius just when they were about to hit crises. Some of the most useful work may be research which has sought to interrogate widely assumed patterns. A good example is the work on tools for innovation which has challenged some of the claims made for radical 'out of the box' innovation made by business gurus and consultancies, showing how these are better understood as combinations of incremental steps which may therefore be rather easier for others to emulate (Markman and Wood, 2009).

Theories of innovation and entrepreneurship

Our next set of sources concerns the agents of change. In Adam Smith's classic account, the combination of markets, legal frameworks, and property rights translates the self-interest and greed of millions of individuals into a force that promotes the prosperity of all. The brilliance of the market mechanism is that it is automatic: by harnessing motives and energies which are already there it avoids the need for a king or a commander to 'run' the economy. Instead the economy runs itself and rewards both performance and innovation. In the eighteenth century, Adam Smith was equally famous for a very different set of writings which looked at the 'moral sentiments' of sympathy and compassion that hold societies together. Although he did not put it in these terms, the two strands of his work can be brought together in the idea that all modern societies depend not only on the invisible hand of the market but also on another invisible hand: the legal and fiscal arrangements that serve to channel moral sentiments, the motivations of care, civic energy, and social commitment, into practical form and thus into the service of the common good (Mulgan and Landry, 1995). Just as markets draw on the energies and creativity of entrepreneurs willing to risk money and prestige, so does social change draw on the often invisible fecundity of tens of thousands of individuals and small groups who spot needs and innovate solutions.

The most influential theorist who has been drawn on to make sense of these processes is Joseph Schumpeter, whose work, often overshadowed in the twentieth century, has enjoyed a great revival of interest over the last decade, partly thanks to the growing importance of innovation in the economy. This revival of interest has been helped by some superb books, such as *The Prophet of Innovation* (McCraw, 2007), and by the vividness of much of Schumpeter's writings. Here are his words on the spirit of social pioneers:

> In the breast of one who wishes to do something new, the forces of habit rise up and bear witness against the embryonic project. A new and another kind of effort of will is therefore necessary in order to wrest, amidst the work and care of the daily round, scope and time

for conceiving and working out the new combination ... This mental freedom presupposes a great surplus force over the everyday demand and is something peculiar and by nature rare.

(1934, p. 86)

Schumpeter's decisive contribution to economic theory was his attention to the role of entrepreneurs in driving change, and pushing markets away from equilibrium. Schumpeter described 'stabilized capitalism as a contradiction in terms', and was interested in the dynamics of change. He was perhaps the greatest advocate for seeing capitalism through the lens of entrepreneurs and entrepreneurship, with the implication that the task for policy is to give them as much free rein as possible, so that they can hunt out value.

The Schumpeterian view of how economies work has become much more widely accepted in recent decades. In his account, the entrepreneur is the decisive actor, seeking out opportunities, spotting under-served markets or unused assets, taking risks (with investors' money), and reaping rewards. His attention to the vital role of credit in providing funds for entrepreneurs to take risks has also become mainstream.

This perspective is very different in spirit to most of mainstream economics. It emphasizes the search for what is not known, what is uncertain and what is immeasurable. In perfect markets with perfect information there is no room for entrepreneurs. Instead, entrepreneurship highlights the difficulty of the world, its resistance to predictable plans, and how we learn by bumping into things, and then navigating around them. What entrepreneurs do is not wholly rational, indeed their success is presented as a kind of magic: in Schumpeter's words, 'the success of everything depends on intuition, the capacity of seeing things in a way which afterwards proves to be true, even though it cannot be established at the moment, and of grasping the essential fact, discarding the unessential, even though one can give no account of the principles by which this is done' (1934, p. 85).

A very different view of entrepreneurship – associated with the work of Israel Kirzner (Kirzner, 1973) – sees it not as the upsetter of equilibrium but as the creator of equilibrium, using information to take advantage of disequilibria and thus push the economy back into balance (Shockley and Frank, 2011). Like Schumpeter, Kirzner saw the entrepreneurial mind as distinct from rational management: it spots emerging patterns and 'weak signals', to use the current phrase: entrepreneurs demonstrate 'the ways in which the human agent can, by imaginative, bold leaps of faith, and determination, in fact create the future for which his present acts are designed' (Kirzner, 1982, p. 150). Entrepreneurship thrives in fields of uncertainty, on the edges of industries and disciplines; much less so in stable contexts or where risk can be calculated.

In either light, entrepreneurship is not peculiar to business, and the Austrian school of economists and philosophers, concerned with action in conditions of uncertainty, recognized this from the start. Schumpeter wrote of entrepreneurship in politics as well as business (and was for a brief period a minister), and saw entrepreneurship as a universal phenomenon, albeit one that was particularly dynamic in capitalist economies. Ludwig Von Mises wrote that entrepreneurship 'is not the particular feature of a special group or class of men; it is inherent in every action and burdens every actor' (Von Mises, 1949/1996). So it has been natural to extend Schumpeter to other fields: to see within universities some academics acting as entrepreneurs, assembling teams, spotting gaps, promoting the superiority of their ideas, and bringing together whatever resources they can find to win allegiance; or to see the founders and builders of great religions as great entrepreneurs, pulling together belief, attraction, and money.

Social entrepreneurship adapts the same ideas to civil society and to social resources; it leads to an interest in the character of entrepreneurs; their motivations; the patterns of creating enterprises and then growing them; and, as with business entrepreneurs, the conflicts between them and the providers of capital on the one hand and the providers of labour on the other (Swedberg, 2009).

Just as Schumpeter's account encouraged a heroic view of the business entrepreneur battling against the resistance of society, so has it affected the view of social entrepreneurs. At one point there were even claims (from one of the leading US support organizations) of a formula – one social entrepreneur for every million in the population (though interestingly, it then went to the other extreme with the more inclusive slogan 'everyone a changemaker') (Drayton, 2006). According to the radical individualistic view, the more that exceptional individuals could be provided with resources, and the more that any constraints could be removed, the more likely they would be to solve social problems.

By contrast, there has been rather less attention to the other key actors in social innovation (the networks, teams, patrons, and investors), though, as in the case of natural science, the more particular cases are studied in detail the more it becomes apparent that individuals only achieve great things because of the complementary skills and institutions that surround them. It is interesting to note that Schumpeter in his later years became increasingly interested in 'co-operative entrepreneurship' within large firms and the role of teams, and was convinced that this was a vital field for study.

The recent discussions of Schumpeter and Kirzner have provided a useful richness to the discussion of social entrepreneurship. They have, for example, opened up research on motivations. Schumpeter recognized that profit was unlikely to be the only or even the main motivation for business entrepreneurs, and clearly for social entrepreneurs a wide range of motives intermingle, from altruism to recognition, financial reward to the hunger for power. Their work also encourages attention to patterns of resistance from existing interests and ways of thought, and to the importance of there being sources of credit and investment for social entrepreneurs and innovators – why, for example, specialized banks (such as Banca Prossima and Banca Etica), or public investment funds for social entrepreneurs (such as the UK's Un Ltd) matter so much.

Neither Schumpeter nor Kirzner, however, addressed the broader question of value. Both treat economic value as an unproblematic concept. Yet one of the keys to their wider use may be to link them to parallel developments in the field of economic sociology, particularly the work of figures such as Harrison White and David Stark. Drawing in creative ways on the work of Luc Boltanski (BoltanskI, 2001), they have shown how societies and economies are made up of systems of 'multiple worth', each with very different ways of thinking about value. Seen through this lens, entrepreneurship is not just about spotting new opportunities for profit. Instead, in David Stark's words, it involves 'the ability to keep multiple orders of worth in play and to exploit the resulting ambiguity' (Stark, 2009). In other words, it goes beyond the ability to exploit uncertainty rather than just calculable risk, but also entails arbitraging, or translating between, distinct fields. This is surely a good description of much social innovation and entrepreneurship, whose most successful practitioners are fluent across fields – medicine and business, voluntary action and education, law and politics – and able to juggle multiple orders of worth. It may also be one of the crucial reasons why attempts to distil social value into single metrics has been largely unsuccessful: by denying the plurality of value systems, these attempt to bring certainty to actions that have to be ambiguous or multiple in nature.

How we think about entrepreneurship, and theorize it, has obvious practical implications. The idea of business entrepreneurship led in time to the idea that states should not only enable it through laws and (light) regulations, but should also support it, and many governments provide tax incentives, training courses, and celebrations to encourage entrepreneurship. Social entrepreneurship, too, has encouraged various kinds of support from governments and foundations: prizes, funds, and networks. In both cases, however, research has still not resolved some fundamental questions: the balance to be struck between backing individuals, teams, and organizations; whether to provide only knowledge and advice or also investment; what attitude to take to risk?

While Schumpeter's celebration of entrepreneurship has entered the mainstream, some of his other frames of analysis have not yet been adequately integrated, in particular his accounts of long-term technological change and the rhythms of business cycles which create opportunities for entrepreneurs (these I cover in a later section). Nor has his account of bureaucratization; Schumpeter lamented in the mid-1940s:

> ... the business of teams of trained specialists who turn out what is required and make it work in predictable ways. The romance of earlier commercial adventure is rapidly wearing away, because so many things can be strictly calculated that had of old to be visualised in a flash of genius.
>
> (1942, p. 132)

The implication is that while every innovator may aspire to scaling and mainstreaming, and more rigorous measurement, they should also be careful what they wish for.

Techno-economic paradigms and the historical context for social innovation

Social innovation has always taken place. But it is powerfully shaped by historical context. What kinds of innovation will be possible at any point will be determined by prevailing technologies, institutions, and mentalities. Wonderful ideas may simply be impossible at the wrong time. Some of the most influential and useful set of ideas for making sense of historical contexts have come from a group of academics led by Christopher Freeman, Carlota Perez, and figures such as Luc Soete (Dosi et al., 1988). Their aim was to understand the long waves of technological and economic change, and to seek out common patterns and congruences between technologies, economics, and social organization. This has also been the concern of the work of figures such as Josef Hochgerner, who have attempted to synthesize perspectives from Weber to Schumpeter with more recent accounts of innovation systems.

Perhaps the most influential current theorist of the connections between technological change and the economy is the Venezuelan economist Carlota Perez, who is a scholar of the successive techno-economic paradigms which define the shape of the economy. She has studied how these intersect with the financial cycles that have repeated themselves again and again during capitalism's relatively brief history. In Perez's account, which builds on Kondratiev and Schumpeter, the cycles begin with the emergence of new technologies and infrastructures that promise great wealth. These then fuel frenzies of speculative investment, with dramatic rises in stock and other prices whether in the canal mania of the 1790s, the railway mania of the 1830s and 1840s, the surge of global infrastructures in the 1870s and 1880s, or the booms that accompanied the car, electricity, and telephone in the 1920s, and biotechnology and the internet in the 1990s and 2000s.

During these phases of technological exuberance, finance is in the ascendant and laissez faire policies become the norm. Letting markets freely grow seems evidently wise when they are fuelling such visible explosions of wealth. During these periods, some investors and entrepreneurs become very rich very quickly. Exuberance in markets may be reflected in exuberance and laissez faire in personal morals – a glittering world of parties, celebrities, and gossip for the rest of the public to lap up and experience vicariously. Entrepreneurs take wild risks and reap wild rewards. The economy appears to be a place for easy predation, offering rewards without too much work, and plenty of chances to siphon off surpluses.

The booms then turn out to be bubbles and are followed by dramatic crashes. The years 1797, 1847, 1893, 1929 and 2008 are a few of the decisive ones when crashes sent values tumbling. They are crashes of stock markets, and brought with them the dramatic bankruptcy of many of the most prominent companies of the booms, like so many railway companies in the later nineteenth century. Sometimes currencies collapse too.

After these crashes, and periods of turmoil, the potential of the new technologies and infrastructures is eventually realized. But that only happens once new social, political, and economic institutions and regulations come into being which are better aligned with the characteristics of the new economy, and with the underlying desires of the society. Radical social innovation plays a key role in making possible much more widespread deployment of the key technologies. Once that has happened, economies then go through surges of growth as well as social progress, like the 'belle epoque' or the post-war miracle.

These patterns can be seen clearly in the Great Depression and its aftermath. Before the crisis of 1929, the elements of a new economy and a new society were already available, and the promise of technologies like the car and telephone encouraged the speculative bubbles of the 1920s. But they were neither understood by the people in power, nor were they embedded in institutions. Then, during the 1930s, the economy transformed, in Perez's words, from one based on:

> ... steel, heavy electrical equipment, great engineering works (canals, bridges, dams, tunnels) and heavy chemistry, mainly geared towards big spenders ... into a mass production system catering to consumers and the massive defense markets. Radical demand management and income redistribution innovations had to be made, of which the directly economic role of the state is perhaps the most important.
>
> (cited in Mulgan, 2009)

What resulted was the rise of mass-consumerism, and an economy: supported by ubiquitous infrastructures for electricity, roads, and telecommunications, and

> ... based on low cost oil and energy intensive materials (especially petrochemicals and synthetics), and led by giant oil, chemical and automobile and other mass durable goods producers. Its 'ideal' type of productive organization at the plant levels was the continuous flow assembly-line ... the 'ideal' type of firm was the 'corporation' ... including in-house R&D and operating in oligopolistic markets in which advertising and marketing activities played a major role. It required large numbers of middle range skills in both blue and white collar areas ... a vast infrastructural network of motorways, service stations, airports, oil and petrol distribution systems ....
>
> (Dosi et al., 1988: 60)

Seen in the light, the Great Depression helped usher in new economic and welfare policies in countries like New Zealand and Sweden that later became the mainstream across the developed world. In the US, it led to banking reform, the New Deal, social security, and unemployment insurance (both backed by big business), and later the GI Bill of Rights. In Britain, it was the Depression, as much as war, that led to the creation of the welfare state and the National Health Service in the 1940s. Social innovation thrived in the wake of the Depression, with a surge of energy in many societies as welfare states were created, along with new arrangements at work and in politics. What emerged were more strongly bonded societies and new commitment devices – the large firm, the welfare state, as well as new and revitalized political parties, all of which were ways of getting people to pre-commit to actions and behaviours that then created value for them. Predatory extremes were reined in (in the USA, marginal income tax rates peaked at 91% in the 1950s), and the dominant spirit in many countries emphasized fairness and fair chances.

An important dimension of these patterns is that phases of entre-preneurial exuberance tend to be followed by phases of consolidation and oligopoly. Industries become more ordered; the products and services they provide become more settled and more reliable, alongside dominance by just a few firms. Bureaucracy wins out over buccaneering risktakers. This happened to the Hollywood film industry, telephony, and cars in the 1920s and then to software and computing 60 years later. Firms like Apple and Amazon are attempting a similar consolida-tion today, using business models that integrate vertically and lock in their customers. For them there are the benefits of monopoly; for their customers, the benefits of stability. Parallel patterns can be found in the social field: periods of intensive innovation and entrepreneurialism (such as the last decades of the nineteenth century) tend to be followed by periods of consolidation, as large NGOs become more bureaucratic and more managerial in approach.

Carlota Perez suggests that we may be on the verge of another great period of institutional innovation and experiment that will lead to new compromises between the claims of capital and the claims of society and of nature. The rise of a low-carbon economy, implying new kinds of arrangement for housing, transport, fuel; the maturing of a broadband economy, with ubiquitous social networks and open data: these are all part of this story, and they provide some of the context for social inno-vations. Examples include the rise of the open source movement and new forms of web-based collaboration; the rise of new types of green NGO and social enterprise which are helping to push up recycling or push down energy usage.

Here, Perez's work intersects with parallel theories which have tried to make sense of the dynamics of societies based on information and communication, and their distinctive patterns of power which have made civic networked forms of organization much more powerful. Manuel Castells's subtle and extensive accounts aim at a synthetic view which stretches from business to identity and social movements (Castells, 1996). His work has shown the inter-relationships between technological innovation, social innovation, and power. Others, like Yann Moulier Boutang, have tried to suggest a new phase of capitalism in which new kinds of enterprise (including ones based on common goods) are thriving (Moulier Boutang; Yann, 2007). Timo Hamalainen has linked these arguments to industrial strategy at the national and regional levels, and there has been a strong strand of research in Europe on the role of regions and places in the social economy.

There is much to debate in these sweeping historical overviews. They can be criticized for being overdeterministic, or for exaggerating the influence of technology. But as Eric Hobsbawm wrote of Kondratiev cycles, they have 'convinced many historians and even some economists that there is something in them, even if we do not know what' (1999, p. 135), and they helpfully force attention to the fit between specific innovations and their larger context.

So, for example, much contemporary social innovation is clearly linked to broader changes happening to the service economy: the rising importance of platforms; the ever more formal structuring of circles of support in ageing or childhood; and the many trends loosely summed up in the term 'personalization'. Care, health, and education are likely to rise significantly as shares of GDP, encouraging a proliferation of new social business models organized around intensive support (Maxmin and Zuboff, 2002). But it is the nature of these moments of change that prediction is impossible. As Perez puts it; 'as at other turning points, imagination has to look forward, not back, and there are no ready-made recipes … What lies ahead are many social conflicts and confrontations, negotiations, agreements and compromises'.

Pragmatism: The epistemology of social innovation

The next family of ideas takes us back to philosophy, and concerns the nature of the knowledge associated with social innovation. Here the most influential and useful set of ideas comes from the late nineteenth century, and in particular the pragmatist school of Charles Peirce, William James, and John Dewey. They are of interest because they accurately describe the types of knowledge involved in social innovation, knowledge which is often rooted in practice, and which is not timeless or universal or abstract in the way that knowledge about physics would be.

This is a good summary by one author of the nature of their ideas:

> … ideas are not out there waiting to be discovered but are tools that people devise to cope with the world in which they find

> themselves ... ideas are produced not by individuals but are social ...
> ideas do not develop according to some inner logic of their own but are
> entirely dependent, like germs, on human careers and environment ...
> and since ideas are provisional responses to particular situations their sur-
> vival depends on not on their immutability but on their adaptability.
>
> (Farrar, Straus and Giroux, 2001, pp. xi–xii)

The pragmatists went out of fashion for a time. But it is striking how many of the most interesting contemporary thinkers have reengaged with them. I have already mentioned Roberto Mangabeira Unger's use of their ideas. Bruno Latour, one of the world's leading thinkers on the place of science in society, is another example of the creative reappropriation of this tradition, notably in his recent book on Walter Lippman and the 'phantom public' which explores the point, funda- mental to much of the work of social innovation, that in processes of social change it may be necessary to create the public that becomes the subject of action. In other words, it is not enough to have a good idea, not enough to promote it or even to show its relevance. At each stage of social development a new kind of collective capacity may be needed which then calls forth the innovation.

On a more prosaic level, the growth of individual social innovations demonstrates a similar pattern. Innovations only grow if there is the right mix of effective supply – which means evidence that the inno- vation works – and effective demand, which means someone willing to pay for it. For innovators, the implication may be that generating demand (for such things as drug treatment or eldercare) can often be more important than promoting supply; that in turn may require the creation of a new kind of public: a public that cares about cutting carbon emission; a public that consciously stands for humanitarian interven- tion to alleviate famine; a public that is willing to put its savings into social investment products.

The other current of contemporary practice which relates to the philo- sophical tradition of pragmatism, and to many of the other theoretical currents described in earlier sections, is what could be called 'experimen- talism': the belief in constant experiment in social forms. This was of course the scientific method, and always intrigued social scientists as well as social reformers. Why couldn't society conduct experiments precisely analogous to those conducted by chemists or physicists? The economist Irving Fisher is generally credited as the inventor of rando- mized control trials, and used them first in agriculture. A couple of decades later, Karl Popper suggested a grander philosophical account of experiment in his book the *Open Society and its Enemies*, advocating a vision of societies and science engaged in perpetual processes of experiment and disproof, with certainty always elusive, and openness to falsification as the true mark of freedom (Popper, 2002).

More recently experiments and randomized control trials (RCTs) have again fired the imagination of social innovators and reformers, notably in fields like criminal justice and economic development. The practice has not always been sophisticated, and not caught up with the debates in medicine where a rather more sceptical view of RCTs has been formed by experience. But the pragmatist spirit is as alive as ever, and its philosophers continue to provide a vital set of theories that make sense of a field which has its roots in practice.

Theoretical approaches to purpose and ends: Well-being and happiness

My final set of sources concerns the ends of social innovation: what it is for. For social movements this was rarely problematic in the past: the goals of ending poverty or spreading rights seemed almost self-evident. But as innovation systems are built up with more significant flows of finance, it becomes ever more important to be specific about ends, to make it possible to judge what works and what does not. Public and social value are now much more prominent as ideas (Moore, 1995), and there is great interest in attempting to map and measure social value, including several hundred competing tools (I have written elsewhere about the practical and intellectual strengths and weaknesses of these tools, and why they are more described than used to guide decisions). In principle a rigorous mapping of social value provides an objective way to assess the ethical question of human advancement.

All of these different tools rest on either implicit or explicit views about what the ends of a society should be. Some treat these ends as unproblematic (and this has been a weakness of much of the work on social value). Others are beginning to link up to a very active debate about societal progress and its measurement (Cho, 2006). This debate led in the past to the development of indices like the Human Development Index (HDI) and assessment tools such as 'Blended Value' and Social Returns on Investment (SROI), first developed by REDF in the United States. But the pace has accelerated in the last decade partly thanks to the work of the OECD under Enrico Giovannini in the 'Beyond GDP' project, which encouraged many statistical offices around the world to experiment with various combinations of indices and new measures of both economic prosperity and societal success. President Sarkozy's appointment of a commission under Joseph Stiglitz, Amartya Sen, and Jean Fitoussi represented a major step forward, setting out a sophisticated critique of current measures of GDP and proposals for a more rounded approach.

For some, the central question is how to measure capabilities, the means for people to exercise freedom (with figures such as Sen arguing that there will inevitably be discussion and disagreement over which capabilities are critical). Many social entrepreneurs and innovators describe their own work in this way: realizing otherwise wasted potential. This is the language used by figures such as Michael Young and Muhammad Yunus. Expanding capabilities is a good in itself, and allows people to decide on their ends for themselves. For others the focus should be on measuring happiness and well-being, seeing these as the common goal for societies to aspire to (Ziegler, 2010). There are many arguments to be had about how to deal with hedonic and eudaimonic measures, and the relationships between pleasure, fulfilment, meaning and other concepts of well-being. Equally challenging is the need to capture both positive and negative dimensions of well-being (since research has shown that these do not inversely correlate).

But the important issue for social innovation is that rapid progress is being made in measurement of outcomes that until recently were thought to be immeasurable. Many governments are now committed to regular statistical surveys, providing a test of impacts. There is, as a result, a real possibility of achieving more consistent and comprehensive assessments of the success of innovations, a comparator equivalent to profit or GDP in economic and business innovation.

What connects all of these arguments is a view of value. Antonio Damasio has argued persuasively that there is a fundamental concept of biological value which is analytically robust, and which is prior to either economic or social value. This is the value of survival and flourishing. Survival depends on homeostasis, preserving the conditions for our bodies to live, with the right temperature, food, water and physical safety. But Damasio argues that we can also extend from this basic value to recognize the conditions under which we are fully alive, mentally stimulated, socially engaged, loved, and cared for: in other words, well-being is indeed a universal value and a solid foundation for constructing more specific measures in fields such as social innovation or action.

These theoretical perspectives can lead to radically different views of what matters – for example, implying a much greater priority to mental prosperity, rather than prioritizing material factors, or focusing attention on psycho-social relationships and their cultivation. More controversially, this turn is bringing the field of social innovation into the controversial debates about the relationship between well-being, economic growth, democracy, and different forms of capitalism. Richard Easterlin, one of the first economists to look systematically at the evidence showing that growth did not reliably lead to happiness, reports in a recent survey of the data that:

> ... [in] sixteen developed countries with time series at least 21 years in length, there is no significant relation between the rate of economic growth and the improvement in life satisfaction. In seven countries transitioning to free market economies with time series that are at least 14 years in length and include a measurement before or close to the beginning of transition, there is no significant relation between the rate of economic growth and the improvement in life satisfaction. In thirteen developing nations spanning Asia, Africa, and Latin America with time series at least 10 years in length (the average being 15 years), there is no significant relation between the rate of economic growth and the improvement in subjective well-being. Pooling the data for all 36 countries above, there is no significant relation between the rate of economic growth and the change in life satisfaction.
>
> (Easterlin, 2009)

Other research seems to confirm the picture with a levelling-off as income rises (Kohut, 2007).

But others dispute this evidence. One reason for the levelling-off of the correlation between happiness and economic wealth is simply that each marginal increment of income produces a smaller absolute increase in happiness. When mapped on a log scale, there is a fairly close fit between income and happiness. More detailed analysis also suggests why the data come out as they do. The Gallup World Poll asks people what emotions they had experienced the previous day. People in relatively rich nations reported themselves as more likely to have felt love and enjoyment and less likely to have experienced anger, depression, or boredom. Patterns over time are similar, with trends towards greater happiness (the US is a particular exception).

Perhaps the more interesting implications of this new field of theory and analysis lie in how it opens up novel questions: Which kinds of consumption most contribute to happiness and which may diminish it? What kinds of work organization are most conducive to well-being? Can philanthropy make up for the unhappiness of a very unequal society?

In an earlier phase of interest in social innovation and entrepreneurship, these issues were largely excluded. It was assumed that if only social enterprises could become more like businesses, they would be more likely to succeed. Their priority was to grow, scale, and establish themselves as equivalent to big business brands. But the focus on well-being shifts the question. It implies that business may have as much to learn from the social sector, and that a field concerned primarily with well-being rather than either profit or GDP growth is bound to reach distinct conclusions. And it forces the field to attend to the quality of growth as well as its quantities.

A few conclusions – and a few gaps

Kurt Lewin famously commented that there is nothing as practical as a good theory. So which of these theories are useful, and if so how? What can we extract from these very diverse and rich theoretical traditions? Clearly, social innovation is not contained or monopolized by any one of them. It is a field of understanding that cuts across disciplines, fields, and areas of knowledge. But there are some common elements which have at least some clear implications for practice.

First, social innovation is an example of the much broader field of evolutionary change that takes place in biology, culture, and societies with some common patterns of mutation, selection, and growth. Like any evolutionary process, it is not easy to plan or predict, but conscious action can make it easier for people and communities to self-organize, and shape the direction of evolution. It follows that the most successful innovation systems will be marked by strong capacities to mutate, select, and grow.

Second, the particular opportunities for social innovation will be heavily shaped by historical circumstance: prevailing types of institution and industry; prevailing technologies; and the availability of freedom or spare capital. So it is important to understand the circumstances surrounding, for example, the diffusion of low-carbon technologies, reactions against globalization, or banking crises with a wide peripheral vision and a sense of how the pieces fit together.

Third, the motivations for social innovation will usually come from tensions; contradictions; dissatisfactions; and the negation of what exists. We can draw from Hegel, Simmel, and others the insight that these tensions are not unfortunate by-products of innovation; they are part of its nature, as is the disappointment and even alienation that innovation processes generate. The very act of innovation is also an act of rejection, and this colours its social and political nature and gives it a necessarily uneasy relationship with any fixed institutions, power structures, and policies. The challenge, it follows, is to capture these tensions and contradictions within institutions rather than to try to iron them out.

Fourth, social innovation as a field seems inseparable from its underlying ethic, which is one of collaboration, acting *with* rather than only *to* or *for*; a belief in rough equality; a cultural commitment to the idea of equality of communication (theorized in more depth by Jurgen Habermas) and perhaps an implicit idea that through collaboration we can discover our full humanity (not just through labour on things). There will undoubtedly be more technocratic and top-down variants of social innovation, but these will be intellectually much less rich, and probably less successful in achieving fundamental change.

Fifth, the nature of the knowledge involved in social innovation is different from knowledge about physics or biology, or indeed the claims made for economic knowledge: it is more obviously contingent, temporary, and often context-bound. It is often as much craft as science, and confirms the key point made by Brian Arthur on the importance of deep craft in technological change. That evidence shows that something works in one place and one time does not imply that the same model will work in another place and another time. As such, it is unlikely that a simple transfer of tools such as randomized control trials will be as successful as many hope. But this perspective also casts light on the urgent need to build the deep craft of social innovation with more systematic attention to skills.

Sixth, social innovation is not yet a fully defined domain. Other domains of technology (not just hardware domains such as aeronautics or structural engineering, but also others such as finance and software) are organized by domain experts who combine rich formal knowledge with the tacit knowledge of experience, that enables them to put together multiple elements in ways that work, with a grasp of systems and sub-systems. It is entirely plausible that within a decade or two, social innovation could be more like these other domains.

Seventh and last, there are signs that the growing interest in wellbeing and capabilities could provide both the theoretical and practical glue to hold social innovation practice together, and provide some common measures of success.

It is interesting to reflect on what are missing from this list. So far there has been surprisingly little serious economic analysis of social innovation. We might expect a plausible micro-economics to have grown up, analysing the dynamics of trade-offs at the level of the enterprise, or for investors concerned with a mix of returns. It is likely that this will emerge: but for now there is a theoretical hole. We might also expect the theorists of business innovation to have paid more attention to social matters. There are a few exceptions, notably Everett Rogers, who took a broad approach to diffusion. A few others have written a bit about the social field, including Clayton Christensen. But so far these writings have lacked the cogency of their work on business, partly perhaps because of a lack of clarity about how the social field is similar to, and different from, business, in its context, motivations, and outcomes. Again, it is likely that this deficiency will be remedied.

Another possible gap is application of the very fertile work that has been done in recent years on commons and collective goods, led by Elinor Ostrom. Much of this work is suggestive for social innovators, particularly those interested in fields such as water conservation, land management, or energy. The lively field of resilience studies shows how much practical use can be made of the best theories in this area (Berkes, Colding, and Folke, 2003). But again, there has so far been little connection to understanding of the dynamics of social innovation.

Finally, we should mention the lack of serious work on the social psychology of social innovation. The lively research that has been done in recent years on the dynamics of co-operation and reciprocity is suggestive of why certain kinds of social enterprise work: how they align hearts and minds, and how through repeated interactions they encourage people to behave in more collaborative ways. But it is waiting to be taken further in relation to particular cases and testable hypotheses.

Each of these is a space to watch, and could become an important part of the network of ideas that will shape the social innovation mind. For now we do not have a single theory of social innovation. But we do have the potential to begin 'joining the dots', to link this network of concepts more coherently together into a useful way of seeing the world, and then of changing it.

References

Ali, R., Mulgan, G., Halkett, R. and Sanders, B. (2008), In and Out of Sync: The Challenge of Growing Social Innovations, London: Young Foundation/ NESTA.

Bacon, N., Brophy, M. Mguni, N. Mulgan, G. and Shandro, A. (2010), *The State of Happiness: Can Public Policy Shape People's Wellbeing and Resilience?* London: The Young Foundation.

Baumol, W. J. (2003), *The Free Market Innovation Machine* Princeton UP.

Berkes, F., Colding, J. and Folke, C. (2003), *Navigating Social-Ecological Systems: Building Resilience for Complexity and Change*, UK: Cambridge University Press.

Boltanski, L. (2001), 'On Justification', in Harrison C. White, *Markets from Networks: Socioeconomic Models of Production*, USA, Princeton University Press.

Boutang, M. and Yann (2007), *Le Capitalisme Cognitif: La Nouvelle Grande Transformation*, Editions Amsterdam.

Castells, M. (1996), The Rise of the Network Society. The Information Age: Economy, Society and Culture Vol. I, 2 and 3 (Oxford: Blackwell, 1996 and later).

Chesbrough, H. (2006), *Innovation Intermediaries, Enabling Open Innovation*, Boston, Harvard Business School Press.

Cho, A. H. (2006), 'Politics, Values and Social Entrepreneurship: A Critical Appraisal', in J. Mair, J. Robinson and K. Hockerts, eds *Social Entrepreneurship*, London: Palgrave Macmillan, 35–56.

Dees, J. G. and Anderson, B. B. (2006), 'Framing a Theory of Social Entrepreneurship: Building on Two Schools of Practice and Thought', in R. Mosher-Williams (ed.) *Research on Social Entrepreneurship: Understanding and Contributing to an Emerging Field* (ARNOVA occasional paper series, 1 (3). Indianapolis: Association for Research on Nonprofit Organizations and Voluntary Action, 39–66.

Defourny, J. and Nyssens, M.(2008), *Social Enterprise in Europe: Recent Trends and Developments*, Social Enterprise Journal, 4 (3), 2008 and J. Defourny and M. Nyssens, 'Conceptions of Social Enterprise in Europe and the United States: Convergences and Divergences', paper presented at the 8th ISTR International Conference and 2d EMES-ISTR European Conference, Barcelona, 9–12 July 2008.

Diener, E., Lucas, R. E. and Scollon, C. N. (2006), Beyond the Hedonic Treadmill: Revisions to the Adaptation Theory of Well-being, *American Psychologist*, 61 (4), pp. 305–14.

Donovan, N. and Halpern, D. (2002), *Life Satisfaction: The State of Knowledge and Implications for Government* (London: Cabinet Office).

Drayton, W. (2006), Everyone a Changemaker: Social Entrepreneurship's Ultimate Goal. Innovations, Winter, 1–32.

Easterlin, R. and Angelescu, L. (2009),'Happiness and Growth the World Over: Time Series Evidence on the Happiness-Income Paradox', IZA Discussion Paper No. 4060.

Easterlin, R. A. (1974), 'Does Economic Growth Improve the Human Lot?', in P. A. David and M. W. Reder (eds) *Nations and Households in Economic Growth: Essays in Honor of Moses Abramovitz* (New York: Academic Press, Inc).

Fagerberg, J., Mowery, D. and Nelson, R. (eds) (2005), The Oxford Handbook of Innovation, OUP.

Freeman, C. and Perez, C. (1988), Structural Crisis of Adjustments, Business, Cycles and Investment Behaviour', in Dosi, G., Freeman, C., Nelson, R., Silverberg, G., and Soete L., *Technical Change and Economic Theory*, London: Printer Publishers, pp. 60–71.

Hirschman, A. (1991), *The Rhetoric of Reaction* Harvard UP.

Hobsbawm, E. (1999), *Age of Extremes: The Short Twentieth Century 1914–1991*, London: Abacus, 87.

Kirzner, I. (1973), *Competition and Entrepreneurship*, Chicago: University of Chicago Press.

Kohut (2007), Global Views on Life Satisfaction, National Conditions and the Global Economy (Pew Global Attitudes Project). http://pewglobal.org/files/pdf/1025.pdf.

Latour, B. (2005), *Reassembling the Social: An Introduction to Actor-Network-Theory*, Oxford: Oxford University Press.

Lundvall, B.-Å. (ed.) (1992) *National Innovation Systems: Towards a Theory of Innovation and Interactive Learning*, London: Pinter.

Managabeira Unger, R. (2007), *The Self Awakened : Pragmatism Unbound*, Harvard UP.

Mandelbrot, B. and Hudson, R. (2008), *The (Mis)Behaviour of Markets: A Fractal View of Risk, Ruin and Reward*, New York: Profile books.

Markman, A. and Wood, K. (eds) (2009), *Tools for Innovation*, Oxford University Press.

Maxmin, J. and Zuboff, S. (2002), *The Support Economy: Why Corporations Are Failing Individuals and The Next Episode of Capitalism*, London: Viking.

McCraw, T. (2007) *The Prophet of Innovation Joseph Schumpeter and Creative Innovation*, Harvard UP.

Menand, L. (2001), The Metaphysical Club: A Story of Ideas in America Farrar, Straus and Giroux, Xi–xii.

Moore, M. (1995), Creating Public Value, Boston: Harvard University.

Morgan, G. (1997), *Images of Organisation Executive*, Berlin: Edition Berrett-Koehler.

Mulgan, G. (2009), 'The Art of Public Strategy', Oxford University Press.

Mulgan, G. and Landry, C. (1995) *The Other Invisible Hand: Remaking Charity for the 21st Century*, London: Demos.

Murray, R., Caulier-Grice, J. and Mulgan, G. (2010) *The Open Book of Social Innovation* London: NESTA/Young Foundation.

Nelson, R. (1982) *An Evolutionary Theory of Economic Change* Harvard UP.

Nicholls, A., ed. (2006), *Social Entrepreneurship: New Models of Sustainable Social Change*, Oxford: Oxford University Press.

Nonaka, I. and H. Takeuchi (1995), *The Knowledge-Creating Company: How Japanese Companies Create the Dynamic of Innovation*, New York: Oxford University Press.

Nussbaum, M. and Sen, A. (eds) (1993), *The Quality of Life*, Oxford: Clarendon Press.

Popper, K. (2002) *The Open Society and its Enemies*, London: Routledge.

Ramalingam, B. and Jones, H. (2008), A good review of literature and possible relevant to development is 'Emploring the science of complexity: ideas and implications for development and humanitarian efforts', ODI Working paper 285.

Rogers, E. M. (2003), *Diffusion of Innovations*, New York: Free Press.

Schumpeter J. (1934) *The Theory of Economic Development: An Inquiry into Profits, Capital, Credit, Interest and the Business Cycle*, Boston: Harvard University Press.

Schumpeter J. (1939) Business Cycles, Volume 1, Harvard University Press, 1939, p. 1011.

Schumpeter J. (1942) Capitalism, socialism and democracy, London: Routledge.

Shockley, G. and Frank, P. (2011), 'Schumpeter, Kirzner and the Field of Social Entrepreneurship', *Journal of Social Entrepreneurship*, 2 (1), pp. 6–26.

Simmel, G. (2010), *The View of Life:Four Metaphysical Essays with Journal Aphorisms*, Translated by A. Y. Andrews and Donald J. Levine; With an Introduction by Donald N. Levine and Daniel Silver, Chicago: University of Chicago Press.

Stark, D. (2009), *The Sense of Dissonance: Accounts of Worth in Economic Life*, Princeton UP.

Stoneman, P. and Diederen, P. (1994),'Technology Diffusion and Public Policy', *The Economic Journal*, 104 (425), 918–30. Oxford, Blackwell.

Swedberg, R. (2009), 'Schumpeter's Full Model of Entrepreneurship: Economic, Non-Economic and Social Entrepreneurship', in R. Ziegler (ed.) *An Introduction to Social Entepreneurship: Voices, Preconditions, Contexts*, Cheltenham: Edward Elgar, 77–106.

Von Hippel, E. (1988), *Sources of Innovation*, OUP.

Von Mises, L. (1949/1996), Human Action: A Treatise on Economics, San Francisco: Fox & Wilkes, pp. 252–3.

Damasio, A. (1994) *Emotion, Reason and the Human Brain*, Putnam NY.

Westley, F., Zimmerman, B. and Patton, M. (2006), *Getting to Maybe: How the World is Changed*, Toronto: Random House Canada.

Young Foundation/SIX report for the Bureau of European Policy Advisers, European Commission, 2010.

Ziegler, R. (2010), 'Innovations in Doing and Being: Capability Innovations at the Intersection of Schumpeterian Political Economy and Human Development', *Journal of Social Entrepreneurship*,1 (2), 255–72, October 2010.

2
Considering Context: Social Innovation in Comparative Perspective

Janelle A. Kerlin

Introduction

'Social enterprise' is a term that is increasingly used across the globe to describe new business solutions to a myriad of social and environmental problems (Alter, 2006). This discourse is often characterized by the shared human sentiments of social justice, sustainability, participation, inclusiveness, and empowerment. In Zimbabwe, the Collective Self Finance Scheme, a micro-finance initiative, pools the savings of associated small- and medium-sized businesses to support lending to members (Masendeke and Mugova, 2009). In Argentina, the 18th of December Workers' Co-operative is an owner-abandoned clothing factory restored to operation by its workers (Roitter and Vivas, 2009). In Italy, the Social Co-operatives of the Consorzio per l'Impresa Sociale are business ventures run largely by former patients of a de-institutionalized mental health facility (Nyssens, 2009). In the Philippines, Cocotech uses coconut coir fibre, formerly a waste product, to employ marginalized people and address soil erosion (Santos et al., 2009). While these socially innovative practices are bound together by approaches that respect humanity at their core, differences in need and socio-economic and cultural context stimulate what are, ultimately, uniquely creative initiatives in different parts of the world.

Comparative research on social enterprise in different countries shows not only variation across borders (Borzaga and Defourny, 2001; SEKN et al., 2006) but also that the types of social enterprise that dominate in a region are often associated with that particular environment's socio-economic strengths (Kerlin, 2009; see also Porter, 1998). It appears successful social innovators are aware of the strongest resources and structures available to sustain innovative projects in a given region. Such resources and structures often include government, the market, civil society, and international co-operation (Nicholls, 2006; Nyssens, 2006; Kerlin, 2009). Equally important, if not more so, is innovators' intimate knowledge of an environment's distinctive culture (Hofstede 2001). Culture at its root is the 'expression of ideals and identity'. (Nussbaumer and Moulaert, 2004, p. 255). As Nussbaumer and Moulaert (2004, p. 255) state, 'The capacity of culture to create bonds enables us to establish the connection between the satisfaction of basic needs, and the various dimensions of social life'. This chapter explores social innovation in the guise of social enterprise in different world regions as a shared, human-focused approach that draws on the institutional resources and culture of a given environment to address specific needs. Such research has important implications for the facilitation of cross-regional dialogue, the transfer and replication of social enterprise ideas, and the structures developed for their support.

Recent research (Kerlin, 2009, 2010) has contributed to the preliminary identification of four broad types of environmental contexts for social enterprise based on available information.[1] This chapter will discuss each type in turn and then provide a series of country case studies of contexts and social enterprise types that correspond with each. While drawing largely on qualitative studies of social enterprise contexts from Kerlin (2009), descriptions of these contexts are also informed by data from five socio-economic databases: the GLOBE study of culture, leadership and organizations (House et al., 2004), World Bank Worldwide Governance Indicators (World Bank, 2009), Models of Civil Society Sectors from the Johns Hopkins Comparative Nonprofit Sector Project (Salamon and Sokolowski, 2004, 2010), the Global Competitiveness Report (Sala-i-Martin, 2009), and World Development Indicators for international aid (World Bank, 2010).[2] Though not discussed in detail here, a theoretical discussion on how different socio-economic factors contribute to contexts and, ultimately, models for social enterprise can be found in Kerlin (2010).

Given the wide range of cultural factors, this preliminary research explores the two aspects discussed in the culture literature deemed most likely to influence social enterprise: level of in-group collectivism (versus individualism) and level of uncertainty avoidance (values) in a society.[3] This literature, as it relates to entrepreneurship, has long supported the idea that individualism rather than collectivism supports entrepreneurial behaviour broadly construed. However, the present research takes the view offered by Tiessen (1997) that collectivism and individualism each support different key functions of entrepreneurialism. Tiessen (1997) argues that individualism specifically supports the generation of variety through innovation (see Shane, 1992; 1993), while collectivism can support the leveraging of resources internally and through external ties. Both the generation of new ideas and the ability to leverage resources are key to economic success on a societal level, and help explain why some largely collectivist countries (the Asian tigers for example) have experienced economic success (Franke et al., 1991). Low levels of uncertainty avoidance have also been associated with innovation (Shane, 1993). The influence of institutional structures including the economy, government, and civil society on social enterprise is more immediate, therefore these factors are addressed directly in the country discussions below.

Contexts for social innovation and enterprise

The following descriptions of contexts for social enterprise are meant to provide an overall framework for understanding the resources and structures that are drawn on in the development of social enterprise ideas in particular types of societies. This discussion thus attempts to highlight large-scale factors that generally appear to differentiate one context relative to another even as it acknowledges variation within and across countries within a regional context. In some cases, countries may diverge somewhat from outlined characteristics though still be considered to align largely with the identified context thus constituting an ideal type. In this sense, the contexts identified in this typology can be viewed as ideal types (see Borzaga and Defourny, 2001 for a similar approach). A few countries may fall in-between the described contexts due to transitioning dynamics (see Sala-i-Martin, 2009). The study also acknowledges the preliminary nature of this investigation and, therefore, the likely existence of other contexts differentiated from and in addition to the four identified here.

Type I, the *village* context, is mostly associated with African and Southeast Asian societies where social enterprise is characterized by individualized small-group efforts of entrepreneurs to provide poverty relief through subsistence employment for themselves and their families and sometimes communities. These activities are at times supported by international aid and can appear in the form of microfinance-supported projects due to the need to provide a sustainable form of assistance and improve small-scale economic development. This type of context is most often characterized by a weak market context and low per capita GDP that underlie a demand for need-based entrepreneurialism where the need for a subsistence livelihood is driving entrepreneurship rather than opportunity (Bosma and Levie, 2010). A low level of government involvement also means that social enterprise draws on the strengths of traditional forms of social interaction in the small village group. Indeed, in terms of culture, this type of context is characterized by a relatively high level of collective, as opposed to individual, activity where individuals maintain close ties and retain a sense of responsibility for one another in the small group.

In Type 2, the *post-authoritarian* context, largely associated with East-Central European and Latin American countries, the context for social innovation is characterized by post-authoritarian, democratic governance structures and a (re)emerging civil society that works to fill in gaps in the economy and state social welfare. Co-operatives, worker 'recuperated' companies,[4] and other mutual assistance activities that provide needed services and employment illustrate predominant organizational forms for social enterprise in this context. Mutualism, introduced by civil society as opposed to the state, may be driven culturally by a relatively high level of uncertainty avoidance in some countries. Also, with a slightly higher per capita GDP there is also a greater possibility of drawing on larger pooled resources for entrepreneurship, either formally or informally. More so than in other contexts, social innovation and social enterprise activities may participate in and be viewed as a form of social activism in part because of a past tradition of civil society working in opposition to an authoritarian state as well as their present efforts to provide a form of social justice for those left behind by the market and state. Thus, social innovators may work autonomously from and sometimes in opposition to the state to address perceived deficiencies in state policies. Socially entrepreneurial activities may be involved in larger-scale manufacturing activities commonly attributed to the efficiency stage of economic development found in these societies.

Type 3, the *welfare state* context, is associated with countries in continental Western Europe and is characterized by the large presence of a welfare state that leaves a narrow space for the development of social enterprise activities. Though social enterprise ideas may develop in the civil society sphere to provide a unique and needed service, once proven, they can become captured (defined) by state welfare policy and dependent on state funding for their activities. Thus social enterprise here runs the danger of only being associated with a narrow sphere of services popularized and supported by the state. An example is the predominance of work-integration social enterprises often organized in social co-operatives that support employment programming for the hard-to-employ (Nyssens, 2006). There may also be occurrences of

local municipalities running social enterprises or partnering with civil
society organizations in order to do so (Spear and Bidet, 2005). In some
countries where the sizeable welfare state does not have a tradition of
working through civil society, there may be fewer and less diverse kinds
of social enterprises with close ties to specific public policies that may
have spurred on their development. In this situation, some few social
enterprises may have originated from the top down due to state privatization of sheltered workshop programmes (Spear and Bidet, 2005).
Continuing economic growth provides the wealth necessary to support
a large welfare state and other institutions that fund social enterprise.
A cultural proclivity that values low uncertainty avoidance in this
region is likely to support innovation.

Type 4, the laissez-faire context, typical of the United States and
Australia, is characterized by a productive market, smaller welfare
state, and a broad array of types of social innovation in part due to less
government involvement. Autonomy from the state, in terms of the
limited subsidies it provides, as well as easy access to strong markets,
also encourages the use of social enterprise as an income generator for
organizations that, at times, run independently of programming for
participants. There is also a highly supportive environment for innovative entrepreneurialism underpinned by a culture of low uncertainty
avoidance and very high individualism. Here a high level of wealth generates private philanthropy rather than government support for social
enterprise. There may also be greater supply and demand for diverse
social enterprise services due to a high-income society's desire for and
ability to pay for them.

Specific country contexts

The four countries discussed below provide examples of the four contexts for social enterprise described above. These are each followed by a
social enterprise case study from the given country that illustrates how
the social enterprise draws on and is shaped by the particular socio-
economic strengths and cultural attributes of its context. Table 2.1
shows the socio-economic data for the four countries used in tracking
large-scale differences across the five societal aspects relevant to social
enterprise.

Type 1: The village context – Zimbabwe

The context for social enterprise in Zimbabwe is characterized by a lack
of government and economic supports for social enterprise as well as a

great need for citizens to find a sustainable means of livelihood. Cultural indicators for Zimbabwe show that citizens have strong resources in their tradition of supportive collective activity. According to the GLOBE analysis, Zimbabweans rate the highest of the four countries in terms of both uncertainty avoidance and in-group collectivism (House et al., 2004). In this sense, collectivism is theorized to support social innovation and enterprise through how individuals in this type of culture 'generate variety through group-based, incremental improvements and changes' and how they 'leverage their own resources by harnessing "clanlike" affiliations, and securing the use of the resources of other firms by building close relational ties' (Thiessen, 1997, p. 368). Given the current instability in Zimbabwe, a feeling or need for more uncertainty avoidance aligns with the situation in the country (House et al., 2004).

World Governance Indicators for 2008 show that Zimbabwe's system of governance has been in decline for over a decade. Although Zimbabwe's governance percentile rankings have been relatively low for a long time, the fall in rankings from 1996 to 2008 (especially steep from 1996 to 2002) indicates a changed environment in the country most likely due to President Mugabe's policies and strong citizen opposition to his ZANU-PF government. Zimbabwe only ranks in the 10th percentile for political stability and the absence of violence. For regulatory quality, including policies that support the private sector, Zimbabwe ranks just above the 0 percentile. The country ranks only slightly higher in terms of government effectiveness in public (2nd percentile) and the control of corruption (just below the 5th percentile) (World Bank, 2009).

The economic situation in Zimbabwe mirrors the weak governance picture. The Global Competitive Report 2009–10 states that Zimbabwe is ranked second to last on the Global Competitiveness Index and has one of the worst institutional environments in terms of property rights, corruption, and basic government inefficiency. Moreover, extreme mismanagement of public finances ranks it last in macro-economic stability. In 2009, skyrocketing rates of inflation forced the government to stop printing Zimbabwean dollars and base the economy on the US dollar. According to the report, Zimbabwe had a GDP per capita of $54.60 and is in the factor-driven stage of economic development (Sala-i-Martin et al., 2009).

In terms of civil society, the National Association of Non-Governmental Organisations in its February 2010 report outlines government suspicion and mistrust of the sector with recent victimization of civil society through arrests and intimidation. The government has also undertaken

Table 2.1 Socio-economic data for four countries

	Culture[1]		Governance[2] (percentile rank/governance score)				Economy[3]		Civil Society[4]	Intl Aid[5]
	In-Group Collectivism (Practices)	Uncertainty Avoidance (Values)	Government Effectiveness (0–100/ −2.5 to +2.5)	Regulatory Quality (0–100/ −2.5 to +2.5)	Rule of Law (0–100/ −2.5 to +2.5)	Control of Corruption (0–100/ −2.5 to +2.5)	Economic Dev Stage (based on GDP per capita)	GCI Ranking (1 = most competitive)	Sector Model (B=Borderline)	per capita (in US $)
Zimbabwe	5.57	4.73	2.4/−1.56	1.4/−2.18	1.4/−1.81	3.9/−1.37	Factor	132	Traditional (assumed)	49
Argentina	5.51	4.66	48.8/−.18	28/−.65	32.1/−.61	40.1/−.44	Efficiency	85	Deferred (B) Democratization	3
Italy	4.94	4.47	66.4/+.39	78.7/+.95	62.2/+.43	62.3/+.13	Innovation	48	Welfare Partnership (B)	—
United States	4.25	4	92.9/+1.65	93.2/+1.58	91.9/+1.65	91.8/+1.55	Innovation	2	Liberal	—

Sources: [1] The Global Leadership and Organizational Behavior Effectiveness (GLOBE) Research Project is a study of 61 cultures/countries reported in *Culture, Leadership, and Organizations: The GLOBE Study of 62 Societies* (House et al., 2004). The study examines culture through nine different dimensions, each in terms of practices and values. This chapter uses the study's findings for two dimensions: In-Group Collectivism in societal practices, which is 'the degree to which individuals express pride, loyalty, and cohesiveness in their organizations or families' (p. 12) (on a scale of 1–7 where higher scores indicate greater In-Group Collectivism in practice) and Uncertainty Avoidance in societal values which is 'the extent to which members of an organization or society *should* strive to avoid uncertainty by relying on established social norms, rituals, and bureaucratic practices' (p. 11) on a scale of 1–7 where higher scores indicate greater Uncertainty Avoidance. Findings for both dimensions correlate with findings for similar dimensions in Geert Hofstede's (1980, 2001) pioneering work, *Culture's Consequences*. Thus work based on Hofstede's dimensions and findings is also likely to hold true for GLOBE findings in these areas.

2 'World Wide Governance Indicators: Governance Matters 2009 Report' provides six governance indicators for 212 of the world's countries and territories. Four of these indicators are referred to in this chapter. Government Effectiveness is the quality of public services, the capacity of the civil service and its independence from political pressures, and the quality of policy formulation. Regulatory Quality is the ability of the government to provide sound policies and regulations that enable and promote private sector development. Rule of Law is the extent to which agents have confidence in and abide by the rules of society, including the quality of contract enforcement and property rights, the police, and the courts, as well as the likelihood of crime and violence. Control of Corruption is the extent to which public power is exercised for private gain, including both petty and grand forms of corruption, as well as 'capture' of the state by elites and private interests (retrieved from [http://info.worldbank.org/governance/wgi/pdf/WBI_GovInd.pdf] (accessed July 2010)).

3 Global Competitiveness Report 2009–10, in addition to a competitiveness ranking of countries, provides a typology of stages of economic development largely based on GDP per capita. In the Factor-Driven stage, economies are largely reliant on the export of mineral goods and have poor infrastructure and supportive policies. The Efficiency-Driven stage is characterized by industrialization where productive efficiency is expanded and product quality improved. The Innovation-Driven stage occurs in countries where a high-standard of living and growth are supported by the continued introduction of unique and innovative products in a sophisticated business environment. The report categorizes 133 countries into the three stages and two transition components. The report also ranks the countries according to global competitiver.ess (Sala-i-Martin et al., 2009).

4 Johns Hopkins Comparative Nonprofit Sector Project. Based on two decades of empirical research, Salamon and Sokolowski's (2010) models of civil society sectors distinguish five types based on differences in empirical data across five dimensions: workforce size, volunteer share, government support, philanthropic support, and expressive share. The first three models – Liberal, Welfare Partnership, and Social Democratic – are all found in developed countries and to a significant degree are shaped by the structure of the welfare state. The last two – Deferred Democratization and Traditional – are influenced to a lesser extent by the welfare state and more so by identifying characteristics of other aspects of government, including the lack of it. Zimbabwe was not included in the Johns Hopkins project; however, its characteristics match other African countries that belong in the Traditional model so Zimbabwe's alignment with this model is assumed.

5 World Development Indicators. International aid data are from the Development Assistance Committee (DAC) of the Organization for Economic Co-operation and Development (OECD), and population estimates from the World Bank. Data are from 2008.

Notes: International aid per capita includes net official development assistance (loans and grants from DAC member countries, multilateral organizations, and non-DAC donors) divided by the mid-year population estimate. Italy and the United States did not receive international aid (data retrieved from the World Bank's World Databank at [http://databank.worldbank.org/ddp/home.do?Step=12&id=4&CNO=2] (accessed July 2010)).

a media campaign accusing civil society organizations of alliances with the opposition and Western countries to remove ZANU-PF from power. Civil society is unable to have a voice of its own to counteract these assertions due to restrictions on freedom of expression in the independent media (NANGO, 2010). As for its civil society sector model, Zimbabwe aligns with other countries belonging to the Traditional model which emphasizes traditional social relationships and forms of helping in the face of limited government support (Salamon and Sokolowski, 2010).

Social enterprise in Zimbabwe is indicative of the village context type because poorly functioning economic and governance institutions not only necessitate need-based social entrepreneurship but also make it difficult to expand and scale up social enterprises. A civil society handicapped by government oppression also does little to provide a supportive home for social enterprise. Thus, international aid appears at times to be the strongest institutional actor. Indeed, Masendeke and Mugova (2009) discuss how social enterprise in Zimbabwe is currently expanding in conjunction with international aid projects. As such, its conceptualization is tied to ideas expressed by the international development community, including microcredit lending institutions and the small businesses they support. They report that high levels of unemployment and the negative social impact of structural adjustment reforms promoted by international financial institutions are the leading reasons behind the recent movement towards social enterprise solutions. Not surprisingly, they discuss the need for market intermediation for the products of social enterprise, the limiting effect the lack of appropriate national-level legislation can have on social enterprise operations, as well as the negative impact of too much financial support by international donors. They provide the following case study of a microfinance initiative in Zimbabwe.

The Collective Self Finance Scheme

The Collective Self Finance Scheme (CSFS) established itself as one of the leading micro-finance institutions (MFI) on the Zimbabwean microcredit landscape. Established in 1989, the scheme started as an association of small and medium enterprises (SMEs) eager to pool savings for purposes of lending to members. HIVOS[5] and the European Commission were among the donors who provided critical funding that enabled the scheme to set up infrastructure and systems during the early years of its existence. By 2000, CSFS had established six branch offices around the country and was arguably one of the largest MFIs in Zimbabwe.

Table 2.2 Performance by CSFS on key indicators, 2004–5 (from Collective Self Finance Scheme, Quarterly and Annual Reports, 2004–6; see Masendeke and Mugova, 2009)

	2004	2005
Resources mobilised locally	20,000 USD	67,000 USD
Loans disbursed	12,416 USD	15,125 USD
Repayment rate	85%	89%
Profitability	5%	15%
Outreach	Country-wide	Country-wide

Beginning in that same year, however, access to donor funding by MFIs drastically decreased due to a number of factors. Rapidly deteriorating socio-economic conditions led to a massive reduction of funding assistance by donors to Zimbabwe. Rising inflation (estimated at 613% in February 2006) led donors to conclude that sustainable micro lending was almost impossible under conditions of hyperinflation. Consequently, it was concluded that little would be achieved by allocating scarce resources to support micro lending activities. There was also the strong belief among donors that MFIs must work towards making their lending programmes self-sustaining if they were to be relevant and play a useful role in enterprise development and poverty alleviation. Given these challenges, CSFS transformed itself from an NGO into a private company in 2004. Soon after the transformation, it embarked on an aggressive mobilization of financial resources from the local community. Table 2.2 summarizes the performance of CSFS over the last two years on key indicators.

This case illustrates various conditions for a social enterprise in the village context including the type of activity (micro-finance), the role of international aid in the start-up phase, the over-involvement of international aid, the impact of the economic situation, and the focus on SME development.

Type 2: The post-authoritarian context – Argentina

Like Zimbabwe, Argentina's indicators suggest there has been a large shift in its socio-economic environment. In particular, the change from authoritarian to democratic rule in 1983 and events including structural adjustment programmes in the late 1990s and the 2001 economic crisis have had a dramatic effect on government policies, the economy, and civil society. Argentina has a moderate risk avoidance rating and a high collectivism orientation, the latter manifesting itself in the many forms of mutual association that have a long tradition in the country.

Worldwide Governance Indicators for 2008 show that Argentina has experienced declines in a number of areas since 1996 reflective of the dramatic changes in the country. In terms of government effectiveness, the country fell from the 70th percentile in 1996 to the 50th percentile in 2008 (with a dip to the 40th percentile in 2002). A similar decline was seen with regulatory quality, where the country was ranked in the 80th percentile in 1996 but fell to slightly below the 30th percentile in 2008. Citizen confidence in the country's laws and legal system also fell, from slightly below the 60th percentile in 1996 to slightly above the 30th percentile in 2008 (with a drastic drop from 2000 to 2002). In terms of the control of corruption, Argentina fell to the 40th percentile in 2008 (World Bank, 2009).

The Global Competitiveness Report 2009–10 finds that though Argentina has improved in some respects and showed strong GDP growth between its economic crises of 2001 and 2008, it has fallen short of expectations based on its strengths, which include relative good health and education policies and a large market. However, high inflation levels brought on by expansionary fiscal and monetary policies, high public debt, and a reduction in tax revenues are a serious problem. Also, a poor institutional environment has engendered pessimism and distrust among those in the business community, particularly in the areas of 'government efficiency and transparency, respect of the rule of law, and even-handedness in dealing with the private sector' (Sala-i-Martin et al., 2009, p. 35). The report, which places the country in the efficiency-driven stage of economic development, also cites the discretionary and rigid market policies of the last two administrations. GDP per capita in Argentina stood at $8,214.10 in 2008 (Sala-i-Martin et al., 2009).

In Argentina, as the governance and economic reports suggest, a number of recent factors have restructured the relationship between civil society and the state and economy. The fall of the authoritarian regime and return to democracy in 1983 saw the restoration of many associations, though they were largely tied to the welfare state at that point. Structural adjustment reforms in the 1990s, however, dramatically changed the landscape for civil society due to a large withdrawal of the state: 'During the 1990s the federal state dismantled the social security system and drastically reduced social expenditures [such] as education, health and other aspects of social welfare, while privatizing public services such as telecommunications, airlines, electricity, water and gas supplies' (Jacobs and Maldonado, 2005, p. 153). The lack of a state welfare net coupled with the economic crisis of 2001 and ensuing jump in unemployment encouraged people to return or turn to mutual forms of civil society organizations including certain types of social enterprise for solutions (see Fiorucci and Klein, 2005; Roitter and Vivas, 2009). Argentina has been categorized as having a borderline Deferred Democratization civil society sector model. In this model, civil society remains small due to repressive or neglectful policies of the state (Salamon and Sokolowski, 2010).

Roitter and Vivas (2009) note that in Argentina co-operatives and mutual benefit societies have a long tradition of following models inherited from European immigrants. More recently, economic decline and high unemployment tied to structural adjustment programmes spurred on variations of these forms, including the rise of the so-called recuperated company: failed companies that have been reorganized into self-managed co-operatives at times in opposition to local authorities. They found that 170 recuperated companies have emerged since the end of the 1990s. Overall, their analysis points to a more politicized discourse for social enterprise in Argentina in the context of a country in the efficiency stage of economic development involved in larger manufacturing initiatives (Sala-i-Martin, 2009). Roitter and Vivas (2009) provide the following case study.

The 18th of December workers' co-operative

When workers arrived at the Brukman clothing factory in Buenos Aires on 18 December 2001, they discovered the owners had abandoned the company. In addition, there had been an ongoing conflict between the owners and the workers mainly due to a large debt the owners had incurred with the employees. The wages of the last few months had not been paid, and social security and ART (Health and Job Risk Insurance) payments had not been made. Upon finding themselves on their own, the employees decided to keep their jobs and reached a consensus about the best way to regain and organize the company. Though the Garment Industry and Accessories Workers Union was indifferent (and in fact supportive of the owner-solicited bankruptcy policy that had left the workers unprotected), the workers found a large support network among university students, Left-wing political parties, workers of other recuperated companies, and neighbours. After a month of worker management the company was able to make its first deals and through reinvestment of the sales the company returned to full, productive activity.

The re-establishment of the company, however, ran into various conflicts for its first two years. In March 2002, a violent attempt to throw the workers out was halted with the help of the factory workers' support network. A month later, however, a second attempt was successful and the police cleared out the workers. The workers tried to enter the factory again a few days later accompanied by more than 10,000 people. Though this attempt also failed, the workers decided to set up camp and sleep in tents on the corner near the company while the struggle to recover their jobs continued.

Over the next eight months things remained unchanged while the dispute moved through the courts and the Buenos Aires City Government. In September, the workers considered the possibility of having the company expropriated and presented an investment, production, and sales feasibility plan to the Buenos Aires City Government. Finally, on 20 October 2003, the owners of Brukman were officially declared bankrupt and ten days later on 30 October the Buenos Aires legislature voted in favour of the Expropriation Law which declared the company's assets to be of public utility. Management of the factory was passed into the hands of the workers now united in a work co-operative called The 18th of December. Authorization to enter the factory was granted on 29 December 2003 and the workers subsequently restored the factory to full operation (Roitter and Vivas, 2009).

This case illustrates how in a post-authoritarian context for social enterprise a weakened post-authoritarian government, reduced welfare state, and poor economic situation spurred on the reconstitution of a manufacturing company by workers who wanted to maintain their jobs. Mutualism was evident in the workers' transformation of the corporation into a co-operative. One of the apparent strengths in this situation was the mobilization of civil society in support of the workers in a form of social activism.

Type 3: The welfare state context – Italy

Italy is much higher on many socio-economic indicators than Argentina, though it still lags behind a number of West European countries. Scores on some governance indicators have slipped over the last decade and the economy is a mix of strong and weak factors. Unlike many other West European countries that value low uncertainty avoidance and have low collectivism, culturally, Italy values moderate uncertainty avoidance and practises moderate in-group collectivism. Similar to other West European countries, however, Italy has a strong welfare state and, consequently, a strong stake in social enterprise, using it to further its policy agenda particularly in the area of work integration for the hard-to-employ.

Worldwide Governance Indicators for 2008 ranked Italy in the 60th percentile for political stability and slightly higher in terms of government effectiveness. For regulatory quality, Italy scored in the 80th percentile in

2008, an improvement from its 70th percentile ranking in 1996. People's confidence in Italy's laws and legal system slipped to the 60th percentile in 2008 after ranking in the 80th percentile in 1996. In terms of the control of corruption, Italy ranked slightly above the 60th percentile in 2008 after peaking in the 80th percentile in 2000 (World Bank, 2009).

The economy in Italy is a mix of strong and weak factors. Categorized as an innovation-driven economy, the Global Competitiveness Index ranked Italy 48th out of 133 countries. In particular, Italy ranked high on business sophistication (20th), high-end goods (14th), and strong business clusters (3rd) as well as large market size (9th). However, the country is held back by low rankings in labour market efficiency (117th), macro-economic stability (102nd), and financial market sophistication (100th). In 2008, Italy had an average GDP per capita of $38,996.20. The GCI report also notes that 'Other institutional weaknesses include high levels of corruption and organized crime and a perceived lack of independence within the judicial system, which increase business costs and undermine investor confidence, with Italy ranked 97th overall for its institutional environment' (Sala-i-Martin, 2009, p. 25).

Historically, civil society in Italy was grounded, among other entities, on the formation of city corporations or guilds. These entities were a self-managed form of mutual assistance and espoused legal and financial autonomy. Over the centuries, civil society in Italy has been influenced by the Catholic Church, political parties, and labour unions. More recently, the development of the welfare state meant the incorporation of many service-oriented civil society organizations into public entities. In the 1980s, however, budget restrictions and dissatisfaction with welfare state services spurred on the development of new forms of civil society organizations, including social co-operatives. These organizations 'revitalized the mutuality sentiments of the guild, and at the same time sought to merge market means with charitable purpose' (Barbetta et al., 2004, p. 251). The civil society sector in Italy is considered to be a borderline Welfare Partnership model which – though it can be large – is circumscribed to certain activities due to a sizable welfare state that both funds and delivers social services (Salamon and Sokolowski, 2010).

Indeed, Italy is particularly known in Western Europe for being the first to promote the social co-operative form of social enterprise through the passage of legislation in 1991 (Borzaga and Loss, 2006). Social co-operatives, a common form of social enterprise in Western Europe, are characterized by multi-stakeholder ownership that includes the involvement of workers, managers, volunteers, costumers, donors, and public authorities who operate with a democratic management style

(Nyssens, 2006). The laws in Italy came about to encourage what was initially a civil society response to a crisis of unemployment among hard-to-employ populations (Borzaga and Loss, 2006). Nyssens (2009, p. 18) notes that the law in Italy 'distinguishes between two types of social co-operatives: those delivering social, health and educational services, called 'type A' social co-operatives, and those providing work integration for disadvantaged people, called 'type B' social co-operatives.'[6] With 'type B', considered a work integration social enterprise (WISE), the law stipulates that 30 per cent of the employed must be disadvantaged, the disadvantaged must be members of the co-operative, and the co-operative receives tax relief and is considered first for public works contracts (Borzaga and Loss, 2006). In the more economically developed north of Italy, social co-operatives focus more on meeting collective needs in terms of childcare, support for the aged, and family and teen services. In southern Italy, where unemployment is higher and family networks stronger, the immediate focus is on creating job opportunities through business ventures that meet individual, private needs such as gardening, laundry, and cleaning (Borzaga and Loss, 2006).[7] The following case study is an example of a social co-operative in Italy.

Social co-operatives of the Consorzio per I'Impresa Sociale

In the early 1970s, the Italian government began de-institutionalizing state psychiatric hospitals, and a young, innovative psychiatrist, Dr Franco Basaglia, was given the task of closing the large state hospital in Trieste and integrating the patients into the community. Basaglia and his former patients (whom they called consumers) quickly came to believe that they could best integrate into Triestine society by finding jobs. Unfortunately, the citizens of Trieste discriminated against the consumers by denying them employment. Undaunted, Basaglia decided to look for more innovative means of employment.

Basaglia discovered that many of the direct care workers at the hospital were earning very poor wages and had taken on second jobs to subsidize their income ranging from carpentry and small agricultural enterprises to more skilled work, including bookbinding. Basaglia encouraged the direct care workers, who were accustomed to inter-acting with people with psychiatric disabilities, to employ consumers to assist them in their second jobs. In a short time, a few of the small enterprises grew into larger businesses that employed an increasing number of consumers. Basaglia arranged for empty hospital wards to be renovated into office and manufacturing space. The old state hospital's central location, accessible by public transport, proved ideal for these purposes.

The environment, now called the 'business park', no longer bears any resemblance to a hospital. The park's small businesses are run as six 'social co-operatives' and consumers are full partners in the enterprises. Employees are organized into small unions, known as guilds, and a majority of the partners must be consumers. Out of the 400 partners in these co-operatives, half have psychiatric disabilities. All of the co-operatives belong to the Consorzio per l'Impresa Sociale, an association established in 1991 to support the co-operatives' administrative and corporate functions. Over the years, these social co-operatives have expanded from carpentry and agricultural ventures to include hi-tech businesses and enterprises requiring highly skilled labour.

The six social co-operatives include:

- The Lavoratori Uniti Co-operative, founded in 1972, is the oldest, employing more than 120 workers with an annual revenue of about 3b lire (€1,321,058). It provides various services including transport, cleaning, and bookbinding.
- The La Collina Co-operative Sociale is considered the artistic co-operative because it works in the fields of photography, graphics, theatre, video, and carpentry. In the carpentry division, furniture is manufactured for schools and hospitals. There are only eight persons in this co-operative, all of whom are consumers. Their revenues exceed 2b lire (€880,705) a year.
- The Il Posto Delle Fragole Co-operative provides tourist services throughout Trieste, operates several restaurants, runs a hotel on the seaside, manages several pubs, and runs a hairstyling centre. There are 21 members, of whom 11 are consumers.
- The Crea Co-operative Sociale, the most recently established, operates a building renovation business.
- The Agricola M.S. Pantaleone Co-operative works in the gardening sector. In addition to contracting with various businesses and private home owners, it also contracts to care for the campus of the business park.
- The Agenzia Socialle assists persons experiencing psychiatric and/or drug addiction problems. In addition to selected case management tasks, it also provides in-home health services.

By law, none of the co-operatives may share profits with partners or stakeholders. Rather, all profits are reinvested into the co-operative and, therefore, are not subject to taxes. The partners are the legal owners. When new partners join a co-operative, they pay an associative fee which is returned when they depart. The sum of all of the partners' shares makes up the company's capital. Thus, all of the partners are entrepreneurs and run the risk of losing their investment. Each partner has one vote, regardless of the shares owned, and the majority of the officers must be active working partners with psychiatric disabilities. (Italian case adapted from Goegren, Renata, as found in Nyssens, 2009[8]).[9]

This Italian case study illustrates the welfare state context for social enterprise through the initial lack of state policy in employment programmes for the disadvantaged and how a civil society initiative, the Consorzio, was developed to fill this particular gap (a common trend in the development of social enterprises in Western Europe). It also shows how social co-operative laws structured and supported the activities of the group, thus illustrating the subsequent involvement of the state.

Type 4: The laissez-faire context – United States

The context for social enterprise in the United States is characterized by governance that is strong in the rule of law and regulation but is limited in the size of the welfare state. Productive markets and a strong civil society sector are also characteristic. The wealth of the country supports social enterprise through private philanthropy rather than government funding as found in the welfare state context. In terms of culture, the US rates low on uncertainty avoidance and low on collectivism, both indicating a culture that drives innovation through the generation of variety.

In 2008, the US ranked slightly below the 70th percentile in political stability, apparently still recovering from the drop in ranking that occurred after 11 September. In terms of government effectiveness, regulatory quality, and the rule of law, the US has hovered at or just under the 95th percentile for much of the decade. The US's control of corruption ranking also has remained constant over the years, always slightly above the 90th percentile.

In terms of its economy, the United States ranked 2nd out of 133 countries, down from 1st in 2008–9. According to the GCI, the US is ranked 1st in terms of efficiency enhancers, market size, and innovation; and, like Italy, it falls into the innovation-driven economic stage. The average per capita GDP in 2008 was $46,859.10. The most commonly reported problematic factor for doing business was access to financing; government instability was the least problematic. The Global Competitiveness Report (2009, p. 21) notes:

> The country continues to be endowed with many structural features that make its economy extremely productive ... The United States is

home to highly sophisticated and innovative companies operating in very efficient factor markets ...The country's greatest overall weakness continues to be related to its macroeconomic stability, where it ranks 93rd, down from 66th last year.

Civil society in the United States is characterized by its large size and autonomy from the state, an aspect that is reflected in its funding patterns. Fees and charges account for almost half of civil society organizations' revenue, with philanthropy and government funding each contributing about a quarter when volunteering is included in philanthropy (Salamon and Sokolowski, 2004, p. 41). Indeed, over the past few decades the non-profit sector in the US has experienced dramatic growth, apparently making it difficult for traditional forms of non-profit revenue to keep up with the demand for new revenue. Kerlin and Gagnaire (2009) suggest that this situation, along with sporadic cuts in government funding, has spurred on the development of social enterprise as a revenue generator for all types of civil society activities (see also Kerlin and Pollak, 2011). Not surprisingly, the civil society sector in the US belongs to the Liberal model, which is characterized by a relatively small welfare state, limited government funding, and a reliance on private support (Salamon and Sokolowski, 2010). The following case is an example of a US social enterprise.

The Georgia Justice Project

Founded in 1986, the mission of the Georgia Justice Project (GJP) is to ensure justice for the indigent criminally accused and to take a holistic approach in helping them establish crime-free lives and become productive citizens. It achieves this through a mixed staff of lawyers, social workers, and a landscaping company. GJP carefully selects the cases it takes on and has the freedom to do this because it receives no government grants. Funding for GJP comes from private foundations, corporations, individuals, and religious congregations. People are initially referred to GJP because they have a criminal case pending and cannot afford a private attorney. They become GJP clients if they are committed to making a life change and being productive members of society. GJP legal, social service, and jobs staff work together with the client to carry out this mission. What makes this approach unique is that it is:

- *Holistic*. The client's initial contact with GJP includes both a legal and social work assessment. A holistic case plan is developed by a team. Services include quality legal representation, individual counselling, substance abuse intervention, educational assistance, and job training and placement. If their clients are convicted, GJP visits them in prison, advocates for their needs while in prison, and provides post-release support.

- *Entrepreneurial.* GJP started a company – New Horizon Landscaping (NHL) – in which all GJP clients are eligible for pre-disposition and post-release employment. NHL has provided quality lawn care services since 1993. It offers an opportunity of job training and steady employment for the clients served by the Georgia Justice Project.
- *Relationship-driven.* At GJP, long-lasting, redemptive relationships with clients are sought. During the initial stage (legal representation), GJP establishes a foundation of trust upon which all subsequent services are built. Staff make sure that representation is both thorough and personal, and that the client is involved in all stages of the representation, not just at the courthouse on the day of trial. And the relationship continues long after the case is over. It is common for staff to spend time with clients whose cases have been over for years through structured services (e.g. counselling, working with NHL) or informal support. GJP clients know that there are GJP staff who care about them.
- *A partnership.* Clients work with staff to develop a case plan outlining goals and expectations, and clients must fulfil their part to continue to receive services.
- *Independent.* The GJP is supported solely by private sources. By not seeking government funding, the organization maintains an independent status with regard to the court system. Thus, GJP has total control of its caseload and can reverse the way legal services have been traditionally available to the poor.
- *Successful.* GJP lawyers and social workers have been using this approach for 20 years. The recidivism rate for GJP clients is 18.8 per cent compared to a national average of over 60 per cent. The incarceration rate for GJP clients is 7.3 per cent compared to an average of 71.30 per cent in a study of urban public defender offices.

(Adapted from: [http://www.gjp.org/about] (accessed January 2009): see Kerlin and Gagnaire, 2009.)

This case of a social enterprise in a laissez-faire context illustrates the autonomy from government and reliance on private contributions and fee-for-service activities that can be found among social enterprises in the US (though some social enterprises in the US do draw on government funding including contracts). While this example provides a case where the social enterprise activity both brings in revenue and provides clients with programming, there are also many social enterprise activities in the US where revenue generation does not have a programming component.

Conclusion

The four broad types of contexts and cases of social enterprise outlined here suggest that different forms and activities of social enterprise develop over time partially in response to environmental factors. Such understanding has implications for the facilitation of cross-regional dialogue, the transfer and replication of social enterprise ideas, and the structures developed for their support. Social enterprise researchers and practitioners working cross-nationally will be able to better engage in discussions of social enterprise knowing that specific forms and processes in different regions may vary though aims and purposes are constant. Such discussions involving a broader range of social enterprise types may in fact facilitate the exchange of ideas. Knowing the context for social enterprise can also support the adaptation of social enterprises in their transfer from one context to the next. If, for example, strong supports from one context are not found in the new, the social enterprise can be adapted to draw on existing resources in the new context. Finally, researchers and practitioners interested in supporting the scalability of social enterprises can identify institutions and policies that may be leveraged in support of such expansion.

Awareness of specific socio-economic and cultural contexts also aids our understanding of how successful social innovators work with and through their environments. As this and other research has found, social innovators appear to seek out and identify the strongest resources and structures available to sustain innovative projects in a given region (Nicholls, 2006; Nyssens, 2006; Kerlin, 2009). Moreover, social innovators are able to combine these resources with their intimate knowledge of culture, expressed as the ideals and very identity of the people in their region. Thus, the study of the development of social innovation should consider the interaction between social innovators and the broader environment in which they operate. This includes specific societal institutions which may facilitate, guide, or impede the work of social innovators and thus ultimately help shape the innovations they design.

While this discussion makes the case for four kinds of contexts for social enterprise, it is only a preliminary effort to identify contextually similar groupings of countries. Other countries with significantly different contexts yet to be explored include India, China, and other Asian and Middle Eastern countries. Also, factors in countries already associated with a given context may call for greater differentiation of the four contexts outlined here. For example, differences across countries in the post-authoritarian context may call for separate categories for Latin American and East European regions. This may also hold true for the village context in terms of greater differentiation between Sub-Saharan African and Southeast Asian contexts. Thus, this chapter is an initial exercise in outlining the most immediately different contexts for social enterprise emerging from recent available comparative research. Future research will explore possible extensions to the contextual framework outlined here.

Notes

1. As of this writing, detailed information on the contexts and types of social enterprise in certain areas of the world (such as China, India, and the Middle East) was not readily available for use in this research.
2. Descriptions of each of the indicators used can be found in the notes to Table 2.1.
3. See Note 1 in Table 2.1 for source and definitions of these culture variables.
4. Recuperated companies are companies that have been abandoned by their owners and are subsequently taken over by the workers in an effort to maintain their employment. They are often established as co-operatives.
5. HIVOS is a Dutch-based funding organization: The Humanist Institute for Development Co-operation. See: [http://www.hivos.nl/eng/About-Hivos/Introduction].
6. Nyssens (2009, p. 18) also notes that in 2006 'an Italian law on social enterprise was enacted that opened this label to various legal forms (not just social co-operatives) and fields of activities, provided that the organization complied with the non-distribution constraint and involved certain categories of stakeholders, including workers and beneficiaries'.
7. Putnam (1993) notes strong regional variation between northern and southern parts of the country.
8. 'Social Cooperative' accessed at [http://www.mentalhealth.org/publications/allpubs/KEN-01-0108/social.asp].
9. 'Social Cooperative' accessed at http://www.mentalhealth.org/publications/allpubs/KEN-01-0108/social.asp.

References

Barbetta, G., Cima, S., Nereo, Z., Sokolowski, S. and Salamon, L. (2004), 'Italy', in L. Salamon and S. W. Sokolowski (eds) *Global Civil Society: Dimensions of the Nonprofit Sector*, Volume Two, Bloomfield, CT: Kumarian Press.

Borzaga, C. and Defourny, J. (eds) (2001), *The Emergence of Social Enterprise*, New York: Routledge.

Borzaga, C. and Loss, M. (2006), 'Multiple Goals and Multi-Stakeholder Management in Italian Social Enterprises', in M. Nyssens (ed.) *Social Enterprise: At the Crossroads of Market, Public Policies and Civil Society*, New York: Routledge.

Bosma, N. and Levie, J. (2010), Global Entrepreneurship Monitor 2009 Global Report. Global Entrepreneurship Monitor. Accessed July 2010 at http://www.gemconsortium.org/about.aspx?page=pub_gem_global_reports.

Fiorucci, F. and Klein, M. (eds) (2005), *Argentine Crisis of the Millennium*, Amsterdam: Aksant Academic Publishers.

Franke, R., Hofstede, G. and Bond, M. (1991), 'Cultural Roots of Economic Performance: A Research Note', *Strategic Management Journal*, 12 (S1), 165–73.

Hofstede, G. (1980), *Culture's Consequences: International Differences in Work Related Values*, Beverly Hills, CA: Sage.

Hofstede, G. (2001), *Culture's Consequences: Comparing Values, Behaviors, Institutions, and Organizations across Nations*, Thousand Oaks, CA: Sage.

House, R., Chhokar, J. and Brodbeck, F. (2004), *Culture, Leadership and Organizations: The GLOBE Study of 62 Societies*, Thousand Oaks, CA: Sage.

Jacobs, J. and Maldonado, M. (2005), 'Civil Society in Argentina: Opportunities and Challenges for National and Transnational Organisation', *Journal of Latin American Studies*, 37 (1), 141–72.

Kerlin, J. (ed.) (2009), *Social Enterprise: A Global Comparison*, Lebanon, NH: Tufts University Press.

Kerlin, J. (2010), 'Historical Institutionalism and Social Enterprise Development: Towards a Comparative Framework for Social Enterprise', Paper presented at the Ninth International ISTR Conference, Istanbul, Turkey, 7–10 July 2010.

Kerlin, J. and Gagnaire, K. (2009), 'United States' in J. Kerlin (ed.) *Social Enterprise: A Global Comparison* (Lebanon, NH: Tufts University Press).

Kerlin, J. and Pollak, T. (2011), 'Nonprofit Commercial Revenue: A Replacement for Declining Government Grants and Private Contributions?', *The American Review of Public Administration*, 41 (6): 686–705.

Masendeke, A. and Mugova, A. (2009) 'Zimbabwe and Zambia', in J. Kerlin (ed.) *Social Enterprise: A Global Comparison*, Lebanon, NH: Tufts University Press.

NANGO ((Zimbabwe) National Association of Non-Governmental Organisations) (2010). 'Early Warning System Report Reporting Period October 2009–February 2010', http://www.nango.org.zw/index.php?option=com_content&view=article&id=72&Itemid=265, date accessed 7 June 2010.

Nicholls, A. (2006) 'Introduction', in A. Nicholls (ed.) *Social Entrepreneurship: New Models of Sustainable Change*, Oxford: Oxford University Press, pp. 1–36.

Nussbaumer, J. and Moulaert, F. (2004), 'Integrated Area Development and Social Innovation in European Cities', *City: Analysis of Urban Trends, Culture, Theory, Policy, Action*, 8 (2), 249–57.

Nyssens, M. (ed.) (2006), *Social Enterprise: At the Crossroads of Market, Public Policies and Civil Society*, New York: Routledge.

Nyssens, M. (2009), 'Western Europe', in J. Kerlin (ed.) *Social Enterprise: A Global Comparison*, Lebanon, NH: Tufts University Press.

Porter, M. (1998), *The Competitive Advantage of Nations*, New York: The Free Press.

Putnam, R. (1993) *Making Democracy Work: Civic Traditions in Modern Italy*, Princeton: Princeton University Press.

Roitter, M. and Vivas, A. (2009), 'Argentina', in J. Kerlin (ed) *Social Enterprise: A Global Comparison*, Lebanon, NH: Tufts University Press.

Sala-i-Martin, X. Blanke, J., Franco, A. and Geiger, T. (2009), 'The Global Competitiveness Index 2009–2010: Contributing to Long-term Prosperity amid the Global Economic Crisis', in K. Schwab (ed.) *The Global Competitiveness Report 2009–2010* Geneva: World Economic Forum. Accessed 10 June 2010 at http://www.weforum.org/pdf/GCR09/GCR20092010fullreport.

Salamon, L. and Sokolowski, S. (2004), *Global Civil Society. Dimensions of the Nonprofit Sector, Volume Two*, Bloomfield, CT: Kumarian Press.

Salamon, L. and Sokolowski, S. (2010) 'Bringing the "Social" and the "Political" to Civil Society: Social Origins of Civil Society Sectors in 40 Countries', Paper presented at the Ninth International ISTR Conference, Istanbul, Turkey, 7–10 July 2010.

Santos, J., Macatangay, L., Capistrano, M. and Burns, C. (2009) 'Southeast Asia', in J. Kerlin (ed.) *Social Enterprise: A Global Comparison*, Lebanon, NH: Tufts University Press.

Social Enterprise Knowledge Network (SEKN), Austin, J. E., Gutierrez, R. and Ogliastri, E. (2006), Effective Management of Social Enterprises: Lessons from Businesses and Civil Society Organizations in Iberoamerica (Cambridge, MA: David Rockefeller Center for Latin American Studies).

Shane, S. (1992), 'Why do Some Societies Invent More than Others?', *Journal of Business Venturing*, 7 (1), 29–46.

Shane, S. (1993) 'Cultural Influences on National Rates of Innovation', *Journal of Business Venturing*, 8 (1), 59–73.

Spear, R. and Bidet, E. (2005), 'Social Enterprise for Work Integration in 12 European Countries: A Descriptive Analysis', *Annals of Public and Cooperative Economics*, 76 (2), 195–231.

Tiessen, J. (1997), 'Individualism, Collectivism, and Entrepreneurship: A Framework for International Comparative Research', *Journal of Business Venturing*, 12 (5), 367–84.

World Bank (2009), 'Governance Matters 2009: Worldwide Governance Indicators, 1996–2008: Country Data Reports',http://info.worldbank.org/governance/wgi/pdf_country.asp, date accessed July 2010.

World Bank (2010), 'World Development Indicators', World Bank World Databank. http://databank.worldbank.org/ddp/home.do?Step=12&id=4&CNO=2), date accessed July 2010.

3

The Loop, the Lens, and the Lesson: Using Resilience Theory to Examine Public Policy and Social Innovation

Michele-Lee Moore, Frances R. Westley, Ola Tjornbo, and Carin Holroyd

Introduction

The role of social innovation and social entrepreneurship in addressing complex problems has increasingly gained traction in policy-making circles with policy practitioners' interest piqued about how governments may best support such innovations (e.g. PRI, 2010). Various governments are attempting to support social innovation through a variety of means. For instance, the Office of Civil Society in the UK and the Australian Centre for Social Innovation are recent attempts by these national governments formally to institutionalize the fostering of social entrepreneurs and social enterprises. Other national governments have chosen simply to promote the 'production' side of innovation, by funding research and development, specifically for the technology sectors (Nelson, 1993). But while there is a growing body of grey literature that mirrors policy practitioners' own interest in this field (e.g. Leadbeater, 2007), scholarship within the social innovation and social entrepreneurship community has largely neglected the role of public policy in supporting or hindering social innovation (for an exception, see Chapman et al., 2007). Yet, without a substantive debate about the relationship between policy and social innovation, both scholars and practitioners will have only a limited understanding about the range of policy options that could best support the process of social innovation.

In response to this gap, this chapter aims to fulfil three objectives. Firstly, it will provide a theoretical framework for exploring the debate about public policy and social innovation by using resilience theory, and in particular its adaptive cycle, as a tool to analyse the process of social innovation. Resilience theory identifies four distinct phases in the adaptive cycle, and in applying this cycle to social innovation, this chapter contends that different policies will suit different phases of social innovation. Secondly, the chapter will support the theoretical arguments put forth about the role of public policy by examining existing social innovation research and case studies. Thirdly, the theoretically informed insights will be used to highlight patterns in the social innovation–policy relationship and are intended better to inform the policy practitioners and social entrepreneurs who are engaged in discussing, championing, and attempting to reform public policy to support social innovations. To meet these objectives, the chapter proceeds in the following manner: it begins by defining social innovation and distinguishing this scholarly domain from social entrepreneurship. Next, resilience theory will be introduced, and a brief description of the lens it provides for examining social innovation cycles will be provided. The chapter will then move to position itself in the debate on the role of government in social innovation, and present the methodological approach. Following that, each phase of the social innovation process will be characterized in detail and supporting case studies will be used to demonstrate optional policy tools that may support each phase. Finally, a single case study on Inuit art will be explored through all of the different phases to illustrate the dynamic policy process that needs to be considered in successfully fostering social innovation.[1]

In keeping with the outline above, given the focus of this book, it is important to clarify the differences between definitions and perspectives on social entrepreneurship and social innovation at the outset. Social innovation is defined here as any new programme, product, idea, or initiative that profoundly changes the basic routines, resource and authority flows, or beliefs of any social system, and successful ones are those with durability and broad impact (Westley and Antadze, 2010). While much energy has been expended on defining social entrepreneurship (Nicholls, 2010), less attention has been paid to social innovation and, in particular, the differences between the two scholarly domains (for some exceptions see Mulgan et al., 2007; Westall, 2007; Phills et al., 2008). For the purposes of this chapter, social innovation is distinguished from social entrepreneurship because of the market orientation of social entrepreneurship (for further distinctions see Westall, 2007; Phills et al., 2008). Social entrepreneurship refers to individuals with a value-based social mission who pursue opportunities within the market context, whether their own organization is considered non-profit, charity, or for profit (Nicholls, 2006). Social innovations do not require the market context and quite often, because of their transformative nature, social innovations may challenge existing economic models and ideologies (Antadze and Westley, 2010).

While both bodies of work are interested in the innovative nature of certain initiatives (Alvord et al., 2004), social innovation is focused on innovations that lead to systemic change (Antadze and Westley, 2010). Whereas a social entrepreneur may be recognized as successful once his/her product diffuses in the market from one to many people, a social innovation, often created by multiple forces, disrupts a larger institutional context and therefore does not rely on mass adoption to be considered a success (Antadze and Westley, 2010). However, given that some social innovations will occur as a result of the work of social entrepreneurs, the two as areas of study and practice do intersect. Thus, social innovation research can be usefully informed by the knowledge that has been advanced about successful social entrepreneurs (e.g. Leadbeater, 1997; Dees, 1998; Nicholls, 2006; Bornstein, 2007). Likewise, the driver of research in both areas is a shared understanding that complex social problems have yet to be addressed effectively by more narrow or traditional approaches (Austin et al., 2006).

Resilience and the process of social innovation

Social innovation is an important component of being resilient – new ideas keep a society adaptable, flexible, and able to learn. Thus, the theory of resilience provides a meaningful lens to build a better understanding of the conditions that enable innovation to emerge and succeed, which includes public sector policy support (Westley et al., 2006). Resilience theory stems from work in ecology in the 1970s (e.g. Holling, 1973) and the adaptive cycle, as represented by an infinity loop, is a key feature. The theory rests upon the idea that any resilient ecosystem is dynamically moving through an adaptive cycle, and that remaining stagnant in a fixed equilibrium is not healthy (Gunderson and Holling, 2002). The adaptive cycle has at least four distinct phases in what is best pictured as a figure of eight: release; reorganization; exploitation; and conservation (Gunderson et al., 1995; Gunderson and Holling, 2002).

Resilience theorists use a forest subjected to fire as a classic example of a resilient ecosystem. Examining Figure 3.1, the theory claims that when a forest burns, biomass is released, and diversity becomes low (Gunderson and Holling, 2002). This is the *release phase* of the adaptive cycle. As resources become available once again and new life begins to proliferate, available carbon and nutrients become attached to a wide diversity of life forms, described as the reorganization phase (ibid.). Eventually, in a competition for resources, some of the diversity dies out and the extra resources are appropriated by the remaining organisms. In the *exploitation stage*, the organisms increasingly accumulate biomass as diversity reduces until the system attains the *conservation pha*se of a mature cycle (ibid.).

While this brief description provides a useful background on resilience theory, this chapter does not focus on ecosystem dynamics; rather it will examine the dynamics of the social innovation process. In doing so, the chapter applies resilience theory and the adaptive cycle and argues that the cycle's four phases (Figure 3.1) provide a meaningful framework for considering the phases that social innovations may go through from inception to implementation (see also Moore and Westley, 2011). Through this application, the conditions of the different phases and how public policy can support or enable the process in each phase can be better understood.

In contrast to the ecosystem and forest fire example, the four phases of complex social innovation dynamics can be briefly described as follows: the release phase is characterized by the collapse of rigid, powerful rules and institutions (Westley et al., 2006). Due to the breakdown,

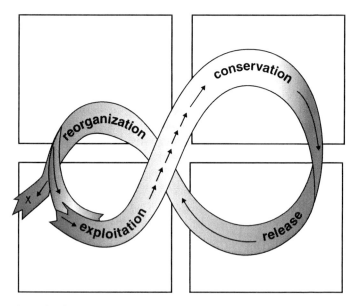

Figure 3.1   The four phases of the adaptive cycle from resilience theory. Adapted from *Panarchy*, edited by Lance H. Gunderson & C.S. Holling. Copyright © 2002 Island Press. Reproduced by permission of Island Press, Washington, D.C.

however, the release phase may also involve new interactions and is the most likely site for creative (re)combinations of ideas, people, and other resources and ultimately, new innovations, as they are released from previous structures and organizations. The reorganization phase involves restructuring individuals around the visions for newly generated innovations, selecting the best options, and trying to establish some level of order without dampening the creative process. The release and reorganization phases are collectively referred to as the back loop (ibid.).

Moving into the front loop, the exploitation phase requires the reorganized groups to leverage the resources that are needed – from establishing legislation to finding financial support – successfully to launch and scale up the innovation (Antadze and Westley, 2010). With those resources leveraged, the innovation may move into the conservation phase which then involves building the formal rules, norms, skill sets, and routine efficiencies as the innovation now becomes mature and the new status quo. Eventually, the reorganized social system will become so rigid with its rules, structures, and dominant authorities and resources that it will become vulnerable to external threats and any event may create a disruption, sending the system back into the release phase once more (Westley et al., 2006).

The characteristics of each of these phases will be explored in greater detail in the 'Phases of social innovation' section below. However, it is important to acknowledge that representing the process of innovation using a cycle has long been identified and discussed in the literature on social and technical entrepreneurship (e.g. Schumpeter, 1937; Utterback and Abernathy, 1975; Van de Venn et al., 1999). The distinct difference however, is that the innovative products of Schumpeter's social enterprises do not require system-altering disruptions. Nor do they create opportunities for portions of society to reorganize or necessarily lead to altered resource flows or sites of authority. Therefore, the resilience framework and adaptive cycle are better suited to understanding the systemic change process associated with transformative social innovations, rather than just innovation or social enterprise in general.

Public policy agendas for social innovation

This chapter posits that government has a role to play in catalyzing social innovation through public policy. Although a consensus on the definition of public policy has not emerged within scholarship, the definition adopted in this chapter is the course of concrete actions selected by a political process to serve the public (John, 1998). But what does the theory of resilience indicate the role of public policy to be with regards to social innovation? Given the dynamic cycle that the theory describes (Berkes et al., 2003; Holling, 2001), the role of public policy will need to be aligned with that dynamism. Likewise, given the growing literature on the need for governments and governance systems to be flexible and adaptive (e.g. Olsson et al., 2004; Folke et al., 2005; Voβ et al., 2006; Duit and Galaz, 2008), it can be inferred that a single, rigid policy is not going to be appropriate for any complex and dynamic process.

Instead, this chapter argues that resilience theory indicates that successfully innovating governments will need to employ a number of different policy tools depending on the phase of the innovation. Some policies need to be geared to the back loop of the adaptive cycle (release and reorganization) and emphasize idea generation, the emergence of new coalitions of actors; and the ability to move quickly to take advantage of available opportunities and resources. Other policy interventions will need to be geared towards the front loop (exploitation and conservation) and be focused on establishing innovations more firmly in the system and to allowing successful innovations to grow rapidly. The difficulty for policy practitioners may be in knowing which policy option to use and when. Thus, the section on 'Phases of social innovation' will explore the characteristics of each phase in depth and present examples of policy tools to highlight their options.

Methodology

In order to build on the phase-based model of policy and innovation developed in this chapter, a number of exploratory case studies are provided. The purpose of these examples is to populate the public policy-social innovation model with cases of actual strategies used by governments or other agencies in examples of successful policy interventions in the social innovation process. It is important to stress that these case studies are only intended to help add richness and detail to the argument, in order to help build hypotheses, and provide suggestions for further inquiry. The cases do not aim to provide firm conclusions, and it is hoped that they will lead to further rigorous empirical work. The methodological approach adopted here is best understood as an example of the explanatory case study approach described by Yin (1994).

Some of the examples are based on primary data collection conducted by one or more of the authors for previous research and case studies. These data were collected through interviews, document analysis, and participant observation in the communities and government settings described. Rather than focusing on examples in a single policy area, the cases presented cover a range of social or ecological problem domains. Problem domains comprise the actors, organizations, and institutions that are concerned and affected by a particular complex problem (Trist, 1983; Westley and Vredenburg, 1991; 1997). This methodology places an emphasis on identifying patterns common to cases instead of focusing on a single variable as a linear, causal effect (Young et al., 2006). Given its complex and dynamic processes, social innovation involves a combination of numerous variables. Policy practitioners will not necessarily be able to adopt each policy option directly or expect to find an exact case in their own work. Rather, this meta-analysis can serve to inform practitioners of the conditions that need to be considered in social innovation and the range of policy options available in different phases or conditions.

Phases of social innovation and relevant policy options

The following section describes the characteristics of the phases of social innovation in more detail as informed by resilience theory, and explores the potential policy initiatives that would be effective in the different phases. Examples are used to illustrate each.

Release phase: Policy approaches for 'sense making' for complex problems and/or when no tangible innovation clearly exists

Prior to the release phase, the problem domain can be imagined as abundant in resources, rules, and institutions. The rigidity of these structures creates homogeneity and a strong resistance to change (Scheffer and Westley, 2007), but also vulnerability due to a lack of diversity (Westley et al., 2006). If a disturbance enters the social system, such as a market crash, a natural disaster, or much less dramatically, a regular democratic election, there may be a breakdown in some existing social structures. The consequence is that resources and capital – including social, intellectual, and financial capital – are released and freed up.

In a phase marked by these characteristics, the greatest need is for new ideas and creative solutions. In this phase, people may be genuinely uncertain about 'what the right idea is' and how to make anything significant happen. In fact, many will not agree yet on the definition of the problem itself (Westley et al., 2006). With the lack of a clear problem definition and the high level of uncertainty about potential solutions that characterize this phase, policy levers that promote discussion, interaction, and social learning are useful for building knowledge

(Hämäläinen, 2007). Research has shown that new knowledge and different ideas are more likely to emerge when diverse actors that do not normally interact closely with one another are exposed to each other's ideas (Burt, 1992; Gilsing and Duysters, 2008). These findings provide a useful foundation for policymakers to consider.

To establish the mix of diverse forms of knowledge, along with the trusting environment that can be critical to the building of new relationships and to the sharing of risks often associated with innovation, public policy instruments that are most useful in this phase are those that convene different individuals or groups together. Multi-stakeholder consultations, Royal Commissions, and participatory planning processes based on models such as Future Search (Weisbord and Janoff, 2000) are all excellent examples of tools that provide a forum for sharing ideas and the range of issues that contribute to the complexity of a problem. For example, the creation of the Central Coast Land Resource Management Planning process for the Central Coast Timber Supply Area in British Columbia brought together a conflict-ridden logging industry, environmental protestors, indigenous peoples, and resource-dependent communities. The process eventually enabled a more nuanced understanding of the complexities of a situation that was not merely a profit versus environment conflict, but a social justice, community economic diversification, and cultural identity issue as well (Tjornbo et al., 2010). The outcome today is the adoption of Ecosystem Based Management practices in what is now known as the Great Bear Rainforest, and a five point deal between the different groups that fundamentally changed the flow of financial resources and the sites of authority (Tjornbo et al., 2010).

The Yukon 2000 Economic Planning Process is another example of this kind of community-based policy development process (see Yukon Territory Department of Economic Development, 1988; Northern Perspectives, 1988–9). In the 1980s, the Yukon Territory of Canada had a resource-dependent economy and had just faced the closure of its major mine, creating great uncertainty for the territory's economic future. In 1986–7, the Territory government brought together the different sectors of the Yukon economy and society – including the mining sector, indigenous peoples, environmental groups, social activists, small businesses, tourism operators, government officials, and village representatives – to set out a new plan for a sustainable economy. Meetings were held across the territory with local consultations focused on infrastructure needs and how to achieve locally controlled finance. Perhaps more importantly, the meetings brought together groups which previously had rarely met and often had antagonistic relationships (Green, 1988). The consultation process was deemed successful, with people deeply engaged in the process and the plans for the future (Coates, 1988).

The Yukon 2000 Process had significant and far-reaching implications. A strong consensus emerged about the need for greater local decision making, territorial venture capital and development funds, and improved access to local administrative and technical support. The process bridged social, cultural, and economic gaps, providing a markedly different environment for the negotiation of land claims and the repositioning of Yukon indigenous people within the territorial order.

Eventually, the collaborations started in the Yukon 2000 meeting carried over into new and mutually beneficial discussions surrounding a new treaty incorporating indigenous concerns into economic and political planning. New programmes, such as the Yukon Economic Strategy, the Yukon Conservation Strategy and the Yukon Training Strategy, came into being as a direct result of this territorial collaboration (Yukon Territorial Assembly, 1989). But the realization that all groups shared common interests helped overcome – if not entirely remove – long-standing divisions in Yukon society, providing a very different foundation for future relationships.

The Yukon 2000 process was not responsible alone for transforming the socio-economic order in the Yukon. But the process initiated formal and face-to-face discussions that all agreed were long overdue and that provided a dramatically different foundation for internal discussions and collaborations in the territory. In many ways, the Yukon 2000 Process illustrated how frank discussion about a fairly simple question – how to diversify the territorial economy – brought to the surface the complexities and subtleties of the territorial order, resulting in a consensus about the need to work collaboratively to solve long-standing and interrelated problems (Downes, 2001).

Proposition 1: When complex problems need to be better understood and new ideas are needed, policies that create and support processes to enable interactions and build trust between previously disconnected groups are helpful to foster new insights, new partnerships, and the generation of social innovations.

Reorganization phase: Policy approaches for reorganizing groups around new ideas, visions, and innovations and policies to ensure selection

In the reorganization phase, the actual definition of the problem is far more clear than in the release phase and the result is that groups, structures, and opinions become formed and organized. In fact, this phase marks a key transition from mere 'idea' or 'talk' to planning for implementation. People will start to cluster around the new ideas that have emerged and in groups with others who share a similar vision for the future (Van de Ven, 1986). Experiments with prototypes on a small scale or in a 'safe' space are likely to occur (Geels, 2002; Voβ, 2007).

Public policies that support social innovation in this phase are those that assist innovators and newly formed groups to develop short- and long-term plans and then encourage a selection process to choose among the range of options or ideas that emerge. That is, forums for the mere generation of new ideas are not needed in this phase; rather, decisions about which innovation will be chosen and, therefore, which one should be invested in become a primary concern. One of the most significant difficulties with selection processes that governments and others face is the lack of appropriate evaluation techniques to measure social innovation and the often intangible benefits it provides. Without appropriate metrics, it becomes difficult to determine which innovation is worth moving towards the next phase. With social innovations, a single 'best' innovation to select may not be obvious – these are transformations that may dramatically shift current resource and authority flows, or norms and beliefs that are at the core of a complex social problem. The most valuable contribution a policy tool provides in this phase is to create a place where people can debate and collectively select an innovation that has emerged as the most appropriate for the relevant group of people, at that time, in that place.

Pilot projects with complete evaluations are effective in this phase. Likewise, challenges that are intended to stimulate, select, and reward innovations are also increasingly popular. For example, the 'Big Green Challenge' was hosted in 2009 in the UK to stimulate community-led responses to climate change. The potential reward was a £1 million prize and the challenge required communities to submit proposals. The organizers selected 100 of the most promising groups, and the Big Green Challenge team then provided technical support to the community groups to develop the ideas into detailed plans. From there, ten finalists were shortlisted who put their ideas into practice to compete for the prize and to reduce CO_2 emissions in their community. While it is still too early to determine the effectiveness of the challenge in generating socially transformative solutions, early indications are that some novel ideas emerged and that they came from communities and actors who would not normally have applied for, or led activities to, reduce carbon emissions (NESTA, 2009).

Another example was demonstrated in Japan in the computer industry (see e.g. Anchordoguy, 1989). In the 1960s, still recovering from the war and with little capital or technology, Japan decided that it wanted to build a computer industry to compete with IBM. As a means to encourage corporations to become involved and to be competitive in the industry, the Japanese government used a variety of strategies to select key innovations and build the industry around those advances. Examples of their policy choices include negotiating for patent permissions from IBM to preclude individual domestic companies bidding against one another, thereby changing the nature of national competition in terms of intellectual property. Additionally, the government devoted substantial financial resources to support seven Japanese companies to begin producing computers – again, a selection mechanism for the entrepreneurs believed most likely to succeed. As well as encouraging the companies to compete against each other aggressively, the government also sponsored co-operative research and development projects in which different companies were assigned different tasks or different approaches to solving the same problem while sharing the results. Not all of the co-operative research projects were immediately successful, but gradually Japan built a successful computer industry; this, in turn, proved critical in launching the country into the high-technology economy of the late twentieth century (Holroyd and Coates, 2007).

At the outset, the case of Japan may appear to be one of promoting technological rather than social innovations. But radical technological innovations require social conditions that enable the technological innovations to take hold, and thus, social and technological innovations are inextricably linked. In fact, social innovations may often provide the platform for multiple technological innovations (Collins, 1997). As Padgett and McLean (2006) demonstrate, the social invention of business partnerships during the Renaissance shifted certain norms and practices and enabled multiple technological innovations. Therefore, public policy options must be informed by the conditions and social reorganization taking place to understand more fully which innovations to select and support.

Proposition 2: policies that not only motivate and reward the generation of innovative ideas but also involve an evaluation or selection process to choose among the many potential innovations that may be legitimate in the current social context is one of the more successful options for the reorganization phase.

Exploitation phase: Policy approaches for leveraging resources and removing barriers to achieving scale

The exploitation phase is characterized by the need to leverage resources to support the development and adoption of the innovations selected in the previous phase.

Often by this phase, an innovation has already been successful at a local level and the goal becomes to scale out the innovation more broadly (Chappin et al., 2009). Many innovations get trapped here because they are unable to ensure support or cannot frame their innovation in a way that it appears legitimate, desirable, and needed; an essential step given that transformative innovations initially do not have an established 'social market' (Geels, 2002; Scheffer and Westley, 2007). Without sufficient resources devoted to these innovations, many never get past the pilot project stage.

Therefore, this phase places less demand on the actual process of innovating and instead emphasizes the need to address any structural barriers to the innovation. Structural change will typically require resources and a source of authority or power that may not previously have existed for those seeking the change (Mulgan and Albury, 2003). Scholars studying social movements, networks, the relevance of social capital, innovation in the private sector, or the increasing role of a range of actors in governance all provide useful insights as to how different people and groups may seek to gain access and legitimately leverage new resources in certain circumstances (e.g. Ernston et al., 2008; Bodin and Crona, 2009). But public policy can also proactively support social innovation and the necessary structural changes. Policymakers may aim to reduce a range of uncertainties that serve as barriers to different actors, for example uncertainty about: available resources; the feasibility of adopting the innovation; the relationship between the innovation and the structures in which it will become embedded; or the risk perceived by both the innovators and adopters (Van de Ven and Polley, 1992; Meijer et al., 2007).

Government incentives for environmental technologies – such as hybrid cars, geothermal heating systems, or water and energy efficient appliances – are good examples of policies that may be useful within this phase because these incentives help to create a market for innovations that are already established or invented (e.g. Braun and Wield, 1994). Policies in this phase are not intended to support the innovation in the phase when it was first trying to create a hybrid car but, rather, support its adoption. In fact, a growing body of research has demonstrated that regulations, taxes, and market mechanisms do not encourage the generation of innovations but may encourage their adoption (Chappin et al., 2009).

While this phase may sound less difficult than some of the other phases, it requires governments to have a strong capacity to adopt innovations. In many cases, the innovation may not have come from within that specific geographic region but rather is the result of external efforts. The capacity to recognize these innovations, adopt them in a timely fashion, and adapt them as needed to the local context is referred to as the 'absorptive capacity' (Cohen and Levinthal, 1990).

An example of a policy attempt to reduce uncertainty and remove structural barriers to ensure adoption is provided by Japan's major recycling initiatives. As the host of the international consultations that led to the Kyoto Protocol on Climate Change, Japan has taken its environmental commitments to heart (Holroyd, 2009). In a series of measures, some of which predated the 1997 accord, the government of Japan undertook steps to address energy consumption, encourage recycling, and otherwise decrease the nation's environmental footprint. These policy initiatives have ranged from procurement changes, regulations, and subsidies to high-profile leadership actions by key national figures, including former Prime Minister Koizumi. Recycling efforts, which have enjoyed considerable success in Japan, are among the most high-profile initiatives (Holroyd, 2009).

The Basic Law for Establishing the Recycling-Based Society, which went into effect in 2000, established a framework for both recycling generally (source reduction or waste prevention, reuse, recycling, energy recovery, appropriate disposal) and extended producer responsibility (EPR) for the recycling of the products and services they produce (Yamaguchi, 2002). A Home Appliance Recycling Law went into effect in April 2001, and stipulated that manufacturers and retailers of home appliances – specifically air conditioners, refrigerators, televisions, and washing machines – are obliged to take back appliances for recycling. Previously, retailers did not accept the return of used appliances, which created a barrier for consumers who were willing to recycle. Manufacturers were consulted extensively while the law was being developed so that they had ample time to redesign their appliances to ensure they could easily be disassembled. The Home Appliance Recycling Law put responsibility for the recycling of these large appliances clearly in the hands of the producers, and gave them a time frame in which to deliver a recycling system that would meet government standards (Ueno, 2002). Together, this created a new legal framework about the responsibilities for recycling and waste. Policy initiatives also channelled efforts and resources specifically into this socially and environmentally innovative area. Eventually, regulation led Japan to become an international leader in recycling and waste diversion (Karpel, 2006).

Proposition 3: Policies that enable social innovation and innovators to access resources – including social, intellectual, and financial capital – are critical to scaling out innovations from local successes to broader systemic change. Policies that create a market or demand for the innovation – whether it is an idea, programme, or technology – are necessary. These policies often involve proactively addressing structural barriers to social innovation, but must be very specific so as not to open opportunities for negative or needless exploitation of scarce resources.

Conservation phase: Policy approaches for institutionalizing the innovation, scaling up, and preparing to be resilient in the face of the next disturbance

During the conservation phase it becomes imperative both to continue the process of completing the existing innovation cycle, and to consider what may happen next, what needs to be adjusted, what consequences and implications have occurred and how best to respond. Therefore, this phase involves two important aspects of the social innovation process: (a) the need to institutionalize and possibly scale up the innovation; and (b) the need to invest in developing the next innovation and prepare to be resilient in the face of the next disturbance.

With regard to the former, social structures that support the innovation need to be established whether this involves certain norms becoming accepted, institutions being created, or regulations being established (for further discussion on social structures, see Giddens, 1979). The specialization of skills, along with the productivity and efficiency of the new programme, product, or initiative, and the social relationships involved, will need to be strengthened and become stabilized (Hämäläinen, 2007). While the freedom for further innovation tends to be negatively affected by the institutionalized nature of this phase (e.g. Braun and Wield, 1994; Chappin et al., 2009), it is equally important for achieving system change as the initial openly creative process.

As the social innovation matures, it may be the most opportune time to determine if the innovation can be scaled up from one successful implementation to other regional or national settings, thereby affecting an even broader system or problem domain. One example of a policy that supports seeking opportunities to scale up innovations involves the government-funded University of Waterloo's International Tobacco Control [ITC] Policy Evaluation Project (Fong, 2006). The project conducts survey research to analyse the effectiveness of anti-smoking policies in various countries, which can inform policy adoption in other countries where comparable policies do not yet exist and smoking rates are still very high. The ITC project first receives a guarantee from the government of the country in question that it will implement the research-based recommendations before the research begins (see [www.ITCproject.org]). Research is then co-ordinated between the central ITC operation and national research institutions to provide local input into the policy development process. In this way, successful innovations may be scaled up but not as a simple policy transfer or mirror adoption. Rather, the ITC seeks to adapt existing practices and policies from different contexts to fit the particular national and/or cultural situation (Fong, 2006).

With respect to investing in the next innovation, it must be recognized that given the nature of the complex problems that these social innovations are designed to address, there will be unforeseen consequences and implications which will create new issues or areas of concern. Additionally, priorities will shift once one problem has begun to be addressed. Thus, at this stage, government policy will want to examine whether other innovations are needed and to begin to understand the complexity of new problems being faced. A real tension exists at this point, given that the more successful an innovation is, the less likely people are to focus on new ideas, needs, and opportunities (Van de Ven, 1986). One approach is that adopted by the Canadian Social Sciences and Humanities Research Council (SSHRC) special project fund which both analyses what has happened and tries to anticipate what will happen next in terms of allocating its funding. The creation of the Forward Scanning Group in the Policy Research Initiative in Canada, whose primary purpose is to analyse trends and develop future scenarios to explore policy strategies, is also a potentially valuable approach. However, the group needs to remain well informed of any current innovation processes in the sector or subject it is analysing to ensure the research focuses on phase-appropriate analysis.

Proposition 4: In this phase, policies that help analyse what has occurred and which new policy priorities have emerged as a result of the innovation are important, along with investing in possible social innovation that will build capacity to be resilient in the face of future change.

Putting it all together

It may be useful to look at the role of public policy through the entire cycle of one social innovation. During the case example described below, and throughout any of the examples provided in this chapter, it must be emphasized that public policy is not the only factor critical to the generation, selection, adoption, and institutionalization or scaling up of social innovations. Indeed, the emphasis on complexity by resilience theory enables one to consider the full suite of social, economic, political, and environmental factors that comprise any complex problem domain. However, this chapter has focused on public policy as the key contextual factor in order better to understand the relationship between social innovation and the role of policy within different phases of the innovation process.

The full social innovation cycle can be explored through an examination of the policies that promoted economic development for the Inuit in the Arctic in the 1950s. During that decade, starvation and hardship led to a situation where life on the land was no longer viable for Inuit peoples – it had become difficult to find wage labour, no clear economic alternatives existed, and there was a dire need for an option other than perpetuating dependency on the Canadian federal government. Few viable alternatives presented themselves beyond traditional harvesting, which was in decline, and occasional/seasonal wage labour, which was uncertain. The worsening conditions served to break down some of the existing social structures – those that provided wage labour for instance. Consequently, the Inuit communities along with the government entered a release phase. The government created a policy to determine the issues that were at the crux of the difficulties and to find economic development ideas for the Inuit: a process described as creating opportunities for 'learning by searching' and 'learning by interacting' (Meijer et al., 2007).

Within this phase, government action was led by a civil servant named James Houston who played a pivotal role in identifying and developing the possibilities for transforming the local livelihoods to include art. Houston was an artist and writer, working as a Northern Service Officer, assigned to the Eastern Arctic. He worked with Inuit artists, whose work had previously been seen as only cultural curiosities, and made connections between northern communities and southern galleries (Houston, 1995). The Government of Canada, eager to find an alternative to the faltering subsistence economy in the Far North, supported the effort, hiring Houston to expand the programme. Inuit sculpture and, later, printmaking attracted global attention, again with significant government investment. By the early 1960s, and largely due to Houston's engagement as a champion, Inuit art had been established as a major cultural and commercial phenomenon (Graburn, 1987).

During the reorganization phase, and as a result of the support for the concept of art as a livelihood, the government created policies that promoted the development of art and sent a clear signal that this vision had been selected as the innovation that would be attempted for now. Examples of the policies included subsidies for promotional efforts and for initial sales, as well as the development of training programmes throughout the North. This clear signal reduced some of the uncertainty about whether Inuit art as an economic development plan was feasible, and helped enable the success of the model throughout the North by creating more secure markets to allow new artists to engage. Arts had to be connected with galleries, and the galleries had to cultivate a substantial and sustainable market. With Houston in the lead, and supported by government funding, the artistic community fostered collectors' interest in Inuit carvings. The process moved with dramatic speed, as Inuit artists developed and displayed a remarkable ability for commercial art and a global market emerged for their soapstone carvings and prints. The challenge, of course, rested with connecting Inuit artists to an international market; the small and remote Inuit communities lacked international business experience to develop sustainable operations (Graburn, 1997). Thus, the exploitation phase involved the Government of Canada developing policy to assist with international marketing activities and leverage support from the Canadian co-operative movement, which provided an opportunity for the Inuit to form their own artistic co-operatives in most of the artistic communities. This, in turn, enabled the innovation to mature and move into the conservation phase as it stabilized artists' incomes, allowed for economies of scale to develop in everything from the purchase of supplies and artist training to shipping and marketing. Communities, particularly Cape Dorset and Holman, and even individual artists became internationally known and able to earn substantial and sustainable incomes (Crandall, 2000).

The Inuit proved just as adept at the management of co-operatives as they were at the creation of Inuit art. With the government of Canada providing most of the capital and operating funds at the early stage, and with professional assistance from the Canadian and international co-operative movement, the Inuit quickly established a network of viable co-operative stores and related operations across the Arctic (the evolution and impact of the Inuit co-operative movement can be traced in Duffy, 1988; Coates and Powell, 1989; Hamilton, 1994). Government and external co-operative organizations placed a great deal of emphasis initially on the training of managers, ensuring that local expertise emerged in very short order to run the increasingly complex and substantial commercial operations (Ketilson, 2004). These steps were all important to facilitating the transition from the exploitation to the conservation phase. Inuit art served as an important element in the commercial viability of the broader co-operative movement, as the co-operative system expanded into other sectors, including retailing, transport, energy supplies, and tourism. Within two decades, the Arctic co-operative movement had emerged as one of the more successful indigenous adaptations to the twentieth-century economy (Young, 1995; Ketilson and MacPherson, 2001).

The conditions created by this innovation enabled the community to undertake further innovations. Perhaps most significantly, the co-operative initiative that combined Inuit artistic activity and local community development became the foundation for Inuit political organization and legal mobilization. Training through the co-operatives developed a region wide network of talented, motivated, and entrepreneurial leaders, many of whom became key figures in Inuit politics in the 1970s and onward. Furthermore, the region wide gatherings for co-operative meetings generated the solid personal connections needed to mobilize Inuit discontent with political, legal, and economic relations. The connections forged during the Art co-operative movement later came to underpin the Inuit land claims and autonomy movements, and created a disruption in the system which moved it into the next release phase. The new interactions in the release phase brought together the two initiatives and the settlement of the Inuit land claim. Moving through the remaining phases of the social innovation cycle, this ultimately led to the creation of the new territory of Nunavut in 1999, an Inuit-controlled jurisdiction in northern Canada. What started as a means of creating employment in isolated communities and meeting regional retail needs became, in fact, the foundation for political mobilization and the transformation of the Canadian Arctic into one of the most innovative indigenous political and economic regions in the world.

Conclusion

Certain policy instruments will have greater impact at specific points in the social innovation process. Recognizing that distinct phases of social innovation exist is central to understanding which policy will be most suitable to supporting the process; that is, different policies are appropriate for the generation, selection, adoption, and institutionalization processes that any social innovation will need to undergo. This chapter has argued that phase-appropriate government interventions facilitate social innovation, and has used resilience theory to explain the characteristics of each phase and to demonstrate that an active role for government is entirely possible and even necessary.

Using a variety of case studies from different problem domains, this chapter examined empirical examples to support the theoretical framework presented. Ultimately, the examples demonstrated the patterns and characteristics described by the phases of adaptive cycle. Four propositions were put forth that outline policy options to support the different phases of social innovation. In doing so, this chapter made a significant contribution by building a deeper understanding of the intricate relationship between public policy and social innovation than has previously been discussed in the social innovation and entrepreneurship literature. Much of the scholarship in the past has focused on innovations that are neither transformational nor systemic in their impact. Likewise, the literature has historically emphasized the role of governments as the primary financial supporters of research and development in the technology sector, which has limited the analysis of the range of policy tools available. Furthermore, although scholars have previously recognized that innovation processes may follow a cycle, the practical realities of aligning policy tools with specific phases of the innovation process has yet to be addressed.

Recognizing that while other factors do contribute to the context in which social innovation may occur, the conceptual framework presented here brings to bear the co-evolutionary nature of policy choices by governments and the social innovations that emerge in various problem domains. Policies influence a system's preparedness for the need for social innovation and then for its generation, selection, adoption, and institutionalization. In turn, the innovation itself affects the type of policy responses that are required by the public sector.

Any scholarly effort has limitations and this chapter is no exception. Adopting a comparative perspective to examine existing cases is difficult given that the methodological approach is not a conventional, quantitative analysis with common techniques to ensure rigour and reliability. But social innovations themselves – as complex, emergent, and nonlinear events that involve multiple actors and multiple scales across time – are not well suited to traditional techniques (Mumford, 2002). Furthermore, a more conventional outcome of such a study may be to recommend a well-defined macro policy framework with specific policy tools listed for each phase. Instead, the outcome of this chapter's analysis is a description of the characteristics of each phase of the social innovation process. However, the chapter is intended to better prepare policy practitioners to recognize similar patterns in their own decision making without reducing the complexity of this process to formulaic problem-solution management approaches. This methodological technique has been recognized as an important tool for analysing complex social-ecological problems previously (Young et al., 2006) and rigour can be improved with more detailed analyses in the future.

Moreover, future research could examine whether certain defined indicators exist that could help governments to more clearly determine how and when to know which policy lever is most appropriate to employ. While some research has begun to explore how policy instruments can be combined (e.g. Foxon and Pearson, 2008), an understanding of the dynamic interaction of multiple policies and innovations will better inform the process of determining phases and selecting phase appropriate policies. Ultimately, the exploration and debate of possible public policy reforms for social innovation has only just begun.

Notes

Acknowledgements: This ongoing research is supported by funding from the J. W. McConnell Family Foundation. Special thanks to the participants of the 2009 International Social Innovation Research Conference and to the Policy Research Initiative of Canada for their insights and support in the continued development of this project.

1. The term 'scaling out' is used in the exploitation phase to refer to the replication of the same innovation in several different locations. The term 'scaling up' is used in the conservation phase to refer to moving an innovation into a broader system. Quite often, to effect transformative change in a broader system, the innovation will be reconfigured into an entirely new form to suit that context. For instance, the PLAN Institute of British Columbia scaled out its original innovation of creating support networks for children with disabilities, setting up networks for different families in numerous locations around the world. However, when it wanted to scale up its innovative thinking to a broader system about how society could provide long-term security for people with disabilities, the social innovation required different tools and involved new legislation and new economic instruments, including the Registered Disabilities Savings Fund. The perspective suggested by this chapter contends that the local networks and the national policies are all part of scaling up a single social innovation.

References

Anchordoguy, M. (1989), *Computers Inc., Japan's Challenge to IBM*, Cambridge, MA: Harvard University Press.

Alvord, S. H., Brown, L. D. and Letts, C. W. (2004), 'Social Entrepreneurship and Societal Transformation', *The Journal of Applied Behavioural Science*, 40 (3), 260–82.

Antadze, N. and Westley, F. (2010), 'Funding Social Innovation: How do We Know What to Grow', *Philanthropy*, 23 (3), 343–56.

Austin, J., Stevenson, H. and Wei-Skillern, J. (2006), 'Social and Commercial Entrepreneurship: Same, Different or Both?', Entrepreneurship Theory and Practice, 30 (1), 1–22.

Berkes, F., Colding, J. and Folke, C. (Eds) (2003), *Navigating Social-Ecological Systems: Building Resilience for Complexity and Change*, Cambridge, UK: Cambridge University Press.

Bodin, Ö. and Crona, B. (2009), 'The Role of Social Networks in Natural Resource Governance: What Relational Patterns make a difference?', *Global Environmental Change*, 19 (3), 366–74.

Bornstein, D. (2007), *How to Change the World: Social Entrepreneurs and the Power of New Ideas*, Oxford, UK: Oxford University Press.

Braun, E. and Wield, D. (1994), 'Regulation as a Means for the Social Control of Technology', *Technology Analysis and Strategic Management*, 6 (3), 259–72.

Burt, R. S. (1992), *Structural Holes*, Cambridge, MA: Harvard University Press.

Chapman, T., Forbes, D. and Brown, J. (2007), 'They Have God on Their Side': The Impact of Public Sector Attitudes on the Development of Social Enterprise', *Social Enterprise Journal*, 3 (1), 78–89.

Chappin, M. M. H., Vermeulen, W. J. V., Meeus, M. T. H. and Hekkert, M. P. (2009), 'Enhancing Our Understanding of the Role of Environmental Policy in Environmental Innovation: Adoption Explained by Accumulation of Policy Instruments and Agent-Based Factors', *Environmental Science and Policy*, 12 (7), 934–47.

Coates, K. S. (1988), 'On the Outside in Their Homeland: Native People and the Evolution of the Yukon Economy', *The Northern Review*, 1, Summer 1988, 73–89.

Coates, K. and Powell, J. (1989), *The Modern North: People, Politics and the Rejection of Colonialism*, Toronto: James Lorimer and Co. Publishers.

Cohen, W. M. and Levinthal, D. A. (1990), 'Absorptive Capacity: A New Perspective on Learning and Innovation', *Administrative Science Quarterly*, 35 (1), 128–52.

Collins, J. (1997), 'The Most Creative Product Ever', Online: http://www.jimcollins.com/article_topics/articles/the-most-creative.html. Accessed: 19 July 2010.

Crandall, R. (2000), *Inuit Art: A History*, Jefferson, North Carolina: Macfarland Publishers.

Dees, J. G. (1998), 'The Meaning of 'Social Entrepreneurship', Report for the Kauffman Centre for Entrepreneurial Leadership, Online: http://www.fuqua.duke.edu/centers/case/documents/dees_SE.pdf. Accessed: June 2010.

Downes, B. (2001), 'Yukon 2000: A Community-Based Planning Effort to Preserve "Things That Matter"', *Northern Review*, 23, Summer 2001, 121–45.

Duffy, R. Q. (1988), *The Road to Nunavut: The Progress of the Eastern Arctic Inuit since the Second World War*, Montreal: McGill-Queen's University Press.

Duit, A. and Galaz, V. (2008), 'Governance and Complexity – Emerging Issues for Governance Theory', Governance: An International Journal of Policy, Administration, and Institutions, 21 (3), 311–35.

Ernstson, H., Sörlin, S. and Elmqvist, T. (2008), 'Social Movements and Ecosystem Services – The Role of Social Network Structure in Protecting and Managing Urban Green Areas in Stockholm', *Ecology and Society*, 13 (2), 39. Online: http://www.ecologyandsociety.org/vol13/iss2/art39/. Accessed: 17 November 2011.

Folke, C., Hahn, T., Olsson, P. and Norberg, J. (2005), 'Adaptive Governance of Social Ecological Systems', *Annual Review of Environment and Resources*, 30 (1), 441–73.

Fong, G., Cummings, K., Borland, R., Hastings, G., Hyland, A., Giovino, G., Hammond, D. and Thompson, M. (2006), 'The Conceptual Framework of the International Tobacco Control (ITC) Policy Evaluation Project', Tobacco Control, 15 (3), iii3–iii11.

Foxon, T. and Pearson, P. (2008), 'Overcoming Barriers to Innovation and Diffusion of Cleaner Technologies: Some Features of a Sustainable Innovation Policy Regime', *Journal of Cleaner Production*, 16 (S1), S148–S161.

Geels, F. W. (2002), 'Technological Transitions as Evolutionary Reconfiguration Processes: A Multi-Level Perspective and a Case Study', *Research Policy*, 31 (8–9), 1257–74.

Giddens, A. (1979), *Central Problems in Social Theory*, Berkeley, California: University of California Press.

Gilsing, V. A. and Duysters, G. M. (2008), 'Understanding in Exploration Networks – Structural and Relational Embeddedness Jointly Considered', *Technovation*, 28 (10), 693–708.

Graburn, N. (1987), 'The Discovery of Inuit Art: James Houston', *Inuit Art Quarterly*, 2 (2) Spring, 3–5.

Graburn, N. (1979), 'Eskimo Art: The Eastern Canadian Arctic', in N. Graburn (ed.) *Ethnic and Tourist Arts: Cultural Expressions from the Fourth World*, LA: University of California Press.

Green, B. (1988), 'The Indian Economy', *Northern Perspectives*, 16 (2). http://www.carc.org/index.php?option=com_wrapper&view=wrapper&Itemid=174. Accessed: 17 November 2011.

Gunderson, L. H. and Holling C. S. (eds) (2002), *Panarchy: Understanding Transformations in Human and Natural Systems*, Washington: Island University Press.

Gunderson, L. H., Holling, C. S. and Light, S. (1995), *Barriers and Bridges to Renewal of Ecosystems and Institutions*, NY: Columbia University Press.

Hämäläinen, T. J. (2007), 'Policy Implications: How to Facilitate the Structural Adjustment and Renewal of Advanced Societies, Ch. 5', in T. J. Hämäläinen and R. Heiskala (eds) *Social Innovations, Institutional Change and Economic Performance: Making Sense of Structural Adjustment Processes in Industrial Sectors, Regions and Societies*, UK: Edward Elgar.

Hamilton, J. D. (1994), *Arctic Revolution: Social Change in the Northwest Territories, 1935–94*, Toronto: Dundurn Press Ltd.

Holling, C. S. (2001), 'Understanding the Complexity of Economic, Ecological, and Social Systems', *Ecosystems*, 4 (5), 390–405.

Holling, C. S. (1973), 'Resilience and Stability of Ecological Systems', *Annual Review of Ecology and Systematics*, 4 (1), 1–23.

Holroyd, C. (2009), 'National Mobilization and Global Engagement: Understanding Japan's Response to Global Climate Change Initiatives', *Asian Perspective*, 33 (2), 73–96.

Holroyd, C. and Coates, K. S. (2007), *Innovation Nation: Science and Technology in 21st Century Japan*, London, UK: Palgrave MacMillan.

Houston, J. (1995), *Confessions of an Igloo Dweller*, Toronto: McClelland and Stewart.

John, P. (1998), *Analysing Public Policy*, London, UK: Continuum.

Karpel, S. (2006), 'Recycling Japan', *Metal Bulletin Monthly*, 424, 33–4.

Ketilson, L. (2004), 'Aboriginal Cooperatives in Canada', *Review of International Cooperation*, 97 (1), 38–74.

Ketilson, L. and MacPherson, I. (2001), A report on Aboriginal cooperatives in Canada. Centre for the Study of Cooperatives: Saskatoon, Canada.

Leadbeater, C. (2007), Social enterprise and social innovation: Strategies for the next ten years. A social enterprise think piece for the Office of the Third Sector. Online: http://www.eura.org/pdf/leadbeater_news.pdf. Accessed: 30 November 2010.

Leadbeater, C. (1997), *The Rise of the Social Entrepreneur*, London, UK: Demos.

Meijer, I. S. M., Hekkert, M. P. and Koppenjan, J. F. M. (2007), 'How Perceived Uncertainties Influence Transitions: The Case of Micro-CHP in the Netherlands', *Technological Forecasting and Social Change*, 74, 519–37.

Moore, M.-L. and Westley, F. R. (2011), 'Public Sector Policy and Strategies for Facilitating Social Innovation', *Horizons*, 11. Online: http://www.policyre search.gc.ca/page.asp?pagenm=pub_index. Accessed: 17 November 2011.

Mulgan, G., Ali, R., Halkett, R. and Sanders, B. (2007), *In and Out of Sync: The Challenge of Growing Social Innovations*, London, UK: NESTA. Available at http://www.socialinnovationexchange.org/node/238. Accessed: 30 November 2010.

Mulgan, G. and Albury, D. Innovation in the Public Sector, 1 (9), 1–40. London: Prime Minister's Strategy Unit/Cabinet Office, 2003. Online: http://www.cabinet office.gov.uk/media/cabinetoffice/strategy/assets/pubinov2.pdf. Accessed: 24 November 2010.

Mumford, M. D. (2002), 'Social Innovation: Ten Cases from Benjamin Franklin', *Creativity Research Journal*, 14 (2), 253–66.

Nelson, R. R. (1993), *National Innovation Systems: A Comparative Analysis*, Oxford, UK: Oxford University Press.

NESTA (2009), 'People Powered Responses to Climate Change: Mapping Community-Led Proposals to NESTA's Big Green Challenge', Full Report commissioned by NESTA, July 2009, London UK.

Nicholls, A. (2010), 'The Legitimacy of Social Entrepreneurship: Reflexive Isomorphism in a Pre-Paradigmatic Field', *Entrepreneurship Theory and Practice*, 34 (4), 611–33.

Nicholls, A. (2006), *Social Entrepreneurship: New Models of Sustainable Social Change*, Oxford, UK: Oxford University Press.

Northern Perspectives (1988–9), Mining the Popular Wisdom, 16 (2), March–April.

Olsson, P., Folke, C. and Berkes, F. (2004), 'Adaptive Co-Management for Building Resilience in Social-Ecological Systems', *Environmental Management*, 34 (1), 75–90.

Padgett, J. F and McLean, P. D. (2006), 'Organizational Invention and Elite Transformation: The Birth of Partnership Systems in Renaissance Florence', *American Journal of Sociology*, 111 (5), 1463–568.

Phills, J. A., Deiglmeier, K. and Miller, D. T. (2008), 'Rediscovering Social Innovation', *Stanford Social Innovation Review*, 6 (4), 34–43.

PRI (Policy Research Initiative) 'Talking About Social Innovation: Summary of International Round Table on Social Innovation', Prepared for: PRI Project on social management of risk, Government of Canada, 2010. Online: http://www.policyresearch.gc.ca/doclib/2010-0047-eng.pdf. Accessed: 1 December 2010.

Scheffer, M. and Westley, F. R. (2007), 'The Evolutionary Basis of Rigidity: Locks in Cells, Minds and Society', *Ecology and Society*, 12 (2), 36. Online: http://www.ecologyandsociety.org/vol12/iss2/art36/. Accessed: 17 November 2011.

Schumpeter, J. A. (1937), *The Theory of Economic Development*, Boston, MA: Harvard University Press.

Tjornbo, O., Westley, F. and Riddell, D. (2010), 'Case Study: The Great Bear Rainforest', University of Waterloo: SiG@Waterloo Case Study 003.

Trist, E. L. (1983), 'Referent Organizations and the Development of Inter-Organizational Domains', *Human Relations*, 36 (3), 269–84.

Ueno, K. (2002), 'Current Status of Home Appliance Recycling in Japan', Environmentally Conscious Products (ECP) Newsletter of the Japan Environmental Management Association for Industry, 18.

Utterback, J. M. and Abernathy, W. J. (1975), 'A Dynamic Model of Product and Process Innovation', *Omega*, 3 (6), 639–56.

Van de Ven, A., Polley, D. E., Garud, R. and Venkataraman, S. (1999), '*The Innovation Journey*', Oxford, UK: Oxford University Press.

Van de Ven, A. and Polley, D. (1992), 'Learning while Innovating', *Organization Science*, 3 (1), 92–116.

Van de Ven, A. (1986), 'Central Problems in the Management of Innovation', *Management Science*, 32 (5), 590–607.

Voβ, J.-P. (2007), 'Innovation Processes in Governance: The Development of "Emissions Tranding" as a New Policy Instrument', *Science and Public Policy*, 34 (5), 329–43.

Voβ, J.-P., Bauknecht, D. and Kemp, R. (Eds) (2006), *Reflexive Governance for Sustainable Development*, UK: Edward Elgar.

Weisbord, M and S. Janoff. Future Search. San Francisco: Barrett-Koehler, 2000.

Westall, A. (2007), How Can Innovation in Social Enterprise be Understood, Encouraged and Enabled? A Social Enterprise Think Piece for the Office of the Third Sector', Online: http://www.eura.org/pdf/westall_news.pdf. Accessed: 30 November 2010.

Westley, F. and Antadze, N. (2010), 'Making a Difference: Strategies for Scaling Social Innovation for Greater Impact', *The Innovation Journal*, 15 (2) article 2. Online: https://www.innovation.cc/all-issues.htm. Accessed: 26 November 2010.

Westley, F. R., Zimmerman, B. and Patton, M. Q. (2006), *Getting to Maybe: How the World is Changed*, Toronto, ON: Vintage Canada.

Westley, F. and Vredenburg, H. (1997), 'Interorganizational Collaboration and the Preservation of Global Biodiversity', *Organization Science*, 8 (4) 381–403.

Westley, F. and Vredenburg, H. (1991), 'Strategic Bridging: The Collaboration between Environmentalists and Businesses in the Marketing of Green Products', *Journal of Applied Behavioral Science*, 27 (1), 65–90.

Yamaguchi, M. (2002), 'Extended Producer Responsibility in Japan', ECP (Environmentally Conscious Products) Newsletter of the Japan Environmental Management Association for Industry, no 19.

Yin, R. (1994), *Case Study Research: Design and Methods* (2nd edn), Beverly Hills, CA: Sage Publishing.

Young, E. (1995), *Third World in the First: Development and Indigenous Peoples*. London: Routledge, 239–45.

Young, O. R., Lambin, E. F., Alcock, F., Haberl, H., Karlsson, S. I., McConnell, W. J., Myint, T., Pahl- Wostl, C., Polsky, C., Ramakrishnan, P., Schroeder, S., Scouvart, M. and Verburg, P. H. (2006), 'A Portfolio Approach to Analyzing Complex Human-Environment Interactions: Institutions and Land Change', *Ecology and Society*, 11 (2), 31. Online: http://www.ecologyandsociety.org/vol11/iss2/art31/. Accessed: 17 November 2011.

Yukon Territorial Assembly (1989), Hansard, Speech from the Throne, 8 March 1989. Online: http://www.hansard.gov.yk.ca/27-legislature/session1/001_Mar_8_1989.html. Accessed: 1 December 2010.

Yukon Territory Department of Economic Development (1988), *Yukon Economic Strategy – Yukon 2000 – Building the Future*, Whitehorse: Government of Yukon.

Yukon Territory (1988), *Yukon Training Strategy December 1988* Whitehorse: Government of Yukon. http://www.education.gov.yk.ca/pdf/yukon_training_strategy.pdf. Accessed: 1 November 2009.

4
The Limits of Economic Value in Measuring the Performance of Social Innovation

Michel Marée and Sybille Mertens

Introduction

Despite considerable discussion of the nature and role of social innovation in recent years (see Phills et al., 2009), there is much less clarity over the best methods with which to assess its effects and impacts. This is, at least in part, because social innovation represents an aspect of 'production' whose effects are not typically mediated by prices. Social innovation is typically expressed, in organizational form, by social enterprises. Social enterprises are often present in markets where purely commercial enterprises, and sometimes even public agencies, are also active. However, it is now well known that even if these types of organization are present in the same markets, they do not produce exactly the same quality of goods or services (Henry et al., 2009). In particular, social entrepreneurship shows a greater ability to generate social and public goods through processes of innovation (Nicholls, 2006). Measuring the impact and performance of social innovation – expressed in social entrepreneurship and enterprise – prompts the following fundamental question: How can we assess the performance of an organization when a part of its production is non-market, that is to say not-mediated by prices? Nowadays, this fundamental question is also being raised by researchers trying to measure what they call the 'social value' of production, more generally, which is in essence non-market outputs (Mulgan, 2010). In reality, this chapter is upstream of these recent developments.

This chapter has two objectives. Firstly, it aims to provide a synthetic presentation of the various methods used to measure the non-market dimensions of production. Secondly, it gives the reader an integrated framework for understanding the advantages and disadvantages of these various methods, by focusing closely on monetary valuation approaches, and specifically on the notion of the economic value of non-market goods. This use of economic value as a criterion for evaluating non-market goods has been gaining ground for some 20 years, in the wake of attempts to provide a monetary assessment of environmental damage.[1]

The chapter consists of three sections. The first defines the concept of performance and the various notions linked to the market and non-market dimensions of production. The second describes the way in which these various dimensions are generally measured in the economic literature, and highlights the advantages and disadvantages of each. Specifically, three types of approach are described: (a) *accounting measures* of production, based on the resources used; (b) measurements of performance through the *use of indicators*, according to the principles of cost-efficiency analysis (CEA); and (c) the *monetary valuation* of production approach based on cost-benefit analysis (CBA). The final section of the chapter demonstrates that, despite their many advantages, methods based on capturing the monetary valuation of non-market production raise many methodological and conceptual questions that may undermine the reliability of the calculations they produce.

The chapter makes a case for an approach to evaluating the production of social enterprises and, more specifically, social innovation, where evaluations are based mainly on non-monetary indicators and on multi-criteria analysis rather than on a single monetary measure. This approach aims to offer the researcher a significant step forward in the use of techniques for measuring the innovation generated by social enterprises and entrepreneurship.

Conceptualizing the performance of social enterprise

Social enterprises are often characterized as producing 'merit goods'; that is, goods whose production generates impacts beyond what is captured through the market. A broad examination of what social enterprises actually produce is, therefore, useful here; one which goes beyond output measurement alone.

Let us consider the example of a work integration social enterprise (WISE), working in the area of waste collection and recycling (Davister et al., 2004). Besides the products linked to recycling, this enterprise produces two services: first, an 'integration' service, provided to disadvantaged persons; and second, a 'collection' service, provided to households. Households and disadvantaged persons are two distinct categories of direct beneficiaries of this enterprise.

These services represent the *achievements* of the enterprise and correspond to the notion of *output* in classical economics. Output is measured by standard indicators such as the total amount of revenue from the sale of recycled goods, the volume of collected waste and the number of hours of training provided.

But beyond these products, the enterprise also generates important effects on economic agents, and these effects need to be taken into account in order to capture fully the impact of the enterprise's activity and to produce valid comparisons with other organizations. A distinction must be made here between the direct and the indirect effects or impacts.

Direct impacts are those that concern the direct beneficiaries of the enterprise. Thus, the persons employed in a work integration enterprise benefit from an increase in their qualification level, which normally leads to better employability in the labour market. This is clearly an important dimension of production, which is not taken into account in the simple accounting of the hours of training and guidance provided within the enterprise. These direct impacts correspond to the notion of *outcomes*.

But agents other than the direct beneficiaries (trainees and households) also benefit from the 'integration' and 'collection' services provided by the work integration enterprise. To the extent that these services contribute to social cohesion, to a better use of resources or to environmental protection, they generate significant *indirect impacts*, which are beneficial to the community. In economic analysis, these impacts are called *externalities*.[2] Goods whose production generates positive externalities are usually called 'merit goods'. This category includes, among other examples, training services, health services, and social action services.

The term 'performance' will be used to refer here to the production of the enterprise, to be understood in its broadest sense, comprising both the enterprise's output and the direct and indirect impacts that it generates. Table 4.1 provides a synthesis of this approach.

Many studies (e.g. Ben-Ner, 2010; Henry et al., 2009) show that direct and indirect impacts – and in particular collective impacts – differ noticeably according to the type of producer (pure commercial enterprise, social enterprise, public agency) and that, as a consequence, an analysis of the productive efficiency of the various producers of a merit good in a market should ideally be based on as complete as possible a definition of performance, including all impacts.

In this context, a fundamental issue of economics lies in the development of tools to measure the impacts linked to production. Indeed, the market cannot be relied upon to set a price reflecting monetarily the value of the increased production: first, as shown in Table 4.1, indirect impacts, by definition, are not taken into account in the market (they are externalities); second, only a proportion of the direct impacts is taken into account in the product's price; finally, in some cases, this price may not even reflect the total value of output.

In the case of a WISE working in the area of waste collection and recycling, the price demanded by this enterprise for its products reflects only a proportion of its output and the direct impacts generated. The market revenues come from the sales of the recycled products to private consumers. The other dimensions (see Table 4.2) show a non-market quality because they are not mediated by prices in the market.

Table 4.1 Dimensions of an enterprise's performance relating to merit goods

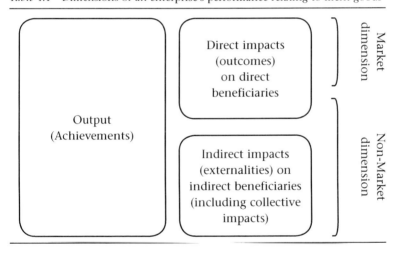

Table 4.2 Market and non-market dimensions of the performance of a WISE

	Market dimension	**Non-market dimension**
Output	Sales of recycled products	Integration Recycling activity
Direct impacts	Utility of users (buying the products)	Increase in employability Waste collection
Indirect impacts		Protection of the environment Social cohesion

In other words, and generally speaking, the price of a merit good only measures part of the social enterprise's performance. Indeed, the enterprise's performance includes a *non-market dimension* whose measure requires the use of specific tools; these tools are presented in the following section.

Measures of non-market production

Since the performance of a social enterprise – which usually produces a merit good – includes a non-market dimension, in order to try to capture quantitatively this dimension, it is necessary to turn to techniques used to measure the production of goods that are not traded on the market.

Table 4.3 synthesizes the various approaches to measuring the production of non-market goods and shows that a distinction needs to be made between 'accounting measures' and 'economic measures' of non-market production.

Accounting measures of the valuation of non-market goods, which involve capturing the flows relating to the costs or funding linked to their production, correspond to the mobilization of resources (production factors) necessary for the activity and are not really representative of the value of the goods produced. It is, therefore, necessary to turn to the so-called economic models, which better distinguish resources and production, inputs and outputs, and aim to obtain a measure of production independent of the resources mobilized.

Table 4.3   Measures of non-market production

Approaches	Accounting measures Resources used	Economic measures		Optimization
Theoretical reference	National accounts	CEA*	CBA*: monetary valuation (Welfare analysis)	
Tools	Accounting value – cost-based approach – revenue-based approach	Indicators + qualitative analysis	Indirect monetary value several [OR various??] techniques**	Economic value (WTP*) – revealed preferences – expressed preferences (CVM*)

* CEA = cost-efficiency analysis; CBA = cost-benefit analysis; WTP = willingness to pay; CVM = contingent valuation method
** Techniques of indirect monetary valuation: effect on production; human capital; human life value; avoided expenditure; replacement cost; opportunity cost; time saving, etc.

Economic measures of non-market production

The 'economic' measures of production result from an *optimization* approach; that is, an approach comparing means and goals, costs, and advantages (Fuguitt and Wilcox, 1999). The goal is to estimate, in one way or another, the value of production, and to justify, by comparison, the amount of resources used. This approach is illustrated by the case of the production of public goods: since these are non-market goods, they must be allocated through a process which differs from market mechanisms, relying mainly on social choice of a political nature. What are the criteria upon which this choice is based? In accordance with the principles of economic optimization, the measure of a non-market product and of the costs that it generates is assumed to allow public authorities to make rational choices regarding the allocation of available resources and to maximize the amount of a product for a given amount of resources. However, the focus on the amount of production is not only a question of costs, despite what many choices of a political nature would tend to suggest.

The optimization calculation is based on two tools to support decisions: *cost-effectiveness analysis* (CEA) and *cost-benefit analysis* (CBA). A third tool, *cost-utility analysis* (CUA) will not be discussed here, as its application is more restrictive. The two tools under discussion – CEA and CBA – differ in the way in which they quantify the 'advantages' side of the comparison. CEA aims to measure production based on physical (i.e. non-monetary) indicators, and its main goal is to compare productive activities, without seeking, in absolute terms, to make a judgement. CBA, by contrast, is based on a monetary benchmark and attempts, by valorizing production in monetary terms, to compare it directly to the cost of the resources mobilized. These two tools represent two ways of measuring non-market goods: measurement through the use of *indicators*, in the case of CEA and through *monetary valorization*, in the case of CBA.

Most tools recently developed to measure the overall production of social enterprises, including social value of production (Mulgan, 2010),[3] use techniques which are based on an optimization approach. Some of these tools define relevant physical indicators for measuring a specific aspect of production while others construct a monetary measure of the social dimensions of production. Therefore, now we go on to discuss CEA and CBA in more detail.

In CEA, the use of indicators to measure non-market goods aims to highlight the presence of impacts produced by a productive activity, to attempt to measure these impacts individually and to allow more realistic comparisons between different types of producers.

The use of such indicators has many limits (Marée, 2005):

- The partial nature of the indicators used: an indicator generally only measures one dimension of performance. It typically applies to a specific impact and thus constitutes only a very partial measure.
- Weighting problems: because of the previously cited issues, several indicators are required in order to capture the overall performance, and this raises the problem of needing to apply weightings to the various indicators.
- The specific character of the indicators: the great diversity of the impacts linked to a product to be measured implies that, for each impact, 'tailor-made' indicators need to be developed; very often, these indicators are specific to a particular economic analysis type of activity and cannot easily be transposed to other types of activity.
- The requirement for inter-disciplinarity: the variety of impacts often implies, as far as the development of appropriate indicators is concerned, that contributions from several disciplines (economics, sociology, health sciences, environmental sciences) be brought together.
- The existence of 'intangible' impacts: some impacts, and in particular collective impacts, have an intangible character, which makes it impossible to reduce them to figures. In this case, the approach based on indicators proves inappropriate, and evaluations of a qualitative nature need to be used.

The *monetary valorization approach* used in the second tool, CBA, is more ambitious. This approach goes beyond the possibility of carrying out comparisons between producers. It aims to assign a 'value' to the performance – considered as a whole (output and impacts) – of a productive activity and to measure its contribution to the welfare of the community. In this sense, monetary evaluation techniques are part of Welfare Economics (Fuguitt and Wilcox, 1999).

CBA was first used in the field of public policy. This tool, which was developed in the USA between the two world wars (Pearce, 1997), became widely used in the 1960s in relation to techniques of the rationalization of public choice, such as the PPBS (Planning Programming Budgeting System), or the RCB (Rationalization des Choix Budgétaires). These techniques aim to optimize the allocation of public resources. In this context, the CBA involves comparing the cost of a project to its advantages or 'benefits', expressed in monetary terms. In this approach, unlike in CEA (in which the calculation only concerns one type of effect), all the aspects of production linked to a project are in principle identified and evaluated in monetary terms, before being aggregated into a single figure. It is, therefore, theoretically possible to calculate the *net actual value* (NAV) of the project, according to the following well- known formula:

$$NAV = \Sigma \, (B_i - C_i)/(1 + r)^i \text{ with } i = 0, \ldots, n,$$

Here B_i and C_i are respectively the benefit and the cost for the year i, r is the actualization rate, and n is the time horizon of the project.

CBA has the advantage over CEA in that CBA facilitates choices between different projects (even relating to different areas such as health, environment, transport, etc.): the various projects can be rated according to their net actual value, and the project with the highest NAV can then be chosen. But this technique also allows a project to be judged in absolute terms; that is, checking that a project is in itself profitable for the collective (NAV > 0). Due to its greater scope, this CBA approach tends to be preferred with increasing frequency (Arrow et al., 1997). As already mentioned, The Social Return on Investment (SROI) method is a well-known example of the recent developments in the CBA approach. It provides financial proxy-values for the impacts that do not have market values. The idea is to use monetary proxies to assess extra-financial value relative to the resources invested in projects or policies (Scholten et al., 2006).

Because various tools aiming at measuring social value include monetary valuation, we next propose a brief overview of the recent developments of this method.

Monetary valuation of non-market production

The CBA of a project or a productive activity obviously only makes sense where it is possible to valorize monetarily all the 'advantages' of the cost-benefits comparison. Among these advantages, some impacts, and in particular collective impacts, are not traded on the market and, as a result, they cannot be assigned a price. Thus, the question of the usefulness of non-market goods' monetary valuation has been raised since the method became more widely used some 50 years ago (Adler and Posner, 2001).

According to the CBA principle, the monetary value of non-market goods must be based on individual valuations. This value is described as 'economic' and its calculation is often a very complex process. Some measuring techniques, mainly developed at the time of the first attempts to apply CBA, attempted to calculate this value. As shown in Table 4.3, two possible ways of valorizing non-market goods can be distinguished. Two types of monetary value correspond to these two ways of calculating, namely *indirect monetary value* and *economic value*.

The *indirect monetary value* of a non-market good is an estimation that does not result directly from the preferences of the agents concerned with this good. It is based on alternative methods, mainly inspired by evaluations carried out in the environmental sector: replacement cost, opportunity cost, avoided expenditure, time saving, human life value, etc. These techniques are widely described in the literature (e.g. Garrod and Willis, 2000).

The *economic value* of a non-market good corresponds to the willingness to pay (WTP) of individuals, such as can be estimated on the basis of their preferences for this good (Smith, 1993), be these preferences *revealed* (*revealed preferences*) through the price of substitute or complementary goods, or *expressed* (*stated* or *expressed preferences*) as part of surveys simulating a fictive market (the so-called contingent valuation method, or CVM).

Indirect methods of valuation have been criticized, and they are being increasingly abandoned in favour of those based on individual preferences. The choice of economic value as a calculation tool seems all the more justified by the fact that economists advocating this method believe that there is always a way of assessing individuals' willingness to pay for non-market goods. Market goods can be considered, to a certain extent, as substitutes for or complementary to the good to be evaluated. In this case, the techniques based on revealed preferences allow, on the basis of the price of these goods, a good approximation of WTP for the non-market good. Alternatively, if it is impossible to identify complementary or substitute goods, direct surveys should allow the identification of individual preferences for the non-market good (Cropper and Oates, 1992).

Prioritizing a priori economic value cannot, however, hide the fact that the techniques used to measure the willingness to pay, when applied to non-market goods, raise several problems. Given the importance these techniques are currently gaining (e.g. in terms of the evaluation of social services and merit goods), these methods deserve to be analysed more thoroughly. This is precisely our objective in the last section of this chapter.

Limits of the application of economic value to non-market production

Traditionally, economic analysis of the value of individual preferences uses observation of the actual behaviour of agents in the markets to *reveal* their preferences. For non-market goods, the revealed preference techniques are assumed to allow the value of these goods to be inferred on the basis of markets for substitute or complementary goods. However, the limits of these techniques have led economists to adopt a new approach, based on the direct collection of the opinions of individuals through surveys. The individuals are invited to *express* their preferences in the form of a willingness to pay for the non-market good within the context of a fictive market. Value is thus no longer determined on the basis of the observation of real behaviours, but on the basis of individuals' hypothetical preferences.

Willingness to Pay (WTP) and the Contingent Valuation Method (CVM)

There are different ways of collecting information regarding individual preferences through surveys. The difference lies in the choice of techniques used to gather that information (e.g. through a bidding process or open questions). However, in all cases, individuals are provided with a description of the functioning of a fictive market: definition of the good, envisaged variation in quantity or quality, ways of funding, etc. The expected answers of individuals (constituting their willingness to pay) are 'conditional' or 'contingent' on this scenario, hence the name given to this approach, referred to as the *contingent valuation method* (CVM).

All CVM surveys involve three stages. In the first stage, the hypothetical scenario or fictive market is described on paper; this includes the definition of the good to be evaluated and the mode of financial contribution. The next stage involves the sampling of the population to be surveyed and the survey itself, which tries to reveal the willingness to pay of the persons in the sample through various methods of questioning. Finally, in the third stage, the answers are processed in order to determine the average willingness to pay of the sample and, by extrapolation to the population, the monetary value or fictive price of the good under consideration.

According to the proponents of CVM, if the good is correctly identified by the individuals questioned through a CVM survey, any type of non-market good, and even more so any collective good, can in principle be evaluated in monetary terms through willingness to pay. This is also true for 'goods' recognized as intangible (reduction in inequalities, increase in social capital, increase in proximity democracy, etc.). CVM has been used for some years to evaluate monetarily collective goods in sectors other than the environment, namely health, culture and, more recently, social action. This can be illustrated by the work of Foster et al.

(2001) which attempts, through CBA, to measure the value of some services provided by nonprofit organizations (NPOs) in the UK.

Methodological and conceptual limitations

Economic value, especially when based on expressed preferences (as in CVM), is increasingly being recommended as a criterion for evaluating non-market goods, both as part of CBA and to measure environmental damage (Fuguitt and Wilcox, 1999). According to the proponents of this method, the use of economic value presents many advantages:

- It is a priori conceptually rigorous, as estimated value (WTP) is integrally explained by consumer theory.
- It is said to be 'objective', because it is based on individuals' preferences.
- It evaluates the product in all its dimensions (including its intangible aspects).
- It ensures coherence with the evaluation of market goods.

As already underlined, these advantages have generated a renewed interest in the monetary valorization of non-market goods. Economic value based on CVM is becoming a key criterion in many political decisions, not only in the USA where the method was first used on a large scale, but also in European and some developing countries.

CVM surveys, though, are far from an ideal solution. The first problem they present is of a purely technical nature: it is not conceivable for public authorities to base all their decisions about matters of collective goods on evaluations obtained through surveys. Given the frequency and the complexity of situations involving such goods, the number of surveys that would be required to produce evaluations makes the generalization of CVM totally unrealistic. In practice, CVM should only be applied in some very specific situations where, on the one hand, a survey would be relatively easy to carry out and where, on the other hand, the limits of CVM would not lead to too significant biases.

CVM raises other types of problem. Many biases can actually affect the measures of the willingness to pay obtained through surveys. These biases reflect the limits of the method, which can be classified into two categories. First, there are *methodological* limits, which are inherent in the various ways of capturing the willingness to pay and calculating economic value. Second, and more fundamentally, there are also *conceptual* limits, which are linked to the hypotheses underlying the model of economic value.

Various comments, sometimes of a very technical nature, have been made regarding the methodological limits at the various stages of the CVM process: the description of the hypothetical scenario, sampling, practical organization of the survey, the way in which preferences are revealed, aggregation of the WTP, validity and reliability tests etc. (e.g. Fuguitt and Wilcox, 1999; Garrod and Willis, 1999). As monetary evaluations of non-market goods made as a result of CVM surveys form a part of CBA, more general questions raised by the net actual value (NAV) formula need to be addressed, in order to provide a more comprehensive analysis.

For many proponents of CVM-based evaluations, all the biases encountered as part of the process of administering and analysing surveys are of a methodological nature. Moreover, these biases are considered as relatively minor, considering the advantages of the method, and, provided that an appropriate response is provided to the questions raised by these biases, CVM is seen as an approach likely to provide a reliable monetary evaluation for non-market goods. However, it should be noted that this 'standard' CVM approach overlooks the fact that some biases generate debates among economists (Hausman, 1993; Adler and Posner, 2001). Among all the biases affecting willingness to pay for a non-market good, the 'embedding effect' is probably the one which raises the most controversy. This effect, highlighted by Kahneman and Knetsch (1992) in the environmental field, notes that an individual's WTP for a specific good depends on the degree of embeddedness of that good within a larger set of goods, defined in the survey protocol: indeed, analyses tend to demonstrate that WTP is inferred for a specific good from the set of goods in which it is included, the estimated value becoming lower the higher the degree of embeddedness. In other words, the WTP for a good tends to be higher when it is evaluated separately, and this can lead to contradictions if this value is subsequently compared to the value of the larger set to which it belongs. Kahneman and Knetsch (1992) cite a series of values obtained from a survey of 14 pairs of goods, each of which included a specific good and a more general good encompassing the specific good (e.g. the protection of the peregrine falcon and the protection of all endangered bird species). In five cases, the average WTP for the specific good was only three to four times lower than the WTP for the general good, even though WTP for the general good included a very high number of goods (e.g. the WTP for the protection of the marmot represented 23.5 per cent of the WTP for the protection of all the small animals in the province). In the other nine cases, the average WTP for the specific good was *higher* than the WTP for the general good (e.g. the WTP for the fight against hunger in Ethiopia was twice as high as the WTP for the fight against hunger in Africa).

This result, which is sometimes referred to as the WTP 'subadditivity effect', is an obvious consequence of the embedding effect. This appears when the value given to a set of goods is lower than the sum of the WTP given to each of its elements. Two other biases are also often cited in the economic literature in relation to the embedding effect, namely the 'scope' or 'scale' effect and the 'order' or 'sequence' effect (Hanemann, 1994). The scope effect refers to the fact that the surveyed individuals do not take into account, in their evaluation, the dimension of a good; for example, the WTP for the protection of a 100-acre area is the same as the WTP for the protection of a 1,000-acre area. The order effect refers to the case where the WTP for a good depends on its place in a sequence of goods to be evaluated: the WTP to pay is lower when the good comes later in a sequence. In other words, when people are given a list of goods to evaluate, they give a higher value to the first goods than to the last ones.

For Kahneman and Knetsch (1992), the very principle of CVM-based evaluations needs to be questioned. Indeed, if the WTP for a good is higher when it is evaluated separately than when it is evaluated as an element belonging to a larger set of goods, what is the correct measure? What level of aggregation is required? Since the choice of the level of aggregation is arbitrary, where no impartial criteria can be defined, the results of CVM surveys may be just as arbitrary. This is something Kahneman and Knetsch consider to be an unacceptable fault: 'This criticism could be fatal. No measuring instrument can be taken seriously if its permitted range of applications yields drastically different measures of the same object' (1992, p. 60).

Moreover, and maybe more fundamentally, Kahneman and Knetsch (1992) consider that the WTP for non-market goods does not really constitute a measure of the subjective value of these goods, but rather represents the price to pay in order to achieve a feeling of moral satisfaction as a result of contributing to this good (the 'warm glow of giving effect'). In other words, far from reflecting an individual's preferences for non-market goods and from constituting a measure of the 'price' of these goods, WTP measures instead the utility linked to the act of giving itself.[4] This interpretation, which has also been endorsed, although with some minor changes, by other analysts (Diamond and Hausman, 1993), would account for some of the biases observed in CVM surveys. In particular, this interpretation would explain why the WTP for the protection of a given area does not differ significantly from the WTP for the protection of several areas (scope effect), or why the WTP for the protection of an endangered species such as the panda (which is a likeable animal) can differ so little from the WTP for the protection of all endangered species (embedding effect), including dangerous species such as some insects.

Kahneman and Knetsch's position can be summarized as being based upon two main arguments. First, CVM, when applied to collective goods, *does not generate results consistent with economic theory* (e.g. the scope effect indicates that WTP does not vary directly according to the quantity of the good to be evaluated). Consequently, CVM does not meet the requirements of a good measuring tool. Second, the WTP for a collective good *does not measure what it is assumed to measure* (i.e. the subjective value of the good), and it includes external elements such as moral satisfaction.

The conceptual basis for using economic value to evaluate non-market goods

The success of CVM can be accounted for by its simplicity, but also by the fact that it is reputed to provide, on the basis of the expression of individual preferences, the 'true value' of goods not traded on the market.

Although the arguments put forward to provide a methodological explanation for the biases in measuring observed in CVM surveys have some merit, it seems necessary to examine more closely the position of those who doubt that economic value applied to collective goods is based on a solid foundation. Indeed, one cannot judge the relevance of WTP without taking a step back from the method and taking into account its underlying hypotheses. Are these hypotheses really valid? For example, is the individual interviewed through a CVM survey really able to order and value her preferences for goods whose definition is not easy, of which she has little experience and which cannot in reality be bought in the market?

A synthesis follows of the criticisms that can be directed, on a theoretical level, at the use of economic value as a criterion for evaluating non-market goods (i.e. through an estimation of WTP).

Economic value as applied to a non-market good is defined in Table 4.4 (see also Marée, 2005).

The total economic value (EV) of a non-market (and, by consequence, collective) good is thus the sum[5] of the subjective values (SV_i) attributed to this good by the individuals making up the population concerned. Following the hypothesis that the preferences of an individual will always

Table 4.4   Definition of the economic value of a non-market good

$EV = \Sigma SV_i,$	for i = 1,...,N, where N is the number of persons concerned
	and
	$SV_i = M(\Delta U_i) = WTP_i,$

The economic value (EV) of a non-market good is the sum of the subjective values (SV$_i$) attributed to this good by all the individuals concerned. Each subjective value corresponds, according to the hypothesis of welfare maximization, to the monetary measure (M) of the individual utility variation (ΔU) induced by the good and assessed through the willingness to pay (WTP), with the individual goals being assumed to be expressed.

lead him to seek to achieve his maximum level of welfare, the subjective value is then defined as the monetary measure of the variation of utility or welfare (ΔU_i) felt by the individual – a value which can in principle be measured by his willingness to pay in order to attain the good.

In addition, the calculation of economic value is embedded in the general issue of the optimal allocation of resources. According to the still prevailing normative economic theory (welfare theory), optimality is assessed on the basis of the maximization of the community's *welfare*; and from such a perspective, the economic value (EV) of non-market goods, as defined above, is the measure that should be used as a basis for informing political decisions.

The conceptual limits of using economic value to evaluate non-market goods

Five propositions can be inferred from the definition of economic value. First, it involves the hypothesis of *utility maximization*. Second, it is possible to *measure monetarily* every individual utility variation induced by the 'consumption' of a good. Third, there is an assimilation of utility to *welfare*. Fourth, economic value is equal to the *sum of subjective values*. Finally, *individual aims* are assumed to be considered as given.

Table 4.5 includes all these elements. The rest of the chapter will show that major objections – likely to account for some of the biases observed in CVM surveys – can be expressed for each of these elements.

Most of the elements that make up the definition of the economic value of a non-market good are based on basic hypotheses of economic theory. These include: individualism; the sovereignty of the consumer (Propositions 1 and 5); individual rationality (1 and 3); and collective preferences seen as the aggregation of individual preferences (4). Proposition 2 presents two hypotheses which are specific to the notion of economic value: by analogy with goods traded on the market, individuals are assumed to be able to assign a price (willingness to pay) to

Table 4.5 The conceptual limits of using economic value to evaluate non-market goods

Conceptual basis of economic value	Limits
1 Maximization of the utility function	Bounded rationality of the consumer => indeterminate preferences
2 Monetary measure of variations in utility	Bounded rationality of the consumer => indeterminate utility variations
3 Assimilation of utility to welfare	Existence of *non-use values* => not reducible to variations in welfare
4 Economic value as the sum of individual subjective values	'Bounded awareness' of the consumer => existence of so-called socially constructed values, distinct from the sum of the individual subjective values
5 Individual goals assumed to be expressed (amorality of the model)	Particular perception of value (paradigm of individualism)

the considered good, which implies, first, the cardinality of its utility function and, second, the possibility of measuring monetarily the variations in utility induced by the good.

The weakness of these hypotheses is the reason why the five elements constituting the model of economic value applied to non-market goods generate many criticisms in the literature. First, the objections directed at Proposition 5 do not have the same impact as those directed at the other four characteristics. The objections to Propositions 1–4 relate to the *efficiency* of the mode of allocation of resources based on the economic value applied to non-market goods. This means that, for this type of good, social choice based on a political decision, which is assumed to counter the inefficiency of market allocation, can also lead to a non-optimal allocation if this choice is based on the willingness to pay.

The limit of the model relating to Proposition 5 is of a different nature; it alludes to the consequences of the lack of reference to *human goals* in the definition of the value based on the willingness to pay. This results from an implicit hypothesis: that is, the goals pursued by individuals (their motivations) are exogenous to the definition of the value. Indeed, there is no reflection on the notion of welfare, or on the building-up of needs felt by individuals or on the way to meet these needs. But, according to some authors, the 'amorality'[6] of the model of economic value would notably favour a rationale of accumulation and of instrumentalization of the world and ultimately an overvaluation of market goods in comparison with non-market goods. In other words, the very concept of economic value, based on the willingness to pay, would induce a very particular conception of value in our society and would thus not be 'neutral'. This is obviously a complex debate, which goes beyond the scope of the present chapter.

Propositions 1–4 can be analysed as follows. First, the notion of economic value is based on the fundamental idea that each individual *maximizes her utility function*. The existence of such a utility function is based on the hypothesis that individuals act in a rational way (through the 'rationality of choices'). According to this hypothesis, individuals are, in principle, able to order rationally their preferences regarding all the possible states of the world, and in particular regarding non-market goods, through complying with the axioms of *completeness* and *transitivity* (Mas-Collel, 1995).[7] The property of completeness, in particular, means that individuals are always able to express their preferences regarding any two states of the world.

But what happens in reality? In cases where choices concern relatively complex situations, or situations with which the individual is not familiar, empirical observations often show that the axioms upon which rationality is based (completeness, transitivity) are not always verified. The concept of individuals having a 'bounded rationality' was introduced by Simon (1982). According to this concept, preferences are characterized by indetermination and they do not allow us to assume the existence of a real utility function (Diamond and Hausman, 1994). The consequence is that ultimately the choices expressed by individuals in such situations, and in particular the expression of their WTP, are prone to be affected by significant biases.

Next, let us assume that a hierarchy of rational preferences concerning all the states of the world exists for each individual, and that it would, therefore, be possible to define a utility function representing this hierarchy numerically. The second characteristic of economic value relates to the shift from the utility function to the definition of the WTP: indeed, it states that each individual is able to *assign a monetary value* (measured by WTP) to the differences between his various levels of utility.

The possibility of measuring monetarily a variation in utility is based, among other things, on the *hypothesis of cardinality* of the utility function.[8] But in complex situations implying non-market goods, such a hypothesis proves highly questionable. Indeed, the consumer's bounded rationality, which already accounts for the indetermination of preferences, also questions the capacity of individuals effectively to quantify the impact of collective goods on their level of utility. From this perspective, we can talk of the 'indetermination of variations in utility'. This constitutes a second element accounting for the biases observed in the use of WTP as an evaluation measure.

Proposition 3 links individual preferences to *welfare*. It explicitly translates the shift from a simple rationality of choices, based only on the criteria of internal coherence of this rationality of choices (completeness and transitivity), to a 'substantive' rationality, where a relationship is established between the choices and the motivations of the individual. The individual would always make her choices with a view to achieving an 'advantage' for herself; that is, an improvement in her own welfare. The utility function, which numerically describes preferences, therefore also becomes a representation of the individual's welfare and thus has a real content. In other words, when asked (e.g. through a CVM survey) about the value that she assigns to a non-market good, an individual would always express her preferences according to the impact of this good on her personal welfare.

Such a hypothesis obviously generated many criticisms when, some 20 years ago, the use of WTP as an evaluation measure started to be applied to environmental goods. Some authors mentioned in this respect the important notion of 'non-use value' (see, among others, Diamond and Hausman, 1993). What value should be assigned to a natural site? To an endangered species, for example? Such a value is linked to the mere existence of the good and does not depend, or not entirely, on its direct use and its impact on individual welfare. In other words, some goods can be assigned a non-use value that could not, by definition, be captured by a model linking individual preferences to sole welfare. Taking the example of the application of CVM to social services, the 'altruistic benefits' gained from this provision clearly correspond to a non-use value.

Proposition 4 suggests that the value assigned to a good by the community is supposed to be integrally reducible to the *sum of individual values*. This is based on the hypothesis that collective preferences result from the simple aggregation of the preferences of individuals considered separately.[9] This hypothesis has commonly been referred to as 'methodological individualism', according to which a social phenomenon is nothing more than the direct reflection of all individual behaviours.

However, this conception disregards the fact that the actual choices made by a community (which is referred to here as 'social choice') often differ significantly from those that would result from the simple aggregation of individual preferences. For example, for the sake of common interest, a community may politically decide to encourage the production of some goods (education, health, etc.) or, conversely, to discourage the production of others (alcohol, drugs, etc.). Taken separately, individuals may make decisions that run counter to their own welfare and that of the community. Here, the consumer could be described as having 'bounded awareness' (Marée, 2005).

Consequently, some authors consider that the value that should be assigned to non-market goods cannot result simply from the addition of individuals' WTP (e.g. Bürgenmeier, 2004). Instead, this value should result from a more complex process of political decision making where 'socially constructed' values differ from the sum of individual values.

A model should generally be constructed based on relatively strict hypotheses, and these hypotheses should build a coherent framework of analysis. But when this framework of analysis is applied to real situations with a view to defining rules for political decision making, one can no longer skip over the analysis of the validity of the hypotheses underlying the framework. CVM surveys collect information for public authorities on individuals' WTP for non-market goods, and does so on the explicit basis of consumer theory. Promoters of these surveys should, therefore, question the appropriateness of their model's hypotheses to the actual behaviours of the surveyed persons.

Leaving aside the other criticisms that CVM methods raise, the indetermination of preferences for non-market goods seems in itself to constitute sufficient reason not to base public decisions regarding such goods on individuals' willingness to pay. Willingness to pay can probably be applied to simple or familiar situations, but it appears inappropriate in many situations characterized by complexity or uncertainty. In such cases, individuals' choices can no longer be interpreted as still meeting the axioms of rational choice, since the indetermination of preferences generates error risks. As Milgrom (1993, p. 424) commented:

> [I]n practical terms, the economic justifications for many kinds of regulations – health and safety regulations, certification standards for various occupations, regulation of medical and financial institutions and of complex products like life insurance – are rooted in the idea that consumers may make serious mistakes because of lack of information, training and experience.

All the more reason, therefore, to question the reliability of evaluations made by consumer individuals in the case of non-market goods, for which markedly more detailed knowledge and judgement capacities are required. Clearly, such individual evaluations are not sufficiently reliable to inform public decisions in this area.

This finding is obviously even more significant if one takes into account not only the sole limit linked to the indetermination of preferences, but all the objections that can be addressed by the WTP model.

Conclusion

Merit goods, and in particular the goods produced by social enterprises, exert impacts on their direct recipients, but also on other agents and even on the community as a whole. Social innovation can be understood as part of those impacts. These impacts, whether direct (outcomes) or indirect (externalities), are part of the production, understood in a broad sense, or the 'performance', of these goods. Therefore, measuring social innovation raises the broader issue of performance measurement.

Some of these impacts, and notably all indirect impacts, have a non-market character because they are not valorized in the price of the good. Traditional methods for measuring non-market production should be used for the quantitative estimation of this type of impact and, in particular, the techniques inspired by the optimization calculation approach. In the present study, two approaches to measuring the production of non-market goods were distinguished: the first approach uses indicators to measure production, as seen in cost-efficiency analysis (CEA); the second approach uses the monetary valuation of production, as seen in cost-benefit analysis (CBA). These two methods are alternatively, and to varying extent, used in different recent tools (like SROI) developed to measure the Social Value.

Among the techniques used in the monetary valuation of production, we focused here on the criterion of economic value based on willingness to pay (WTP) for evaluating non-market goods. In the wake of the attempts made in the last two decades to evaluate environmental goods, the contingent valuation method (CVM), in which information on individuals' willingness to pay is collected directly through surveys, has developed and become the preferred method for evaluating non-market goods.

This chapter has shown that evaluation based on willingness to pay does, however, present various types of limit. Limits of a methodological nature are relatively well known, but the conceptual problems raised by WTP (indetermination of preferences, problems linked to the cardinalization of utility, the difficulty of taking into account non-use values, etc.) are far from being clearly identified. This is probably why contingent valuation provokes much debate and has failed to gain unanimous support among economists (Hausman, 1993).

This work suggests that, even though calculating economic value could constitute a reliable tool to evaluate non-market goods, it can only be applied in specific cases; and in any case, it is not sufficient in itself to inform stakeholders who are interested in the Social Value. The approaches based on *non-monetary indicators* of non-market production and on *multi-criteria analyses* probably constitute a solution that has been insufficiently explored. Despite their own limits (the problem of intangibility of some collective goods, the problem of non-homogeneity of measures, etc.), the evaluations based on multiple indicators present many advantages in comparison with a single/sole monetary measure. Therefore, to take into account the different aspects of a productive activity, social measurement methods should be based primarily on physical indicators rather than on monetary valuations.

The anticipated progress in this area thus takes on a specific significance, given the stakes linked to the current requirement for greater 'visibility' of the impacts generated by economic activities, and by social innovation in particular.

Notes

The authors are very grateful to Sophie Adam (EMES European Network) for her editorial assistance.

1. Throughout this chapter, there will be a strong focus on public sector methods of calculating performance impacts. Historically, these issues were first raised in a context of public policy evaluation before being used to assess the social value of production in a more general context. See Mulgan (2010).
2. The notion of externality (introduced by Pigou (1932) originally derives from the distinction between private costs and social costs: there is an externality when the action of a producer has an impact (be it positive or negative) on the costs incurred by another producer, without this impact being taken into account by the market; that is, without the impact affecting the costs of the first producer. The social cost therefore differs from the private cost. More generally, the term 'externalities' is applied to situations where the action of another agent directly affects the utility of a consumer or the production function of a company. The word 'directly' means that all the effects mediated by prices are excluded.
3. While Mulgan (2010) presents CEA and CBA as tools among others (SROI, value-added assesment, etc.), we argue that these are 'generic tools' that inspired the various current approaches.
4. According to Kahneman and Knetsch (1992), the explanation for the existence of the warm glow effect lies in the fact that these goods are not bought through the market but as the result of a political decision: in such a context, any voluntary contribution would be linked to moral considerations rather than to consumption behaviour.

5. The total value of the good to be evaluated in CVM surveys is generally obtained by multiplying the average WTP of the sample by the number of individuals in the population, which amounts to assuming that the function of social welfare (W) has a simply additive form (the so-called Bentham function).
6. Sen (1993) considers that economics is historically based on two traditions, namely the *ethical tradition*, which establishes a link between the economy and human goals, and the *mechanistic conception*, according to which goals are considered to be given and which is mainly concerned with issues of efficiency and 'logistics' (allocation of means to the achievement of goals). Modern economics comes closer to this second conception, which justifies the use of the term 'amoral' here.
7. Transitivity refers to the way in which preferences are logically transferred. If product A is preferred to product B and product B is preferred to product C, then it follows that product A is preferred to product C.
8. The hypothesis of cardinality of the utility function refers to the capacity of individuals to measure any variation of their utility.
9. Since Bergson (1938) and Samuelson (1947), the function of collective utility built on the basis of the sole functions of individual utility has been referred to as the 'social welfare function'.

References

Adler, M. and Posner, E. (eds) (2001), *Cost-Benefit Analysis – Legal, Economic, and Philosophical Perspectives* Chicago: University of Chicago Press.

Arrow, K., Cropper, M., Eads, G., Hahn, R., Lave, L., Noll, R., Portney, P., Russell, M., Schmalensee, R., Smith, V. and Stavins, R. (1997), 'Is there a Role for Benefit-Cost Analysis in Environmental, Health and Safety Regulation?', in *Environment and Development Economics*, May 1997, Cambridge, 2 (2), pp. 196–201.

Ben-Ner, A. and Ting, R. (2010), 'Ownership and Performance in Markets with Asymmetric Information: Evidence from Nursing Homes', Research paper, Carlson School of Management, University of Minnesota-Twin Cities, December 2010.

Bergson, A. (1938), 'A Reformulation of Certain Aspects of Welfare Economics,' *Quarterly Journal of Economics*, Cambridge, MA: MIT Press, 52 (2), pp. 310–34.

B.Bürgenmeier, B. (2004), Economie du développement durable, De Boeck, Bruxelles.

Cropper, M. and Oates, W. (1992), 'Environmental Economics: A Survey', reprinted in R. Stavins (ed.) *Economics of the Environment: Selected Readings* New York: W. W. Norton, 2000.

Davister, C., Defourny, J. and Grégoire, O. (2004), 'Work Integration Social Enterprises in the European Union: An Overview of Existing Models', EMES Working Papers no. 04/04, EMES European Research Network, Liège.

Diamond, P. and Hausman, J. (1994), 'Contingent Valuation: Is Some Number Better than No Number?', reprinted in R. Stavins (ed.) *Economics of the Environment: Selected Readings*, New York: W. W. Norton 2000, pp. 295–315.

Diamond, P. and Hausman, J. (1993), 'On Contingent Valuation Measurement of Nonuse Values', in J. Hausman (ed.) Contingent Valuation: A Critical Assessment, North Holland, Amsterdam, pp. 3–38.

Foster, F., Mourato, S., Pearce, D. and Ozdemiroglu, E. (2001), *The Price of Virtue – The Economic Value of the Charitable Sector*, Cheltenham, Brookfield: Edward Elgar.

Fuguitt, D. and Wilcox, S. (1999), *Cost-Benefit Analysis for Public Sector Decision Makers*, London: Quorum Books.

Garrod, G. and Willis, K. (2000), *Economic Valuation of the Environment: Methods and Case Studies*, Cheltenham, Northampton: Edward Elgar.

Hanemann, W. (1994), 'Valuing the Environment through Contingent Valuation', reprinted in R. Stavins (ed.) Economics of the Environment: Selected Readings, New York: W. W. Norton, 2000, pp. 268–94.

Hausman, J. (ed.) (1993), *Contingent Valuation: A Critical Assessment* Amsterdam: North Holland.

Henry, A., Nassaut, S., Defourny, J. and Nyssens, M. (2009), Economie plurielle et régulation publique. Le quasi-marché des titres-services en Belgique, Politique Scientifique Fédérale/Academia Press, Gand.

Kahneman, D. and Knetsch, J. (1992), 'Valuing Public Goods: the Purchase of Moral Satisfaction', in *Journal of Environmental Economics and Management*, Amsterdam: Elsevier, 22 (1), pp. 57–70.

Marée, M. (2005), 'Les impacts collectifs de l'insertion. Définition, typologie et techniques de mesure', in Nicaise, I., Nyssens, M. and Marée, M. (eds) Economie sociale, inclusion sociale et intérêt général, Politique Scientifique Fédérale/Academia Press, Gand.

Mas-Collel, A., Whinston, M. and Green, J. (1995), *Microeconomic Theory*, New York-Oxford: Oxford University Press.

Milgrom, P. (1993), 'Is Sympathy an Economic Value? Philosophy, Economics and the Contingent Valuation Method', in Hausman, J. (ed.) Contingent Valuation: A Critical Assessment, Amsterdam: North Holland, pp. 417–41.

Mulgan, G. (2010), 'Measuring Social Value', Stanford Social Innovation Review (Summer), pp. 38–43.

Nicholls, A., (2006) *Social Entrepreneurship: New Models of Sustainable Social Change*, Oxford University Press.

Pearce, D. (1997), 'Benefit-Cost Analysis, Environment, and Health in the Developed and Developing World', in *Environment and Development Economics*, May 1997, Cambridge, 2 (2), pp. 210–14.

Phills, J. A., Deiglmeier, K. and Miller, D. T. (2008), 'Rediscovering Social Innovation', in *Stanford Social Innovation Review* (Fall), Standford.

Pigou, A. (1932), *The Economics of Welfare*, 4th edn, London: Macmillan and Co.

Samuelson, P. (1947), *Foundations of Economics Analysis* Harvard: Harvard University Press.

Simon, H. (1982), *Models of Bounded Rationality*, Cambridge, MA: MIT Press.

Sen, A. (1993), *Ethique et économie* Paris: PUF.

Scholten, P., Nicholls, J., Olsen, S. and Galimidi, B. (2006), *SROI A Guide to Social Return on Investment*, Amstelveen: Lenthe Publishers.

Smith, V. (1993), 'Nonmarket Valuation of Environmental Resources: An Interpretive Appraisal', reprinted in R. Stavins (ed.) *Economics of the Environment: Selected Readings* New York: W. W. Norton, 2000.

Part II
Strategies and Logics

5
Social Innovation, Co-operation, and Competition: Inter-organizational Relations for Social Enterprises in the Delivery of Public Services

Fergus Lyon

Introduction

Social innovation is seen as a way of developing new approaches to addressing social problems (Phills et al., 2008; Murray et al., 2010). As with innovation in other contexts, collaborative relations are often a factor in successful cases of social innovation, although little is known about how co-operation is built up and maintained. This chapter sets out an argument for understanding how these inter-organizational relationships operate.[1] This is necessary in order to go beyond the empty rhetoric of terms such as 'partnership', 'collaboration' and 'co-operation', and understand how these complex forms of organizing are built and maintained (Hastings, 1996; Atkinson, 1999). There has been much discussion of the need for collaboration (OTS, 2009) and co-operation between organizations is given as a core value of some forms of social enterprises such as co-operatives (Spear, 2000), but very little work has been carried out on understanding the process of building these relationships. This chapter examines the context of collaboration with the state for public services, reviews the literature on collaboration and social enterprise, and draws on the literature of inter-organizational relationships to present a framework for understanding how collaboration is built and maintained.

The chapter will go beyond assumptions concerning how organizations are expected to behave, and will examine the constraints and barriers being faced by organizations and the economic and social institutional contexts in which their actions are embedded (Granovetter, 1985). In particular, attention will be given to how organizations build relationships in 'quasi markets' and in an environment of emerging competition for the delivery of public services (Le Grand and Bartlet, 1993). These may involve partnerships between commissioners and those delivering services (what can be termed 'vertical relationships') and also collaborations between providers of products and services (what can be termed 'horizontal relationships'). For horizontal relationships, organizations may be both competing and collaborating. Some refer to this as 'co-opetition' (Nalebuff and Brandenburger, 1996), although there has not been any attention given to how this may be different for social enterprises compared to private sector businesses.

A broad definition of social enterprise is used here, as proposed by the UK government's 'Social Enterprise: A Strategy for Success' document: 'A social enterprise is a business with primarily social objectives, whose surpluses are principally reinvested for that purpose in the business or in the community, rather than being driven by the need to maximize profits for shareholders' (DTI, 2002). As mentioned elsewhere, this definition is kept deliberately open so as to be inclusive (Lyon and Sepulveda, 2009). This results in a huge diversity of organizations with different forms, different sizes, different origins (coming from individual social entrepreneurs, community activity, voluntary organizations, private sector or as public sector spin outs) and operating in different sectors.

The scope of this chapter is limited to inter-organizational relationships and co-operation within these. It does not examine the issues of intra-organizational relations but recognises that there are important issues related to the development of trust there too (Mollering, 2006). The chapter does not examine the impact of social enterprise and third sector organizations on trust or social capital in other parts of the economy (Putnam, 1993; Fukuyama, 1995), nor is it able to examine the extent to which users or customers trust social enterprises (Anheier and Kendall, 2002).

This chapter makes a theoretical contribution to understanding the nature of social enterprises and civil society more broadly. In particular it sheds more light on the relationships between public and third sectors, demonstrating the overlapping nature of these spheres. While social enterprises are presented as a hybrid form of organization combining the financial imperative of the private sector with social aims, there is a need to examine different theories of how relationships develop outside of the purely private and public sectors. This chapter does not assume that effective partnerships will spontaneously emerge when needed, but rather recognises that the social relations behind collaboration are contingent on and embedded in historical and spatial contexts (Granovetter, 1985; Amin et al., 2002).

The chapter addresses three research objectives. First, it examines various types of inter-organizational relationships and details the motivations for building trust. Second, it explores the processes of building co-operation, looking in particular at issues of trust and power in inter-organizational relationships. Third, it examines issues of the moral economy and conflicting norms of behaviour that underpin the inter-organizational relationships and participation by social enterprises in competitive markets for public services. The conclusion identifies some theoretical and policy implications, and identifies a future direction for research in this area.

Types of inter-organizational relationships

While there has been considerable academic research on inter-firm relationships and how they can be managed (Huggins, 2010), there has been little on interpersonal relationships of social enterprises or not-for-profit organizations (Hardy et al., 2003). In the context of public service delivery, the need for closer relationships with commissioners is discussed in much policy documentation with the recognition that social enterprises may not be sharing their experience and commissioners may not be using the knowledge of local areas held by social enterprises (IFF, 2007). In the UK, there has been a range of programmes trying to encourage social enterprises, particularly smaller ones, to become more involved in procurement (Wilson, 2009). Similarly, there are programmes for commissioners to understand issues facing social enterprises and how to build relationships with the sector. Munoz and Tindsley (2008) point out the need to overcome barriers with respect to the attitude of procurement professionals, although the government's Audit Commission found that the public sector commissioners were nervous of engaging too closely with those delivering services (Audit Commission, 2008).

The more horizontal relationships rely on linkages between more equal parties that are not hierarchical or market-based interactions (Hardy et al., 2003). This may comprise consortia to win contracts or even a move towards the merging of organizations. It may be less formalized with co-operation aimed at innovation through sharing knowledge and ideas (Westall, 2007), or to share contacts, referrals, or equipment. Such collaboration is one of the co-operative values set out by the co-operatives movement (ICA, 1994), although there has been limited research on how these forms of social enterprise implement this ideal in practice when operating in a more competitive environment.

Finally, Amin et al. (2002) identify relationships with the private sector for absorbing trainees. Their study of four locations in the UK found that these relationships were strongest and worked best where the private sector and local economies were stronger, and were less effective in places where there are fewer economic opportunities and less economic growth.

Dijkstra and Knottnerus (2004, p. 33) refer to informal ties as the social bonding required by social enterprises that will support the 'structural bonding', with larger contracts relying on more formalized written agreements. Spear refers to the difference between soft and hard public service contracts:

> Earlier adversarial, conflict-based 'hard' or tightly specified contracting models have sometimes given way to 'soft' relational contracting models that allow for more flexibility because a more trusting relationship has been developed. However, this may only be easy for smaller contracts, since larger contracts are subject to the full EU procurement regime.
>
> (Spear, 2008, p. 44)

Munoz and Tindsley (2008) found that there are relationships with the public sector that remain informal with a fear of losing a contract if the organization asks to formalize the relationship.

The processes of building co-operation

Much research on partnerships and co-operation describes the potential outcomes and the types of relationships, but does not explore the actual processes by which trust is built up. This is partly due to assumptions running through much of social and economic theory that motivations and incentives will be adequate to drive this forward (Williamson, 1983). In this chapter, it is argued that these factors are necessary but not enough on their own, and that there is a need to understand more about how and why co-operation occurs in one place and not another. A more nuanced understanding is required that takes into consideration context and how these linkages based on trust are embedded in existing social relations (Granovetter, 1985; 1994).

Trust can be defined as an expectation of others' behaviour (Zucker, 1986, p. 54; Gambetta, 1988, p. 217) with confidence based on personal relationships or knowledge that there are institutions that can ensure or enforce expected behaviour. Trust also requires an element of willingness to embrace vulnerability and expectation that the other party will act responsibly (see Mayer et al., 1995; Rousseau et al., 1998). Well-placed trust is based on active enquiry, often extended through questioning and listening over time, rather than on blind acceptance (O'Neill, 2002, p. 76). This may be a conscious action based on calculations of vulnerability, risks, and rewards, or it may be more instinctive and based on habitual action (Lyon, 2006; Mollering, 2006).

Zucker (1986, pp. 60–5) distinguishes three 'central modes of trust production', namely: process-based where trust is tied to past or expected exchange; characteristic-based, where trust is tied to a person and their background; and institutionally-based, such as membership of associations, use of bureaucracy and legal institutions. Lyon (2006) also stresses the importance of building trust through working relationships, existing relationships, and intermediaries who are known to each party. This latter group of actors plays key roles as bridge builders and boundary spanners (Williams, 2002), particularly where there is more of a cognitive distance between parties in terms of culture (ethnic, professional, etc.). While these issues are rarely examined in research on social innovation, they are referred to in research on inter-organizational relationships internationally. Mawdsley et al. (2005, p. 77) stress the importance for NGOs of building up trust through face-to-face interaction, while NCVO (2008a) identifies recent research on international NGO relationships that also require this interaction.

Co-operation does not arise solely through the people wanting to act reciprocally. In each case there may be an element of being coerced into actions by the sanctions and controls of others. Much literature on the nature of trust now accepts that there is a 'duality of trust and control' with blurred boundaries and each assuming the existence of the other (Reed, 2001; Mollering, 2005). The issue of power in relationships involving social enterprises is much more noticeable in vertical relationships such as between commissioner/funder and those contacted. Craig et al. (2002) question the use of the term 'partnership' when there are unequal power relations between local authorities and the third sector organizations. Munoz and Tindsley (2008) found that many social enterprises were delivering services for the public sector without a contract and not covering their full costs, but that they felt powerless to change this. Murdock (2007) similarly found that social enterprises were fearful of commissioners and not demanding 'full cost recovery', instead using charitable resources to cover the shortfall in income from the public sector. Curtis (2008) identified the powerful co-opting force of the state but also notes the forms of resistance shown by social enterprises with actors subverting the intended norms of commissioners in order to meet alternative social outcomes.

Morality, collaboration, and competition

Underpinning both issues of trust and power in co-operation are the moral norms of behaviour that define what is deemed right or acceptable. There is a set of literature on generalized morality (Moore, 1994; Platteau, 1994a; 1994b) related to co-operation. These include issues such as reciprocity, altruism, friendship, keeping agreements, and market-specific norms. The rhetoric of social enterprises and the voluntary and community sector stresses the sector-specific norms, particularly in relation to co-operation with other parts of the sector (ICA, 1994; Williams, 2008). While altruism is an important factor underlying the third sector, there is a need to distinguish between altruism towards beneficiaries or clients and altruism towards other providers.

In addition there are norms related to the sanctions that can be used against other parties if they break agreements. These range from peer pressure, shaming, and damaging personal reputations to exclusion from specific fora (Lyon and Porter, 2007). These sanctions can only be implemented if they are underpinned by a set of norms such as whether the sanction is considered fair, whether the community will exert peer pressure, or whether there is a professional community that is willing to exclude others.

Norms cannot be created at will. The production of norms is based on what Platteau (1994a, p. 536) refers to as 'historically-rooted cultural endowments', upon which norms of a more generalized morality can be encouraged when the right conditions arise. Portes and Sensenbrenner (1993: 1324–5) use the term 'bounded solidarity' which can lead to 'the emergence of principled group-oriented behaviour ... If sufficiently strong, this emergent sentiment will lead to the observance of norms of mutual support, appropriable [sic] by individuals as a resource in their own pursuits'. Research on the emergence of new market systems found that while markets erode some social relationships and norms, new relationships are formed and new moral values can be generated by the market, its practices and incentives. (Moore, 1994, p. 826)

Context of social enterprises and public services in the UK

While social enterprises are considered to occupy the interstices between the state and market, many have become increasingly involved in public service delivery in the UK (Amin et al., 2002; NCVO, 2009; Peatie and Morely, 2009). The UK public sector increasingly views social enterprises as a source of innovation and an effective model of delivery, and is keen to increase the proportion of its public spending to these forms of organization (Murdock, 2007; Munoz and Tindsley, 2008). This has also resulted in much of the social enterprise and voluntary sector becoming involved in contracts and trading. This situation is highly dynamic with a growth in public sector spending between 1997 and 2009, and a growing proportion of this spend going to competitive public service markets involving private and third sector organizations. Throughout the growth of this sector and more recent threats of reduction, there have been calls for greater partnerships and collaborative activities (OTS, 2009).

In the UK, the reforms to the public sector, started by the Conservatives and continued by the New Labour Government since 1997, have resulted in a dramatic increase in the proportion of public spending being contracted out. In 2008, total public procurement for goods and services was £142b or 25 per cent of total public expenditure; of this, £79b or 14 per cent of total spending is estimated to be on public services (HMT, 2008). The total spend on external procurement has grown from £31b in 1996, with a levelling-off since 2005. This growth has been part of the public sector reforms and the growth of 'quasi markets'. This involves a range of providers competing to deliver services and attempts to provide users of services with a choice (in terms of who provides and where).

There are no clear data for social enterprises as a whole but evidence from the NCVO (2009) on charities shows that £12b of their income comes from statutory or public sector sources, of which almost £8b is in contracts rather than grants, what NCVO refer to as social enterprise activity. This equates to 10 per cent of all public service procurement in England. This only covers those organizations registered as general charities, which are estimated to be one-third of the total value of civil society in the UK that include housing associations, universities, co-operatives, Community Interest Companies and Companies Limited by Guarantee that are not also charities. The value of this source of funding is just less than the value of charities' voluntary income (donations, etc.) (NCVO, 2009). However, the public service industry is still dominated by the private sector. There are considerable geographical differences, with 60 per cent of third sector organizations in the most deprived areas receiving statutory funding, compared to only 30 per cent in the least deprived areas (Clifford et al., 2010).

While many organizations have reported a shift in their income from grant to contract funding in the past (Craig et al., 2002), the overall growth of statutory funding has come from additional funding for contracts. It is not clear which part of the third sector is receiving this increased funding, but some evidence suggests that it is the larger organizations (Clifford et al., 2010), with some commentators calling for greater collaboration among smaller organizations in order to compete (Williams, 2008).

Public sector actors have been attracted by claims of the innovative approaches of social enterprises (Amin et al., 2002; Westall, 2009) including the development of new services and meeting a wide range of policy objectives related to social inclusion. In particular, social enterprises have the potential to have multiple objectives related to economic, social, and environmental outcomes with benefits for users, staff, local economies, and local communities that allow the public sector to meet a number of goals (Lyon, 2009). Social enterprises are also perceived to be closer to communities and able to articulate the needs of people and deliver services to them. Anheier and Kendall (2002) refer to the need for the state to use non-profit enterprises as they are trusted intermediaries between supply and demand, particularly where they can draw on existing trust due to their links to the community (e.g. community or religious organizations).

However, there is only limited evidence of this and the state's interest has been based more on expectation than on hard evidence. The growth of the sector has been related to public sector interest and this is likely to continue with the social enterprise model at the heart of the ideology of the Conservative/Liberal Democrat Coalition Government that came to power in the UK in May 2010 (Conservative Party, 2008; 2010; Big Society Network, 2010). A range of new policies are giving a greater emphasis to having a 'plurality of provision' and a model of 'any willing provider' regardless of the organizations' ownership and governance. At the same time there is growing interest in supporting social enterprises in the delivery of public services as part of the Coalition's Big Society Agenda.

With the growth of public service markets, social enterprises and the third sector more widely are put in challenging positions of needing to compete and collaborate. This presents contradictions in their relationships with other social enterprises, particularly when there has been an ethos of co-operation in the past. Little is known about the motivations of social enterprises and third sector organizations in competitive public service delivery contexts.

The following sections will examine the range of inter-organizational relationships found in the case study, and examine how these relate to the context of the delivery of public services in a competitive environment. In particular, the issue of how co-operation is built up is examined. The dearth of literature on this subject presents challenges for understanding how co-operation between organizations can be encouraged, although frameworks can be drawn from research in the international development field and from research on trust building in the private sector. These can then present an agenda for future research that can inform public policies attempting to encourage collaborative relations in public service delivery.

Case study results

These issues are examined by taking the case of public sector-funded support for the self-employed, focusing on services for unemployed people. The funding of support is through a 'prime contractor' model with one social enterprise or private company having the contract delivered through sub-contracting to other social enterprises.

The case study material is based on interviews with training and self-employment support providers in the UK. The nature of the research questions demanded a qualitative approach with case study organizations. The use of multiple cases strengthened the findings and enabled the research to draw out common themes, conclusions, and theoretical implications (Yin, 2003). In-depth interviews were carried out with 34 social enterprises, private providers, and public sector providers. With the small sample sizes, the interviewees were selected purposely to ensure a cross section of respondents from five contrasting locations (Durham, Staffordshire, Cornwall, Leicestershire, and Norfolk) and offering different services. Semi-structured interviews were carried out face-to-face or by telephone. Based on the analysis of data and comparison of cases, key themes are drawn out (Yin, 2003). The data presented here have been anonymized due to the sensitive nature of some comments and the need for these organizations to continue ongoing relationships.

There are various means available for start-up support providers to co-ordinate their support and also to learn from other providers. However, the ability to co-ordinate depends to a large extent on the relationships of trust that have been built between organizations. These relationships are built at both the organizational level and by individuals working within these organizations. The types of co-ordination can be divided between those that are 'horizontal' (i.e. with complementary or competing organizations) and those that are 'vertical (i.e. sub-contractors and suppliers). A division can also be made between those relationships that are formalized through written agreements and those that are informal.

Means of co-ordination

In many cases, the term 'partnership' is used to describe the relationship between support organizations. However, use of the term is vague and refers to a range of relationships that can be divided into six types with varying degrees of intensity of interaction:

- Close alliances/shared investment: for example, the Chamber of Commerce and local authorities/regeneration bodies form organizations that win the contract to deliver Business Link-franchised services. This was found in the Staffordshire case study.
- Collaborative delivery by consortia: for example, a group of enterprise agencies in Staffordshire came together to get the contract to deliver support. Through this partnership, one enterprise agency has secured funding for a community liaison officer to increase awareness of opportunities and encourage people to think about self-employment.
- Discussion groups for sharing information and social innovation: examples of these were found at the county, regional and national levels where a diverse range of support providers, government departments, and business representatives were brought together to share information on support needs, existing provision, and new sources of funding. One member of a group referred to a concern at the risk of participating in these activities: 'We go to update each other ... I suppose they are competition and my boss is a bit worried ... but I go for curiosity, see [public sector] people who attend, and we can learn from each other, see how others do it, talk about the paperwork'.
- Joining other organizations' management boards: in three of the case study areas, key personnel were invited to sit on the management boards of local organizations. For example, advisors from one organization were invited onto the funding panel of a micro-finance organization, and the Head of Operation of a private sector contractor is on the local advisory boards of two other social enterprises that also deliver for them.
- Sub-contracting relationships: many of the interviewees referred to the importance of relationships with funders or contractors as a means of co-ordinating support. These 'vertical relationships' may be in the form of sub-contracting with bilateral relationships built up

over time. These relationships were found to be strengthened when organizations were co-locating in the same building or had staff seconded to the sub-contractors.

- Partnerships hosted by the funding body and involving all sub-contracting bodies. Attendance at these 'partnerships' is compulsory and is a way in which the prime contractor organizations can ensure their sub-contractors co-ordinate their delivery. However, this form of co-ordination is based on coercion rather than voluntary co-operation, with the result that participants felt that they were unlikely to continue the partnership unless they were forced.

Building trust

While the formal means of co-ordination are important, successful partnerships and collaborative working are usually underpinned by personal relationships built up through informal interaction. Continued and reciprocal referrals are an important way of building relationships and trust between both organizations and individuals in each of the organizations.

Previous experience of working together was also considered important by support providers. 'Churning' or moving of staff from organization to organization helps to strengthen inter-organizational linkages, particularly when individuals have worked together on previous start-up support programmes. For example, enterprise agency staff in one area reported that they have exceptionally good relationships with the staff of the prime contractor with whom they have contracts. This is built up over many years because of the movement of staff from the (now superseded) Training and Enterprise Councils to the enterprise agencies. Seconded staff also help build up these links, which can continue when people return to their original organization. Another referred to the benefits of informal links with prime contractors which they have developed since co-locating and sharing offices.

Participation in formal fora also provides individuals with an opportunity to develop informal relationships with others. This demonstrates the long-term – and often serendipitous – impact of short-term collaborative activities. An interviewee from an enterprise agency stressed the importance of informal links with local authorities: 'We are strengthening our links with the Economic Development Units of District and Borough Councils. These tend to be informal links. We have regular briefing sessions, liaise with them and swap a lot of information'.

The ability of support organizations to work together is dependent on trust and the relationships between individuals in different organizations. The examples given in the previous section demonstrate the importance of recognizing the role of relationships in partnerships. Trust is drawn on when there is confidence in others despite the risk of them acting 'opportunistically'. In many cases there is competition between organizations (for funding as well as clients) offering support, and so co-operation results in an element of risk. For example, support providers in one case-study area felt that they were exposing themselves to risk when sharing information on funding sources or when admitting their own weaknesses in front of other organizations.

Trust is built up through experiences of working together and through having information on the reputation of others. The ability to acquire this information is shaped by the business support infrastructure in a locality and the types of opportunity for collaboration outlined above. Business support organizations were found to be more likely to start co-operating on relatively low-risk activities such as information sharing and discussion groups before attempting more intensive forms of partnerships with greater implications (such as joint projects) if they were to fail.

The issue of distrust was brought up by several interviewees, particularly with regard to conflicts following competitive bids for the specific contracts such as the franchise to deliver a support service. The extent of the distrust in one case-study area was exacerbated by accusations that other providers were carrying out 'bias sign-posting' by referring their clients to favoured organizations. Trust can also be built up by working through trusted intermediaries such as organizations attempting to remove themselves from delivery, enabling them to play a brokerage role. One organization attempting to do this stated: 'In the past we would compete with other organizations for start-up business. Now we very much take a broker's role – we do not deliver ourselves. We see ourselves as having a co-ordinating role'. Where there is a large number of funding organizations, this research found evidence that there was competition for the role of broker, as this position provides the organization with an element of control over the whole business support infrastructure.

Some funding agencies encourage or require organizations to form consortia despite the lack of experience of working together or having trust-based relationships. In such cases, the consortia tend to be led by one party, with other 'partners' acting more as sub-contractors. In an extreme case of lack of co-ordination, one of the support providers in the Durham case study area found that they had been included as a partner in a bid without being aware of it: 'There is lots of duplication of bids by different bidders for funding. We have even found ourselves classed as partners on bid applications when we have known nothing about it'.

In the past 20 years competition among support organizations has been encouraged, although the extent to which there is competition varies between areas depending on the history of start-up support funding. Competition can lead to innovation, with organizations encouraged to find new ways of delivering services. This was observed in the case-study areas, with the two areas with more competition having a more diverse range of support which differed to traditional forms of self-employment support.

Competition and its associated disruption can also contribute to a breakdown of trust, making it harder to bring people together to co-operate, when antagonism has built up due to competition. The case studies show that competition does not have to be antagonistic, with some enterprise agencies working closely together on some programmes while having an element of rivalry when not working together. For example, the enterprise agencies in Staffordshire were found to be applying for new forms of funding independently, as partners or as sub-contractors for each other, while also delivering services together, as well as participating in a number of partnerships.

Discussion

The terms 'collaboration' and 'co-operation' are often used in loose ways without clear understanding of the range of types of inter-organizational relationships. This discussion identifies a range of different characteristics of these relationships and presents frameworks for greater understanding. The types of relationships differ based on who is involved, how they operate, what activities are carried out, and how often they are used.

The case-study material shows how inter-organizational relationships can be divided into two types: first, relationships with buyers, funders, and sub-contractors (what can be termed 'vertical relationships' in a supply chain); and second, relationships with other service providers (what can be termed 'horizontal'). These types of relationships can be both formal (based on contract) and informal (based more on word-of-mouth and a common understanding). In many cases, formalized relationships required a level of informal relationship for starting consortia.

Table 5.1 Types of co-operative relationships (based upon Lyon and Smallbone, 2003)

	Formal	Informal
Horizontal	Joint ownership of a delivery organization Discussion Groups Joint delivery Invited to be board members Partnership membership	Referrals Worked together in the past Co-locating Personal relationships built from formal activities
Vertical	Sub-contracting Combine funding sources	Build relationships with contract managers

Table 5.1 shows how both formal and horizontal relationships have elements for formal and informal relationships.

Types of inter-organizational relationship also vary depending on the depth and intensity of the relationship. Hardy et al. (2003, p. 337) assessed the intensity through the 'level of engagement' in terms of the frequency of meetings and the extent to which a range of people within each organization were interacting with people in the partner organization. They found that this varied from infrequent meetings between leaders to regular meetings of staff at all levels of each organization. Similarly, this was found in the case studies with interaction through co-location helping to build trust.

However, this approach does not examine other elements of the relationships such as the degree of risk taken. In the private sector, the degree of risk can be assessed in financial terms – i.e. the amount of financial resources that could be lost if the collaboration fails. The hybrid nature of social enterprises (with both social and financial imperatives), makes assessing the risks more complex as social enterprises with a not-for-profit legal form do not entail financial risk for a particular individual but rather for a group or community. Furthermore, there are other risks in terms of damaging the reputation and relationship of the social enterprise (or individuals associated with it).

The case material also shows how trust can be built, especially with repeated informal ties and the movement of staff who take their ties from job to job. Trust is shown to be important and coming from existing ties, new working relationships, and through the use of intermediaries known to all parties. As Nicholls (2008) points out, demonstrating legitimacy is an important element of building trust with a wide range of stakeholders; and, as found in all parts of the economy, the role of audits and other forms of assessment can play a role in creating that perceived legitimacy and trust (Power, 2003).

The analysis of the case study material also shows forms of 'coercive co-operation' when power is exerted by commissioners in the form of requiring sub-contractors or those organizations receiving funding to work together; arrangements similar to what Hastings (1996) refers to as 'financially driven partnerships'. The funding organization also has the ability to shape the structure, operation, and subjects for discussion in these situations (Atkinson, 1999). In such cases, power relations can be very unequal with financial control exerted by one party.

This power is exerted through explicit threats of applying sanctions, such as ending a contract or damaging the reputation of a sub-contracting organization. Power may also be less explicitly articulated through the role of surveillance (Clegg et al., 2002; Lukes, 2005). The case-study material includes examples of the use of monitoring and evaluation as surveillance. Similarly, Mawdsley et al. (2005, p. 77) present evidence of an increasingly bureaucratized and formalized system of monitoring in international NGOs that 'have taken the form of a micro-managing obsession with audits, targets and performance indicators'.

The breakdown of relationships and the build-up of distrust are identified in the cases, often in relation to competition. In the context of quasi-markets for public services, there is a range of different norms related to competition. Carmel and Harlock (2008, p. 156) argue that the state has played a crucial role in shaping these norms and changing behaviours, stating: 'The governance of the third sector not only privileges market-like behaviour and market-style organizational forms, but assumes their necessity'. The types of competition may vary with different norms for each of these parts of the market system. For example, there can be competition with other providers, including the private and public sector for public sector contracts. There can also be competition for clients who can be supported (Lyon and Smallbone, 2003). The latter form of competition is growing with increased emphasis on outcomes (such as people placed in work), rather than outputs (training provided) with funding tied to performance. There is also competition between prime contractors and sub-contractors for a larger share of contracts once they have been awarded.

Norms of competition relate to what is considered acceptable behaviour. In a purely commercial market, this is clearer. In the delivery of public services, acceptable norms in the purely private marketplaces (such as withholding information from competitors, not referring customers) may have severe impacts on social outcomes. This raises questions over whether or not social enterprises have different moralities and professional norms that change the way they collaborate, the way they compete, and their involvement in public service delivery, when compared to the private sector. To a certain extent the third sector as a whole has always been involved in a competitive environment competing for restricted resources (Kotler and Andreasen, 1996; Williams, 2008). This has led to the emergence of a set of common norms around acceptable ways of competing in different contexts such as for winning customers, competing between charity shops, or competing for fundraising. For example, there are norms against comparing the impacts of one charity with another when trying to increase fundraising, while still allowing for considerable investment in marketing related to increasing donations. However, this is changing as organizations use a range of social impact measurement tools to demonstrate their potential greater impact compared to other providers.

Competition and markets do not remove collaborative relationships but rather change them. As mentioned earlier, in many competitive markets there is a need for organizations to collaborate with partners on some issues while competing with the same partners on others – what some refer to as 'co-opetition'. The extent to which this occurs and how it works in practice in a social enterprise context is not known. Social enterprises, as hybrid forms combining the economic imperative and social objectives, might therefore be expected to be better suited to the contradiction of competition and collaboration, and able to evolve a range of norms that allow them to operate in the complex quasi-markets for public services.

With more of an emphasis on competition, it is not known how those using the services will perceive the motives of third sector organizations. Anheier and Kendall (2002) state that non-profit organizations are well suited to play the trusted intermediary role between state and client, and there is a risk that this role may be lost. Williams (2008) is more optimistic about competition, seeing it as a way for the third sector to grow its role, impact, and visibility while retaining its defining features.

Conclusion

This chapter has argued for a greater understanding of the dynamics of inter-organizational relationships involving social enterprises in public service markets. There is a mutual attraction between social enterprises and the public sector. Social enterprises benefit as they have a valuable income source that may be less affected by economic downturns. It also allows them the opportunity to scale up their impact either in terms of reaching a wider range of service users or to reach a wider geographic area (Wilson, 2008). The public sector is attracted by the innovative potential of these organizations, offering new ways of delivering services, having greater social impact, and (at times) offering services more efficiently.

As the size of these markets has been growing, social enterprises have been developing a range of co-operative forms in order to access opportunities and to encourage innovation. There is, therefore, a need to look beyond single *organizations* and consider the market systems and forms of *organizing*. This is in a period of flux with public sector reforms bringing in new market relationships. These will bypass some relationships and require new relationships to be formed.

This chapter presents a framework for understanding collaboration in a social enterprise context with vertical and horizontal relationships manifesting themselves in ways that are formal, informal, or having elements of both. These relationships allow services to be developed and new innovative configurations to be identified.

The chapter explores how co-operation is built up, with issues of trust and power explored in the context of the social enterprise model. The issue of moral norms is identified as an area of academic exploration that has not been given adequate attention and which is of central importance to social enterprises as they try to balance their financial and social objectives. The process by which social enterprises build co-operation is also shown to be embedded in existing social relations and local contexts that shape the nature of the relationships and how the relationships are built up. Therefore, understanding the process of building co-operation is more important than trying to describe the 'model' types of co-operative forms.

The final part of the chapter has explored how the competitive environment being faced by social enterprises is shaping the collaborative relationships and norms of behaviour. While little research has been carried out in this area, lessons can be learnt from other studies looking at the emergence of new market forms. There is a need to understand how different types of collaboration are operating in specific contexts which are becoming increasingly dominated by market forces in the UK and internationally (Carmel and Harlock, 2008; Eikenberry, 2009; Sepulveda, 2009). Research that links morality and different forms of the economy may shed more light (Sayer, 2004). This work identifies a range of perspectives on moral economies that may relate to the morality of products and service deliveries, the morality of balancing social and financial aims within a social enterprise, the morality of the inter-organizational relationships, and finally the morality of institutions such as quasi-markets and competition.

There are a number of policy and practical implications arising from this chapter. As mentioned at the beginning, there is a growing interest among policymakers and social enterprises on increasing collaboration. The research presented here provides insights into how co-operation can be strengthened and encouraged. There are no easy fixes, and examples of good practice can be found that demonstrate useful processes, but should not be used for identifying the exact form that organizations should follow. However, key factors include recognizing the importance of existing networks and relationships, and creating the opportunities for groups to work together on smaller activities. The case study data show the importance of recognizing the historical context of collaboration that shapes the types of activities, the public sector funding and the individuals' career trajectories. These are the institutional contexts that should be taken into consideration.

There are questions over the extent to which greater collaboration is beneficial. Being overly close to the public sector can lead to co-option and limiting the advocacy role of independent organizations, mission drift from serving the beneficiary to serving the funder, and reducing innovation as organizations try to deliver in line with the status quo and commissioners' expectations.

There are also risks of dependence if public policies change or there is a reduction in public expenditure available. Mocroft and Zimmeck (2004) found that:

> Funding of voluntary and community organizations expands and contracts more markedly than government spending as a whole. In other words, central government departments appear to treat this kind of funding as a more flexible or discretionary element, to be increased or decreased in response to economic exigencies or policy changes in high-profile areas such as homelessness, unemployment or crime.
>
> (Mocroft and Zimmeck, 2004, p. 19)

The issue of competition in quasi-markets is also likely to grow, and there will be a growing need to understand the nature of relationships and the moral norms that evolve in these changing economies.

Research on the topic of collaboration and public service delivery needs to understand why it occurs, where it does, and what constrains it elsewhere. Much literature describes the benefits of collaboration without examining the processes by which social enterprises reach it. There is an assumption that co-operation should appear when there are clear benefits in terms of reducing costs and maximizing impact. This ignores the importance of context and how the actions of individuals or their organizations are embedded in existing social relations. There is a need to examine how collaboration is built up in different types of relationships (e.g. vertical versus horizontal, formal versus informal, high stakes versus low stakes). There are also differences based on the type of organizations and their histories, while recognizing that there are rapid changes continuing in many organizations as they cope with the recession, potential future cuts in spending, and public sector reforms. This has to be an interdisciplinary project involving hybrid research that mirrors the hybrid nature of social enterprises. It should draw on a range of disciplines that allows an understanding of both the economic and social aspects of social enterprise activities and their collaborations.

Note

1. This chapter is part of a programme on social enterprise being carried out at Middlesex University as part of the Third Sector Research Centre. The support of the Economic and Social Research Council (ESRC), the Office of the Civil Society (OCS), and the Barrow Cadbury UK Trust is gratefully acknowledged. I am grateful for inputs at different stages from Ian Vickers, Pete Alcock, Leandro Sepulveda, David Smallbone, and Alex Nicholls. All views expressed are those of the author.

References

Amin, A., Cameron, A. and Hudson, R. (2002), *Placing the Social Economy* London: Routledge.
Anheier, H. and Kendall, J. (2002), 'Trust and Voluntary Organisations: Three Theoretical Approaches', *British Journal of Sociology*, 53 (3), pp. 343–62.
Atkinson, R. (1999), 'Discourses of Partnership and Empowerment in Contemporary British Urban Regeneration', *Urban Studies*, 36 (1), pp. 59–72.
Audit Commission (2008), *Hearts and Minds: Commissioning from the Voluntary Sector* Audit Commission.
Barney, J. (1991), 'Firm Resources and Sustained Competitive Advantage', *Journal of Management*, 17 (1), pp. 99–120.
Big Society Network (2010), What is Big Society? http://thebigsociety.co.uk/what-is-big-society/.
Burgess, S., Propper, C. and Wilson, D. (2005), 'Will More Choice Improve Outcomes in Education and Health Care? The Evidence from Economic Research', *Centre for Market and Public Organisation (CMPO)*.

Carmel, E. and Harlock, J. (2008), 'Instituting the "Third Sector" as a Governable Terrain: Partnership, Performance and Procurement in the UK', *Policy and Politics*, 36 (2), pp. 155–71.

Clegg, S., Pitsis, S. T., Rura-Polley, T. and Marosszeky, M. (2002), 'Governmentality Matters: Designing an Alliance Culture of Inter-organisation Collaboration for Managing Projects', *Organization Studies*, 23 (3), pp. 317–37.

Clifford, D., Geyne Rajme, F. and Mohan, J. (2010), 'How Dependent is the Third Sector on Public Funding?', TSRC Working Paper 45. Available at http://www.tsrc.ac.uk/LinkClick.aspx?fileticket=TiDxGXmS2Ko%3d&tabid=500.

Conservative Party (2008), 'A Stronger Society: Voluntary Action in the 21st Century, Responsibility Agenda', Policy Green Paper No. 5.

Conservative Party (2010), *Building a Big Society* London: Conservative Party.

Craig, G., Taylor, M., Wilkinson, M. and Bloor, K. (2002), *Contract or Trust: The Role of Compact in Local Governance* Bristol, UK: The Policy Press.

Curtis, T. (2008), 'Finding that Grit Makes a Pearl: A Critical Re-reading of Research into Social Enterprise', *International Journal of Entrepreneurial Behaviour & Research*, 14 (5), pp. 276–90.

Department of Trade and Industry (DTI) (2002), *Social Enterprise: A Strategy for Success* London: Social Enterprise Unit, DTI.

Dijkstra, P. and Knottnerus, S. (2004), 'Successful Partnerships for Social Enterprise, Social enterprises in partnership with the public and private sector as a source of inspiration and renewal in local and regional development [online], [accessed 1/12/2010] http://www.deverandering.com/mple/pdf/engcross.pdf.

Eikenberry, A. (2009), 'Refusing the Market: A Democratic Discourse for Voluntary and Nonprofit Organisations', *Nonprofit and Voluntary Sector Quarterly*, 38, p. 582.

Fukuyama, F. (1995), *Trust* New York: Free Press.

Gambetta, D. (1988), 'Can we Trust Trust?', in D. Gambetta (ed.) *Trust: Making and Breaking Cooperative Relations* Oxford: Blackwell, pp. 213–37.

Granovetter, M. (1985), 'Economic Action and Social Structure: The Problem of Embeddedness', *American Journal of Sociology*, 91 (3), pp. 481–510.

Granovetter, M. (1985), 'Economic Action and Social Structure: The Problem of Embeddedness', *American Journal of Sociology*, 91 (3), pp. 481–510.

Granovetter, M. (1994), 'Business Groups', in N. J. Smelser and R. Swedburg (eds) *The Handbook of Economic Sociology* Princetown, NJ: Princetown University Press, pp. 454–75.

Hardy, C., Phillips, N. and Lawrence, T. (2003), 'Resources, Knowledge and Influence: The Organisational Effects of Interorganisational Collaboration', *Journal of Management Studies*, 40 (2), pp. 289–313.

Hastings, A. (1996), 'Unravelling the Process of "Partnership" in Urban Regeneration Policy', *Urban Studies*, 33 (2), pp. 253–68.

OTS (2009), *Real Help for Communities: Volunteers, Charities and Social Enterprise* London: Office of the Third Sector, Cabinet Office.

Huggins, R. (2010), 'Forms of Network Resource: Knowledge Access and the Role of Inter-firm Networks', *International Journal of Management Reviews*, 12 (3), pp. 335–52.

IFF Research Ltd (2007), 'Third Sector Market Mapping' for the Department of Health, http://www.dh.gov.uk/en/Publicationsandstatistics/Publications/PublicationsPolicyAndGuidance/DH_065411.

International Co-operative Alliance (ICA) (1994), *Draft Statement on Cooperative Identity* Geneva: ICA.

Kotler, P. and Andreasen, R. (1996), *Strategic Marketing for Nonprofit Organisations* Fifth Edition, New Jersey: Prentice Hall.

Le Grand, J. and Bartlet, W. (1993), *Quasi Markets and Social Policy* Basingstoke: Palgrave Macmillan.

Lukes, S. (2005), *Power: A Radical Review* London: Palgrave Macmillan.

Lyon, F. (2006), 'Managing Co-operation: Trust and Power in Ghanaian Associations', *Organization Studies*, 27 (1), pp. 31–52.

Lyon, F. (2009), 'Measuring the Value of Social and Community Impact', in Paul Hunter (ed.) *Social Enterprise for Public Service: How Does the Third Sector Deliver?* London: The Smith Institute.

Lyon, F. and Porter, G. (2007), 'Market Institutions, Trust and Norms: Exploring Moral Economies in Nigerian Food Systems', *Cambridge Journal of Economics* doi:10.1093/cje/bem008.

Lyon, F. and Sepulveda, L. (2009), 'Mapping Social Enterprises: Past Approaches, Challenges and Future Directions', *Social Enterprise Journal*, 5 (1), pp. 83–94.

Lyon, F. and Smallbone, D. (2003), 'Joining-up Entrepreneurship Support: Coordination and Partnership amongst Start Up Support Providers in England', Proceedings of the Regional Studies Association Annual Conference.

Mawdsley, E., Townsend, J. and Porter. G. (2005), 'Trust, Accountability and Face-to-face Interactions in North–South NGO Relations', *Development in Practice*, 15 (1), pp. 77–82.

Mayer, R. C., Davis, J. H. and Schoorman, F. D. (1995), 'An Integration Model of Organizational Trust', *Academy of Management Review*, 20 (3), pp. 709–34.

Mocroft, I. and Zimmeck, M. (2004), *Central Government Funding of Voluntary and Community Organisations* London: Home Office.

Mollering, G. (2005), 'The Trust/Control Duality: An Integrative Perspective on Positive Expectations of Others', *International Sociology*, 20 (3), pp. 283–305.

Mollering, G. (2006), 'Understanding Trust from the Perspective of Sociological Neo-Institutionalism', in R. Bachmann and A. Zaheer (eds) *Handbook of Trust Research* Cheltenham: Edward Elgar.

Moore, M. (1994), 'How Difficult is it to Construct Market Relations? A Commentary on Platteau,' *Journal of Development Studies*, 30 (4), pp. 818–30.

Murdock, A. (2007), 'No Man's Land or Promised Land? The Lure of Local Public Service: Delivery Contracts for Social Enterprise', Paper presented at the fourth UK Social Enterprise Research Conference, London South Bank University, July.

Munoz, S. A. and Tindsley, S. (2008), 'Selling to the Public Sector: Prospects and Problems for Social Enterprise in the UK', The Journal of Corporate Citizenship, December.

Murray, R., Caulier, G. and Mulgan, G. (2010), *The Open Book of Social Innovation* The Young Foundation and NESTA.

Nalebuff, B. and Brandenburger, A. (1996), *Co-opetition* London: HarperCollins.

Nicholls, A. (2008), 'Capturing the Performance for the Socially Entrepreneurial Organisation: An Organisational Legitimacy Approach', in J. Mair, J. Robertson and K. Hockerts (eds) *International Perspectives on Social Entrepreneurship* Basingstoke: Palgrave Macmillan.

National Council for Voluntary Organisations (NCVO) (2008), 'Collaboration without Borders: What can UK Organisations Learn about Collaboration from International NGOs?', available at www.ncvo.org.uk.

National Council for Voluntary Organisations (NCVO) (2009), *The UK Civil Society Almanac 2009* London: NCVO.

HMT (2008), *Accelerating the SME Engine* London: HM Treasury, http://www.ogc. gov.uk/documents/Accelerating_the_SME_Economic_Engine.pdf.

Office of the Third Sector (OTS) (2009), *Real Help for Communities: Volunteers, Charities and Social Enterprises* London: OTS.

O'Neill, O. (2002), *A Question of Trust* Cambridge: Cambridge University Press.

Phills J. A., Deiglmeier, K. and Miller, D. T. (2008) 'Rediscovering Social Innovation', Stanford Social Innovation Review Fall 2008.

Platteau, J. P. (1994a), 'Behind the Market Stage where Real Societies Exist, Part I: The Role of Public and Private Order Institutions', *Journal of Development Studies*, 30 (3), pp. 533–77.

Platteau, J. P. (1994b), 'Behind the Market Stage where Real Societies Exist, Part II: The Role of Moral Norms', *Journal of Development Studies*, 30 (4), pp. 753–817.

Portes, A. and Sensenbrenner, J. (1993), 'Embeddedness and Immigration: Notes on the Social Determinants of Economic Action', *American Journal of Sociology*, 98 (6), pp. 1320–50.

Power, M. K. (2003), 'Auditing and the Production of Legitimacy', Accounting, Organizations and Society, 28 (4), pp. 379–94.

Putnam, R., Leonardi, R. and Nanetti, R. (1993), *Making Democracy Work: Civic Traditions in Modern Italy* Princeton, NJ: Princeton University Press.

Reed, M. (2001), 'Organisation, Trust and Control: A Realist Analysis', *Organisation Studies*, 22 (2), pp. 201–28.

Rousseau, D., Sitkin, S. B., Burt, R. S., Camerer, C. (1998), 'Not so Different after All: A Cross-discipline View of Trust', *Academy of Management Review*, 23 (3), pp. 393–404.

Sayer, A. (2004), 'Restoring the Moral Dimension: Acknowledging Lay Normativity', mimeo, published by the Department of Sociology, Lancaster University. Available at www.comp.lancs.ac.uk/sociology/papers/sayer-restoring-moral-dimension.pdf.

Sepulveda, L. (2009) 'Outsider, Missing Link or Panacea? The Place of Social Enterprise (with)in and in Relation to the Third Sector', TSRC Working Paper 15. Available at http://www.tsrc.ac.uk/LinkClick.aspx?fileticket=DusBIXssUUA%3d&tabid=500.

Spear, R. (2000), 'The Co-operative Advantage', Annals of Public and Co-operative Economics, 71 (4), pp. 507–24.

Spear, R. (2008), 'European Perspectives on Social Enterprise', in P. Hunter (ed.) *Social Enterprise for Public Service: How Does the Third Sector Deliver?* London: The Smith Institute.

Van Slyke, D. M. (2007), 'Agents or Stewards: Using Theory to Understand the Government–Nonprofit Social Service Contracting Relationship', *Journal of Public Administration Research and Theory*, 17 (2), pp. 157–87.

Westall, A. (2007), 'How can Innovation in Social Enterprise be Understood, Encouraged and Enabled?', A Social Enterprise Think Piece for the Office of the Third Sector, London: OTS.

Wilson, A. (2009), 'Social Entrepreneurs and Public Service Delivery', in Paul Hunter (ed.) *Social Enterprise for Public Service: How Does the Third Sector Deliver?* London: The Smith Institute.

Williams, I. (2008), 'What does Competition and Collaboration Mean in the Voluntary and Community Sector? Compete or Collaborate', Seminar jointly organized by the NCVO Third Sector Foresight Project and Performance Hub.

Available at http://www.ncvo-vol.org.uk/uploadedFiles/Third_Sector_Foresight/ Third_Sector_Foresight_Events/IWCompetitionCollaborationPaper2.pdf.

Williams, P. (2002), 'The Competent Boundary Spanner', Public Administration 80 (1), pp. 103–24.

Williamson, O. E. (1993), 'Calculativeness, Trust, and Economic Organization', *Journal of Law and Economics*, 36 (1), pp. 453–86.

Yin, R. (2003), *Case Study Research: Design and Methods*, London: Sage Publications.

Zucker, L. G. (1986), 'Production of Trust: Institutional Sources of Economic Structure, 1840–1920', *Research in Organisational Behaviour*, 8, pp. 53–111.

6
Agency in Social Innovation: Putting the Model in the Model of the Agent

Kirsten Robinson, David Robinson, and Frances Westley

Introduction

Westley defined social innovation as 'an initiative, product or process or program that profoundly changes the basic routines, resource and authority flows or beliefs of any social system and has durability and broad impact' (Westley and Antadze, 2010, p. 2). Intentionally creating social innovations requires the kind of agents who can understand and actively change the rules and the structure of the system. These agents are, in the language of this chapter, 'projective agents' (Emirbaayer and Mische, 1998). They emphasize the orientation to the future, responsive choice, and inventive manipulation of the physical and social worlds. This chapter deals primarily with features of the projective agent that are useful in formally modelling social innovation as a process. Modelling is just one of several approaches to understanding, but it complements empirical and applied investigation (Macy and Willer, 2002).

The features needed for modelling agents who engage in social innovation are present in the conventional understanding of how to develop entrepreneurs and how to help individuals or groups promote innovation. However, these features are still under-theorized, and this weakness inhibits the flow of ideas between practitioners and educators, on the one hand, and theorists attempting to develop formal models, on the other. This chapter does not present a complete model of agency; it simply explicates a problem inherent in modelling society. The problem is, however, critical for understanding the process of social innovation. While the focus of this chapter is on an aspect of the formal exercise of modelling, its basic insights have implications for the practical business of understanding and promoting social innovation more generally.

The central argument put forward here is that the agent in social innovation differs in a fundamental way from the agent as it is usually modelled in the social sciences. The typical modelling solution for the social sciences, especially economics, is to treat agents essentially as automata constrained by the system's rules and structures. An agent consciously promoting change, however, is actively shaping the rules and structures of the system. Such an agent must have a model of the system they are attempting to change. The challenge for modelling change is, therefore, to put the model of the system into the model of the agent and then to put the agent into the model of the system.

This chapter briefly reviews some developments in the simulation of social systems, drawing in particular on the history of economic modelling and the emergence of agent-based modelling. It then describes the problem of placing a model of the system into the model of an agent, framing this as an extension of the classic problem of projectivity that can be traced back to Aristotle (Emirbayer and Mische, 1998). This work illustrates the problem in the context of social innovation, introduces existing precursors to models of projective agents, and sketches what remains to be done.

Despite analytical difficulty, building formal models that include social innovators is important because it then becomes possible to ask questions with the model, explore computationally the effect of numerous interacting innovators, and test what factors shape the ultimate impact of particular kinds of innovation. The recent success of research on networks that explores computationally the impact of activities and ideas with different patterns of connectivity among agents shows the potential power of this type of approach (Newman et al., 2006).

Modelling agents

The term 'modelling' in this chapter is used to refer to the process of studying a system by examining an analogue. In its most extended sense, modelling includes the use of metaphor, but our focus is on simulation models of social situations, and within that class, the sub-class of agent-based models (ABMs). By social situation, we mean any social configuration in which people are making decisions. Agent-based models (ABMs) are computational models for simulating the actions and interactions of autonomous agents. They consist of dynamically interacting rule-based 'agents'. As Hammil (2010, p. 23) noted, ABM 'has made most progress among economists', suggesting that economists are more open to ABM because building models is already a widely practised methodology in that discipline. An alternative explanation is that the nature of the problems economists choose is amenable to formal modelling. Whatever the explanation, formal reasoning based on explicit models of individual behaviour in economics goes back at least to August Cournot early in the nineteenth century.

Analytic approaches

Long before simulation methods were available, Cournot described the working of an economy with thousands or perhaps millions of players by radically simplifying his description of individual behaviour (1927). The utilitarian movement in philosophy proposed that people in general seek to maximize their utility. For the purpose of analysing most market behaviour, utility could be understood as an unobserved function of the goods and services bought in markets. Calculus provides the observation that a differentiable function is maximized only where the derivative is zero.[1] It followed that if an agent is maximizing in a situation that can be described by continuous functions, agents will only accept values of the choice variables that make the derivative zero. That statement describes an equation or a set of equations that can often be solved to identify a situation of interest. Situations that satisfy the equations have come to be called a Cournot-Nash equilibrium. In such equilibria, no agents want to unilaterally change what they are doing because small changes cannot increase their utility.

This approach, which characterizes economists' modelling of social situations, is an application of mathematical analysis. Analysis is the branch of pure mathematics that includes the theories of differentiation, integration and measure, limits, infinite series, and analytic functions. Using calculus, a rule is derived for a plausible model of agent behaviour. The rule allows economists to identify the outcomes that result from a model of behaviour in an interesting class of cases. It provides prescriptions that might be applied by real-world agents, and it may yield testable hypotheses about behaviour.

Extending models of agents

The basic model is limited in several ways. One problem is that it does not tell us how society gets to an equilibrium. Economists recognize this point and describe the method as 'comparative statics': an approach that focuses on the properties of equilibria. A second problem is that because of the difficulty of finding analytical solutions to any but the simplest cases, economists have historically restricted themselves to 'tractable', which is to say 'easy', functions and a great deal has been achieved in economics with relatively simple models (Hudson, 1977). A third limitation is that the difficulty of finding analytical solutions tends to limit the number of agents employed, and indeed economist have frequent recourse to what they call 'the representative agent': results derived mathematically for a single `representative' agent are assumed to hold true for all agents (Hartley, 1996).

In principle, this style of analysis can incorporate preferences of any sort, including altruistic feelings, moral constraints, risk preference, imperfect information, evolving tastes, erratic behaviour, mistakes or imprecision in choice, and so on. It is possible to add additional rules to the model of the agent to take into account the many errors and biases in perception and decision making (Kahneman, 2003).

There have been several major methodological innovations in modelling technique in the last half century. One of the most important limitations in the application of the basic economic model was that it tended to focus attention on the optimal choices of individual agents. Economists knew that humans are aware of each other, but the available techniques were not well adapted to modelling agents who were aware of other agents. The development of game theory by von Neumann and Morgenstern (1943) was a major innovation in economic modelling that spread rapidly to other fields, including law (Baird et al., 1994), philosophy (Sugden, 1991) and biology (Maynard Smith, 1982). The striking feature of game theory is that it adds techniques that allow modellers to explicitly condition agent responses on their views about what other agents think.

A third innovation in modelling focuses on the implications of specifying relationships among agents. Network theory adds additional structure to multi-agent models (Newman et al., 2006). Understanding the effect of network structures also makes significant computational demands. Social network analysis (related to network theory) has emerged as a key technique in modern sociology. Although understanding the effect of network structures also makes significant theoretical and computational demands, network theory adds additional structure to multi-agent models (Newman et al., 2006).

A second major innovation, made possible by the introduction of cheap computing, is the use of simulation models. Simulation models allow analysts to explore out-of-equilibrium behaviour much more easily. They allow analysts to introduce large numbers of agents, identical or otherwise. Simulation models require that agents contain rules for behaving in out-of-equilibrium situations. They make it relatively easy to follow the evolution of a system and to examine the robustness of the patterns observed over numerous repetitions with different parameters (Tesfatsion and Judd, 2006).

Computational models

Computational models for simulating the actions and interactions of autonomous agents are relatively new. Despite the fact that ABMs open new areas to Model-based exploration, many problems remain to be solved. Agent behaviour must be specified for more agents, both in- and out-of equilibrium, and for an expanding range of situations.

ABMs have not been adopted as readily in fields like sociology as they have been in economics, and even there they have not penetrated to the point that they are mentioned in introductory or even intermediate textbooks (Hamill, 2010). Nonetheless, because ABMs remove the constraints imposed by earlier analytical approaches, they will reduce the reliance on optimizing agents and simple self-interest that has characterized much of the most successful modelling in economics and has, perhaps, given formal modelling a bad name among other social scientists. The traditional focus on distributed self-interest was, at least in part, a computational convenience rooted in tractability as much as ideology. Arguably, the fields of social entrepreneurship and social innovation represent the generalization from the study of distributed self-interest in economics and management to the study of a wider selection of distributed interests.

To some extent, the newer techniques have already facilitated an enriched view of society and even human nature. Axelrod's use of computational models, for example (Axelrod, 1980a; 1980b), helped to make co-operation a credible subject by showing that it could emerge in a situation where previous analysis predicted it could not. By making it easy to dispense with the self-interest and rationality assumptions, these approaches open the way for models in which selfishness is just one possible way to motivate agents. If social innovation is something other than privately motivated entrepreneurship, a modelling approach that supports agents with more complex motives than simple self-interested rationality will be needed.

Computational models have also opened up the door to studying complexity and emergence systematically. 'Emergence' is the common term for the spontaneous appearance of features at one level of organization that are not built into the units that constitute the system at a smaller level of organization. For example, predator–prey population cycles are not a feature of either the predator or the prey. Similarly, rules of syntax are not a feature of the underlying human biology, and in Conway's Game of Life (Gardner, 1970) the gliders and other persistent patterns are simply not present in the cellular automata that populate the field. Evolution and aggregation regularly throw up features not present in the precursors. It is important to note that the emergence of new features in human society is not simply a result of the automatic working of the rules governing individual behaviour: human beings consciously introduce innovations out of an imaginative engagement with the future (Emirbayer and Mische, 1998), while the agents in the game of life, for example, simply respond in the present to signals in the present. The intentional and strategic activity of projective agents may not have any direct analogue in physical systems (Anderson, 1972).

The opportunity landscape

A valuable metaphor for the opportunity landscapes in which social innovators operate comes from the literature on complexity in bio-logical and ecological systems (Holling, 1973; Holling and Gunderson, 2001; Westley, 2006). In the language of complex adaptive systems, a social system may have the capacity to sustain several distinct of behaviour. These patterns, or attractors, could be classic equilibria or cycles, but they are more commonly something like 'strange attractors' around which the state of the system 'orbits' without exactly repeating previous patterns. As a result of some cumulative process, a system may spontaneously jump from one such 'basin of attraction' to another. In the bottom panel of Figure 6.1, the basins of attraction are represented as depressions in a surface. The surface is sometimes called the stability landscape. Deeper indentations are more stable. Over time the land-scape itself may evolve. The possibility of evolution is represented by a second version of the landscape at a later time (above) the first.

The state of the system is imagined as a point in motion orbiting in one of the basins. In this case, the two dimension of the surface repre-sent two variables that describe important and changing features of the system; for example, opposition to a regime and the level of inequality under the regime. Rising inequality might increase opposition, while rising opposition might increase the tendency to reform. Such a system might exhibit repeated cycles. A stable cycle in a landscape evolving through time is illustrated by the heavy spiral connecting the basin in the lower and upper sections of Figure 6.1.

At some time the cycles might grow so large that the point represent-ing the state of the system runs over the lip of one basin and falls into

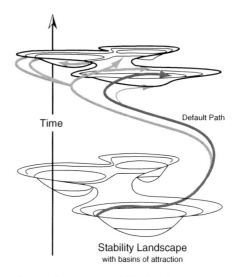

Time

Default Path

Stability Landscape
with basins of attraction

Figure 6.1 Innovation as choice in a stability landscape

another. Changing the regime need not be a result of the mindless dynamics that characterize simple dynamical systems. Individuals may attempt to steer the system to a different basin of attraction, a process illustrated in Figure 6.1 as lighter lines diverging from the default path. Innovation is possible when the neighbourhood in the 'stability landscape' presents states that a decisive individual or coalition can access by modifying or by taking advantage of the dynamics of the system at a particular moment.

Figure 6.1 can be used to illustrate the inherent difficulty of directing social change. The challenge for an agent is to identify alternate basins of attraction, determine which are accessible, and evaluate the system dynamics in alternative basins. An agent must somehow construct a sufficiently clear idea of the attractiveness of a situation in a hypothetical future using current and past information. This is not far from Dewey's description of human intelligence as being based upon the capacity to 'read future results in present on-goings' (1981). It is clear that at least some individuals attempt these feats of imagination and some succeed, although the roles of intentionality, strategy, chance, and opportunity are far from clear. Such thinking has much in common with social movement theory that explores the mobilization of cognitive frames in social change action.

Mental models

In order to choose an action leading to a different basin of attraction the agent must have a mental model of the dynamics of the system. Describing the dynamical system and identifying potential basins of attraction are challenging tasks. How individuals with limited information are able to develop what amounts to a working model of the dynamics, select actions that can change the trajectory of a significant part of the system, and convince others to support those actions is neither fully understood in practice nor adequately theorized.

In the context of social innovation, the agent makes purposive choices among alternative possible futures. Since the future is not available for observation, the agent must generate alternative futures from experience and memory. Emirbayer and Mische term the capacity to generate possible futures 'projectivity', and track the history of the notion back to Aristotle (1998). To model a society containing such an agent appears to require agents that possess a model of how the system evolves.

Introducing the future into economic models is not new. Keynes's *General Theory of Employment, Interest and Money* (1936) features one chapter entitled 'The State of Long-term Expectation' that discusses how investors' expectations are formed and how they affect investor behaviour. A variety of approaches has been tried, including the rational expectations hypothesis suggested by Muth (1961) and popularized by Lucas (1972). One version of the hypothesis states that agents' predictions of the future value of economically relevant variables are not systematically wrong. This statement is usually interpreted to mean that agents employ a correct model of the system of which they are part. The model is usually implemented by forcing the expected value of a variable to be equal to the value predicted by the model. This is equivalent to assuming agents have a consistent model – one that is not contradicted by any observation they may make.

Examples of formal modelling of agents abound, and the variety as well as the sheer virtuosity of some of the efforts are impressive. Some explicitly model aspects of agents' model formation and refinement. For example, Thagard at the University of Waterloo and his colleagues have presented a theory of *explanatory coherence* that has been applied to a variety of cases of scientific belief change, including major scientific revolutions and climate change debates (Thagard, 1992). Propositions are coded as either cohering with or being incoherent with other propositions. A proposition is accepted if including it maximizes coherence. 'Maximizing coherence' is rigorously defined and is implemented in a programme which searches for the set of propositions that maximize coherence (Thagard and Findlay, forthcoming).

Explanatory coherence is an approach to modelling the agent's mental model, which is, in this case, a set of propositions. Predictions about the behaviour of individuals with respect to, say, climate change, are expected to change as the agents' model of the human–climate interactions changes. It is especially interesting that the agent's model evolves as it is confronted with new information: the agent updates his or her picture of the world.

When a new proposition comes along, representing either newly discovered evidence or a newly generated explanatory hypothesis, then this proposition is added to the overall set, along with positive and negative constraints based on the relations of coherence and incoherence that the new proposition has with the old ones. Then, an assessment of coherence is performed, with the results suggesting what to accept and what to reject.

There are other, less formal, accounts of how scientific beliefs change that are essentially hypotheses about an agent's mental models. These include Popper's conjectures and refutations (2004), Hempel's confirmation theory (1945), Kuhn's paradigm shifts (1962), and Lakatos's methodology of research programmes (1980). Other formal approaches include Bayesian models that explain belief change using probability theory, and logicist ones that use ideas about logical consequence in deductive systems (Thagard and Findlay, forthcoming). The discussion is rooted in the notion that agents have mental models, that these can be scientifically modelled, and that the way they change can also be modelled.

More generally, a wide variety of learning approaches has been implemented in simulations and in analytical models. Although many ABM learning models are quite limited (sometimes being little more that than collections of reflexes), the notion of learning itself implies that agents must contain models. A learning model is a specification of how an environment alters the behaviour of an agent. It implies that the agent contains an information structure that affects its behaviour and that the agent's behaviour is altered by changes in the information structure. Learning is clearly necessary but not sufficient in a model of an innovating agent.

Thagard and his colleagues are also refining the notion of cognitive maps to include feelings, creating 'cognitive-affective' maps (Thagard, 2010). In order to do so they have developed an appropriate *graph semantics* that allows them to attach emotional values to concepts represented as nodes in a graph. The emotional affix provides information on whether the presence of one concept supports or obstructs the introduction of another. Knowing that, for another person, certain concepts have negative affect would clearly provide some guidance in winning support for new ideas. They argue that these maps will help groups and individuals to reduce conflict and find new solutions. It is a very small step from this to recognizing that techniques for developing such maps could create a body of systematic knowledge to help social innovators.

In another example, Pape (2008) investigates agents with differing mental models of the same phenomenon. Pape devises a representation of how causally coherent agents incorporate information. Given ambiguous information, identical agents may develop different, but, perfectly consistent, theories of how the world works and may, therefore, rationally choose different strategies. Pape goes on to show that in a simple dynamic information economy, agents with different theories of the world can engage in predator/prey relationships that, in turn, produce natural population cycles of behaviour. The predator/prey relationship emerges only from their different interpretations of common data. A striking feature of Pape's model is that it describes a world of competing mental models. There is complex emergent behaviour in a social system, but the evolution occurs in the models and not in the physical stocks of the outside world.

Human agents come equipped with models of the world. The typical modelling strategy in economics has been to treat agents as relatively simple automata. In modelling social innovation, however, researchers are imagining agents who examine the constraints they face and consider how they might be changed. Social innovators necessarily attempt to understand the social system and make forecasts. In doing so, they may use the tools and results of the social sciences. Standard equilibrium models cannot capture agents who are actively using the tools of the other social sciences. These agents act on the system at the same time as responding to it. Unlike the agents who would be found in the economist's model, they are conducting analysis that may be as sophisticated as the economist's or the sociologist's, often in an eclectic, interdisciplinary, and creative way. It goes without saying that it is hard to incorporate an agent like this into the kind of modelling traditional in economics or the other social sciences.

A major challenge will be to find ways to represent existing situations so that models of projective agents can generate interesting innovations. Kauffman has a preliminary version of this. He imagines a series of strings of 1's and 0's that can bang into each other and recombine according to particular rules to create new strings (Kauffman et al., 2008). As the strings collide, they can get longer or shorter. A longer string offers an expanded space of possibilities. The current set of strings determines what is possible in the next step. He calls the space of variants that can be reached in one step the 'adjacent possible'. This space evolves over time and, in what he calls 'autocatalytic sets', more possibilities emerge. He argues that his model captures what happens both in biological systems as organisms evolve and in technological systems as new technologies emerge. A television, for example, creates the opportunity for a remote control, and a car creates the opportunity for a car seat and an automated parking system. Removing one element eliminates not just that option but also the class of options dependent on it. This process introduces genuinely novel goods and services. Eric Bienhocker of McKinsey and Company estimates that there are 10 billion goods and services available just in New York (2006). Furthermore, the emerging organisms and technologies depend not on general laws, but on the particular configuration of precursors.

Social innovators operate within a space of possibilities something like Kaufmann's adjacent possible. Kaufmann's model, however, is almost perfectly abstract and the simple model does not contain intentional agents. In modelling social innovation, the goal is to have intentional agents operate on a space which resembles in some sense the space of what is possible in the human world, and to reach variants that are recognizably different within that world.

Table 6.1 lists some of the major developments in modelling agents. To model a social system in which some agents are social innovators will require new modelling techniques. An agent-based model of social innovation would require one or more agents capable of identifying feasible alternatives and evaluating them. Such agents would be able to identify the barriers to reaching the preferred state. A model might include other agents who can find ways to surmount those barriers and agents capable of mobilizing other agents to overcome the barriers, as well as agents capable of being mobilized on behalf of an imagined future.

A similar problem remains unsolved in the economics literature. In economic theory, the entrepreneur is analogous to the agent required for modelling social innovation. Entrepreneurs identify opportunities, mobilize resources, and invest effort to realize possibilities that other agents often cannot imagine. Entrepreneurs play a minimal role in predictive models in economics precisely because they act in highly specific rather than generic situations, and are fundamentally unpredictable.

Table 6.1   Some developments in modelling

Analytic models	Cournot (1838)	Agents select points that satisfy optimality conditions: maximizing, rational, representative agents
Computational models		Rely less on representative agents, may not impose rationality
Simulation models		
Agent-based Models		Rule-based behaviour, open to complexity and emergent behaviours
Projective models	Keynes (1936)	Agents forecast the evolution of the system (have expectations)
Game theoretic models	von Neumann & Morgenstern (1943)	Agents forecast behaviour of other agents
Rational expectations models	Muth (1961)	Agents forecast correctly
Models of model selection		Agents choose or create models
Explanatory coherence	Thagard (1992); Pape (2008)	Agents use consistency criterion
Cognitive affective modes	Thagard et al. (2010)	Agent choice influenced by emotional associations
Models of innovation	Kauffmann (2007)	Models with selection of improvements but no agents

They change the rules that are the foundations of prediction. The term 'social entrepreneur' is used in contexts where the objective includes social well-being and not just private gain (Phills et al., 2008).

An innovating agent in context

Several features of the innovating agent are illustrated in Etmanski's work on building a culture of belonging (Wesley, 2006). Etmanski's daughter had mental disabilities, which meant that she would always require support and never live entirely independently. Like many parents of children with disabilities, he worried about what would happen when he was no longer able to provide for her. He began working with a group of parents with similar concerns and together they founded Planned Lifetime Advocacy Network (PLAN), which assists families address the financial and social well-being of a relative with a disability, particularly after their parents die. Their strategy was to build networks of support centred on each child with a disability. PLAN began in Vancouver, but its programmes became successful and the model was replicated across Canada.

Over time, Etmanski realized that even if this programme were to be universally adopted, the institutional barriers that made it difficult for those with disabilities to form meaningful connections and contribute to their communities would remain. He pulled back from PLAN and began to focus on changing how people talk and think about mental disabilities. He and his wife organized a series of dialogues with thought leaders and intellectuals in which they asked speakers to consider the role of belonging and contribution. They then tracked how the ideas that were developed in these conversations were taken up in public discourse. They found that the ideas did begin to shift public discourse.

Building on this shift in the public dialogue, Etmanski began to work on building institutional support to allow those with disabilities to achieve greater financial independence. At the time, people had to use up all of their assets before becoming eligible for disability payments. This meant that they remained perpetually vulnerable unless they had others who could support them financially. Etmanski worked with the government to develop a new Registered Disability Savings Program (RDSP) similar to Canada's Registered Retirement Savings Program (RRSP) and Registered Education Savings Program (RESP). Since friends and acquaintances as well as family could contribute to the disability savings plans, it reinforced the networks that PLAN worked on building as well as increasing the independence of those with disabilities.

The example illustrates several features of the projective agent. Etmanski imagined a change and set out to achieve it. In the process he continued to learn about structures, but also about the understanding (models) of others. He began to work directly on the model in the minds of other agents, taking care to make the way others understood the situation support the changes he needed and to make sure that the changes he introduced reciprocally supported the change in the mental models of others. He seems to have experimentally developed an understanding of the dynamics of change and helped steer the system to a nearby state in which a new institutional form was self-sustaining.

The story also illustrates the way innovation may propagate from the bottom up. Unlike the traditional problem of designing policy-level changes that are implemented at the level of the society, these changes began with small and local innovations. Although in general, profound changes are rare and most challenges to structures and resource flows leave the larger society almost unaffected (Westley 2006), local innovations can in certain cases have significant aggregate effects or trigger changes in larger systems. Some people seem to be able to intentionally drive this kind of change.

Conclusion

The concept of agent proper to the analysis of social innovation differs from the notion of the agent commonly employed in the established social sciences, particularly in economics. Where existing models typically put automata-like agents into models of the system, a model of social innovation requires a model of creative and autonomous agents who themselves contain models of the system within which they act.

Developing a model of an innovating agent that contains a model of the system is useful because it helps to characterize formally important requirements of the social innovation process and helps to identify aspects of the social innovator. It also lays the groundwork for exploring the large-scale, aggregate behaviours of systems with a richer class of agents embedded in them. Even partial solutions to the problem of modelling social innovators will be useful for asking different questions about social innovation, and will also be of interest to agent-based modellers as they address some of the most difficult problems in modelling agency and its interaction with existing structures.

This chapter has reviewed some developments in the simulation of social systems, drawing in particular on the history of economic modelling and the emergence of agent-based modelling. Each of the modelling approaches described suggests techniques that might eventually be incorporated in a general model of a social innovator. Integrative modelling work that draws on and synthesizes modelling innovations from across different fields is, therefore, needed.

Note

1. In this context, a derivative is a measure of how a function changes as its input changes or, put more simply, how much one quantity changes in response to another.

References

Anderson, P. W. (1972), 'More is Different', *Science*, 177 (4047), pp. 393–6.
Axelrod, R. (1980a), 'Effective Choice in the Prisoner's Dilemma', *Journal of Conflict Resolution*, 24 (1), pp. 3–25.

Axelrod, R. (1980b), 'More Effective Choice in the Prisoner's Dilemma', *Journal of Conflict Resolution*, 24 (3), pp. 379–403.

Baird, D., Gertner, R. and Picker, R. (1994), *Game Theory and the Law*, Cambridge, MA: Harvard University Press.

Beinhocker, E. D. (2006), *Origin of Wealth: Evolution, Complexity, and the Radical Remaking of Economics*, Boston: Harvard Business School Press.

Cournot, A. (1927), *Researches into the Mathematical Principles of the Theory of Wealth*, New York: The Macmillan Company.

Dewey, J. (1981), 'The Need for a Recovery of Philosophy', in J. J. McDermott (ed.) *The Philosophy of John Dewey*, Chicago: University of Chicago Press, pp. 58–97.

Emirbayer, M. and Mische, A. (1998), 'What Is Agency?', *The American Journal of Sociology*, 103 (4), pp. 962–1023.

Gardner, M. (1970), 'Mathematical Games: The Fantastic Combinations of John Conway's New Solitaire Game "life"', *Scientific American*, 223 (10), pp. 120–3.

Hamill, L. (2010), 'Agent-Based Modelling: The Next 15 Years', *Journal of Artificial Societies and Social Simulation*, 13 (4), p. 7.

Hartley, J. E. (1996), 'Retrospectives: The Origins of the Representative Agent', *The Journal of Economic Perspectives*, 10 (2), pp. 169–77.

Hempel, C. G. (1945), 'Studies in the Logic of Confirmation', *Mind*, 54 (214), pp. 1–26.

Holling, C. S. (1973), 'Resilience and Stability of Ecological Systems', *Annual Review of Ecology and Systematics*, 4 (4), pp. 1–23.

Holling, C. S. and Gunderson, L. H. (2001), 'Resilience and Adaptive Cycles', in L. H. Gunderson and Holling, C. S. (eds) *Panarchy: Understanding Transformations in Human and Natural Systems*, Washington, DC: Island Press, pp. 25–62.

Hudson, P. (1977), 'Simple Mathematics in Simple Economic Modelling', *The Mathematical Gazette*, 61 (416), pp. 105–19.

Kahneman, D. (2003), 'Maps of Bounded Rationality: Psychology for Behavioral Economics', *The American Economic Review*, 93 (5), pp. 1449–75.

Kauffman, S., Thurner, S. and Hanel, R. (2008), 'The Evolving Web of Future Wealth', *Scientific American*, available at: http://www.sciam.com/article.cfm?id=the-evolving-web-of-future-wealth. Accessed 5 March 2009.

Keynes, J. M. (1936), *The General Theory of Employment, Interest and Money*, London: Macmillan.

Kuhn, T. S. (1962), *The Structure of Scientific Revolutions*, Chicago: University of Chicago Press.

Lakatos, I., Worrall, J. and Currie, G. (1980), *The Methodology of Scientific Research Programmes*, Cambridge: Cambridge University Press.

Lucas, R. E. (1972), 'Expectations and the Neutrality of Money', *Journal of Economic Theory*, 4 (2), pp. 103–24.

Macy, M. W. and Willer, R. (2002), 'From Factors to Actors: Computational Sociology and Agent-Based Modeling', *Annual Review of Sociology*, 28 (1), pp. 143–66.

Maynard Smith, J. (1982), *Evolution and the Theory of Games*, Cambridge: Cambridge University Press.

Morgenstern, O. and Neumann, J. V. (1943), *Theory of Games and Economic Behavior*, New York: John Wiley and Sons.

Muth, J. F. (1961), 'Rational Expectations and the Theory of Price Movements', *Econometrica*, 29 (3), pp. 315–35.

Newman, M., Barabasi, A. and Watts, D. J. (2006), *The Structure and Dynamics of Networks*, Princeton: Princeton University Press.

Pape, A. D. (2006), *Agents' Mental Models*, Dissertation. Ann Arbor: University of Michigan.

Popper, K. R. (2004), *Conjectures and Refutations: The Growth of Scientific Knowledge*, London: Routledge.

Sugden, R. (1991), 'Rational Choice: A Survey of Contributions from Economics and Philosophy', *Economic Journal*, 101 (407), 751–85.

Tesfatsion, L. and Judd, K. L. (eds) (2006), *Handbook of Computational Economics: Agent-Based Computational Economics*, Amsterdam: North-Holland.

Thagard, P. (1992), 'Computing Coherence', in R. Giere (ed.) *Cognitive Models of Science, Minnesota Studies in the Philosophy of Science* Minneapolis: University of Minnesota Press, pp. 485–8.

Thagard, P. (2010), EMPATHICA: 'A Computer Support System with Visual Representations for Cognitive-affective Mapping', in K. McGregor (ed.) *Proceedings of the Workshop on Visual Reasoning and Representation*, Menlo Park, CA: AAAI Press, pp. 79–81.

Thagard, P. and Findlay, S. (forthcoming), 'Changing Minds About Climate Change: Belief Revision, Coherence and Emotion', in E. Olsson (ed.) *Science in Flux: Belief Revision in the Context of Scientific Inquiry*, Berlin: Springer.

Westley F. and Antadze N. (2010), 'Making a Difference: Strategies for Scaling Social Innovation for Greater Impact', *The Innovation Journal*, 15 (2).

Westley, F., Zimmerman, B. and Patton, M. (2006), *Getting to Maybe: How the World Is Changed*, Toronto: Random House Canada.

7
The 'Porcupine in the Room': Socio-Religious Entrepreneurs and Innovators within the Framework of Social Innovation

Randy M. Ataide

Introduction

In *Parerga und Paralipomena* (1851), Schopenhauer created a parable about the dilemma faced by porcupines in cold weather. He described a 'company of porcupines' who 'crowded themselves very close together one cold winter's day so as to profit by one another's warmth and so save themselves from being frozen to death. But soon they felt one another's quills, which induced them to separate again, and so on. The porcupines were 'driven backwards and forwards from one trouble to the other', until they found 'a mean distance at which they could most tolerably exist'. Freud, and others, would later pick up on Schopenhauer's metaphor related to the long-term nature of human relationships, and our desire to both crave and be repelled by intimacy and understanding in human relationships across cultures, settings, and times (see Prochnik, 2011).

In the same way, the pressing needs of society and our compulsion for intimacy often drives 'human porcupines' together, only to be mutually repelled by the many prickly and disagreeable qualities of our natures, beliefs, and motivations. Indeed, in many places it is hard to conceive of a more potentially 'disagreeable quality' than the issue of religion. Social, business, and scholarship codes of politeness and decorum typically sanitize conversations and considerations of religion, or if such bonds fail to hold we can easily polarize when it comes to social discourse and religion. This has been titled 'the privatization of religion' where 'Science therefore belongs in the public realm and can be appealed to in the public discourse, while religious faith is banished to the private sphere and its contribution to public discourse is gagged' (Avis, 2009, p. 353–4).

While it is certainly true that great progress has been made in the field of social innovation research, discovering the capacity to discuss differing and at times conflicting values and cultures, especially religion, remains a formidable and unresolved task for many scholars. 'The question of how to engage and incorporate values into social entrepreneurship and other development initiatives is a daunting one [as] the very conflicts that characterize hard places often emanate from and are expressed in the idiom of worldviews, both secular and religious' (Haskell et al., 2009, p. 536). It has also been argued that there is 'a danger in social entrepreneurship highlighting the business aspects of entrepreneurial approaches in contrast to voluntary and public sector approaches, and not placing enough emphasis on the inherently political nature of bringing about social change' (Grenier, 2002, p. 2).

This chapter is an attempt to expand the discussion beyond Foster's observation regarding religion in the UK: 'For many of course the Church of England has long been of no significance and its fate does not matter. Yet despite the need to raise human and financial resources to keep the Church itself going, it still so often has human and financial capacity over to offer for social objectives – it is only that it might do better with opportunities that it proactively encounters and otherwise seeks out' (Nicholls, 2006, p. 200). Similarly, a 1998 study on religion and entrepreneurship provided some affirmation of the theories of British secularization suggesting that the power of religion on entrepreneurial activity may not be a significant factor (Dodd and Seaman, 1998, p. 83). But there are contradictory signals when it comes to social entrepreneurship and religion: 'In the context of a pluralistic moral basis for entrepreneurship, both mainstream and religious sects continue to motivate, and provide strong links to legitimacy and resources for social entrepreneurs' (Keynes, 2007, p. 13).

This would suggest that questions of engaging and incorporating religion into the social entrepreneur dialogue should not be defined by any one particular geographical, ethnic, cultural tradition, or other setting of shared values. For example, in sharp contrast to the negative British attitudes on religion, during this same period religious interest continues to increase in other parts of the world. Despite formidable state restrictions on the practice of religious beliefs, active Chinese religious believers are estimated to exceed 100m, including not only Catholics and Protestants, but also a wide variety of other faiths including Buddhism, Daoism, Islam, and folk religions. Unregistered Christian 'house churches' are growing rapidly and are estimated to be at least double the number of patriotic registered Christian churches

(Potter, 2003). A study of several hundred US companies concluded that 92 per cent of executives and managers viewed religion or spirituality positively and most wanted more integration of religious practices into their lives and work, and that such integration would lead to enhanced profits and firm results (Mitroff and Denton, 1999). Interestingly, there is evidence that contemporary religious belief especially among Muslims and Christians in Europe is undergoing a sort of renaissance:

> After decades of secularization, religion in Europe has slowed its slide toward what had seemed inevitable oblivion. There are even nascent signs of a modest comeback ... and belief in heaven, hell and concepts such as the soul has risen in parts of Europe, especially among the young, according to surveys. Religion, once a dead issue, now figures prominently in public discourse.
>
> (Higgins, 2007)

It is the thesis of this chapter that while religious entrepreneurship and social entrepreneurship are fundamentally different, a category of actor exists where these two poles meet – that of the *socio-religious entrepreneur and innovator*. It is a response to the finding that while 'there is substantial evidence for high trust religious networks supporting entrepreneurship among smaller religious groups and sects, however there is not so much evidence of *social* entrepreneurship here' (Keynes, 2009, p. 12). This conclusion results from the lack of identification of a distinct sub-group of socio-religious entrepreneurship within social entrepreneurship. Social entrepreneurship serves as an appropriate, overall, definitional category and academic framework for a variety of hybrids and variations, and scholars and practitioners are increasingly entering into deeper conversations than was true in the early years of scholarship. Bill Drayton of Ashoka has suggested that the results-based, transformational, power of the citizen sector and a rapidly expanding pool of social entrepreneurs and innovators can change the world: 'This virtuous cycle, catalyzed by leading social entrepreneurs and local changemakers, is the chief engine now moving the world towards an "everyone a changemaker" future' (Drayton, 2006, p. 1). No matter how difficult or 'prickly', it is the contention of this chapter that Drayton's vision of 'everyone a changemaker' might include those involved in social entrepreneurship motivated and operating according to their religious beliefs and values, as well as those working towards environmental, social, humanitarian, altruistic, or other equally important and compelling objectives.

The problem of definition

Social entrepreneurship has been a focus of academic study since the 1980s across multiple fields and disciplines (Spear, 2006, p. 399 identified 20 distinct fields of study). Given the considerable range of scholarly approaches to the subject, it is, perhaps, unsurprising that the field lacks a common unifying theory or even definition of social entrepreneurship and innovation. Furthermore, the applied forms and frameworks for social entrepreneurship and innovation continue to develop and are likely to continue in the same process for the foreseeable future. Despite a multiplicity of definitions still in use across the scholarly community, four key elements of social entrepreneurship appear to have general support (Dees, 1998; Nicholls and Cho, 2006):

1. They advance a social mission.
2. They apply innovative processes and technologies.
3. They have a measurable and scalable impact.
4. They often integrate financial sustainability and demonstrate a pronounced, though often nuanced, market orientation.

Mair and Marti (2006, p. 4) summarized a range of definitions of social entrepreneurship to synthesize their own: 'it is a process that catalyzes social change and/or addresses important central needs in a way that is not dominated by direct financial benefits for the entrepreneurs'. Roberts and Woods proposed that 'social entrepreneurship is the construction, evaluation and pursuit of opportunities for transformative social change carried out by visionary, passionately dedicated individuals' and noted the tension between academic and practitioner definitions and terminology in the field (2005, pp. 48–9).

Outside of academe, the Global Entrepreneurship Monitor (GEM) provided a working definition of social entrepreneurship that addressed the intersection between social innovation and the market:

[S]ocial entrepreneurship is any attempt at new social enterprise activity or new enterprise creation, such as self-employment, a new enterprise, or the expansion of an existing social enterprise by an individual, team of individuals or established social enterprise, with social or community goals as its base and where the profit is invested in the activity or venture itself rather than returned to investors.

(Harding, 2007 p. 11)

A hybrid definition has been developed from the GEM and Roberts and Woods's definitions that suggested that 'social entrepreneurship is a revenue generating, innovative and unique approach to solving a social problem where profits are reinvested in the mission regardless of the structural distinction between nonprofit or commercial enterprise' (Lucas, 2010, p. 14).

In 2007, Martin and Osberg argued that the field lacked appropriate definition and was overly broad and inclusive. They held that social entrepreneurship should build upon the foundational principles of entrepreneurship, namely the combination of context, opportunity, personal characteristics, and the creation of a particular outcome. The authors suggested that social entrepreneurship is best defined as processes that aim to change a stable but inherently unjust equilibrium and forge a more socially just stable equilibrium.

While it is clearly important that scholarship in the field of social entrepreneurship and innovation should broaden its focus beyond the setting of definitions alone, in doing so there is a need to remain open to new thinking that can shape these definitions. It may well be that religion remains a complicated, generally overlooked, and 'porcupine-like' variable that, nevertheless, has relevance for better understanding issues of interest in the field of (social) innovation such as individual motivation and models of enterprise creation. Indeed, the matter of religion and entrepreneurship has been properly identified as a 'thorny and unresolved issue' and that 'although the entrepreneurship literatures suggest that value structures may form an important construct in a theory of entrepreneurship behavior, their magnitude and overall importance is still relatively unknown' (Dodd and Seaman, 1998, p. 71). The next section develops this point further.

Religious and socio-religious entrepreneurs

Certain historical figures or groups have been identified both as religious and entrepreneurial: indeed, many could be seen, in today's language, as path-finding 'social entrepreneurs'. These include a range of Roman Catholics, Jews, Quakers, Muslims, and Hindus (Bornstein, 2004, pp. 240–7; Spear, 2007, pp. 5–10). Much of this research has been recently classified as 'Values-Driven Entrepreneurship', building upon Weber's influential thesis of Protestantism and the rise of capitalism (Spear, 2007, pp. 1–3). However, there is little published research concerning how religious beliefs impact the ordinary entrepreneur, social or otherwise, or conversely how entrepreneurship impacts the religious community. There is even less information on the relationship between religious entrepreneurs and non-religious entrepreneurs. While religion is obviously a component of private religious universities throughout the world – and some public universities devote curriculum and research time to religious issues across various subject areas – business and management scholars have generally ignored religion as an important component of better understanding entrepreneurial activities. Indeed, contemporary business textbooks on entrepreneurship typically ignore religion and its relationship to entrepreneurship.[1] Conversely, social entrepreneurship has a very limited presence within the teaching of private Christian universities and colleges across the world. A survey of the United States found that only 17 of the 109 members of the Council of Christian Colleges and Universities currently offer courses in social entrepreneurship, and only three member institutions offer either a BA or BSc degree in social entrepreneurship (Lucas, 2010, p. 16).

It is clear today that 'entrepreneurship' is being extended well beyond its original application to business activities alone. There is wide discussion of 'intellectual entrepreneurship', a cross-disciplinary approach to undergraduate education,[2] as well as 'norm entrepreneurship' (meaning the use of political scandals to effect cultural change utilized by lower-level French governmental officers).[3] Of particular relevance here, adherents of modern secular or humanist movements are sometimes known as 'spiritual entrepreneurs' (Goossen, 2004, p. 48), and the phrase 'religious entrepreneurship' has been applied to the origins of jihad.[4] However, despite this, there is only a limited discussion of religious entrepreneurship currently available in the scholarly literature and definitions are few. However, one example is as follows: 'religious entrepreneurs can be differentiated by two drivers: the extent that success of the organization is measured by monetary rewards, and the extent that the organization's operations are guided by the owners' religions' (Goossen, 2004, p. 53). However, there remains no widely accepted definition of religious entrepreneurship. Part of this is because some definitions have included religious entrepreneurship as examples of businesses that sell religious goods and services or which operate religious camps and schools. As will be illustrated in the following section, while these individuals and organizations may well possess some entrepreneurial elements, they should be excluded from serious consideration as social entrepreneurs for they do not have *as a primary goal* the advancement of a social vision, beyond offering a product or service that is religious in its nature, type, or substance. This chapter suggests that, while religious entrepreneurs are distinct from social entrepreneurs, there exists a hybrid category of entrepreneurs linking religious motivation with socially entrepreneurial behavior and models.

So, how can a classification be developed for those entrepreneurial individuals and organizations working from a religious motivation, foundation, or framework? A potential starting point is to review some of the other working definitions of religious entrepreneurship, for example:

- A religious entrepreneur is an opportunity exploiter typically focused upon a specific set of products or services for niche markets (Bradley et al., 2007, 12–13).
- A high-trust religious network supportive of entrepreneurial activity (Spear, 2007).
- An organized group such as the Salvation Army with a stated mission 'to preach the gospel of Jesus Christ and to meet human needs in His name without discrimination'.[5]
- Religious entrepreneurial activity for the benefit of a specific community and operating in direct furtherance of broader religious purposes and system, such as Islamic Entrepreneurship.[6]
- Someone who uses entrepreneurial endeavors as the vehicle through which to satisfy their spiritual desire for meaning and purpose in life (Goossen, 2004, p. 39).

For the purposes of this chapter, it is apparent that the first two of these definitions are not suitable for further consideration in the context of social entrepreneurship and innovation, because additional examination shows either little evidence of any connection between this form of entrepreneurship and social entrepreneurial activities (Spear 2007, p. 12), or that their products and services are primarily a method of self-employment and not to further social causes or needs more widely. In other words, they are a sub-group of traditional entrepreneurship and not social entrepreneurship per se. As to organizations such as the Salvation Army, while they have a long and rich history of social causes and service 'without discrimination', there is no separating this mission from the stated purpose of personal religious renewal in those who serve. For Islamic Entrepreneurship, its activities are often placed in the context of furthering Islamic economic practices and establishing Islamic economics.

The definition offered by Goossen – the 'Spirituality Model' of entrepreneurship – appears to have some merit as a working definition for use in this chapter. However, Goossen went to great lengths to critique his own model as being a self-interpreting, personal narrative rather than an association with a recognized religious group or organization. The ultimate focus, Goossen concluded, is on self rather than on others, something which is broadly incompatible with the mission of most social entrepreneurship and innovation (Goossen 2004, pp. 48–9).

This chapter proposes that there exists across these various definitions of religious and social entrepreneurs another category: *the socio-religious entrepreneur*. These entrepreneurs can be defined as entrepreneurial individuals or groups who by virtue of their personal and shared religious values and ideology are compelled to create social enterprises with the primary goal of achieving non-religious social purposes. This definition of entrepreneurship combines both social and religious elements and embodies:

- widely accepted entrepreneurial components
- a common and well-defined set of religious values
- religious values which motivate and propel social entrepreneurial activities
- a religious mission present but subordinated to the social enterprise purposes
- substantially similar entrepreneurial components unique to social entrepreneurs

Figure 7.1 demonstrates that the three types of entrepreneurship illustrated here all share Martin and Osberg's (2007) common entrepreneurial elements of context, characteristics, and outcomes. Socio-religious entrepreneurs are generally similar to social entrepreneurs except for a religious mission, but this remains subordinated to the social mission. However, it is clear that religious entrepreneurship does not identify with social entrepreneurship in any significant way beyond these common elements and is typically highly focused on its products, customers, and markets.

This issue is not merely one of semantics, respect, or inclusion; rather, it is important prima facie to the social entrepreneur and social innovator. There is emerging support for a more positive view of the role of religion and vocation within society, even within the academy, which is only reinforced by the recent assertion that 'companies built on belief systems tend to outlast those without them, boding well for ventures founded on a system of religion such as Christianity' (Bradley et al., 2007, pp. 3–4). Simply stated, 'religion both shapes and is shaped by society' and 'investigating the relationship between the individual's

Religious Entrepreneurs	Socio-Religious Entrepreneurs	Social Entrepreneurs
• Religious mission primary • Ambiguous social mission • Niche products • Niche markets • Religious enclaves • Exclusive	• Social mission primary • Religious and other missions secondary (influence, conversion, etc.) • Identifiable social entrepreneur components • Inclusive	• Social mission primary • Other Missions Secondary (public policy, opinion, economic policy, etc.) • Identifiable social entrepreneur components • Inclusive
Common Entrepreneurial Contexts, Characteristics and Outcomes		

Figure 7.1   A typology of socio-religious entrepreneurs

religion and enterprise shows that religion affects a believer's entrepreneurial activity, influencing their decision to become an entrepreneur, enterprise management, and the entrepreneur's contact network' (Dodd and Seaman 1998, p. 71).

Beyond these general observations, it is also likely that in many situations the social and socio-religious entrepreneur do very similar work and that there must be opportunities for both to come together to develop new and enhanced value creation. In the current era of economic uncertainty with escalating needs and opportunities and declining resources, it is in the interests of both socio-religious and social entrepreneurs alike mutually to support one another and to converse and connect.

Socio-religious entrepreneurs in context

Examples of the interfaces between entrepreneurship and faith/spirituality serve to illustrate a new socio-religious context for innovation. Countries including Turkey and Malaysia have been at the forefront of a movement in the Islamic world to begin a serious, significant, and official consideration of what in the *hadith* (i.e. the words and deeds of the prophet Muhammad) is historical and what is cultural. As but one example, a group of theologians at Ankara University is examining early Islamic sources in order to distinguish core elements from the accretions of later history: 'a believer **can** well accept that there are problems in the 'cultural baggage' of Islam – and that the time has come to deal with them'.[7] Prominent Christian author Alan Roxburgh strikes a similar note with respect to the ineffectiveness of contemporary Christian churches:

> The old skills and identities no longer work but there are, as yet, neither new skills nor identities. This is the ambiguous sense of being out of control, exposed and unable to see what the demand and chall-enges might be that have to be faced. Because of this tension, the instinct to create the illusion that little has changed, or to integrate change resources into current organizations is very high.
>
> (Roxburgh and Regele, 2000, p. 66)

Roxburgh and Regele asserted that this was not a situation that requires only minor adjustments and course corrections, but a fundamental rethinking of the frameworks and paradigms that have shaped the church over the last half-century (ibid.). Moreover, *Time Magazine* observed of Rick Warren, best-selling author and pastor of one of the largest Christian churches in the United States: 'he is both leading and riding the newest wave of change in the Evangelical community: an expansion beyond social conservatism to causes such as battling poverty, opposing torture and combating global warming'. The piece went on to describe Warren's evaluation of the Presidential candidates in 2008: 'there will be no Christian religion test. I want what's good for everybody, not just what's good for me' (Van Biema, 2008, p. 38).

Beyond the reformation efforts of theological and religious organiza-tions, there are other innovations evident in many countries linked to entrepreneurship and religion. For example, in contemporary India, it has been observed that:

> Tamil leaders are abandoning traditional dynastic business and re-structuring enterprises through Japanese or American business plans and management techniques. This brings them into dialogue with contemporary global Islam in its reformist and modernist trends. Their preoccupations of how to shift the Muslim community away from practices or lifestyles considered 'backward' and towards modern Islam is what marks out the parameters of their life goals ... [and] entrepreneurship can stand at the core of a Muslim identity and of contemporary reformulations of Muslim morality.
>
> (Osella, 2007, p. 9)

Similarly, Malaysia has recently taken steps to position itself as a bridge between Muslim countries and the United States, pointing to its capacity to use Islamic entrepreneurial principles to foster better understanding between Islamic and non-Islamic economic systems and countries.[8]

In the area of university curricula, religious approaches and frameworks to economic, business, and entrepreneurial issues are on the rise. In the United States, a prominent American Protestant voice has been 'Business as Mission' (BAM), which is based on the principle of developing an holistic mission that attempts to bring all aspects of life and holiness into an organic whole and includes 'business related issues such as economic development, employment and unemployment, economic justice and the use and distribution of natural and creative resources among the human family'.[9] Among private universities, Regent University's Center for Entrepreneurship is a good example of a business school that has extensively incorporated BAM into their mission and curriculum.[10] Furthermore, to keep up with the demand for graduates with skills in Islamic finance, Western universities are increasingly offering courses and even graduate degrees in the subject.[11]

These efforts underscore the reality that religions do not represent monolithic groups of people with a common belief, world outlook, or identity. While at a very basic level of understanding there are certain religious tenets of a commonly held set of beliefs, the applications of these beliefs vary greatly among many categories including gender, geography, socio-economic background, nationality, and age (Keynes 2007, 186–98). As noted in the introduction to this chapter, there are wide differences in the positive and negative effects of religion in two countries that share much in common; the UK and the United States. However, in comparing the differences between various regional religious practices, it has been observed that 'church buildings tend to claim a relatively central site in both settings, but with a crucial difference. In the Eurasian instances, a single structure almost always dominates the scene, whereas in the United States we find multiple denominations and their quarters manifested at or near the center, generally, inter alia, Methodist, Episcopal, Presbyterian, Baptist, Lutheran, United Church of Christ, and, depending on the region, Roman Catholic' (Zelinksy 2001, p. 566). This underscores the decentralized and dispersed nature of religious organizations in the United States, something quite different from many other countries. The rapid growth over recent years in the number of Islamic mosques, non-denominational and interdenominational Christian congregations, and scores of other emerging religious groups can be added to this diversity in understanding contemporary religious practices.

While it is not a great surprise that research on religious entrepreneurship has asserted that religious beliefs have led entrepreneurs to play significant roles in the formation of religions (Stark and Bainbridge, 1987; Lu, 2005), it is probably not as widely expected that Christians appear to be attracted to entrepreneurship for similar reasons as others who seek to bring about change and share common values (Murphy, 2006). For other religious groups, including those outside of mainline Christianity such as Quakers, Mennonites, and the Amish, or in the case of non-Christian religions such as Islam and Judaism, entrepreneurship has often been a way of responding to prejudice and a practice of mutual support in a dominant, alien culture (Aldrich and Zimmer, 1985, p. 14; Granju, 1997). Internationally, a large-scale study of nearly 90,000 workers in India examined the influence of religion on the decision to become an entrepreneur. The study found that not only was religion an important determinant of entrepreneurial decision making but that, following Weber, some religions such as Islam and Christianity, were more conducive to entrepreneurship while other world religions tended to inhibit entrepreneurial activities (Audretsch et al., 2007).

There are also numerous organizational and practical examples of newly imagined religious frameworks, paradigms, and innovations across many faiths throughout the world. For example, the Indian Muslim Welfare Centre in Batley, West Yorkshire (UK) is an affiliation of six neighborhood organizations founded in the 1960s. Originally a place of worship, it evolved to cover a range of cultural needs for the local Asian community including elder care, women's support, youth services, training, weddings, funerals, and health education. The Centre's goal is to generate income to be self-sufficient, which is a distinguishing characteristic from traditional religious charities (Thompson et al., 2000, p. 328; Foster, 2006). In the Philippines, the Catholic University of Santo Tomas, Manila, created the Entrepreneurship and Ethics Education Towards Equity Program in the 1990s. The Program's mission is that 'The Triple E Program is a center of excellence that forms entrepreneurs who, inspired by the ideals of ethics, social responsibility and social justice, serve low income groups with goods, services and paid work' (Loanzan, 2007, p. 345). In Ramallah on the West Bank of Israel, one of the most war-torn and religiously tense areas of the world, small and medium-size enterprises dominate the economy and it was recently noted that 'Indeed, the IMF has reported that the Palestinian economy is on track to grow 8% in 2010. Israeli and Palestinian negotiators may equivocate over peace, but an economy is breaking out in the West Bank.'[12]

There are, clearly, many potential points of connection between socio-religious entrepreneurship and social entrepreneurship. To illustrate this, the next section of this chapter presents an analysis of three examples of existing socio-religious organizations that deal with identifiable socially entrepreneurial goals and objectives. These examples demonstrate the similarities between socially and socio-religiously entrepreneurial organizations. The examples provided will be in the provision of clean water to the world's poor, fair-trade coffee, and education for African nationals.

Socio-religious entrepreneurs in context

WaterPartners International is a United States-based, non-profit organization committed to providing safe drinking water and sanitation to people in developing countries. Working in partnership with donors and local communities, it has helped thousands of people develop accessible, sustainable, community-level water supplies.[13] Co-founded by Gary White and actor Matt Damon, the organization has a long history of doing significant and transformational service in addressing this formidable problem in many countries and regions.

Similarly, Healing Waters International states that 'we affect lasting change in the cities of developing countries with passion, entrepreneurship and creativity by providing safe water through local partners'.[14] However, a further look at the website of Healing Waters International reveals that it is a Christian organization: they describe their vision as 'to see safe water provided in the name of Jesus in every poor community of the world'. However, it is also made clear that the organization, both in policy and practice, 'will work with any individual or organization that wants to help us provide affordable, safe water to the poor including churches, companies, foundations and civic organizations'.[15] WaterPartners International and Healing Waters International are strikingly similar in every other way bar this reference to religion.

A second example is that of Fair Trade, which is defined as 'a trading partnership, based on dialogue, transparency and respect that seek greater equity in international trade. It contributes to sustainable development by offering better trading conditions to, and securing the rights of, marginalized producers and workers – especially in the South. Fair Trade Organizations, backed by consumers, are engaged actively in supporting producers, awareness raising and in campaigning for changes in the rules and practice of conventional international trade'.[16] A prominent example of social entrepreneurs engaged in Fair Trade coffee is Dean's Beans, based in Orange, MA, United States. The firm states that, 'besides only roasting organic coffees, Dean's Beans only purchases beans from villages and importers that are committed to Fair Trade and working towards better economic opportunity, improved health and nutrition in the villages. We promote local empowerment and self-reliance through our <u>Fair Trade purchases</u> and our work with <u>local grassroots development</u> and human rights groups'.[17]

A similar Fair Trade coffee firm is Equal Exchange, founded in 1986 and located about 100 miles from Dean's Beans in West Bridgeport, MA. This organization defines itself as follows:

> Equal Exchange has created *Big Change* since 1986. Our founders envisioned a food system that empowers farmers and consumers, supports small farmer co-ops, and uses sustainable farming methods. They started with fairly traded coffee from Nicaragua and didn't look back. Today, we continue to find new and powerful ways to build a better food system. We partner with co-operatives of farmers who provide high-quality organic coffees, teas, chocolates and snacks from farmers all over the world. [18]

The only indication that that there is any difference between Dean's Beans and Equal Exchange is in the listing of the Interfaith Coffee Program on Equal Exchange's website, where it states that it 'works in partnership with faith-based relief, development and human rights organizations to help communities of faith learn about and promote Fair Trade'.[19] The religious motivations behind Equal Exchange can only be inferred from statements like 'not all coffee is equal, and it is important for Christians to link consumptive choices to take care of the global economic household. The basic assumption of the Interfaith Coffee Program is that Christians should and do care, and will in fact vote redemptively in the marketplace when given the information and opportunity to do so'.[20]

A final area of comparison is that of education in Africa. Dr Senyo Adjibolosoo, Professor of Economics at Point Loma Nazarene University, is a native Ghanaian who frequently returns to his home African country. In 1999, Adjibolosoo, who is a Christian, developed the theory of 'The Human Factor' that has a basic thesis suggesting that leadership is fundamentally a reflection of personal ethics. He has since expanded his Human Factor theory into a number of books, articles, and curricula for undergraduates. In 2006, Adjibolosoo started the Human

Factor Leadership Academy (HFLA) in Akatsi, Ghana. This initiative was defined as follows:

> [O]ur vision is to improve Human Quality ... We believe the world can be a better place for all humanity, and are dedicated to improving the human condition through our academy. Our programs will generate honest and compassionate leaders who will transform lives through knowledge acquisition and its application through clear understanding. Most educational institutions concentrate on schooling rather than education. Our primary goal is to use our curriculum and methods of transformational development education to accomplish our vision and mission at the HFLA.[21]

The non-profit organization Educate! offers a similar model of education for Africa. It states that its mission is 'to educate and empower the next generation of socially responsible leaders in Africa', and with its five core values of personal leadership, innovation, ethical action, powerful relationships, and exponential empowerment, the organization achieves its educational goals: '[T]hrough the study of leadership and social entrepreneurship, Educate! equips scholars with the knowledge and vision to create a vision of positive change'.[22] As with the HFLA, it has a US base of operations to support its Uganda focus, and has developed key strategic partnerships. There is great similarity between both organizations, except for Dr Adjibolosoo's statement of personal religious beliefs.

It is important to note that Healing Waters International, Equal Exchange, and the HFLA all have a global vision, one which has specific outcomes that are large-scale and envision a systems change towards a new, stable equilibrium (cf. Osberg and Martin, 2007). Nor are these three examples tied to the individual or founder – all have sought from the inception to create financial sustainability through strategic alliances, network building, and connections with multiple stakeholders. Each example operates in multiple countries or regions yet each is motivated, organized, and functions according to clear religious beliefs. Notwithstanding their religious motivation and support, Healing Waters, Equal Exchange, and the HFLA are nearly identical to their 'non-religious' counterparts. Each of these organizations and many others is highly entrepreneurial as well as having clearly defined social entrepreneurial objectives. All three do not aim at religious proselytizing and their religious motivations are subtly portrayed and projected.

The comparison between the organizations illustrates precisely what Martin and Osberg identified: 'having created a definition of social entrepreneurship and distinguished it from social service provision and social activism, we should recognize in practice, many social actors incorporate strategies associated with these pure forms or create hybrid models' (Martin and Osberg, 2007, p. 38). Moreover, the authors noted that 'in the real world, there are probably more hybrid models than pure forms' (ibid.). This is precisely what can be observed with socio-religious entrepreneurship here.

Conclusion

Dodd and Seaman (1998) emphasized the social constructionist impact of religion: 'it [religion] supports power structures, gives meaning and shape to a society's ethical structures, rewards and punishes certain kinds of behavior: providing norms for social action ... religion [also] explains and justifies social institutions and social roles' (p. 71). From this perspective, the entrepreneur's belief systems are often the product of normative, cultural contexts In societies where religion plays a significant role, personal motivation, including religious motivation, is often the link between socially entrepreneurial action and the socio-religious entrepreneur. As Gerard and Zahra (2007) noted, 'culture is an important and complex construct. Likewise, entrepreneurship captures a wide spectrum of activities and is multifaceted ... The addition of social institutions to the repertoire of cultural icons is a step forward in behavioral research on the nexus of culture and entrepreneurship' (p. 6). The linkage between religion and personal motivation is clear, 'the meaning system provided by religion and the sacred symbols of a religion bring together or synthesize a people's ethos – the tone, character, and quality of their life, its moral and aesthetic style and mood – and their world view' (Geertz, 1985, p. 67). The socio-religious world view can, thus, transcend traditional religious functions, methods, and models and embrace other spheres of action and institutional logics.

This does not mean that socio-religious entrepreneurs are non committal about their religion: rather it is that the religious model provides a personal or collective world view, which then develops particular motivations that lead to social entrepreneurial activities: as Goossen (2004) noted, 'a worldview is simply the sum total of our beliefs about the world, the big picture that directs our daily decisions and actions' (p. 49). Also the socio-religious entrepreneur's resource base, leadership, and support structures are primarily from other like-minded religious individuals and organizations whose own personal values resonate with the mission of the enterprise.

Prothero (2010) has written of the need for religious literacy as opposed to religious knowledge, and noted that while faith is more 'robust' in the United States it is not an irrelevant force in Europe and elsewhere (p. 7). He went on to suggest that religions should be an important part of public education and discourse, including higher education across many disciplines (Prothero, 2010, pp. 17–18). Avis (2009) contended: 'It is dangerous for religion to be banished to the dark corners of private life, for there abuses and fanaticism will flourish unchecked. Religion needs public exposure, but for this to happen its tenets must be taken sufficiently seriously to be discussed and argued about' (p. 353).

Similarly, the opportunities and challenges to social and socio-religious entrepreneurs are formidable yet the rewards may be great. Within their own different spheres of activity, each may be engaged in very similar activities. It is a key conclusion of this chapter that the divergent voices, interests, organizations, religions, professions, and disciplines that have, perhaps, viewed each other with skepticism or ignorance in the past could now usefully engage in a fresh dialogue. This attitude and willingness to explore common interests could be an appropriate meeting ground for socio-religious entrepreneurs and social entrepreneurs to exchange ideas, models, and inspiration.

On Freud's desk in Austria, adjacent to his famous couch, there is a bronze porcupine, a gift from an American friend to remind him of Schopenhauer's parable of the company of porcupines. It is a heavy and somewhat foreboding creature, and in no way does it appear to be something that attractive to touch. However, it holds a surprise for those who dare to touch it: while the spines are indeed needle-like when they are softly touched they produce a melodic, harp-like sound. This capacity is hidden from those who care only to glance at the porcupine's quills.[23] Religious beliefs and organizations generally, and socio-religious entrepreneurs particularly, should not be ignored in the study of social entrepreneurship for they too have the capacity to participate in the diverse and multi-faceted music of social innovation and change in the future.

Notes

1. For example, popular collegiate textbooks on entrepreneurship that fail to even mention religious issues or beliefs and entrepreneurship include: Steve Mariotti, *Entrepreneurship: Starting and Operating a New Business*, Prentice Hall, New Jersey (2006); Peggy A. Lambing and Charles R. Kuehl, *Entrepreneurship* (94th edn), Prentice Hall, New Jersey (2007); Bruce R. Barringer and R. Duane

Ireland, *Entrepreneurship: Successfully Launching New Ventures* (2nd edn), Prentice Hall, New Jersey (2008).

2. The University of Texas at Austin, 'Intellectual Entrepreneurship: A Cross-Disciplinary Consortium' Accessed on October 19, 2008 at https://webspace. utexas.edu/cherwitz/www/ie/.

3. Ari Adut 'Scandal as Norm Entrepreneurship Strategy: Corruption and the French Investigating Magistrates', *Theory and Society* 33 (October 2004): 529–78.

4. Joshua Sinai, 'Religious Entrepreneurs: A Study in the Origins of Jihad.' *Washington Times*, July 24, 2007. Accessed 12 September, 2011 at http://www. washingtontimes.com/news/2007/jul/24/religious-entrepreneurs-10349648.

5. The mission statement of the Salvation Army. Accessed November 11, 2010 at http://www.salvationarmy.org/ihq/www_sa.nsf/ce952dea4507ee7780256c f4005d2254/2af3956053a88a5e80256d4e003b4965!OpenDocument.

6. Nawawi Mohd Jan. Theories and Concepts of Islamic Entrepreneurship, Course Module. Accessed October 4, 2010 at www.perlis.uitm.edu.my

7. Mustafa Aykol. 'Turkey's Islamic Reform: Roots and Reality', *Open Democracy*, March 4, 2008. Accessed October 11, 2010 at http://www.opendemocracy. net/article/democracy_power/future_turkey/islamic_reform_roots_reality

8. 'Malaysia can Promote Islamic Entrepreneurship.' April 10, 2010. *The Star Online*. Accessed October 19, 2010 at file://localhost/U:/Data/Missional Religious Entrepreneurship/Malaysian Islamic Entrepreneurship.htm

9. Regent Center for Entrepreneurship, Regent University, 'Definition of Business as Mission (BAM)'. Accessed October 5, 2008 at http://www.regen tentrepreneur.org/paradigm.html.

10. Regent Center for Entrepreneurship, Regent University, 'Resources & Research.' Accessed October 5, 2008 at http://www.regententrepreneur.org/ index.html

11. Hariett Swain. 'Islamic Finance Gives Universities a Boost', The Guardian Online, July 28, 2009. Accessed October 9, 2010 at http://www.guardian. co.uk/education/2009/jul/28/business-schools-islamic-finance

12. Accessed October 10, 2011 at http://www.time.com/time/magazine/ article/0,9171,2024235,00.html#ixzz1aR4vcLEj.

13. WaterPartners International, Water.org, 'About Us.' Accessed May 19, 2009 at http://www.water.org/

14. Healing Waters International, 'About'. Accessed May 19, 2009 at http://www. healingwatersintl.org/abouts/view/stuff-people-always-ask-us

15. Healing Waters International, 'About' (ibid.).

16. European Fair Trade Association, 'EFTA: Joining Fair Trade Forces'. Accessed May 20, 2009 at http://www.european-fair-trade-association.org/efta/Doc/ What.pdf

17. Dean's Beans, 'Fair Trade Roadmap'. Accessed May 20, 2009 at http://www. deansbeans.com/coffee/fair_trade_roadmap.html. Equal Exchange, 'About Our Co-Op'. Accessed May 20, 2009 at http://www.equalexchange.coop/our-co-op

18. Equal Exchange, Ibid.

19. Equal Exchange, 'Interfaith Program.' Accessed May 20, 2009 at http://www. equalexchange.coop/interfaith-program

20. Equal Exchange, Ibid.

21. 'Human Factor Leadership Academy on Target for Completion', *Business Wire*. Accessed May 20, 2009 at http://www.allbusiness.com/education-training/education-systems-institutions/11762880-1.html
22. Educate! Empowering Africa's Future Leaders, 'Educate! Concept Paper'. Accessed May 20, 2009 at http://www.experienceeducate.org/storage/Concept Paper.pdf
23. George Prochnik. 'The Porcupine Illusion' (ibid.).

References

Aldrich, H. and Zimmer, C. (1985),'Entrepreneurship through Social Networks', in *The Art and Science of Entrepreneurship*, edited by Raymond Smilor and Donald Sexton, Cambridge: Ballinger.

Audretsch, David B., Boente, W. and Tamvada, Jagannadha P. (2007), Religion and Entrepreneurship. Jena Economic Research Papers in Economics, Friedrich-Schiller-University Jena, Max-Planck-Institute of Economics, pp. 2007–75.

Avis, P. (2009), 'Review of Religion in Public Life: Must Faith be Privatized?', by R. Trigg, *Ecclesiastical Law Society*, 11(3), pp. 352–3.

Berger, P. L., Berger, B. and Kellner, H. (1973), *The Homeless Mind: Modernization and Consciousness*, New York, NY: Random House.

Biema, D. Van (2008), 'The Global Ambition of Rick Warren', *Time Magazine*, 18 August 2008.

Bornstein, D. (2005), *So You Want to Change the World?* Toronto: Hart House.

Bradley, Don B. III, Drinkwater, Dawn, Rubach, Michael J. (2007), 'Spiritual and Religious Entrepreneurs: Studying Christian Entrepreneurs as Opportunity Exploiters and Social Entrepreneurs', paper presented at the International Conference of the Academy of Entrepreneurship, Jacksonville, Florida, 11–14 April 2007. (Unpublished paper.)

Creswell, J. W. (2008), *Research Design: Qualitative, Quantitative and Mixed Methods*, Approaches Thousand Oaks: Sage.

Dees, J. G. (1998), 'The Meaning of 'Social Entrepreneurship', Report for the Kauffman Centre for Entrepreneurial Leadership, Accessed on 14 November 2011 at: http://www.fuqua.duke.edu/centers/case/documents/dees_SE.pdf.

Dodd, S. Drakopoulo and Seaman, P. T. (1998), 'Religion and Enterprise: An Introductory Explanation', *Entrepreneurship Theory and Practice*, 23 (1) (Fall 1998), pp. 71–87.

Drayton, B. (2007), *Everyone a Changemaker*, Boston: MIT Press.

Evans, D., Vos, Ronald J. and Wright, K. P. (2003), *Biblical Holism and Agriculture*, Pasadena: William Carey Press.

Geertz, C. (1985), *Religion as a Cultural System in Religion and Ideology*, Edited by R. Bocock and K. Thompson. Manchester: Manchester University Press.

Gerard, G. and Zahra, S. A. (2002), 'Culture and Its Consequences for Entre-preneurship', *Entrepreneurship Theory and Practice*, 26 (4) (Summer 2002), pp. 5–9.

Golstein, J. A., Hazy, J. K. and Silberstang, J., ed. (2009), 'Complexity Science & Social Entrepreneurship: Adding Social Value Through Systems Thinking', 3, Litchfield, AZ: ISCE Publishing, pp. 529–58.

Goossen, R. J. (2004), 'Entrepreneurship and The Meaning of Life', *The Journal of Biblical Integration in Business*, Fall 2004, 11, pp. 21–74.

Granovetter, M. (2000), 'The Economic Sociology of Firms and Entrepreneurs', *Entreprenership: The Social Science View*, 11, pp. 244–75.

Grenier, P. (2002), 'The Function of Social Entrepreneurship in the UK', Draft paper presented at the ISTR Conference, Cape Town, July 2002.

Harding, R. (2007), 'Understanding Social Entrepreneurship', *Industry & Higher Education*, 21 (1), pp. 73–84.

Haskell, D. L., Haskell, J. H. and Kwong, J. W. (2007), 'Spiritual Resources for Change in Hard Places: A Values-Driven Social Entrepreneurship Theory of Change', in *Complexity Science & Social Entrepreneurship*, Vol. 3.

Goldstein, J., Hazy, J. and Higgins, A. (2007), 'In Europe, God is (Not) Dead', *Wall Street Journal*, 14 July 2007, A1.

Silberstang, J. (eds) (2009), *Complexity Science and Social Entrepreneurship*: *Adding Social Value through Systems Thinking*. A Volume in the *Exploring Organizational Complexity Series*: Volume 3. Edited by: Jeffrey A. Goldstein, James K. Hazy and Joyce Silberstang. (2009) ISCE Publishing, Litchfield Park, AZ.

Keynes, M. (2007), 'Religion and Value-Driven Social Entrepreneurship', Conference Presentation, 3rd International Social Entrepreneurship Research Conference, Copenhagen Business School, Frederiksberg, Denmark, 18–19 June 2007.

Lindsay, D. M. (2008), 'Evangelicalism Rebounds in Academe', *The Chronicle of Higher Education*, 9 May 2008.

Loanzan, J. (2007), 'Toward Equity: The Poor and University Students', *Political Theology*, 8 (3), pp. 341–70.

Lucas, T. (2010), 'Social Entrepreneurship: Exploring the Link between Concept, Definition and Application in Christian University Business Programs', Paper Presentation at the Christian Business Faculty Association, Southeastern University, Lakeland, Florida, October 2010.

Mair, J. and Marti, I. (2006) 'Social Entrepreneurship Research: A Source of Explanation, Prediction and Delight', IESE Business School, Navarra, Spain. Revised April 2005.

Martin, R. and Osberg, S. (2007), 'Social Entrepreneurship: The Case for Definition', *Stanford Social Innovation Review*, 5, 2 (Spring 2007), pp. 29–39.

Mitroff, I. and Denton, E. A. (1999), *A Spiritual Audit of Corporate America: A Hard Look at Spirituality, Religion, and Values in the Workplace*, San Francisco: Jossey-Bass.

Mohd Jan, N. B. (2009) 'Theories and Concepts of Entrepreneurship', Course lecture and presentation for Entrepreneurship 300.

Nicholls, A. (ed.) (2006), *Social Entrepreneurship: New Models of Sustainable Social Change*, Oxford: Oxford University Press.

Nicholls, A. and Cho, A. (2006), Social Entrepreneurship: The Structuration of a Field', in A. Nicholls (ed.) *Social Entrepreneurship: New Models of Sustainable Social Change*, Oxford: Oxford University Press, pp. 99–118.

Osella, C. and Osella, F. (2007), 'Muslim Entrepreneurs between India and the Gulf', *ISIM Review*, 19, Spring 2007.

Potter, P. B. (2003), 'Belief in Control: Regulation of Religion in China', *The China Quarterly*, No. 174, Religion in China Today (June 2003), pp. 317–37.

Prochnik, G. (2011), 'The Porcupine Illusion', Accessed 20 November 2010 at http:www.cabinetmagazine.org/issues/26/prochnik.php.

Roberts, D. and Woods, C. (2005), 'Changing the World on a Shoestring: The Concept of Social Entrepreneurship', University of Auckland Business Review, 7 (1), pp. 45–51.

Roxburgh, A. and Regele, M. (2000), *Crossing the Bridge: Church Leadership in a Time of Change*, Chicago: Percept Group.

Spear, R. (2006), 'Social Entrepreneurship: A Different Model?', *International Journal of Social Economics*, 33 (5/6), pp. 399–410.

Thompson, J., Alvy, G. and Lees, A. (2000), Social Entrepreneurship – A New Look at the People and the Potential', *Management Decision*, 38 (5), pp. 328–38.

Zelinsky, W. (2001), 'The Uniqueness of the American Religious Landscape', *The Geographical Review*, 91 (3), pp. 565–88.

8
Social Entrepreneurs in the Social Innovation Ecosystem

Heather Cameron

Introduction

This chapter uses social innovation as an analytical concept (Phills et al., 2008) to explore the socially entrepreneurial ecosystem (Bloom and Dees, 2008). Specifically, this chapter aims to contribute to a better understanding of the processes in this ecosystem by investigating how social entrepreneurs emerge and how they locate themselves with regards to the social innovation ecosystem and universities in particular. These issues will be approached from two perspectives: theoretically and through empirical research.

The concept of the social entrepreneur will be compared with another social agent: the 'specific intellectual' proposed by Foucault (1984b). This comparison with an established social agent allows the strengths, weaknesses, and risks to the social entrepreneur to be seen in a different light than previous comparisons to conventional entrepreneurs or social activists. The specific intellectual, like the social entrepreneur, is a reaction to older forms of social agency, in this case the heroic universal intellectual. This chapter will compare the specific intellectual with the social entrepreneur in the following four respects: function, methods, risks, and position in relation to the university.

The university offers opportunities and obstacles to social entrepreneurs in the social innovation ecosystem. Universities are present and recognized all over the world as privileged sites of education. Understanding how the university functions as a meeting place, legitimator, and knowledge producer is part of finding scalable, system-changing ways to sustain existing social entrepreneurs and encourage new ones.

The empirical data presented here were collected during the annual Skoll World Forum on Social Entrepreneurship (SWF) held at the Said

Business School, University of Oxford, in 2009. This site was chosen because the SWF represents a key part of the global social innovation ecosystem. The data in this chapter are based upon an analysis of 41 semi-structured interviews with people engaged in social innovation attending the SWF. Key themes that were explored included the function of social entrepreneurs, the risks and strengths of social entrepreneurship, and the role of the SWF and universities in general in supporting the emergence of social entrepreneurs. This chapter concludes with recommendations as to how to foster a greater critical awareness of the tensions and risks of social entrepreneurship and how the university can provide an enabling environment from within which social entrepreneurs may emerge.

The social innovation ecosystem

Dees and Bloom (2008) argued that social entrepreneurs can benefit by understanding their work is a part of a wider ecosystem of social entrepreneurship. An ecosystem 'includes the resources (financial, human, social/political, and intellectual capital) essential for the success of social entrepreneurs, and the environmental conditions (such as public policy and politics, media, economic and social conditions, and related fields) that could support or undermine the practice of social entrepreneurship' (CASE, 2008, p. iv).

Thus, ecosystem mapping is positioned by the authors as an important strategic planning exercise to help social entrepreneurs be more aware of their operating environment and its risks and opportunities. Such an approach also helps to broaden the theory of social innovation beyond a focus on the social entrepreneur as heroic individual:

> An ecosystems framework, ... incorporates the broader environment within which organizations operate. ... This framework is particularly important for social entrepreneurs, who must leverage complex systems of interacting players in rapidly evolving political, economic, physical, and cultural environments.
>
> (Dees and Bloom, 2008, p. 48)

Despite an increasing focus on systems thinking, it is still common to accredit considerable agency to social entrepreneurs, in the sense that they are depicted as needing to 'leverage' systems. It is, however, still novel to see the social entrepreneur embedded in a wider system. The question of the influence of (eco)systems on the social entrepreneur is of central interest to this chapter.

A consensus has emerged that social entrepreneurship involves the recognition, evaluation, and exploitation of opportunities that result primarily in social value creation, as opposed to personal or share-holder wealth (Austin et al., 2006). Santos (2009) has also suggested that there is an important separation between value creation and value appropriation for social entrepreneurs, with a key focus on the former ahead of the latter. Social entrepreneurship can further be defined as any action that displays three key characteristics: sociality, innovation, and market orientation (Nicholls, 2006). Both for-profit and not-for-profit organizations may engage in social entrepreneurship, which is also found in the public sector. Mair and Marti (2004) suggested that entrepreneurial processes can be used to identify and exploit innova-tive solutions to social and environmental problems. Dees (2001) has suggested that though both involve innovation and an orientation towards opportunity, social entrepreneurship can be differentiated from conventional entrepreneurship by the criteria used for its evalua-tion. While businesses are evaluated based on profits for shareholders, social entrepreneurs measure their performance above all on creating social value. In the search for ways better to analyze the real nature of socially entrepreneurial value creation, researchers have begun to challenge a dominant archetype of social entrepreneurial agency. This archetype is an ideal type of the individual actor typified by the Ashoka Fellowship model that selects individuals on account of his or her innovative ideas, overall creativity, entrepreneurial qualities, and ethical fibre (see Ashoka, 2010).

Light (2006) offered a more inclusive definition of the social entre-preneur not just as an individual but as organizations, networks or alliances of organizations. His definition increases the pool of potential social entrepreneurs: 'the amount of social entrepreneurship can be increased by supporting more potential entrepreneurs as they cross over to actual engagement' (Light, 2008, p. 14). Light focused on redefining the scope of social entrepreneurship not necessarily its effectiveness, compared to more exclusive models. Bill Drayton, the founder of Ashoka, also embraced the idea that everyone can play a role in social entrepreneurship. But Drayton did not call everyone a social entrepreneur – reserving that title for a few individuals – rather he made a distinction between a select group of individuals who were 'pattern changing leading social entrepreneurs' and the general public, each of whom had the potential to be a 'changemaker'. Changemakers are people who are inspired by a social entrepreneur's example and, while not generating systems changes themselves, take up the ideas of others and make changes in their local community (Drayton 2006, p. 84). People who fit the Ashoka criteria to be fellows are rare, while anyone can become a changemaker according to Ashoka. Ashoka has only elected over 2,000 fellows worldwide, but Drayton argues that if there is a focused effort on youth participation then there is a potential for many to become changemakers:

> A generation hence, probably 20 to 30 percent of the world's people, and later 50 to 70 percent, not just today's few percent, will be changemakers and entrepreneurs. That world will be fundamentally different and a far safer, happier, more equal, and more successful place.
>
> (Drayton, 2006, p. 95)

Light argued for a debate concerning how to get more people involved in social entrepreneurship by broadening the definition of a social entrepreneur. Unlike Drayton, he did not just add a new category in which more people can participate, but, instead, attempted to expand an existing category by reclassifying other behaviours as social entrepreneurship. Some have suggested that 'this stretches the fundamental meaning of entrepreneurship' (Phills et al., 2008, 43, footnote 4), but Light's point is still well taken: in order to engage more people in socially entrepreneurial activities, a wider conceptual net must be cast to capture all the things that make social entrepreneurship possible.

By focusing on social innovation more broadly, rather than on a single person or organization, a clearer understanding of the mechanisms of social change, understood as the interconnected parts of a complex process, is possible (Phills et al., 2008). Social innovation draws attention to the importance of networks, ecosystems and the systems in which social entrepreneurship is embedded. It also suggests that strategic management of such networks and connections can create opportunities to increase the effectiveness for social entrepreneurs. However, even with a clearer focus on mechanisms for change, the scope of the agency of social entrepreneurs remains an issue, as Drayton argued:

> Multiplying society's capacity to adapt and change intelligently and constructively and building the necessary underlying collaborative architecture, is the world's most critical opportunity now. Pattern-changing

leading social entrepreneurs are the most critical single factor in catalyzing and engineering this transformation.

(Drayton, 2006, pp. 82–83)

Words such as 'architecture' (Drayton, 2006) or 'mechanism' (Phills et al., 2008) still suggest agency and human purpose within a given environment or social structure, rather than a reciprocal relationship of influencing and shaping. Referring to an 'ecosystem', however, where the focus is on how the various members of the system are impacted and shaped by each other (Bloom and Dees, 2008, p. 48), opens up more conceptual space to imagine different types of agency and visibility for social entrepreneurs in social innovation systems. This is akin to Giddens's (1984) analysis of structuration within social theory (see also Nicholls and Cho, 2006).

In the next section, this chapter introduces Foucault's concept of the 'specific intellectual' as a social agent embedded in a larger social frame or 'truth regime'. By comparing and contrasting the social entrepreneur and the specific intellectual this chapter will better articulate a possible paradigm shift for the field from focusing on the qualities of specific visible individuals to a focus on wider systems of change, emergence, and social innovation.

The specific intellectual

The 'specific intellectual', described by Foucault, can be seen as part of a system rather than as a discrete individual. He is defined more by his privileged position with regard to (re-)producing power and knowledge than by his subjective qualities. Foucault (1980; 1994) defined the specific intellectual in contrast to an earlier model of the universal intellectual who spoke in the name of the masses and who was positioned as a heroic man of justice and conscience. Foucault gave as an example of the universal intellectual the writer Emile Zola, who published 'J'accuse!' as an open letter to the French President accusing the French government of anti-semitism in the case of Alfred Dreyfus.

The universal intellectual was typically a writer, who spoke for those who could not articulate their thoughts. Foucault contrasted this earlier power to speak of universal values in the name of others with a new type of social agency brought about by the growing technocratic state. Foucault suggested:

A new mode of the 'connection between theory and practice' has been established. Intellectuals have become used to working, not in the modality of the 'universal,' the 'exemplary,' the 'just-and-true-for-all,' but within specific sectors, at the precise points where their own conditions of life or work situate them.

(Foucault, 1980, p. 68)

The specific intellectual is described as someone with particular expertise and the technical know-how to solve problems of great relevance to many people. Foucault gave the example of the nuclear physicist Oppenheimer. Specific intellectuals are privileged because of their positions to create meaning and shape discourses directly in the institutions of which they are part and with the wider public in general. Specific intellectuals are seen as 'multipliers' and as content providers through the use of the mass media or teaching, especially at the university: 'the university and the academic emerge, if not as principle elements, at least as "exchangers", privileged points of intersection' (Foucault, 1980, p. 127).

Why are intellectuals 'privileged' exchangers or points of intersection? Foucault argued that:

The essential political problem for the intellectual is not to criticize the ideological contents supposedly linked to science, or to ensure that his own scientific practice is accompanied by a correct ideology, but that of ascertaining the possibility of constituting a new politics of truth. The problem is not in changing people's consciousnesses – or what's in their heads – but the political, economical, institutional regime of the production of truth.

(Foucault, 1980, p. 133)

In the case where changing the regime of the production of truth is defined as the key problem for the intellectual, having institutional legitimacy through being attached to a university, research centre, or major media outlet is an advantage. The specific intellectual can use her position relative to current power and knowledge regimes to make these regimes more self-evident and reveal them more clearly as the consequences of particular power relationships. The intellectual, because she is both formed by and herself forms these systems, is in a position to seek out the gaps in the system and use them as opportunities to put the system in question and change its rules of operation.

Foucault's critiques of the clinic (1973), the prison (1977a), and the factory (1977a) were not just negative, in the sense that they could only identify or break down constructed limits, but were positive, and could be used to test the possibility of new horizons. The third volume of his *History of Sexuality, The Care of the Self* (Foucault, [1984a] 1990) articulated an ethos that added a productive aspect to the process of critique, referred to as a 'critical ontology', which was concerned with the constitution of subjectivity:

> The critical ontology of ourselves must be considered not, certainly, as a theory, a doctrine, nor even as a permanent body of knowledge that is accumulating; it must be conceived as an attitude, an ethos, a philosophical life in which the critique of what we are is at one and the same time the historical analysis of the limits imposed on us and an experiment with the possibility of going beyond them.
>
> (Foucault, [1984a] 1990, p. 319)

Foucault's ethos of critical ontology, of an analysis of limits with a view to going beyond them, helps mitigate the risks that accompany the new positioning of the specific intellectual. The same closeness to local and specific struggles that is the specific intellectual's strength keeps him also at the level of 'conjunctural struggles, pressing demands related to particular sectors' (Foucault, 1980, p. 130). This is the first of three risks identified by Foucault. Second, he also runs the 'risk of letting himself be manipulated by the political parties or union apparatuses directing these local struggles' (ibid.). Foucault saw the third and most important risk as 'being unable to develop these struggles for want of a global strategy or of outside support; the risk too of not being followed, or only by very limited groups' (ibid.).

This chapter argues that the risks to the specific intellectual are also broadly applicable to the social entrepreneur. The specific intellectual was defined by a shift away from universal to local struggles and from speaking for all from a point of moral authority to making localized interventions based on specific technical expertise. The social entrepreneur is also often engaging at a local level, not simply calling for things to be done by others, but using technical skills and local insights from his community to create change himself. Foucault drew attention to the shift away from a writer, like Zola, to a scientist, like Oppenheimer. Social entrepreneurs may also be experiencing this shift from a projection of themselves as 'moral icons' to being recognized more for their technical expertise within a given system. Bornstein presented many social entrepreneurs as technically adept insiders who know the specific strengths and weaknesses of a given system and so are able to navigate and use the system more effectively than done before. For example, he profiled a South African nurse who created a new way to treat AIDS patients at home. Her technical expertise and knowledge of the limits of the current healthcare system and how to surmount them were key to her success (Bornstein, 2004). Many Ashoka fellows are professionally qualified, for example water treatment specialists in the Environmental Innovation Initiative (see http://www.ashoka.org/eiiprojects).

Foucault's discussion of truth regimes and the specific intellectual drawing power from her relationship to them is also relevant to social entrepreneurs. As acknowledged pragmatists, social entrepreneurs often work within systems to change them. Even if the hoped for result is a revolution in the way the system works, social entrepreneurs can still create change from within. This is particularly true in the case of social enterprises that use the market to bring about social or environmental objectives (see Alter, 2006). Foucault identified some risks to the specific intellectual in terms of being limited to particular sectors, of being manipulated by others directing the struggle, and of being unable to grow due to a lack of strategy or support. In what follows, these risks will be assessed for their relevance to, and implications for, the social entrepreneur. Using Foucault's specific intellectual as a foil for the social entrepreneur provides a rich theoretical framework informed by post-structuralist and social-constructivist theory. This theoretical heritage poses new questions and identifies different risks to those which have been discussed in previous attempts to define and locate the social entrepreneur within the social innovation ecosystem. Table 8.1 summarizes these risks.

Methodology

The Skoll World Forum on Social Entrepreneurship (SWF) at the University of Oxford presents itself on its webpage as 'the premier gathering of the world's leading social entrepreneurs. Prominent figures from the social, academic, finance, corporate and policy sectors engage for three days and nights in a series of debates, discussions and work sessions focused on accelerating, innovating and scaling solutions to some of the world's most pressing social issues' (Skoll Foundation, 2010a). Though strongly informed by Anglo-American traditions, it hosts a wide variety of delegates from outside North America and the UK, including a large contingent of European delegates who bring another social-cultural perspective and academic tradition to the forum. The SWF has been referred to as the 'Davos of Social Entrepreneurship' (Hutton, 2005), reflecting the event's convening power and exclusivity. The SWF website also states that its aims to 'accelerate the impact of

Table 8.1 Foucauldian risks for social entrepreneurs

	Risk 1	Risk 2	Risk 3
Specific Intellectual	Limited to conjunctural struggles	Manipulated by political parties or union apparatuses directing these local struggles	Want of global strategy, being followed only by small groups
Social Entrepreneur	Restricted to criticizing the system from within the system	Manipulated by fickle funding and investment priorities and needs to have a market orientation to earn income	Lack of scale, lack of transfer to larger population groups
Examples	Solving a problem with water delivery to a specific location does not challenge the system of privatization of water.	Being required to earn income to pursue projects sustainably requires the social entrepreneur to apply a market logic and discount opportunities to act where costs cannot be recovered in favour of those which can be profitable.	Social Entrepreneurs can be fixed on solving a particular problem and not have the skills or desire to take the solution to scale.

the world's leading social entrepreneurs by uniting them with essential partners in a collaborative pursuit of learning, leverage and large scale social change' (Skoll Foundation 2010a). Today, the SWF is an invitation-only event. People apply online with biographical information and their reasons for wanting to attend months in advance. The participants are then selected by the conference organizers on the basis of 'who will contribute to our mission of accelerating the impact of the world's leading social entrepreneurs' (Skoll Foundation, 2010b).

This chapter is informed by 41 semi-structured interviews with delegates of the SWF held in 2009. With respect to a theoretical framework derived from Foucault's specific intellectual, key themes explored in the interviews included: the function of the social entrepreneur; risks to social entrepreneurship; measuring impact; the role of the university; the role of the SWF itself. The interviewees were videotaped in order to make their contributions available later as a web-based teaching resource for social entrepreneurship.

The interviews were not designed to be a representative sample but rather a set of key informant interviews from leading members of the global social entrepreneurship and innovation community. In 2009 the SWF hosted approximately 800 delegates. The 41 interviews analysed here, therefore, represent approximately five per cent of all the attendees. The interviewees categorized themselves as follows: social entrepreneurs (22), including Ashoka or Skoll fellows (5), academics whose research focus includes social entrepreneurship (5), prominent journalists and authors publishing on social entrepreneurship (3), employees of foundations working with social entrepreneurs (8), and social investors (3). Of the 41 interviewed, 32 stated they had been in the field for over five years, 9 for less. Of the 41, 15 were based outside Europe and North America. Women comprised 20 of the 41. A range of interesting themes emerged from the interviews. These are considered below in terms of a Foucauldian analysis of the social entrepreneur as specific intellectual.

The dangers of moral heroism

Several interviewees identified a set of risks that resonate with Foucault's description of the specific intellectual as not deriving her power from moral heroism but from technical expertise, within a power/knowledge regime. In the selections from interviews below, the interviewees acknowledged the relevance of this theme of the social entrepreneur as adopting, or being put into, the role of a moral ideal-type, a highly visible charismatic leader, or, even, a 'rock star':

> I also have a certain amount of, I think, healthy self-awareness around, like the social entrepreneur rock star pitfalls, I think [they are] somewhat real and people can take themselves a little too seriously, and then I think that can lead to bad things, and current priorities being askew.
>
> (Interviewee 7)

> If we get caught up in the vanity, in the seduction, in the ego-things of Social Entrepreneurship, then I think our own enterprise will disappear. But so long as we can stay true to the mission, so long as we can keep measuring the impact of our work and looking to increase that impact, then I think social entrepreneurship has got a very, very exciting future.
>
> (Interviewee 8)

> I think one of the biggest obstacles is the extent to which social entrepreneurs get too caught up in who they are and what they do instead of the impact of their work.
>
> (Interviewee 5)

The interviewees showed an awareness of the risks of assigning too much responsibility to the heroic personality or the moral example of the social entrepreneur rather than focusing on the impact and the function of the social entrepreneur in a wider context. Some interviewees suggested an alternative model:

> The entrepreneur is a mechanism to bring together a lot of people in a framework that is self-correcting, and growth-oriented, and responsive to solve the big problem. I am much more comfortable talking about the mechanism of social entrepreneurship or the process of social entrepreneurship (which is a very organic, and adaptive and self-correcting process), rather than only speaking in terms of the social entrepreneur as the individual who launches this.
>
> (Interviewee 1)

This interviewee drew attention to the importance of not confusing the visibility and media-friendly deployment of the founder with the belief that the social entrepreneur is responsible as an individual for the social value created by a larger group of people. Rather, the social entrepreneur is one function (albeit an attractive, attention grabbing function) of a wider adaptive and self-correcting process in which many people necessarily play a part.

The challenges of systems change from within

According to Foucault, specific intellectuals work within the dominant political system to understand the rules of the system and to exploit this knowledge to shift the rules where possible and thereby change the system. Many of the interviewees also drew attention to this strategy of immanent critique by the social entrepreneur. Here, an interviewee drew a distinction between an old and the new strategy:

> It is a dramatic difference. … the old strategy was shaming, and blaming, and attacking. The strategy … of social entrepreneurs … is: 'There are real problems in the world', 'How can I use a positive approach?', 'How can I get in there with my skills?', 'How can I make a difference?' Rather than saying: 'It is somebody else's fault', or 'I am waiting for the government to do it', or 'It is hopeless' – [they say] 'I really believe that I can make a contribution … It is a very new approach, but it is not an approach that requires destroying the existing structure.
>
> (Interviewee 2)

In this case, the interviewee emphasizes using a positive approach and taking action within existing structures:

> I am a realist. I would love the world to be a very different place. … I recognize that change happens slowly and particularly if you have got to dismantle the existing power structure. So, I am much more interested in people who are saying: 'Okay, they can be over there doing their thing, meanwhile we are going to be making change this way by being creative with the system that already exists'.
>
> (Interviewee 2)

This interviewee, by contrast, explicitly acknowledged that existing power structures may need to be dismantled for change to happen, but also suggested that different groups can work on parallel strategies. Some people can work on dismantling the existing power structure while at the same time others use creative means within the current system to effect change:

> The basic assumption [of activists] is that other people have the power and your job is to move those other people in the direction that society needs to go. The assumption of social entrepreneurship is in fact: The power is not necessarily in other institutions. We actually have the power to build new institutions ourselves.
>
> (Interviewee 1)

Foucault's specific intellectuals are seen as part of the knowledge/power structure that makes an institution through their deployment of knowledge and expertise. The quote above refers to the power of existing structures. The interviewee made the point later that existing social structures and actors do not necessarily know what to do to solve a problem. It is not always the case that they are choosing not to act, and need to be moved by protest to take action, but that they cannot act because they do not know what to do. They rely on outsiders to develop innovative solutions to problems they have not been able to solve. In some cases the social entrepreneur can provide the technical insights to solve the problem. While Foucault's specific intellectuals are described as aligning themselves with powerful existing institutions that they helped build and critically maintained, the social entrepreneur is not unnecessarily impressed by the established power and authority of existing institutional arrangements.

In the following interviews, the interviewees spoke of operating within the 'mindset' of the current system, specifically with the goal of using the power of market structures to create greater impact for social causes. According to one approach argued below, one first finds common ground with the 'enemy', changes their behaviour, and then re-aligns the incentives in the prevailing system so that the system can create new social good and positive outcomes:

> I think the exciting thing about this movement and this opportunity is that by working within the system, by working with the so called 'enemy', you can find common ground and ultimately deepen the impact that you want to see ... What is great about social entrepreneurship and one of the key strategies of what it means to be a social entrepreneur is to build those bridges and to change the behaviour of the enemy, whether that means working with the corporate bad guy and realizing that business can actually serve a really profound social good. We just have to figure out how to align its incentives, how to get the right people involved in that conversation.
>
> (Interviewee 21)

This quote shows a belief in the value neutrality and malleability of market systems, by proposing a realignment of incentives so that business can serves a social good. But it is less clear what are the limits to such a realignment of incentives or what restrictions in the current system compromise the ability of social entrepreneurs to create lasting change. Self-identifying as a 'social entrepreneur' can be seen in itself as an attempt to make social change making more comprehensible and recognisable to dominant interests:

> The reason why people use terms like 'social value' or even 'social entrepreneurship' rather than other terms, in the past we would call someone 'humanitarian'; instead of social value we would talk about helping people. Why do we use these terms? There is a co-opting of terms that have become very powerful in the world, and whole mindsets and frameworks of understanding that in the past twenty years have become unchallenged in the world in terms of how economies are organised, what people study and what the accepted ways of doing things are .... [They are] trying to help people understand what they are talking about (who are already deeply vested in those [business sector] systems) and you meet them half way: you use terms, you use references that seem to be palatable, or seem to be recognisable to them.
>
> (Interviewee 1)

But do arguments for action conceived and phrased in a way which is intelligible to business threaten to make some lines of argument, some premises, unintelligible? For example, is it still possible to frame market discourses in terms of the necessary role of the public sector, the state or basic, human rights? Another interviewee mentioned the missing role of the public sector:

> Although we are very inspired by this enthusiastic movement, I would say that the role of the government, the role of state, the role of the public sector is underdeveloped in this area. The focus is very much on a very innovative combination between civil society, third sector, NGO's enthusiastic individuals, and the business world. Society in this global era consists of three sectors: state, market, and civil society. And is more or less only the public sector that can secure rights of people. Not only the opportunities, but the rights.
>
> (Interviewee 5)

This interviewee referred to the 'underdevelopment' of the state's role in social innovation in public discourses at the SWF, and other leading organizations – such as Ashoka – are, at best, ambivalent about the role the public sector can play in social entrepreneurship. Nevertheless, at the SWF in 2008, Farmer made the following remarks regarding the importance of seeing the limits of certain ways of thinking and the necessity of protecting the public sector:

> We need to be aware of the limitations of any culture that sees all services as commodities and very few as rights [...]. Even though we're not from the public sector, we need to do everything in our power to make sure that the public sector does not shrivel and die. Why? Not only because a functioning public health or education system is often the only way to bring a novel program to scale, and not only because we need the participation of governments to address the current environmental crises at the transnational scale needed to make a difference. There is another reason to fight the neoliberal gutting of the public sector: only governments can confer rights ... and without rights ... then the world's poor do not have hope of a future.
>
> (Farmer, 2009, p. 24)

This focus on rights as something only government can provide, shows the need for social entrepreneurs to be aware of the risks of explaining and basing their work too deeply within an exclusive business logic.

The risk is that if the government is excluded as part of the solution, public sector logics of problem solving are lost, reducing the 'toolbox' of concepts and practices with which to conceptualize and solve problems. Social entrepreneurs create a bridge, or translation space, in order to work within multiple logics and to escape the threat of being 'manipulated', in Foucauldian terms, by either one logic or another (though see Dart, 2004). If the goal is to remain able to innovate, then it is necessary to be aware of the ways thinking is shaped by certain rule systems which are not explicit and sometimes stay obscured (see Lukes, 1974). Social entrepreneurs can adopt the ethos of Foucault's specific intellectuals of constantly hunting for, questioning, and sharing with others, the rules governing the game in which they are playing. As they play the game they are also constantly testing how rules can be shifted.

Another social entrepreneur explained how sustainability and irreversibility were achieved through creating a new mindset in people outside the organization:

> I very much want to make sure that we build the organisations in each of those cities that are going to last way past me and way past the existence of [my organisation] itself; and that along the way we will really change how [people] think ... To achieve that kind of change, you need to build a sustainable organisation. But, I also think that key to building sustainability is to win the hearts and minds of people outside the organisation – a much bigger approach.
>
> (Interviewee 4)

Working within the dominant system to create a new equilibrium (Martin and Osberg, 2007) is another way of discussing Foucault's understanding of the intellectual working within the truth regime to change the way it functions. What is often missing from the discussion concerning social entrepreneurship, however, is what may be lost, hidden, or unthinkable by framing social innovation through particular logics, language, and processes (see Nicholls, 2010). What falls in the space of the possible and what is made impossible by this way of operating, as compared to other historical forms of organizing social innovation?

Lack of institutional support for growth

The final risk Foucault identifies for the specific intellectual is 'the risk of being unable to develop ... for lack of a global strategy or outside support; the risk too of not being followed or only by very limited groups' (Foucault 1980, p. 130). Social entrepreneurs share in this risk in the sense that they can fail to grow beyond their local or national context due to a lack of strategic, external support and resources.

The fact that Ashoka has a special programme to globalize social innovations draws attention to this problem:

> I think it is a revolution to ... take the best of the business sector and put it into the social sector and see how we can globalise patterns of social change. We have so many great ideas ... but these ideas never make it beyond their countries. Ashoka brings these ideas to the surface, globalises them and creates an open source network of social innovations.
>
> (Interviewee 18)

Many of the social innovations brought about by social entrepreneurs locally turn out to be difficult to adapt to other contexts. Some interviewees attributed this to the local nature of the networks that nurture a social entrepreneur, others pointed out that most social entrepreneurs were motivated to solve a particular problem in their area of influence, and did not have the network skills or interest in leading an organization tasked with spreading their solution elsewhere. Another potential challenge to growth identified by an interviewee was that social entrepreneurs often offer niche products and services tailored to a specific group, and have similarly tightly tailored funding strategies for it:

> One potential trap for social entrepreneurs is that only when you have a very focused thing you are doing, can the funders understand it and write cheques for it.
>
> (Interviewee 16)

As the work done by the social entrepreneur goes to scale – in this case from funding a specific sort of operation for children to the funding of health clinics in general – funders may no longer attribute normative value to an organization or project and may cut the flow of resources to it. Foucault brought to the fore similar themes of intelligibility and how truth regimes frame what is understood and is impossible to understand. This applies here to the situation of funders who no longer understand an investment or its logics under conditions of systems change. This simple example of a funder not understanding the logics of an organization's actions shows the powerful effects of truth regimes that can make ideas incoherent to funders and, as a result, block resources to support social innovation.

Risk mitigation: The role of the university

Foucault argues that a university can function as an exchanger of information and an intersection point for specific intellectuals. This makes universities 'politically ultrasensitive areas' (Foucault, 1980, p. 127). Several interviewees agreed that the university indeed played this exchange and intersection role for social entrepreneurs. When reflecting on the SWF, as an event closely associated with a prestigious university, interviewees expressed particular emotional effects including excitement, belonging, and enthusiasm:

> That was what has been most exciting about Skoll for me – just listening to people who have a totally radical way of doing something. That is what gets me excited. In five to ten years, I am hoping we are going to see new 'service delivery models' or 'business models' for social entrepreneurs, hopefully enabled by technology, that are inconceivable from our vantage point today.
>
> (Interviewee 16)

Another interviewee spoke of meeting up with her 'tribe':

> I think the importance of partnership, the importance of being here at the Skoll World Forum is so valuable to me because I see like minds – I found my tribe here. It is people who do not tell you, you cannot do something but they are like: 'There is a person over here you need to meet'.
>
> (Interviewee 22)

Alongside the opportunities to be exposed to radical new ideas and new people to advance the work of social innovation, interviewees valued the personal experiences of providing 'a very enthusiastic atmosphere' (Interviewee 5) or a 'social entrepreneur family reunion' (Interviewee 21). People at the SWF 'do not tell you, you cannot do something, but instead understand and try to assist you', said one interviewee.

When asked to reflect on how the university can help advance social entrepreneurship, similar answers were often offered. One interviewee gave a vision of the university in the future where social entrepreneurs do not 'feel alone' and 'respon[d] to relevant needs':

> [I]n 5–10 years we are no longer looking at bodies of people ... faculty or students ... who feel alone ... that there is an ongoing

and sustained conversation, and universities are really responding to relevant needs, and actually playing very relevant and rigorous role in the world.

(Interviewee 25)

The interviewee continued to say that university students can form:

[a] community of like minded individuals to say that you are not alone in wanting to change something here and giving them access to one another and a platform for that kind of exchange so that they can share ideas.

(Interviewee 25)

Some interviewees responded that they wanted universities to help them measure their impact or use their legitimating function to put a stamp of approval on their projects. One interviewee (who worked at a university) spoke of the importance of research and teaching skills at the university, along with the need to 'show enthusiasm':

I think there is a demand from students to engage in this new language, in this new movement, if you wish ... so the universities should really go for it, pick it up, be enthusiastic in our approaches but remember why we here in the world. We are here to do research and research based education.

(Interviewee 5)

This quotation shows apparent, possible tension between the demands from the students and the purpose of the university according to the interviewee. This raises the question of a possible disconnect between various groups in and around the university (CASE, 2008). The creation of a better relationship between researchers and practitioners – beyond teaching and dissemination – was also identified as offering a contribution towards a more meaningful role for the university in the social innovation ecosystem.

Interestingly, the majority of interviewees did not speak specifically about the teaching of social entrepreneurship, but rather said that the university should provide opportunities for like-minded faculty and students to be in regular contact with each other and not feel isolated. As with the comments concerning the SWF itself, several interviewees believed that social entrepreneurs could be supported by an enthusiastic and engaged university population.

Conclusion

This chapter has used the Foucauldian concept of the specific intellectual to analyse some of the risks faced by the social entrepreneur as specific intellectual in the wider social innovation ecosystem. The risks that Foucault set out for the specific intellectual – being stuck at the level of particular sector, being manipulated by political forces that control the terms of the debate, not being able to grow because of a lack of resources –, were shown to be shared by social entrepreneurs. Also following Foucault, it has explored how the university can provide an enabling environment from within which social entrepreneurs can emerge. Foucault identified the university as playing a central role as an exchange mechanisms and intersection point for specific intellectuals. Furthermore, the specific intellectual is closely linked to the production of knowledge at universities. The university also exercises remarkable legitimating and excluding power as the site where a wide variety of discourses intersect. The interviewees in this study confirmed the importance of the legitimating role of the university as a place to give new knowledge the chance to be integrated into academic tradition. The university was also valued as a place where action could be taken to make potential social entrepreneurs less isolated, join a community of practice, and become active in social entrepreneurial activity. A related point was made that events like the SWF often provided individuals the chance to meet with 'their own tribe'.

This chapter has argued that a paradigm shift is underway from an understanding of social entrepreneurs as heroic individuals to social entrepreneurs being seen as actors embedded in a larger system of innovation. This study suggests several lines of future research. For example, drawing on Foucault, new research could explore in detail how social entrepreneurs are affected by – and, in turn, affect – other actors within a given ecosystem. An analysis of the risks of being manipulated by political forces that control the terms of the debate may also provide a particularly fruitful area for future research, since the political aspects of social entrepreneurship have been under-researched to date. Two other linked areas for future research could be: first, an explorations of what is lost and what is gained by framing the work of social innovation within terms adapted from the logics of business and the market; second, to consider the ontological implications of adopting a specific conceptual and normative stance on the work of social entrepreneurs.

This chapter has attempted to use a methodology derived from Foucault's ethos of critical ontology to examine social entrepreneurship and social innovation. This work has also drawn attention to another area where a further juxtaposition of the specific intellectual and the social entrepreneur could be fruitful, namely on methods of reflection and seizing opportunities for systems change. The method of creative destruction assigned by Schumpeter to the entrepreneur suggests a comparison with the genealogical method of Foucault. Both Schumpeter (1934) and Foucault (1977b) owe a debt to Nietzsche and Marx that would be profitable to explore further to provide another theoretical underpinning to the critical and reflective practices of the social entrepreneur.

References

Alter, K. (2006), 'Social Enterprise Models and Their Mission and Money Relationships', in A. Nicholls (ed.) *Social Entrepreneurship: New Models of Sustainable Social Change*, Oxford University Press.

Ashoka (2010), *Selction Criteria*, http://www.ashoka.org/support/criteria, accessed: 30 December 2010.

Austin, J., Gutierrez, R. and Ogliastri, E. (2006), *Effective Management of Social Enterprises: Lessons from Business and Civil Society Organizations in Ibero-America* Rockefeller/Inter-American Development Bank.

Bloom, P. N. and Dees, G. (2008), 'Cultivate your Ecosystem', in *Stanford Social Innovation Review*, Winter 2008, pp. 47–53. Available also at: https://www.self-help.org/about-us/about-us-files/SH_SSIR_Ecosystems.pdf (accessed: 30 December 2010).

CASE Report (2008), 'Developing the Field of Social Entrepreneurship', A Report from the Center for the Advancement of Social Entrepreneurship (CASE) Duke University: The Fuqua School of Business, June 2008. Available at: http://www.caseatduke.org/documents/CASE_Field-Building_Report_June08.pdf (accessed: 30 December 2010).

Dart, R. (2004), 'The Legitimacy of Social Enterprise', in *Nonprofit Management and Leadership*, 14 (4), Summer 2004, pp. 411–24.

Dees, J. G. (2001), 'The Meaning of Social Entrepreneurship', Duke University, Fuqua School of Business, Center for the Advancement of Social Entrepreneurship. Available at: www.fuqua.duke.edu/centers/case/documents/dees_sedef.pdf (accessed: 30 December 2010).

Drayton, W. (2006), 'Everyone a Changemaker: Social Entrepreneurship's Ultimate Goal', in *Innovations: Technology/Governance/Globalization*, Winter 2006, Cambridge: MIT Press, pp. 80–96. Available also at: http://www.ashoka.org/files/innovations8.5x11FINAL_0.pdf (accessed: 30 December 2010).

Farmer, P. (2009), 'Three Stories, Three Paradigms, and a Critique of Social Entrepreneurship', in *Innovations: Technology/Governance/Globalization*, Special Edition for the Skoll World Forum 2009, Cambridge: MIT Press, pp. 19–27.

Foucault, M. [1977] (1994), Dits et écrits. 1954–1988 par Michel Foucault. Édition établie sous la direction de Daniel Defert et François Ewald. III 1976–1979. Paris: Éditions Gallimard.

Foucault, M. (1973), *The Birth of the Clinic: An Archaeology of Medical Perception*, London: Routledge.

Foucault, M. (1977a), *Discipline and Punish: The Birth of the Prison*, London: Penguin Books.

Foucault, M. (1977b), 'Nietzsche, Genealogy, History', in *Language, Counter-Memory, Practice: Selected Essays and Interviews*, edited by D. F. Bouchard, Ithaca: Cornell University Press.

Foucault, M. (1980), 'Truth and Power', in Power/Knowledge: Selected Interviews and Other Writings 1972–1977 (ed.) Colin Gordon, Trans. C. Gordon, L. Marshall, J. Mepham and K. Soper, New York: Pantheon Books.

Foucault, M. [1984a] (1990), *The History of Sexuality Vol. 3: The Care of Self*, London: Penguin.

Foucault, M. (1984b), 'What is Enlightenment?', in P. Rabinow (ed.) *The Foucault Reader*, New York: Pantheon Books, 1984, pp. 32–50.

Giddens, A. (1984), *The Constitution of Society: Outline of the Theory of Structuration*, Berkeley: University of California Press.

Hutton, W. (2005), 'How would Confucius Vote?', in: *The Observer*, Sunday, 27 March 2005. Available at: http://www.guardian.co.uk/politics/2005/mar/27/election2005.uk1 (accessed: 31 December 2010).

Light, P. C. (2006), 'Searching for Social Entrepreneurs: Who They Might Be, Where They Might Be Found, What They Do', Paper prepared for the 34th annual conference of the Association for Research on Nonprofit Organizations and Voluntary Action. Washington, DC, 17–18 November 2005. Reprinted in *Research on Social Entrepreneurship: Understanding and Contributing to an Emerging Field*, edited by R. Mosher-William, pp. 13–37. Occasional Paper Series, vol. 1, no. 3 (Indianapolis: ARNOVA).

Light, P. C. (2008), *The Search for Social Entrepreneurship*, Washington, DC: Brookings Institution Press.

Lukes, St ([1974] 1986), *Power: A Radical View* [London] Oxford: [Macmillan] Blackwell.

Mair and Marti (2004), 'Social Entrepreneurship: What Are We Talking About? A Framework for Future Research', Working Paper. University of Navarra, IESE (Instituto de Estudios Superiores de la Empresa) Business School (International Graduate School of Management).

Martin, R. and Osberg, S. (2007), 'Social Entrepreneurship: The Case for Definition', in *Stanford Social Innovation Review*, Spring 2007, pp. 28–39. Available also at: http://www.ssircview.org/imagcs/articlcs/2007SP_feature_martinosberg.pdf (accessed: 30 December 2010).

Nicholls, A. (ed.) (2006), *Social Entrepreneurship: New Models of Sustainable Social Change*, Oxford University Press.

Nicholls, A. and Cho, A. (2006), 'Social Entrepreneurship: The Structuration of a Field', in A. Nicholls (ed.) *Social Entrepreneurship: New Models of Sustainable Social Change*, Oxford University Press, pp. 99–118.

Nicholls, A. (2010), 'The Legitimacy of Social Entrepreneurship: Reflexive Isomorphism in a Pre-Paradigmatic Field', in *Entrepreneurship Theory and Practice Journal*, July 2010, pp. 611–33.

Phills, Jr, J. A., Deiglmeier, K. and Miller, D. T. (2008), 'Rediscovering Social Innovation', in *Stanford Social Innovation Review*, Fall 2008, pp. 34–43.

Santos, F. (2009), 'A Positive Theory of Social Entrepreneurship', Working Paper: INSEAD 2009/23/EFE/ISIC.

Schlumpeter, J. (1934), *The Theory of Economic Development: An Inquiry into Profits, Capital, Interest, and the Business Cycle*, Cambridge, MA: Harvard University Press.

Internet References quoted in text:

The Skoll World Forum (2010a), Skoll World Forum. http://www.skollfounda tion.org/skollworldforum/index.asp (accessed: 4 January 2010).

The Skoll World Forum (2010), Skoll World Forum Registration. http://www. skollworldforum.com/forum-2010/register (accessed: 4 January 2010).

Part III
Sustainability and Environmental Innovation

9
Social-Ecological Innovation and Transformation

Per Olsson and Victor Galaz

Introduction

Humanity has entered the anthroposcene era; human activity has become a major driving force in the history of the planet. It is critical to find ways to increase our ability to understand and guide human–environment interactions. Our point of departure in this chapter is the contention that human and biophysical systems are closely inter-connected. Yet not only have scientists and practitioners largely failed to recognize the tight coupling between these systems, the stakes of failing to harness the dynamic behaviour of social-ecological systems are getting higher (Gunderson and Holling, 2002; Rockström et al., 2009). Consequences of such failure include the loss of vital ecosystem services[1] at a global scale (Millennium Ecosystem Assessment, 2005) and the extensive societal challenges posed by global environmental change (Steffen et al., 2004).

Although analysts can project some future impacts on ecosystems and livelihoods, other effects will surface unexpectedly due to our limited understanding of the inter-connectedness of social and biophysical systems. The mismatch between governance systems at local to global levels and the dynamics of biophysical systems has been referred to as 'the problem of fit' (Folke et al., 1998; Young, 2002; Folke et al., 2007; Galaz et al., 2008). In order to deal with the environmental challenges that humanity is facing and find more sustainable pathways, new management and governance systems are acutely needed (Duit and Galaz, 2008; Walker et al., 2009). More specifically, there is a need for radical shifts to new approaches that can enhance the fit between human and biophysical systems and improve the capacity of ecosystems to generate services for human well-being. This chapter addresses the role innovations can play in these transformations.

The need for innovation and creative solutions to deal with the problems of global environmental change is widely recognized. In complex social-ecological systems, innovation is crucial to steer away from potential critical thresholds and open up new trajectories of sustainability. A topic within the social innovation and sustainability transitions literature is a more in-depth concern with the conditions and dynamics of innovations and their role for a broader transformation of patterns in social organization and collective decision making (Rotmans et al., 2001; Geels and Shot, 2007; Loorbach and Rotmans, 2010). However, this research tends to miss the ecological dimension of such shifts. This chapter argues that addressing only the social dimension will not be sufficient to guide society towards sustainable outcomes. Societies may undergo major transformations without improving their capacity to learn from, respond to, and manage environmental feedback from dynamic ecosystems. For example, a systemic shift to biofuels might slow climate change but lead to destructive land-use change and biodiversity loss (Grau and Aide, 2008). This in turn can lead to further ecological degradation, regime shifts, and lock-in traps in social-ecological systems that are difficult to get out of.

A major challenge is to secure, restore, and develop the capacity of ecosystems to generate ecosystem services. Such capacity is the very foundation for social and economic development. Hence, the interactions between societies and ecosystems can create dynamic feedback loops in which humans both influence and are influenced by ecosystem processes. This calls for integrated approaches that span problem domains and sectors, and that address the interface between humans and the environment. The resilience literature generally uses the term 'social-ecological systems' to highlight the inter-connectedness and co-evolution of human-environmental systems and human dependence on the capacity of ecosystems to generate essential services (Berkes and Folke, 1998; Berkes et al., 2003). Berkes and Folke (1998) underscore the need to address the interplay and fit between social and ecological systems by relating management practices based on ecological understanding to the social mechanisms behind these practices in a variety of geographical settings, cultures, and ecosystems. The key message here is that humans are part of ecosystems and ultimately depend on the capacity of ecosystems to generate services.

This chapter draws on the literature on resilience and social-ecological systems to outline some important considerations when applying social innovations[2] and entrepreneurship research and development to sustainability issues. The chapter outlines key sustainability challenges and then identifies some initiatives that promote innovations and sustainability transitions, and offers a critical view on such initiatives from a social-ecological systems perspective. Furthermore, it provides insights from studies on resilience and social-ecological systems that could help widen the concept of social innovation, strengthen research, and develop radical shifts in the context of sustainability. This chapter argues that this linking of perspectives can help speed innovation and up-scaling processes, and improve human well-being without degrading the biosphere and its life support systems in the process.

Social-ecological systems, resilience, and the problem of fit

Institutions, planning processes and policy prescriptions that fail to acknowledge the tight inter-connection between human and biophysical systems are likely not only to provide ill-founded guidelines, but also to steer societies onto undesirable pathways. An environmental policy or regime cannot be effective unless it incorporates an understanding of the larger social, economic, and political context and its dynamics. But no matter how adaptive it is, a social system cannot succeed in being sustainable if its practices are 'ecologically illiterate'.

Ecosystems are complex and adaptive systems, characterized by historical dependency, non-linear dynamics, threshold effects, multiple basins of attraction, and limited predictability (Levin, 1999). Ecosystems can have multiple stable states, a certain one of which may be more desirable from an anthropocentric point of view, due to the ecological services associated with it. For example, a coral reef state may provide more ecological services than an algae-dominated reef. Ecosystems go through natural cycles of collapse and renewal, as with a forest continuously developing in the face of a disturbance regime of fires, storms, and insect outbreaks without changing state (Holling, 1986). However, ecosystems can become vulnerable to the same or new disturbances if the resilience of the system is reduced, which may cause practically irreversible shifts. Resilience is the capacity of a system, such as an ecosystem, to cope with disturbances without shifting into a qualitatively different state. A resilient system has the capacity to withstand and continue to develop in the face of shocks and surprises, including to rebuild itself if damaged. Resilient systems can, in other words, sustain the supply of ecosystem services in the face of disturbance.

Galaz et al. (2008) describe four types of mismatch between ecosystems and governance systems): (a) spatial mismatches, which occur when governance does not match the spatial scales of ecosystem processes; (b) temporal mismatches, which occur when governance does not match the temporal scales of ecosystem processes; (c) threshold behaviour mismatches, which occur when governance does not recognize (or is unable to avoid) abrupt shifts in social-ecological systems; and (d) cascading effect mismatches, which occur when governance amplifies or is unable to buffer cascading effects. The factors behind this governance failure lie not only in weak environmental legislation, lack of enforcement power or poor monitoring systems (United Nations Environment Programme, 2007), but also in attempts to control a few selected ecosystem variables in efforts to deliver efficiency, reliability, and optimization of ecosystem goods and services (Holling and Meffe, 1996). Such governance can be called a command-and-control approach, and can bring considerable benefits to humans in the short term. However, treating a set of desirable ecosystem goods and services as stable can create mismatches between institutions and ecosystems that can in turn introduce or increase vulnerability to the systems affected, and also lead to undesirable regime shifts and ecological surprises (Gunderson and Holling, 2002; Folke et al., 2003).

For example, Gordon et al. (2008) show how agricultural modifications of hydrological flows can produce a variety of ecological regime shifts that operate across a range of spatial and temporal scales ranging from soil structure to salinization and vegetation patchiness. These shifts can have severe implications for food production, the quality and quantity of freshwater resources, and other ecosystem services such as climate regulation and downstream coastal ecosystems. Allison and Hobbs (2004) describe how adaptive behaviour that fails to respond to environmental feedback in agricultural systems can result in a 'lock-in' trap.

Gunderson and Holling (2002) refer to rigidity traps where people and institutions try to resist change and persist with their current management and governance system despite a clear recognition that change is essential. The tendency to lock into such a pattern comes at the cost of the capacity to respond to new problems and opportunities. In rigidity traps, a high degree of connectivity and the suppression of innovation prolong an increasingly rigid state, which can result in an undesired regime shift in the system. For example, archaeological studies show that people of the Hohokam region, in the Southwest of the United States, developed a way of life that offered few alternatives, which led to a societal collapse (Hegmon et al., 2008). Although conditions worsened, households failed to relocate despite generations of poor health conditions, until the social and physical infrastructure ultimately fell apart. Hence the misfit between social and ecological systems and the inability to respond to feedbacks can push inter-connected social-ecological systems into undesirable pathways from which it is hard to escape, and which may lead to societal collapse and major human suffering.

Within the social sciences and humanities, this problem is referred to as 'path dependence'. A system is path-dependent if initial moves in one direction elicit further moves in the same direction; in other words, if there are self-reinforcing feedback mechanisms (Kay, 2003). Some institutions encourage actors to learn from their mistakes and actively seek new solutions from a variety of sources. Others lock in actors and organizations; they repeat the same strategies (Ostrom et al., 1993). Historical institutionalists see institutions as one of the key factors that drive development along a set of paths (Hall and Taylor, 1996) and have focused on explaining how institutions lock societies into such paths. This includes studies of how institutions structure a nation's response to new challenges. Shifting to new pathways may be very difficult due to stabilizing feedback mechanisms. For example, attempts aimed at implementing new integrated, ecosystem-based approaches for managing and governing marine resources in the United States have been severely constrained by inflexible institutions, a lack of public support, and difficulties developing acceptable legislation (Crowder et al., 2006). In other words, attempts and initiatives to move towards ecosystem management can fail because there are mechanisms operating at different scales – including opinions and worldviews, incentives, power relations, and institutions – that do not support such shifts. Berkes et al. (2006) show how trade flows of marine resources at the global scale and a lack of legislation to deal with 'roving bandits' fishery can stifle attempts to move towards ecosystem-based management at the local/regional level. Understanding drivers, feedbacks, traps, and path dependence, and identifying barriers to change at a specific scale or institutional level are important for developing strategies for transformations in social-ecological systems.

Applying a 'resilience lens' to the study of social-ecological systems emphasizes three aspects:

- *persistence* (buffer capacity, robustness): the most common interpretation of resilience in the literature
- *adaptability*: the capacity to reconfigure or reorganize within the same social-ecological regime in the face of disturbance

- *transformability*: the capacity to create a fundamentally new system when ecological, economic, or social conditions make the existing system untenable.

From a resilience perspective, unsustainable social-ecological regimes can be very difficult to change due to path dependence and inertia in the system. This suggests that resilience as persistence is not necessarily a good thing and that building resilience is not an end in itself, especially if in a trap or on an unsustainable path (Folke et al., 2010). The question is how the persistence of the undesired social-ecological systems regime can be reduced in order to enable shifts to a new regime.

Initiatives for large-scale transformations

The recent global food and climate change crises have triggered a number of initiatives that promote innovation for creating large-scale transformations towards sustainability. Many of these focus on developing countries and technological innovation that can improve livelihoods and enhance human well-being. For example, the Development Marketplace is a competitive grant programme administered by the World Bank. A 2009 global competition – in partnership with the Global Environment Facility (GEF), the International Fund for Agricultural Development (IFAD), and Ministry of Foreign Affairs of Denmark – focused on innovative approaches and technologies that help prepare for and respond to the immediate and potential impacts of climate change. The programme promotes indigenous peoples' communities and organizations' development of innovative ways to conserve agriculture, land, water, and soil management practices. The World Ecological Forum [www.worldecologicalforum.com] (accessed 10 Oct 2011) offers a platform for innovation and active cross-over collaboration, and focuses on catalyzing action for sustainable development and ecological solutions. Rework the World [www.reworktheworld.org] (accessed 10 Oct 2011) is a global initiative that seeks to mobilize young people around the efforts that drive sustainability and create green jobs, from advancing solar energy in East Africa and India to water security and forest conservation in Brazil. The Baltic Sea Action Group [http://en.bsag.fi] (accessed 10 Oct 2011) has a regional focus on sustainability, and their New Challenges programme aims to identify big-gain, high-risk solutions that can make a difference. An example of a project that this programme notes as interesting is the oxygenation of sediments in the Baltic Sea area.

In 2006, with support from the Rockefeller Foundation and the Gates Foundation, the Alliance for a Green Revolution in Africa (AGRA) was founded. The AGRA is an association of farmers, agricultural businesses, scientists, and research institutions that explores innovations in crop production and adjustments to national and international assistance policies to better support African agriculture (Blaustein, 2008). Its intentions are to increase agriculture productivity and thereby improve the welfare of Africa's most struggling communities. However, organizations including the US-based Institute for Food and Development Policy warn that AGRA's policies can exacerbate social and ecological issues because they rely on technological innovations that increase productivity without sufficient considerations of local, social institutions and ecological factors. AGRA's technological innovations may well be an example of what Sterner et al. (2006) call 'quick fixes': innovations that address symptoms but not their underlying causes. Quick fixes can provide short-term solutions to environmental problems such as flooding, poor soil quality or drought, but often have long-term negative consequences that fall upon future generations to address (Foley et al., 2005). There is already evidence that the so-called Green revolution in Asia, supported by USAID since the 1960s, produced dramatic increases in crop yields but displaced millions of small landowners and irreversibly damaged fragile ecosystems in the process. Sander van der Leeuw, a scientist at Arizona State University, also sees some cause for concern; as he stated at a recent The Long Now Foundation meeting, 'It is the rampant innovations of the last two centuries that has led us to the crisis where we currently are' (video available at www.longnow.org) (accessed 10 Oct 2011).

This is not to say that technological innovation has no role in addressing social-ecological sustainability issues. Indeed, Galaz et al. (2010) find that some technological innovations that incorporate a social-ecological systems focus can be critical tools for environmental management. For example, web crawlers can be used to detect early warning signals of ecosystem change. The challenge is to develop reflexive approaches (Voß et al., 2006) to environmental governance that can identify appropriate social and technological innovations in a way that substantially improves current conditions without diminishing the benefits that future generations obtain from ecosystems.

Innovation is the result of experimentation and, therefore, requires management systems that are flexible and even leave room for failure. Indeed, failure can be an important source of feedback and learning. However, this suggests that applying innovations such as new technologies in fragile ecosystems is a risky business with a low margin for error. Quick fixes can push social-ecological systems closer to thresholds and tipping points, reducing the resilience of these systems to further disturbances.

Both research and development activities tend to focus more on technological innovation than on institutional and social innovations (Evans et al., 2010). Social innovation, including new governance and management approaches, can be an important tool for sustainability but also requires critical review. Resource management systems that perform in a socially and economically resilient manner, with well-developed collective action and economic incentive structures, may unintentionally degrade the capacity of ecosystems to provide ecosystem services. The Maine lobster fishery system, for example, is a sophisticated collective action and multi-level governance system that has sustained and regulated economically valuable lobster fisheries. It has been considered one of the classic cases of successful people-oriented local management of common-pool resources. However, when the linkage of the social domain to the production of lobsters is taken into account, the Maine fishery seems to have followed the historical pattern of fishing-down food webs (Jackson et al., 2001). Depletion of the cod fishery opened up space for the expansion of species lower down in food webs, like lobsters. Currently the coastline is massively dominated by lobsters, like a coastal monoculture, with the bulk of the lobster population artificially fed with herring supplied as bait in lobster pots. The lobster has a high market price and sustains the social organization and the fishery. However, such simplification of marine systems through removal of functional diversity has created a highly vulnerable social-ecological system waiting for an accident, like a lobster disease, to happen. If such a 'surprise' occurs, the lobster population might be decimated over huge areas, perhaps triggering a shift into a very different social-ecological system in which coastal waters no longer provide a viable livelihood for local fishermen (Steneck et al., 2011). Because lobster fishing is central to regional identity, the potential loss of lobster fishing could have severe social as well as economic impacts. Another example is the mobilization of Belizean coastal fishermen into cooperatives, which was socially desirable and economically successful, but led to excessive harvesting of stocks of lobster and conch (Huitric, 2005). Such behaviour may cause a shift to a degraded ecosystem state (Sheffer et al., 2001) that in turn feeds back into the social and economic domains, risking unpleasant surprises and undesirable social-ecological regime shifts (Folke et al., 2003).

Similarly, focusing only on the ecological or biological aspects as a basis for decision making for securing ecological integrity and promoting sustainable development may lead to conclusions that are too narrow. A case in point is the establishment of the Maya Biosphere Reserve in Guatemala (Manuel-Navarrete et al., 2004). The goal was to preserve the remaining rainforest that co-evolved with Mayan culture for centuries. The Guatemalan Congress established the reserve in 1990 according to strict biological criteria dictated by outside experts. The response from local people and resource users was violent, and the establishment of the reserve resulted in a decade of struggle between conservationists and local people. This, in turn, led to the development of more participatory conservation strategies, but the integrity of the Mayan forest remained at stake. Similar issues have been described around the failures of many marine protected areas (MPAs) (Ferse et al., 2010). The Maine, Belize, and Guatemala case studies illustrate that a focus on inter-connected social and ecological systems is of crucial importance but is a difficult challenge.

Resilience thinking and the dynamics of social-ecological systems

Although the social and economic dimension is prevalent in the social innovation and entrepreneurship research and development field, the ecological dimension needs strengthening when addressing sustainability. Analyses of social-ecological systems generally differ from analyses of social or ecological systems alone. An observed shift in a lake from a desired to a less desired state, for example, may indicate that the lake has lost resilience from an ecological perspective. However, if there is capacity in the social system to respond to change and restore the lake, the social-ecological system is still resilient (Bodin and Norberg, 2005). Resilience thinking can help develop frameworks for research and development that incorporate a complex adaptive social-ecological system perspective.

Multiple-stable states and thresholds

In the existence of alternate stable states in social-ecological systems, three considerations become important. The first has to do with identifying and monitoring thresholds. For example, an aquatic system might have a safe level of nutrient input, regulated by internal feedbacks, before it shifts into an undesired state. This means that a system can appear healthy and stable up until it abruptly shifts to a new state. Walker et al. (2009) use a resilience-based approach to assess sustainability in the Goulburn-Broken catchments, Australia, and identify ten biophysical, economic, and social thresholds. Crossing these thresholds might result in irreversible change in goods and services generated by the region. In the Kruger National Park, South Africa, a collaborative process is used among stakeholders to identify 'Thresholds of Potential Concern' (Biggs and Rogers, 2003). At a global scale, Rockström and others (2009) have identified and quantified planetary boundaries and biophysical thresholds that, if crossed, could cause unacceptable environmental change and have devastating consequences for humanity. There are, however, a range of uncertainties regarding these thresholds and boundaries, and the interactions between them. Such uncertainty poses a great challenge for monitoring and a great deal of research focuses on early warning signals to detect thresholds before they have been passed. (e.g. van Nes and Scheffer, 2007; Biggs et al., 2009).

A second important consideration is how to steer clear of critical thresholds and avoid regime shifts to undesired states. Once a threshold is identified it is possible to steer away from it. In the Kruger National Park, for example, managers use a reflexive, adaptive management approach to treat policy goals and targets as hypotheses that are revised in the light of new knowledge when approaching a Threshold of Potential Concern (Biggs and Rogers, 2003). Biggs et al. (2009) argue that avoiding ecological regime shifts depends on the ability rapidly to respond to early warnings of change, and that there must also be policy windows for such intervention. In the case of planetary boundaries (Rockström et al., 2009), the challenges include developing global governance approaches that can help humanity stay within a 'safe operating space.'

A third consideration has to do with enabling regime shifts from undesired states to more desired states, which requires actively passing thresholds. Self-reinforcing feedbacks keep a system in a certain state, which makes it hard to shift out of, a phenomenon called hysteresis. This poses a challenge for restoration efforts. Moreover, thresholds are often dynamic, but understanding threshold dynamics can help design effective restoration strategies. Holmgren and Scheffer (2001) show how restoration strategies can make use of wet El Niño Southern Oscillation (ENSO) years to induce vegetation and ecosystem restoration and shift from a 'bare soil' to a 'woody' state. Similarly, the Baltic Sea ecosystem has gone through a number of undesired regime shifts (Österblom, 2008), and discussions about how to counter-act these trends involve using a good saltwater inflow year (which comes from the North Sea and happens irregularly) that can temporarily lower the threshold and enable a shift to a more desirable state (Österblom et al., 2010).

Diversity and connectivity

Biological diversity plays an important role in the health and resilience of ecosystems, and provides the ingredients for regenerating an ecosystem within its current state after disturbance. For example, Hughes et al. (2004) show the role of herbivorous fish in preventing undesired regime shifts in the face of disturbance events like coral bleaching (coral die-off caused by increases in water temperature due to global warming). In the absence of grazing fish, algae can move in and colonize the reef, keeping coral larvae from resettling, and causing an 'ecosystem flip'. In the presence of fish, however, the algae are kept at bay and the coral reef can recover.

Response diversity refers to species that can carry out the same ecosystem functions, like algal-grazing fish on coral reefs, but that respond differently to disturbances (Elmqvist et al., 2003). As observed by Folke and colleagues (2004), the loss of response diversity leads to more fragile ecological systems. This means that an ecosystem where disturbances were previously buffered and that may have helped revitalize the system after prior disturbances can undergo practically irreversible shifts if diversity is diminished. The result, in turn, can be states with less capacity to support social welfare. This applies to both small- and large-scale ecological systems, including shallow lakes, coral reefs, landscapes, and even the global climate system (Scheffer et al., 2001; Folke et al., 2004; Schneider, 2004).

A major task of ecosystem stewardship is to identify and manage the role of functional groups of organisms, their redundancy, and their response diversity in relation to ecosystem services at the landscape and seascape scales (Elmqvist et al., 2003; Nyström, 2006). Management that focuses on using protected areas and reserves as reservoirs of biodiversity to strengthen resilience is gaining ground (e.g. Bengtsson et al., 2003). This builds on the notion that different habitats and ecosystems in a landscape depend on each other for ecosystem renewal and resilience (Nyström et al., 2001). For example, patches of coral reef in a seascape can be connected by 'mobile links' (biological or physical processes that link patches on a landscape) (Moberg and Lundberg, 2003) that help recolonize a disturbed reef. But the coral patch might also be dependent on other habitats like sea grass beds and mangroves for the same reasons. Brondizio et al. (2009) describe the limitations of conserving 'islands of resources' and the governance challenges of addressing landscape heterogeneity and connectivity in relation to the resilience of social-ecological systems. The connectivity between patches is equally important and can be addressed through management practices. For example, to enhance the resilience to climate change and secure ecosystem services of the Great Barrier Reef in Australia, 70 different reef and non-reef habitats were identified and a marine zoning plan was used to create a network of protected areas which included at least 20 per cent of each of the 70 habitats (Fernandes et al., 2005; Olsson et al., 2008; McCook et al., 2010).

While research shows that maintaining biophysical diversity helps prevent threshold effects, some researchers argue that institutional diversity is also important. As discussed by Low and colleagues (2003), redundancy and diversity in environmental and resource regimes can become a major source of stability and strength, as they can provide multiple ways of coping with, or reorganizing after, change and unexpected events. The argument is that redundant systems can compensate for human errors and for unpredictable changes in circumstances. One simple example of this is technical redundancy in engineered systems such as the Boeing 777. Multiple components that assume the same function can work as backup in case of partial technical failure or provide redundant strength, hence allowing for a higher margin of error. Both types of redundancy can provide robust performance despite changing and uncertain environments (Low et al., 2003).

Cross-scale interactions

Kinzig et al. (2006) provide a number of projections of social, economic, and ecological conditions in the Australian wheat belt and reveal a number of interacting thresholds. Abrupt shifts from sufficient soil humidity to saline soils and from freshwater to saline ecosystems could render agriculture non-viable at a regional scale. This in turn might trigger migration, unemployment, and weakened social capital. They also provide illustrations of the governance challenges posed by cascade effects or the possibility of causing such effects. Building resilience at one scale can erode resilience at another scale (Folke et al., 2010). Building resilience is scale-dependent and requires an understanding of cross-scale interactions.

Interactions occur between both temporal and spatial scales. Changes at faster scales can trigger changes at slower scales and changes at larger scales can open up windows of opportunity for transformations at regional to local scales. For example, the diffusion of small-scale farming innovations can have large-scale impacts on re-greening Africa's drylands and the Sahel in particular (Reij et al., 2008). These dynamics are a central part of the panarchy[3] theory (Gunderson and Holling, 2002). Shifts from one social-ecological regime will often require novelty and innovation, drawn from other scales or other systems. This has been referred to as social-ecological memory (Barthel and Folke, 2010). For example, Gelcich et al. (2010) describe how a new governance approach for marine resources emerged in the late 1980s in Chile at a time of marine resource crisis and political turbulence. The resource crisis triggered a few collaboration initiatives between fishers and scientists who, for different reasons, started to solve their problems together. Political turbulence in the late 1980s provided a window of opportunity for fishermen to organize and influence the new national fishery legislation. Hence, transformations at one scale do not take place in a vacuum but in a cross-scale context.

Discussion

This section discusses ways of combining perspectives on social innovation and entrepreneurship with resilience thinking and research on social-ecological systems. This can increase our understanding of patterns in innovation and transformation, particularly regarding shifts to more adaptive, integrated, collaborative approaches for governing and managing social-ecological systems.

Researchers in social sciences and the humanities have long recognized that rigidity, lock-in traps, and path dependence are common characteristics of institutional development and public policy making. They have deepened our understanding of the drivers of sudden change and 'punctuated equilibrium' where long periods of stability and incremental change experience abrupt, non-incremental, large-scale change (e.g. Baumgartner and Jones, 1991; True et al., 1999). For example, in 1970 the US experienced an abrupt burst of environmental policy innovations and a number of environmental laws were passed in rapid succession (Repetto, 2006). This period lasted for about five years and was exceptional in terms of public concern over environmental protection, political mobilization, and legislative consensus. The literature on punctuated equilibrium recognizes that there are critical junctures and branching points from which historical development moves onto a new path. Understanding the sequence of events that leads to such junctures and the role of innovation is of crucial importance for understanding transformative capacity.

Resilience research in transformability focuses on how to 'unlock' a locked-in regime or escape from traps. Gunderson et al. (2009) argue that there are at least two ways to unlock a system. One is the experience of a crisis, an external variation that overwhelms system resilience. Crises, like the current climate change crisis, food crisis, and financial crisis, can potentially be used productively to stimulate experimentation, innovation, novelty, and learning within society. The other way is a more 'quiet revolution' where internal processes, sometimes eroded by broader scale processes and drivers, reduce the resilience of the system and the resistance to change. Lock-in mechanisms operate at different levels and scales and in different parts of the system (social, economical, ecological), and strategies need to be developed to understand such mechanisms and find ways to unlock them. In order to do so this chapter concurs with Lane et al. (2009) that there is a need to move from simple linear models of innovation and diffusion and transformation to more complex models that reflect phase shifts, bifurcation points, and thresholds as well as cross-scale interactions.

Recent research explores the links between disturbance/crisis, opportunity, and innovation for creating radical shifts and transformations in social-ecological systems (Biggs et al., 2010; Chapin et al., 2010). It focuses on the mechanisms for linking social innovations to a specific opportunity context (of which crisis and disturbance can be a part) and the emergence of new ecosystem-based management approaches. These studies confirm that there are no blueprints or recipes for sustainability transitions. Instead empirical studies show that transformations are multi-level and multi-phase processes that involve incremental as well as abrupt change (Olsson et al., 2004). There are at least three recognizable phases of transformation in social-ecological systems: (1) preparing for transformation; (2) navigating the transition; and (3) building resilience of the new governance regime. Phases (1) and (2) are linked by a window of opportunity. Provide a more detailed analysis of such shifts and identify mechanisms that support phase transitions, including the role of innovation, sense-making strategies, enabling conditions, dynamic networks, and institutional entrepreneurs.

There is a need to focus on key features for reducing the resilience of undesired regimes and the capacity to unlock social-ecological regimes (Gunderson and Holling, 2002; Gunderson et al., 2009). More specifically, studies on social innovation and transformative capacity need to focus on inter-connected social-ecological systems, especially on changes in feedback loops (Chapin et al., 2009). One challenge is to understand the mechanisms for breaking up self-reinforcing feedback loops that keep a system on an undesired trajectory (Gunderson and Holling, 2002). For example, Enfors (2009) maps the drivers and feedback loops that keep small-scale agricultural social-ecological systems in dry land sub-Saharan Africa in a poverty trap. This mapping helps to clarify when, where, and how small-scale farm innovations can break these loops and enable communities to escape poverty traps, shift livelihoods, and secure long-term provisioning of ecosystem services (Enfors, 2009). In a similar way, Sendzimir et al. (2008) map the structure of two competing sets of feedback loops in a water management regime in the Tiscza River, Hungary, where the dominating loop keeps the system on an unsustainable trajectory. However, their research shows that there is a new management approach emerging in an informal network or shadow network that is beginning to challenge the old paradigm and create new feedback loops.

Shadow networks are informal networks that emphasize political independence outside the fray of regulation and implementation in places in which formal networks and many planning processes fail (Gunderson, 1999; Olsson et al., 2006). Shadow networks are incubators for new ideas and approaches for governing social-ecological systems. Similarly, Pelling et al. (2008) discuss the role of shadow spaces and organizations in fostering innovation and experimentation for social learning and adaptation to climate change. In the Chile case described above, actors within informal networks experimented with new ecosystem management approaches, innovations that were ready to be scaled up when a window of opportunity opened. In Kristianstad Vattenrike, a shadow network initiated collaborative experiments to reduce nutrient loads to the rivers. In the Great Barrier Reef, experiments showed that the biomass of coral trout was up to six times lower on heavily fished near-shore reefs compared with adjacent no-take areas. These experiments generated innovations that became the seeds for developing new approaches that could help steer clear of potential thresholds and enhance the fit between the ecosystem and governance systems. This is in line with the findings of scholars in transition management (e.g. Loorbach, 2010) who argue that the ability to co-ordinate experiments that contribute to system innovation is of crucial importance to release lock-ins and enable shifts into new trajectories. In other words, experimentation requires resilience – but building resilience requires experimentation (see also Gunderson, 2003).

Experiments such as those described here can be important when preparing for a transformation by 'beta testing' alternative policy options that can be ready when an opportunity comes along. These windows of opportunity can be triggered by biophysical factors as in the cases of semi-arid ecosystems and ENSO and the Baltic Sea and the saltwater inflow described earlier. In Australia, change agents used a national election as a political window of opportunity for implementing a new zoning legislation for the Great Barrier Reef (Olsson et al., 2008). Olsson et al. (2006) highlight the role of individual actors or bridging organizations[4] that scan for and use windows of opportunity to develop and utilize ties with various different actors at different scales and launch new initiatives and scale up innovations. Hence, institutional entrepreneurs successful in scaling up social innovations within an opportunity context have an ability to create the right links, at the right time, around the right issues (Westley et al., 2006).

In order for a social innovation to have a broad, durable impact, the social innovation must 'cross multiple social boundaries to reach more people and different people, more organizations and different organizations, organizations nested across scales (from local to regional to national to global) and linked in social networks' (Westley and Antadze, 2009).

There are other factors that support and frame the scaling-up of social innovations, including scenario planning, conflict resolution, trust building, bridging organizations, and sense making. In the context of social-ecological systems, sense-making processes can be important for interpreting ecosystem changes and creating a meaningful order. The sense-making process helps link ecosystem changes and degradation to social factors including values and perspectives, organizational structures, and institutions at multiple levels. In both Kristianstads Vattenrike Biosphere Reserve (Olsson et al., 2004) and the Great Barrier Reef (Olsson et al., 2008), raising awareness of pending social-ecological crises helped change public perceptions and attitudes, which was important for unlocking and changing existing regimes. Shifts to more integrated forms of water management in the Netherlands (van den Brink and Meijerink, 2005) have been preceded by a change in collectively held mental models, from 'fighting the water' to 'living with the water'. In the Kristianstad, Great Barrier Reef, and Chile case studies, changes in attitudes among a few local politicians marked a critical tipping-point into new social-ecological trajectories (Olsson et al., 2004; Olsson et al., 2008; Gelcich et al., 2010). This shows that links to the political arena are of crucial importance in order to move from an idea, shared by a small informal network of engaged actors, to the institutionalization of a new environmental governance and management approach.

Scenario building is another key tool for collectively identifying possible futures and plausible alternative pathways for the social-ecological system (Carpenter and Folke, 2006; Peterson et al., 2007; Enfors et al., 2008). Scenario planning can frame the process of scaling-up and help define the arena for collaboration, connect and coordinate ongoing activities, and develop social networks.

There is a need to further develop our understanding of diffusion and up-scaling of social innovations and the impact they have on social-ecological systems, including new national and global environmental governance solutions applicable to challenges at these scales. For example, Voß (2007) studies the diffusion of the emissions trading policy instrument; from when it was a policy proposal by the US Environmental Protection to a global standard in environmental governance. Marinova and Todorov (2009) argue for a globally coordinated Global Green System of Innovation for dealing with climate change. Although these studies can help shift the focus of analysis to include a global dimension they also point to two problems and research gaps. One is that they tend to focus on technological innovations. The other is that these analyses tend to involve a single sector (like energy) or one problem (like climate change). However, the linked nature of environmental problems (Lenton et al., 2008; Rockström et al., 2009; Walker et al., 2009) calls for global, integrated approaches that can focus on innovative ways of addressing the interface between sectors and problems (Galaz et al., forthcoming), like new multi-level governance solutions for addressing the interface between climate change, biodiversity, and ocean acidification.

Conclusion

This chapter has used insights from resilience thinking and research on social-ecological systems to argue for a focus on inter-connected social-ecological systems to address interacting environmental problems. It suggests 'social-ecological innovation' as an organizing concept to link research in perspectives on social innovation and entrepreneurship with resilience thinking and research on social-ecological systems. Social-ecological innovation is defined as social innovation, including new strategies, concepts, ideas, institutions, and organizations that enhance the capacity of ecosystems to generate services. These have the potential to enhance human well-being and reduce vulnerability to present and future challenges. Social-ecological innovations can enhance the fit between ecosystems and governance systems, help move to new trajectories of sustainability, and contribute to the overall resilience of social-ecological systems.

A key question identified in this chapter that requires further attention is the role of social innovation in transforming multi-level governance and management regimes and reversing the current trends that challenge critical thresholds and tipping points in the Earth system.

There are ongoing, large-scale transformations in society, influenced by such things as information and communication technology, nano- and biotechnology, and new energy systems. Such innovations have the potential significantly to improve peoples' lives. However, if the globalized society fails to incorporate the capacity of the biosphere to provide ecosystem services in framing their development, there is a risk that they may reinforce unsustainable development pathways. History has shown us numerous examples of major socio-technological advances, like the Industrial Revolution, that have improved human life but at the same time degraded the life-support systems on which it ultimately depends. The concept of social-ecological innovation can help identify new models that open up transformative trajectories of sustainability, avoid lock-in traps, and steer away from potential earth-system thresholds and tipping points.

Notes

1. Ecosystem services are resources and processes supplied by ecosystems that benefit humankind. They include products like clean drinking water and processes such as the decomposition of wastes. Although the term 'ecosystem services' has been around for decades, it was brought to a wider audience through the Millennium Ecosystem Assessment (2005). This worldwide, four-year study grouped ecosystem services into four categories: provisioning, such as the production of food and water; regulating, such as the control of climate and disease; supporting, such as nutrient cycles and crop pollination; and cultural, such as spiritual and recreational benefits.
2. This chapter uses Westley and Antadze's (2009) definition of social innovations: 'Social innovation is a complex process of introducing products, processes or programs that profoundly change the basic routines, resource and authority flows or beliefs of the social system in which they arise' p.5.
3. The interdisciplinary panarchy theory focuses on cross-scale interactions in social-ecological systems. 'Its essential focus is to rationalize the interplay between change and persistence, between the predictable and unpredictable … Panarchy is the structure in which systems, including those of nature (e.g. forests) and of humans (e.g. capitalism), as well as combined human-natural systems (e.g. institutions that govern natural resource use such as the Forest Service), are interlinked in continual adaptive cycles of growth, accumulation, restructuring, and renewal' (Gunderson et al., 2002).
4. 'Bridging organizations provide arenas for multisector and/or multilevel collaboration for conceiving visions, trust-building, collaboration, learning, value formation, conflict resolution, and other institutional innovations. Bridging organizations lower the transaction costs of collaboration and crafting effective responses' (Malayang et al., 2005). Bridging organizations facilitate interaction, offer leadership, and identify incentives for coordinated actions (Hahn et al., 2006).

References

Allison, H. E. and Hobbs R. J. (2004), 'Resilience, Adaptive Capacity, and the "Lock-in Trap" of the Western Australian Agricultural Region', *Ecology and Society*, 9 (1), 3. [online] URL: http://www.ecologyandsociety.org/vol9/iss1/art3/. Accessed: 10 October 2011.

Barthel, S., Folke, C. and Colding, J. (2010), 'Social–Ecological Memory in Urban Gardens – Retaining the Capacity for Management of Ecosystem Services', *Global Environmental Change*, 20 (2), pp. 255–65.

Baumgartner, F. R. and Jones, B. D. (1991), 'Agenda Dynamics and Policy Subsystems', *Journal of Politics*, 53 (4), pp. 1044–74.

Bengtsson, J., Angelstam, P., Elmqvist, T., Emanuelsson, U., Folke, C., Ihse, M., Moberg, F. and Nyström, M. (2003), 'Reserves, Resilience and Dynamic Landscapes', *Ambio*, 32 (6), pp. 389–96.

Berkes, F., Colding, J. and Folke, C. (eds) (2003), *Navigating Social-ecological Systems: Building Resilience for Complexity and Change*, Cambridge, UK: Cambridge University Press.

Berkes, F. and Folke, C. (eds) (1998), *Linking Social and Ecological Systems: Management Practices and Social Mechanisms for Building Resilience*, Cambridge, UK: Cambridge University Press.

Berkes, F., Hughes, T. P., Steneck, R. S., Wilson, J. A., Bellwood, D. R., Crona, B., Folke, C., Gunderson, L. H., Leslie, H. M., Norberg, J., Nyström, M., Olsson, P., Österblom, H., Scheffer, M. and Worm, B. (2006), 'Globalization, Roving Bandits and Marine Resources', *Science*, 311 (5767), pp. 1557–8.

Biggs, H. C. and Rogers, K. H. (2003), 'An Adaptive System to Link Science, Monitoring, and Management in Practice', in *The Kruger Experience: Ecology and Management of Savanna Heterogeneity*, edited by J. T. du Toit, K. H. Rogers and H. C. Biggs, pp. 59–80, Washington, DC: Island Press.

Biggs, R., Carpenter, S. R. and Brock, W. A. (2009), 'Turning Back from the Brink: Detecting an Impending Regime Shift in Time to Avert It', Proceedings of the National Academy of Sciences, USA, 106, pp. 826–31.

Biggs, R., Westley, F. R. and Carpenter, S. R. (2010), 'Navigating the Back Loop: Fostering Social Innovation and Transformation in Ecosystem Management', *Ecology and Society*, 15 (2), p. 9. [online] URL: http://www.ecologyandsociety.org/vol15/iss2/art9/. 10 October 2011.

Blaustein R. J. (2008), 'The Green Revolution Arrives in Africa', *BioScience*, 58 (1), pp. 8–14.

Bodin, Ö. and Norberg, J. (2005), 'Information network topologies for enhanced local adaptivemanagement', *Environmental Management*, 35 (2), pp. 175–93.

Brondizio, E. S., Ostrom, E. and Young, O. R. (2009), 'Connectivity and the Governance of Multilevel Social-Ecological Systems: The Role of Social Capital', *Annual Review of Environment and Resources*, 34, pp. 253–78.

Carpenter, S. R. and Folke, C. (2006), 'Ecology for Transformation', *Trends in Ecology and Evolution*, 21 (6), pp. 309–15.

Crowder, L. B., Osherenko, G., Young, O., Airamé, S., Norse, E. A., Baron, N., Day, J. C., Douvere, F., Ehler, C. N., Halpern, B. S., Langdon, S. J., McLeod, K. L., Ogden, J. C., Peach, R. E., Rosenberg, A. A., and Wilson, J. A., (2006) 'Resolving Mismatches in US Ocean Governance', *Science*, 313 (5787), pp. 617–18.

Chapin III, F. S., Carpenter, S. R., Kofinas, G. P., Folke, C., Abel, N., Clark, W. C., Olsson, P., Stafford Smith, D. M., Walker, B., Young, O. R., Berkes, F., Biggs, R., Grove, j. M., Naylor, R. L, Pinkerton, E., Steffen, W. and Swanson, F. J. (2010), 'Ecosystem Stewardship: Sustainability Strategies for a Rapidly Changing Planet', *Trends in Ecology and Evolution*, 25 (4), pp. 241–9.

Dovers, S. R. and Handmer, J. W. (1992), 'Uncertainty, Sustainability and Change', *Global Environmental Change*, 2 (4), pp. 262–76.

Duit, A. and Galaz, V. (2008), 'Governance and Complexity – Emerging Issues for Governance Theory', *Governance*, 21 (3), pp. 311–35.

Elmqvist, T., Folke, C., Nyström, M., Peterson, G., Bengtsson, J., Walker, B. and Norberg, J. (2003), 'Response Diversity, Ecosystem Change and Resilience', *Frontiers in Ecology Environment*, 1 (9), pp. 488–94.

Enfors, E. I., Gordon, L. J., Peterson, G. D. and Bossio, D. (2008), 'Making Investments in Dryland Development Work: Participatory Scenario Planning in the Makanya Catchment, Tanzania', *Ecology and Society*, 13 (2), p. 42. [online] URL: http://www.ecologyandsociety.org/vol13/iss2/art42/.

Enfors, E. (2009), 'Traps and Transformations: Exploring the Potential of Water System Innovations in Dryland Sub-Saharan Africa', Doctoral Thesis in Natural Resource Management, Department of Systems Ecology, Stockholm University.

Evans, A., Jones, B. and Steven, D. (2010), 'Confronting the Long Crisis of Globalization: Risk, Resilience and International Order', *Brookings/CIC*, 2010, p. 21, available: http://www.humansecuritygateway.com/documents/BROOKINGS_ConfrontingLongCrisisGlobalization.pdf.

Ferse, S. C. A., Mánez Costa, M., Schwerdtner Mánez, K., Adhuri, D. S., Glaser, M. (2010), 'Allies, not Aliens – Increasing the Role of Local Communities in Marine Protected Area Implementation', *Environmental Conservation*, 37 (1), pp. 23–34.

Fernandes, L., Day, J., Lewis, A., Slegers, S., Kerrigan, B., Breen, D., Cameron, D., Jago, B., Hall, J., Lowe, D., Innes, J., Tanzer, J., Chadwick, V., Thompson, L., Gorman, K., Simmons, M., Barnett, B., Sampson, K., De'ath, G., Mapstone, B., Marsh, H., Possingham, H., Ball, I., Ward, T., Dobbs, K., Aumend, J., Slater, D. and Stapleton, K. (2005), 'Establishing Representative No-take Areas in the Great Barrier Reef: Large-scale Implementation of Theory on Marine Protected Areas', *Conservation Biology*, 19 (6), pp. 1733–44.

Foley, J. A., DeFries, R., Asner, G. P., Barford, C., Bonan, G., Carpenter, S. R., Chapin, F. S., Coe, M. T., Daily, G. C., Gibbs, H. K., Helkowski, J. H., Holloway, T., Howard, E. A., Kucharik, C. J., Monfreda, C., Patz, J. A., Prentice, I. C., Ramankutty, N., Snyder, P. K. (2005), 'Global Consequences of Land Use', *Science*, 309 (5734), pp. 570–74.

Folke, C, Carpenter, S., Walker, B., Scheffer, M., Chapin, T. and Rockström, J. (2010), 'Resilience Thinking: Integrating Resilience, Adaptability and Transformability', in press *Ecology and Society* 15 (4), p. 20. [online] URL: http://www.ecologyandsociety.org/vol15/iss4/art20/. Accessed: 17 November 2011.

Folke, C., Colding, J. and Berkes, F. (2003), 'Synthesis: Building Resilience and Adaptive Capacity in Social-Ecological systems', in F. Berkes, J. Colding and C. Folke (eds) *Navigating Social-ecological Systems: Building Resilience for Complexity and Change* Cambridge, UK: Cambridge University Press, pp. 352–87.

Folke, C., Pritchard, L., Berkes, F., Colding, J. and Svedin, U. (1998), 'The Problem of Fit between Ecosystems and Institutions', IHDP Working Paper No. 2. International Human Dimensions Programme, Bonn, Germany.

Folke, C., Pritchard, L., Berkes, F., Colding, J. and Svedin, U. (2007), 'The Problem of Fit between Ecosystems and Institutions: Ten Years Later', Ecology and Society, 12 (1), 30 (online) URL: http://www.ecologyandsociety.org/vol12/iss1/art30/. Accessed: 10 October 2011.

Folke, C., Carpenter, S., Walker, B., Scheffer, M., Elmqvist, T., Gunderson, L. and Holling, C. S. (2004), 'Regime Shifts, Resilience and Biodiversity in Ecosystem Management', *Annual Review of Ecology Evolution and Systematics*, 35, pp. 557–81.

Galaz, V., Olsson, P., Hahn, T., Folke, C. and Svedin, U. (2008), 'The Problem of Fit among Biophysical Systems, Environmental and Resource Regimes, and Broader Governance Systems: Insights and Emerging Challenges', in O. R. Young, L. A. King and H. Schröder (eds) *Institutions and Environmental Change – Principal Findings, Applications, and Research Frontiers*, Cambridge, MA: The MIT Press, pp. 147–82.

Galaz, V., Crona, B., Daw, T., Bodin, Ö., Nyström, M. and Olsson, P. (2010), 'Can webcrawlers revolutionize ecological monitoring?' *Frontiers in Ecology and Environment* 8, pp. 99–104.

Galaz, V., Crona, B., Österblom, H., Olsson, P. and Folke, C. (forthcoming), 'Polycentric Systems and Interacting Planetary Boundaries – Emerging Governance of Climate Change – Ocean Acidification – Marine Biodiversity'. Forthcoming in *Ecological Economics*.

Geels, F. W. and Schot, J. (2007), 'Typology of Socio-technical Transition Pathways', *Research Policy*, 36 (3), pp. 399–417.

Gelcich, S., Hughes, T., Olsson, P., Folke, C., Defeo, O., Fernández, M., Foale, S., Gunderson, L. H., Rodríguez-Sickert, C., Scheffer, M., Steneck, R. and Castilla, J. C. (2010), 'Navigating transformations in governance of Chilean marine coastal resources.' Proceedings of the National Academy of Sciences, USA, 107 (39) 16794–99.

Gordon, L. J., Peterson, G. D. and Bennett, E. M. (2008), 'Agricultural Modifications of Hydrological Flows Create Ecological Surprises', *Trends in Ecology & Evolution*, 23 (4), pp. 211–19.

Grau, H. R. and Aide, M. (2008), 'Globalization and Land-use Transitions in Latin America', *Ecology and Society* 13 (2), p.16. [online] URL: http://www.ecologyandsociety.org/vol13/iss2/art16/. Accessed: 10 October 2011.

Gunderson, L. H. and Holling, C. S. (eds) (2002), *Panarchy: Understanding Transformations in Social-ecological Systems*, London, UK: Island Press.

Gunderson, L. H. (2003), 'Adaptive Dancing: Interactions between Social Resilience and Ecological Crises', in F. Berkes, J. Colding and C. Folke (eds) (2002), *Navigating Social-Ecological Systems: Building Resilience for Complexity and Change*, Cambridge, UK: Cambridge University Press, pp. 33–52.

Gunderson, L., Allen, C., Holling, C. S. (2009), *Fundamentals of Ecological Resilience*, Washington, DC: Island Press.

Hahn, T., Olsson, P., Folke, C. and Johansson, K. (2006), 'Trust-Building, Knowledge Generation and Organizational Innovations: The Role of a Bridging Organization for Adaptive Co-management of a Wetland Landscape around Kristianstad, Sweden', *Human Ecology*, 34 (4), pp. 573–92.

Hall, P. A. and Taylor, R. C. R. (1996), 'Political Science and the Three New Institutionalisms', *Political Studies*, 44 (5), pp. 936–57.

Hegmon, M., Peeples, M. A., Kinzig, A., Kulow, S., Meegan, C. M. and Nelson, M. C. (2008), 'Social Transformation and Its Human Costs in the Prehispanic US Southwest', *American Anthropologist*, 110 (3), pp. 313–24.

Holling, C. S. and Meffe, G. K. (1996), 'Command and Control and the Pathology of Natural Resource Management', *Conservation Biology*, 10 (2), pp. 328–37.

Holmgren, M. and Scheffer, M. (2001), 'El Niño as a Window of Opportunity for the Restoration of Degraded Arid Ecosystems', *Ecosystems*, 4 (2), pp. 151–9.

Huitric, M. (2005), 'Lobster and Conch fisheries of Belize: A History of Sequential Exploitation', *Ecology and Society*, 10 (1), p.21. http://www.ecologyandsociety.org/vol10/iss1/art21/. Accessed: 10 October 2011.

Jackson, J. B. C., Kirby, M. X., Berger, W. H., Bjorndal, K. A., Botsford, L. W., Bourque, B. J., Bradbury, R. H., Cooke, R., Erlandson, J., Estes, J. A., Hughes, T. P., Kidwell, S., Lange, C. B., Lenihan, H. S., Pandolfi, J. M., Peterson, C. H., Steneck, R. S., Tegner, M. J., Warner, R. R. (2001), 'Historical Overfishing and the Recent Collapse of Coastal Ecosystems', *Science*, 293 (5530), pp. 629–38.

Kay, A. (2003), 'Path Dependency and the CAP', *Journal of European Public Policy*, 10 (3), June 2003, pp. 405–20.

Kinzig, A. P., Ryan, P., Etienne, M., Allison, H., Elmqvist, T. and Walker, B. H. (2006), Resilience and Regime Shifts: Assessing Cascading Effects', *Ecology and Society*, 11 (1), p. 20. [online] URL: http://www.ecologyandsociety.org/vol11/iss1/art20/. Accessed: 10 October 2011.

Lane, D., van der Leeuw, S., Pumain, D. and West, G. (eds) (2009), *Complexity Perspectives in Innovation and Social Change*, New York, NY: Springer.

Lansing, J. S. (1991), *Priests and Programmers: Technologies of Power in the Engineered Landscape of Bali*, Princeton, NJ: Princeton University Press.

Lenton, T. M., Held, H., Kriegler, E., Hall, J., Lucht, W., Rahmstorf, S., Schellnhuber, H.-J. (2008), 'Tipping Elements in the Earth's Climate System', *Proc. Natl. Acad. Sci. USA*, 105 (6), pp. 1786–93.

Levin, S. (1999), *Fragile Dominion: Complexity and the Commons*, Reading, PA: Perseus Publishing.

Loorbach, D. (2010), 'Transition Management for Sustainable Development: A Prescriptive, Complexity-Based Governance Framework', *Governance*, 23 (1), pp. 161–83.

Loorbach, D. and Rotmans, J. (2010), 'The Practice of Transition Management: Examples and Lessons from four Distinct Cases', *Futures*, 42 (3), pp. 237–46.

Low, B., Ostrom, E., Simon, C. and Wilson, J. (2003), 'Redundancy and Diversity: Do they Influence Optimal Management', in F. Berkes, J. Colding and C. Folke (eds) *Navigating Social–Ecological Systems*, Cambridge: Cambridge University Press, pp. 83–114.

Lundberg, J. and Moberg, F. (2003), 'Mobile Link Organisms and Ecosystem Functioning: Implications for Ecosystem Resilience and Management', *Ecosystems*, 6 (1), pp. 87–98.

Malayang III, B. S., Hahn, T. and Kumar, P. (2005), 'Responses to Ecosystem Change and to their Impacts on Human Well-being', in Millennium Ecosystem Assessment, Findings of the Sub-global Assessments Working Group, Chapter 9, pp. 205–08. *Island Press*, Available at http://www.maweb.org. Accessed: 17 November 2011.

Marinova, D. and Todorov, V. (2009), 'Climate Change and Global Green System of Innovation', Conference paper presented at the 5th Dubrovnik conference on sustainable development of energy, water, and environment system, the 30 Sept–3 Oct 2009: University of Zagreb and Instituto Superior Tecnico. Available at http://www.clubofrome.at/2009/dubrovnik/supi2009/dl_oct_marinova.pdf. Accessed: 17 November 2011.

Manuel-Navarrete, D., Kay, J. J., Dolderman, D. (2004), 'Ecological Integrity Discourses: Linking Ecology with Cultural Transformation', *Human Ecology Review*, 11 (3), pp. 215–29.

McCook, L. J., Ayling, T., Cappo, M., Choat, J. H., Evans, R. D., De Freitas, D. M., Heupel, M., Hughes, T. P., Jones, G. P., Mapstone, B., Marsh, H., Mills, M., Molloy, F. J., Pitcher, C. R., Pressey, R. L., Russ, G. R., Sutton, S., Sweatman, H., Tobin, R., Wachenfeld, D. R., Williamson, D. H. (2010), 'Adaptive Management of the Great Barrier Reef: A Globally Significant Demonstration of the Benefits of Networks of Marine Reserves', *Proceedings of the National Academy of Sciences, USA* [Available online].

Millennium Ecosystem Assessment (2005), *Ecosystems and Human Well-being: Synthesis*, Washington, DC: Island Press.

Nyström, M. (2006), 'Redundancy and Response Diversity of Functional Groups: Implications for the Resilience of Coral Reefs', *Ambio*, 35 (1), pp. 30–5.

Nyström, M. and Folke, C. (2001), 'Spatial Resilience of Coral Reefs', *Ecosystems*, 4 (5), pp. 406–17.

Olsson, P., Folke, C. and Hahn, T. (2004), 'Social-ecological Transformation for Ecosystem Management: The Development of Adaptive Co-management of a Wetland Landscape in Southern Sweden', *Ecology and Society*, 9 (4), p. 2 (online) URL: http://www.ecologyandsociety.org/vol9/iss4/art2. Accessed: 10 October 2011.

Olsson, P., Gunderson, L. H., Carpenter, S. R., Ryan, P., Lebel, L., Folke, C. and Holling, C. S. (2006), 'Shooting the Rapids: Navigating Transitions to Adaptive Governance of Social-ecological Systems', *Ecology and Society*, 11 (1), p.18 (online) URL: http://www.ecologyandsociety.org/vol11/iss1/art18/. Accessed: 10 October 2011.

Olsson, P., Folke, C. and Hughes, T. P. (2008), 'Navigating the Transition to Ecosystem-based Management of the Great Barrier Reef, Australia', *Proceedings of the National Academy of Sciences, USA*, 105 (28), pp. 9489–94.

Österblom, H., Hansson, S., Larsson, U., Hjerne, O., Wulff, F., Elmgren, R. and Folke, C. (2007), 'Human-induced Trophic Cascades and Ecological Regime Shifts in the Baltic Sea', *Ecosystems*, 10 (6), pp. 877–89.

Österblom, H., Gårdmark, A., Bergström, L., Müller-Karalis, B., Folke, C., Lindefren, M., Casini, M., Olsson, P., Diekmann, R., Blenckner, T., Humborg, C., Möllmann, C. (2010), 'Making the Ecosystem Approach Operational – Can Regime Shifts in Ecological and Governance Systems Facilitate the Transition?', in Marine Policy, 34 (6), 1290–99.

Ostrom, E., Schroeder, L. D. and Wynne, S. G. (1993), 'Institutional Incentives and Sustainable Development', Boulder, CO: Westview Press.

Pelling, M., High, C., Dearing, J. and Smith, D. (2008), 'Shadow Spaces for Social Learning: A Relational Understanding of Adaptive Capacity to Climate Change within Organisations', *Environment and Planning A*, 40 (4), pp. 867–84.

Peterson, G. D. (2007), 'Using Scenario Planning to Enable an Adaptive Co-management Process in the Northern Highlands Lake District of Wisconsin', pp. 289–307, in F. Berkes, D. Armitage and N. Doubleday (eds) *Adaptive Co-Management: Collaboration, Learning, and Multi-level Governance*, Vancouver, British Columbia, Canada: UBC Press.

Reij, C. P. and Smaling, E. M. A. (2008), 'Analyzing Successes in Agriculture and Land Management in Sub-Saharan Africa: Is Macro-level Gloom Obscuring Positive Micro-level Change?', *Land Use Policy*, 25 (3), pp. 410–20.

Repetto, R. (ed.) (2006), *Punctuated Equilibrium and the Dynamics of US Environmental Policy*, New Haven, US: Yale University Press.

Rockström J., Steffen, W., Noone, K., Persson, Å., Chapin, F. S. III, Lambin, E. F., Lenton, T. M., Scheffer, M., Folke, C., Schellnhuber, H. J., Nykvist, B., de Wit, C. A., Hughes, T., van der Leeuw, S., Rodhe, H., Sörlin, S., Snyder, P. K., Costanza, R., Svedin, U., Falkenmark, M., Karlberg, L., Corell, R. W., Fabry, V. J., Hansen, J., Walker, B., Liverman, D., Richardson, K., Crutzen, P., Foley, J. A. (2009), A Safe Operating Space for Humanity', *Nature*, 461 (7263), pp. 472–5.

Rotmans, Jan, René Kemp, and Marjolein van Asselt (2001), 'More Evolution Than Revolution: Transition Management in Public Policy', *Foresight*, 3 (1), p. 17.

Scheffer, M., Carpenter, S. R., Foley, J. A., Folke, C. and Walker, B. (2001), 'Catastrophic Shifts in Ecosystems', *Nature*, 413 (6856), pp. 591–696.

Schneider, S. H. (2004), 'Abrupt Non-linear Climate Change, Irreversibility and Surprise', *Global Environmental Change, Part A: Human and Policy Dimensions*, 14 (3), pp. 245–58.

Sendzimir, J., Magnuszewski, P., Flachner, Z., Balogh, P., Molnar, G., Sarvari, A. and Nagy, Z. (2008), 'Assessing the Resilience of a River Management regime: Informal Learning in a Shadow Network in the Tisza River Basin', *Ecology and Society*, 13 (1), 11. [online] URL: http://www.ecologyandsociety.org/vol13/iss1/art11/. 10 October 2011.

Steffen, W., Sanderson, A., Tyson, P. D., Jäger, J., Matson, P. M., Moore III, B., Oldfield, F., Richardson, K., Schellnhuber, H. J., Turner II, B. L., Wasson, R. J. (2004), *Global Change and the Earth System: A Planet under Pressure*, New York: Springer.

Sterner, T., Troell, M., Aniyar, S., Barrett, S., Brock, W., Carpenter, S., Chopra, K., Ehrlich, P., Hoel, M., Levin, S., Mäler, K. -G., Norberg, J., Pihl, L., Söderqvist, T., Wilen, J., Vincent, J., Xepapadeas, A. (2006), 'Quick Fixes for Environmental Problems: Part of the Solution, or Part of the Problem?', *Environment*, 48 (10), pp. 20–7.

Steneck, R. S., Hughes, T. P., Cinner, J. E., Adger, W. N., Arnold, S. N., Berkes, F., Boudreau, S., Brown, K., Folke, C., Gunderson, L., Olsson, P., Scheffer, M., Stephenson, E., Walker, B. H., Wilson, J., and Worm, B. (2011), Creation of a gilded trap by the high economic value of the Maine lobster fishery. *Conservation Biology* 25 (5), pp. 904–12.

True, J. L., Baumgartner, F. R. and Bryan, D. J. (1999), 'Explaining Stability and Change in American Policymaking: The Punctuated Equilibrium Model', in P. Sabatier (ed.) *Theories of the Policy Process*, Boulder, CO: Westview Press, pp. 97–115.

United Nations Environment Programme (2007), 'Global Environment Outlook: Environment for Development', Vol. 4, Valletta, Malta: Progress Press Ltd.

Vignola, R., Locatelli, B., Martinez, C., Imbach, P. (2009), 'Ecosystem-based Adaptation to Climate Change: What Role for Policy-makers, Society and Scientists?', *Mitigation and Adaptation Strategies for Global Change*, 14 (8), pp. 691–96.

van den Brink, M. and Meijerink, S. (2005), 'Implementing Policy Innovations: Resource Dependence, Struggle for Discursive Hegemony and Institutional Inertia in the Dutch River Policy Domain', Paper prepared for the ERSA Congress, Amsterdam, pp. 23–27, August 2005.

van Nes, E. H. and Scheffer, M. (2007), 'Slow Recovery from Perturbations as a Generic Indicator of a Nearby Catastrophic Shift', *The American Naturalist*, 169 (6), pp. 738–47.

Voß, J.-P., Bauknecht, D. (Eds) (2006), *Reflexive Governance for Sustainable Development*, Cheltenham: Edward Elgar Publishing.

Voß, J.-P. (2007), 'Innovation Processes in Governance: The Development of "Emissions Trading" as a New Policy Instrument', *Science and Public Policy*, 34 (5), pp. 329–43.

Walker, B. H., Barrett, S., Galaz, V., Polasky, S., Folke, C., Engström, G., Ackerman, F., Arrow, K., Carpenter, S. R., Chopra, K., Daily, G., Ehrlich, P., Hughes, T., Kautsky, N., Levin, S. A., Mäler, K. -G., Shogren, J., Vincent, J., Xepapadeous, T., and de Zeeuw, A. (2009), 'Looming Global-scale Failures and Missing Institutions', *Science*, 325 (5946), pp. 1345–6.

Walker, B. H., Abel, N., Anderies, J. M. and Ryan, P. (2009), 'Resilience, Adaptability and Transformability in the Goulburn-Broken Catchment, Australia', *Ecology and Society*, 14 (1), p. 12. [online] URL: http://www.ecologyandsociety.org/vol14/iss1/art12/. Accessed: 10 October 2011.

Westley, F. R., Zimmerman, B. and Patton, M. Q. (2006), *Getting to Maybe: How the World is Changed*, Canada, Toronto, Ontario, Canada: Vintage.

Westley, F. and Antadze, N. (2009), 'Making a Difference: Strategies for Scaling Social Innovation for Greater Impact', *Social Innovation Generation*, University of Waterloo, Canada.

Young, O. R. (2002), *The Institutional Dimensions of Environmental Change: Fit, Interplay, and Scale*, Cambridge, MA: The MIT Press.

10

Green Technology Implementation in Developing Countries: Opportunity Identification and Business Model Design

Benedetto Cannatelli, Antonio G. Masi, and Mario Molteni

Introduction

In the last decade the concepts of social entrepreneurship and social innovation have received increasing attention from both the academic and professional communities as promising tools that can inspire socially committed individuals to act in response to long-standing issues that affect humanity around the globe (e.g. Dees, 1998; Austin et al., 2006; Nicholls, 2006; Phills et al., 2008). The traditional aid and welfare models – whereby the government plays the role of provider of basic services to populations in need – have failed in the context of global, social and environmental problems such as the HIV pandemic, extreme poverty, rising inequality and global warming, especially in less developed regions like Eastern Asia and Africa (Prahalad, 2004; Certo and Miller, 2008; Moyo, 2009). The contingent failure of welfare and market mechanisms in serving people 'at the bottom of the pyramid' (Prahalad and Hart, 2002; Prahalad, 2004) has created space for private initiatives to address social issues by designing entrepreneurial and financially sustainable solutions able to last in the long term (Mort et al., 2003; Seelos and Mair, 2005; Peredo and McLean, 2006; Leadbeater, 2007).

In his milestone book, Prahalad (2004) suggested that the 'bottom of the pyramid' constitutes a substantial opportunity for private organizations to accomplish organizational growth and profit seeking, while contributing to the improvement of humankind. In particular, he identifies the areas that lack modern infrastructure and products to meet basic human needs as an 'ideal testing ground for developing environmentally sustainable technologies and products for the entire world' (Prahalad and Hart, 2002). From this perspective, a range of drivers offers new opportunities for the development of market innovation, including: deregulation and the diminishing role of government; reduced international aid; the need to discourage migration to overcrowded, urban centres; global overcapacity combined with intense competition in established markets (Prahalad and Hart, 2002; Prahalad, 2004).

It has been suggested that, in order to transform global social issues into market opportunities, social entrepreneurs and social ventures should develop innovative business models challenging the traditional rules of welfare and markets. Examples of for-profit and not-for-profit organizations have been reported in the extant literature as best practices of successful achievement of social, economic, and – in several cases – environmental sustainability. Such business models – identified as functioning according to a double, or triple, bottom line – represent potential forms of social innovation. However, although Bottom of the Pyramid models have received considerable attention as potential new solutions to global problems like poverty and failing health care in developing countries, the processes leading to the conception and design of such innovative business models is an under-explored field. In particular, the potential conflicts coming from an overlap of different logics for opportunity identification – such as social, economic, and environmental – and how organizations balance them successfully, are relevant issues that still need to be properly researched.

This chapter contributes to the academic literature on social innovation by advancing a theoretical model linking the criteria for the identification of social opportunities – suggested by the behavioural theory of the firm – to the business model design process. This is accomplished by focusing on Greentecno S.A., a Switzerland-based, for-profit organization that provides case evidence about how potential conflicts between opportunities identified according to different social, economic, and environmental logics are managed and solved by designing a comprehensive business model. The findings here constitute a first step towards conceiving innovative business models that balance conflicts caused by the contextual implementation of heterogeneous rationales and institutional logics. In particular, the beneficial effects accrued from including environmental sustainability criteria through the implementation of green technologies is emphasized here. This is particularly relevant for social organizations pursuing a triple-bottom-line strategy and relying on green technologies as the main source of innovation.

The chapter proceeds as follows: first, a review of the literature on innovation, business modelling and opportunity recognition in the social sector is provided; second, the methodology used for data collection and analysis is set out combined with a brief presentation of the Greentecno case; third, information about Greentecno is critically analysed according to a theoretical framework, and findings are discussed; last, theoretical and practical implications, limitations, and indications for further research are advanced.

Social innovation and business modelling

Social innovation has been defined as a construct that crosses institutional boundaries and that can be applied to a wide spectrum of entities ranging from for-profit organizations to social movements (Mulgan, 2007; Westall, 2007; Phills et al., 2008). Mulgan (2007, p. 3) defined social innovation as 'new ideas that work, which address social or environmental needs'. Such a broad definition encompasses various different forms that social innovation can take within different settings. According to the strategic focus of an organization, a social innovation can be defined by principles, values, programmes, organizational. and business models, and technologies (Dees, Anderson and Wei-Skillern, 2004; Mulgan, 2006; 2007).

Social innovation in market settings can be differentiated from other types with respect to a focus on outcomes rather than processes (Phills et al., 2008). This chapter aims to explore this type of social innovation particularly since Mulgan (2006) observed this is an overlooked topic that calls for further research. Moreover, in order to better understand the scope of the social innovation process, social needs can be recast in terms of new opportunities; for example, the availability of new technologies leading to new business models for exerting social impact (Mulgan, 2006). Such an approach is also consistent with Mair and Schoen (2005), who called for a shift from the 'who' to the 'how' question in the social entrepreneurship field.

From this perspective, Prahalad and Hart (2002) suggested four main activities that account for the process of creating innovative solutions for communities in need: creating buying power; shaping aspirations; improving access; and tailoring local solutions. Such a wide range of activities can be accomplished, on the one hand, by enhancing innovation in technology, business models; and management process; and, on the other, by establishing lasting relationships within a value network (Mair and Schoen, 2005; Chesbrough et al., 2006).

Business modelling can play an important role in creating social-innovation solutions to alleviate poverty. Chesbrough and colleagues (2006) argued that 'the vital role of a business model is the one reason why the fortune at the bottom of the pyramid has gone untapped for so long'. Their comments stress the need for a theoretical linking of strategies for creating economic and social value (Seelos and Mair, 2005). The literature offers several examples of business models that succeeded in pursuing social, economic, and environmental value creation simultaneously (such as Grameen Bank, Kickstart, One World Health, among others). Bloom (2009) suggested that successful business models in the social field vary accordingly to the nature of the social need to be addressed. He identified seven theories of change in a typology that varies according to the nature of the outcome created and its purpose in the wider spectrum of poverty alleviation: capital provision; business development assistance; education; resource matching; information provision and advocacy; health improvement; providing products/services for the poor (Bloom, 2009).

Opportunity recognition for social improvement

Developing effective business models serving people at the bottom of the pyramid implies facing the challenge of making economic, social, and environmental logics coexist. Organizations aiming at exerting a social impact in under-developed areas design business models in which multiple logics are in equilibrium and potential trade-offs between economic and social-driven opportunities are resolved (Patzelt and Shepherd, 2010). Indeed, Zahra and colleagues (2008) suggested that researchers can 'gain insights into the choice of the *business model* employed to exploit these opportunities, as this model is likely to build on entrepreneurs' talents, skills, and background'. This suggests the importance of connecting an opportunity – as identified by the entrepreneur according to the economical, social, and environmental perspectives – and the business model with which it can be exploited.

The need for understanding the dynamics according to which the different dimensions of entrepreneurial opportunity interact has been recognized in the literature (Cohen and Winn, 2007; Dean and McMullen, 2007; Zahra et al., 2008; Patzelt and Shepherd, 2010). Identifying opportunities for social improvement is a complex and inherently contested topic due to the co-existence of heterogeneous goals, rationales, and institutional logics (Baker et al., 2005; Weerawardena and Mort, 2006). Recently, Zhara and colleagues (2008) declared the need for advancing a conceptualization of social opportunities to overcome the assumption of profit maximization shared by the traditional perspectives employed in the commercial field. Indeed, a failure to recognize the value – and inter-connection – of both economic and non-economic goals has previously hampered the conceptualization of opportunities in contexts lacking traditional market mechanisms, such as are often found in developing countries. To address this need, they proposed an approach based on the behavioural theory of the firm, shifting from a profit maximization perspective to a satisfying one within the notion of bounded rationality (Simon, 1979). Therefore, rather than relying on profit maximization criteria, individuals and organizations considering an intervention in contexts of social or environmental need might identify opportunities for social improvement by using a different set of criteria. Zhara and colleagues (2008) proposed a list of five attributes of pressing social opportunities: prevalence, relevance, urgency, access by others, and radicalness.

There is clearly a divergence between the conventional criteria that lead to opportunity recognition from a commercial as opposed to a social perspective. This calls for a deeper analysis of how ventures pursuing value creation from both perspectives succeed in designing business models to balance potential trade-offs and conflicts. This issue is even more critical for organizations committed to an environmental perspective and evoking a triple bottom line. By focusing on Greentecno's experience, this chapter explores how multiple strategic criteria for the identification of (social) innovation opportunities are likely to engender trade-offs between the commercial and the environmental perspectives. Particular attention is paid to how the business model of the organization is designed to solve potential trade-offs integrating these three dimensions.

Methodology

The empirical research provided in this chapter is based on a qualitative case study with an exploratory purpose. The case focuses on Greentecno S.A., a for-profit organization headquartered in Switzerland that designs and produces green technology solutions for developing countries. This study seeks to understand the causal linkages among the theoretical constructs discussed in the literature review section above. Consistent with the complexity and under-researched nature of this topic, this research aims at contributing to the extant literature through a hypothesis-generating, rather than a hypothesis-testing, approach. Indeed, in-depth, qualitative case studies have been used by researchers to provide the kinds of information that allow the identification of relationships that would not be captured by more quantitative methodologies (Yin, 1984).

As pointed out by Glaser and Strauss (1967), theoretical sampling cases are often chosen for theoretical, not statistical, reasons. Specifically, the case used here well suits the aim of this research for at least two reasons. First, at the time of the study, the company was in the start-up stage, when the opportunity-identification process was a central function, making direct observation by one of the authors an effective source of information. Second, the authors had access to a wide range of sources of information related to the business. These two factors account for an opportunity to approach a significant phenomenon under privileged circumstances through a single case study, as pointed out by Eisenhardt and Graebner (2007).

Data were collected between January and June 2009 from multiple sources. The use of multiple methods is ideal to allow for the convergence and triangulation of findings (Jick, 1979). First, two rounds of semi-structured interviews with Greentecno managers were conducted. The first round aimed at clarifying their business goals, history, and background, and outlined Greentecno's profile, with specific regard to its organizational structure, areas of activity, opportunities, challenges, and expected social, economic, and environmental impacts. The second round of interviews was aimed at verifying the understanding of documents and other secondary material, as well as at gathering further specific information about perceived opportunities, planned activities, timings, and partnerships being established with local actors. Second, corporate documents such as Greentecno's business plan, financial statements, and a detailed description of each project were collected (about 200 pages in total). Third, one of the authors had the opportunity to conduct direct observations by attending several business meetings during the period of study.

As reported by Eisenhardt (1989), in building theory from case studies, an overlapping of data analysis with data collection is likely to occur. Actually, data analysis began during the first interview. Notes taken during each meeting served as the basis for the development of the interview protocols. Interviews were registered and transcribed verbatim, backed up by a systematic review by the interviewee. Also, data were analysed and codified separately by two of the authors and then systematically tested to enhance validity and reliability of the constructs (Yin, 1984).

Such a process generated comprehensive data with regard to the criteria according to which social, economic, and environmental opportunities were identified and internalized by Greentecno's managers. A systematic review of internal documents contextualized the business model used in terms of the management's strategic vision.

Greentecno S.A.

Greentecno S.A. is a company based in Chiasso (Canton Ticino – Switzerland) and operating in the renewable energy sector. It was set up in 2006 within the Solar 3 S.A. Group, also comprising TC Systems S.A. which is leader in information and communication technology in Switzerland. Greentecno claims that it is envisioning a world where everybody can satisfy his/her basic needs while having the chance of developing the skills allowing him/her to give his/her contribution to his/her Country's development and well being. Specifically, attention is being paid to three main issues: a lack of potable drinking water; a lack of access to electricity; a lack of an effective educational system and of educational tools.

To accomplish those goals, Greentecno bases its corporate philosophy on two concepts expressed as '3-P' and '3-E'. The 3-P concept refers to the company's commitment to *people* (whose needs are expected to be the basis of every business initiative), to the *planet* (whose needs should always be taken in account in order not to undermine humanity's future), and to *profit* (that allows the enterprise to satisfy its financial needs and positively impact on society). The 3-E concept comprises a focus on *ethics, ecology, and equity* and refers to Greentecno's goal to demonstrate the viability of a business strategy based on the triple bottom line.

Greentecno's core activity is to design, build, and commercialize equipment and concrete solutions to the three issues mentioned above: electricity generation from renewable energy sources; the production of drinkable water; and the provision of primary education in developing countries, particularly in rural and suburban areas. In 2007, Greentecno received the European Renewable Energy Entrepreneurial Company of the Year Award from the London-based company Frost and Sullivan.

Specifically, Greentecno has developed three main products that can be purchased either individually or integrated in a single package. The first product, LWH_1000_GOGO, is a hybrid wind-photovoltaic module for electricity generation. It is targeted to villages, specific buildings (schools, clinics, public buildings) and stand-alone consumers in rural areas, whose electricity needs may be met through either off-grid generation or local grid developments. Until now, diesel generators have been widely employed in this context, even though they are a major source of green house gases and can lead to oil dependence.

The second product, WD – Water Device, artificially reproduces evaporation and condensation processes[1] to provide safe drinkable water. Through a condensation-filtration process, this technology can produce from 0.7 to 5.0 litres of drinkable water per hour, depending on the relative atmospheric humidity and temperature. It starts producing drinkable water at a relative humidity of 40 per cent, ensuring a high level of water purity through a four-phase filtration process and subsequent UV-ray sterilization process.

Lastly, Edu Computer is a low-cost and low-energy-consumption computer that offers an innovative tool to support the creation of local education communities. It is designed to resist extreme climatic conditions where dust and other factors would otherwise cause damage and break-down. Basic programs using a Linux platform come pre-installed, while educational software and applications can be regularly updated from 'local mirrors' that communicate with Greentecno's central server via satellite or fibre optic technologies.

Greentecno decided to start its activities in Africa, where the largest part of the world's poor live and where innovation in development approaches is most clearly needed. In particular, South Africa has been chosen as a starting point because the local political-economic environment was considered to be most suitable to sustain Greentecno's efforts.

Analysis: Opportunity recognition

In this study, the five attributes of social need proposed by Zhara et al. (2008) are employed as analytics to explore the strategies adopted by Greentecno in identifying opportunities for creating social impact. These are: prevalence, relevance, urgency, accessibility, and radicalness. In particular, the analysis strives to establish the extent to which each of the criteria affected managers' perceptions of the nature of opportunity from the perspective of a triple bottom line. In other words, each criterion is evaluated with regard to its suitability in helping identify a viable and blended, social, commercial, and environmental opportunity for the organization. Empirical evidence supporting these relationships is shown in Table 10.1. Each criterion is now considered in turn.

Table 10.1 Opportunity dimensions and identification criteria

Criterion	Dimension		
	Social opportunity	Commercial opportunity	Environmental opportunity
Prevalence	+	−	+
Relevance	+	+	−
Urgency	+	−	−
Accessibility	−	−	+
Radicalness	+	−	+

Prevalence

The prevalence of social problems refers to the extent to which a social problem is diffused and is easily observable by potential social entrepreneurs and innovators around the globe. Greentecno targets poverty based on limited access to basic utilities and services for rural populations in developing countries. The widespread diffusion of such a social issue represents a significant driver for the firm's objectives. As the managing director reported himself:

> In western countries like Switzerland or Italy you are used to get what you need pretty easily ... but try to imagine how your life would be if you had to walk for three hours every time your family need to be fed. Now, think that this condition is not so uncommon around the world and millions of people struggle in providing water to their children.

However, the high prevalence of a social issue does not imply that a viable commercial opportunity must follow. In most cases a social problem persists because market mechanisms fail. This holds also for Greentecno:

> We realize that having a wide range of potential beneficiaries does not automatically mean having a wide range of potential income, even at a lower rate. You have to find a way to be sustainable even when the market is significantly smaller than the number of beneficiaries.

Widespread social or environmental issues in developing countries may sometimes be addressed by technologies that are less effective in developed countries. In this case, most African countries share a high potential in terms of natural resources that could be exploited by implementing the LWH_1000_GOGO energy generator, as pointed out by the technical design manager:

> LWH_1000_GOGO maximizes the value of local renewable energy sources that is often underestimated in developed countries, even though they are an abundant resource in rural African areas.

Hence, according to the criterion of prevalence, a trade-off emerges between the social and commercial viability of the opportunity. At the same time, the high prevalence of the social opportunity also has a positive influence on the environmental perspective, constituting a valuable driver for creating awareness around ecological issues.

Relevance

A prevalent social issue accounts as relevant for a venture when a balance between the need to be addressed and organizational resources is evident. In other words, relevance refers to the extent to which the social organization owns suitable assets – whether they be values, skills, knowledge or resources – effectively to respond to the need/opportunity. In the case of Greentecno, the relevance of the social issue is a source of its commercial viability. Specifically, the technical knowledge developed by the organization constitutes a substantive resource for competitive advantage in addressing specific issues by implementing relevant new technologies. As Greentecno's marketing manager declared:

> Greentecno's competitive advantage relies on pursuing social goals that are consistent with what we can actually offer from a technical standpoint. Easy access to energy and drinking water can be no more than a dream for many people. This need can be met thanks to our commitment to developing new technologies over time.

While the relevance of the social issue is perceived mainly as a viable pattern for commercial and social opportunities to emerge as a consequence of high technological competences, the same cannot be assumed for the environmental dimension. Specifically, the high relevance of the problem of poverty in rural areas appears unrelated to the emergence of an environmental opportunity.

Urgency

Urgency is an attribute shared by many social issues and represents a powerful driver in the search for viable solutions. This term mainly refers to circumstances characterized by pressing time constraints that call for rapid action. This is often the case with natural disasters, epidemics, and wars. While urgency is a key criterion that social entrepreneurs take into account when setting their priorities of action, limited time and resources sometimes make it harder to identify commercial opportunities quickly in the same context. Greentecno's marketing manager suggested that the potential trade-off between the commercial and social rationalities is more stressed under situations of emergency:

> In these circumstances it is almost impossible to make out opportunities for sustainable solutions. First, because the opportunity is likely to expire quickly, and second, because you feel like you are

taking advantage of people in high need. Usually, in these situations the most viable solution is pure charitable work.

Moreover, since urgency can catalyze public attention towards a social need that requires a quick solution, the potential opportunity for environmental sustainability to emerge is significantly reduced. The technical design manager commented:

> When catastrophes occur the environmental issue is seen as a second order priority.

The urgency of social issues, therefore, represents a potential source of conflict between the social and the commercial and environmental perspectives.

Accessibility

High accessibility to the social issue by multiple typologies of institutions such as governments and traditional welfare providers reduces the need for social entrepreneurial solutions. The option to get involved in these contexts typically appears less attractive for private organizations looking for opportunities to exert their impact for good. The same holds for a commercial opportunity that is reduced by the presence of low barriers to entry. Surprisingly, accessibility seems to have the opposite result on the identification of environmental opportunities. The potential to create environmental benefits, such as reduced gas emissions or lower energy consumption, may represent a source of competitive advantage compared to extant providers focusing just on a single or a double bottom line. Greentecno's managing director commented:

> Pursuing social change through a triple bottom line strategy ... is not just good 'per se'. Each perspective is likely to strengthen the others, starting a virtuous circle ... Proposing technologies that are not only effective – but also eco-friendly – will make our products more appealing than other traditional solutions available in that context.

So, the emergence of an environmental opportunity in serving needs characterized by a high accessibility to other sectors led Greentecno to consider working in contexts that would otherwise be disregarded from a purely social or commercial perspective.

Radicalness

The radicalness of a social issue is connected to the innovation of the solution required and is an attribute typical of entrepreneurship, rather than bureaucratic government institutions that often struggle to find such solutions. Also, engaging in complex problem-solving tasks is often attractive to (social) entrepreneurs. However, providing highly innovative solutions implies high transaction costs in research and development activities that may reduce profitability and increase risk. This rationale can be inferred by the following extract from an interview with Greentecno's marketing manager:

> I think that reversing the rules is the best part of this job ... actually, we try to create technical solutions for addressing social needs where others have failed. Investing in R&D always implies uncertainty in the outcomes ... in our context, uncertainty is even higher due to the price policy that we adopt in our target markets.

The radicalness of the solution is also positively related to the emergence of environmental opportunities. Technological developments and environmental sustainability have been conceived as a joint set of mission objectives in a wide range of industries. Reducing environmentally negative impacts can be a major achievement of technological development:

> Nowadays, green technology is our brand. We want better technologies. Meaning more effective and more respectful of the environment.

Therefore, assessing the trade-offs between social and commercial viability – in addressing issues requiring radical solutions – can also be linked to environmental innovation that challenges the status quo.

Designing a business model

In the case of Greentecno, each of the five attributes of social need affects the identification of social, commercial, and environmental opportunities. The above analysis suggests that each attribute played either a supportive or a discouraging role in the company's decision-making process around social, commercial, and environmental considerations. The case evidence suggests that one of the three dimensions typically played a driving role with regard to each criterion of social need, while the remaining two were positively or negatively affected. This meant that, in some cases, the company faced difficult trade-offs between the course of action suggested by the driving dimension and the others related to another dimension.

Providing an effective solution to such trade-offs was considered to be a crucial issue by Greentecno's managers. In fact, the blended-value model that lay behind the organization's internal logic drove them to design a business model that pursued social, economic, and environmental objectives simultaneously. Thus, the organization aimed to contribute effectively to the promotion of local, durable, social-economic development, while also ensuring the organization's economic viability and pursuing local environmental value creation.

The company's managers recognized that these three entrepreneurial dimensions were closely related to each other, even though balancing them was sometimes difficult. This led them to pay great attention to balancing environmental, social, and economic issues in designing products, identifying, assessing, and exploiting geographical implementation opportunities, organizing product distribution and operations, and setting prices. Greentecno's business model (shown in Figure 10.1) demonstrates that these three dimensions are considered to be equally important and, consequently, qualified to receive equal management attention.

On the left-hand side of Figure 10.1, the environmental dimension is emphasised. This aims to create environmental value by means of green-energy production devices and/or low (green) energy-consumption products and/or services. In the middle is the social dimension that aims to promote local sustainable development by helping locals to exploit their resources. This is achieved by creating products conceived of to meet local people's needs and to be easily and cheaply maintained by local technicians as well as by setting prices that are affordable to as wide a group of local people as possible. On the right hand of the figure is the commercial dimension that aims to ensure economic profitability by identifying, evaluating, and exploiting the market opportunities as well as by setting prices that do not threaten the organization's financial sustainability. In order to balance environmental, social, and economic sustainability, Greentecno's managers have strived to provide an effective solution to a series of trade-offs while identifying and assessing the opportunities for the accomplishment of their intended social, commercial, and environmental objectives.

The prevalence attribute led the company to identify operating opportunities along the social dimension that offered a contribution to combat deep poverty and the social issues that affect a large part of the people living in the rural and suburban areas of developing countries. Specific attention has been paid here to the three main issues: lack

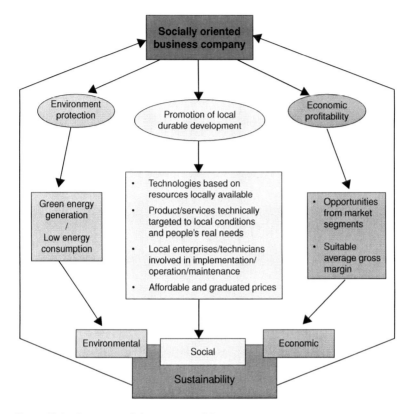

Figure 10.1   Greentecno's business model

of access to drinking water; shortages of energy; lack of information technology within education. The marketing manager of Greentecno contextualized their objectives in terms of larger issues such as the relationship between the lack of access to drinking water and political instability. Moreover, the lack of an effective educational system and of educational tools may be considered to be one of the major factors preventing most developing countries from achieving sustainable development. Finally, the lack of access to modern and sustainable electricity is a widespread issue in most developing countries, particularly in rural and remote areas where electricity grids are not typically present due to logistical and financial barriers. With regard to prevalence – and contra the problematic role played by the commercial dimension – the social dimension played a driving role in the decision-making process.

The criterion of relevance led to the identification of opportunities along both the social and the commercial dimensions, even though a dominant role was played by the latter. Greentecno defined its mission as based on designing, building, and commercializing equipment and concrete solutions for electricity generation from renewable energy sources, for the production of drinkable water, and for the provision of primary education in developing countries. However, the technical design manager claimed that, unlike purely commercial enterprises, Greentecno focused not only on manufacturing and commercializing its products, but also on providing rural people with solutions that effectively met their needs for energy, water, and education. Consequently, products were developed by considering the environmental, social-economic, and logistical conditions of developing countries and emerging economies. They were, therefore, designed to be very tough and resistant to extreme climate conditions, and also, thanks to their modular design, to easily be transported, assembled, and even adapted to either single user or community needs.

The company's marketing manager was confident that effective and pragmatic solutions, suiting local environmental and logistical conditions, could be provided by hiring staff with long-standing experience in developing countries. He also noted that Greentecno aimed at providing a total service to developing-country communities that included needs assessment, project development, and implementation support and advice.

In terms of the urgency criterion, Greentecno solved the trade-off between the social and commercial dimensions by giving priority to the latter. The firm made a strategic decision to start its activity in Africa, since this is where many of the world's poor live. Nevertheless, instead of geographic contexts affected by wars, natural disasters, and epidemics, the company chose the Republic of South Africa as a starting point, because the local political-economic environment was considered to offer the most stable and viable market. Furthermore, the South African market was attractive for several other reasons. First, since it represented an opinion leader among other developing countries and emerging markets, both in Africa and worldwide. Second, since Greentecno already had existing contacts with key decisionmakers in target sectors there. Third, there was good availability of highly skilled labour at a low cost and a modern and functional infrastructure. Finally, the country had an efficient banking and financial systems. Nevertheless, despite a focus on developing markets, the firm was clear that green technologies alone do not automatically allow target communities to gain any direct income benefits. According to the managing director, renewable energy projects should, therefore, be linked with other projects that specifically encourage local economic growth through the development of entre-preneurial skills in local communities so that they may benefit fully from the economic opportunities provided by such projects. Local tech-nicians, for example, might be trained to take care of equipment opera-tion and maintenance and even to set up local businesses by employing the skills gained.

The radicalness dimension led to a conflict between the opportunities to achieve social objectives (here specifically supported by the envi-ronmental benefits expected) and the high costs stemming from the relevant R&D and implementation investments needed. The managing director centralized the R&D and administrative services, while decen-tralizing production, warehousing, and operation/maintenance serv-ices in each territory. This strategy reduced sunk costs but also offered project ownership to local stakeholders. In such a way, the high quality standards of Swiss-made technology and services were combined with proximity to clients and markets also fostering local entrepreneurship.

At the same time, as clarified by the marketing manager, affordable and competitive prices were fixed in order to compete with established products while maintaining a suitable average gross margin. Greentecno was also willing further to reduce its commercial margins in order to enable rural communities and institutions to purchase its full range of products. Furthermore, different pricing structures were set to take into account various market segments: NGOs, communities, and develop-ment projects; government and other institutions; corporate, tourist facilities, and private purchasers.

Greentecno's managers typically focussed on medium-, rather than short-term, profitability via cooperation with local institutions and stakeholders. They aimed to foster the development of revenue streams and micro-finance mechanisms that supported the establishment of local independent-power-producers who were able to take care of products' operation and maintenance. In order to enhance capacity for project development and management, partnerships with local suppliers, dis-tributors, and project developers were created. In addition, training for the day-by-day device maintenance was provided to local technicians.

Conclusion

This chapter contributes to the extant literature on social innovation in terms of a deeper understanding of the link between opportunity recognition and business model design processes. Underlining the causal relationship between these constructs is of critical importance as it explicates how organizational solutions can be conceptualized as responses to a set of different rationalities based on social, commercial, and environmental aims.

Five criteria from behavioural theory have been applied as an analytic framework to a single case study to explore aspects of the opportunity identification process. Empirical evidence suggests that these criteria – prevalence, relevance, urgency, accessibility, and radicalness – are likely to engender trade-offs in the identification of opportunities according to social, economic, and environmental rationalities. From this perspective, the present study constitutes a follow-up to the contribution provided by Zahra et al. (2008) by enhancing the validity of using approaches from the behavioural theory of the firm as a useful framework to explain the process of identifying viable and sustainable opportunities for social innovation.

A further contribution is provided here by the inclusion of an environmental dimension in the identification of opportunities for creating social value. Although environmental issues have emerged as a relevant subject for debate in the social innovation and social entrepreneurship fields, analyses that explore the relationship of social and environmental opportunities are still under-researched.

The Greentecno's case study contributes to the discussion by suggesting viable criteria for social ventures to manage potential conflicts in opportunity recognition and business modelling. This emphasizes the importance of business models to social entrepreneurship as they serve as primary tools in shaping organizational priorities and opportunity recognition. Social entrepreneurs could benefit by systematically considering the advantages and disadvantages of any opportunity in terms of each of the three strategic dimensions and the consequent potential trade-offs. For example, though a social rationale usually represents the primary driver for social ventures, financial sustainability – and consequently, organization's efficiency in the long term – can be analysed by using a commercial lens to test the opportunity at hand.

Moreover, the analysis here emphasizes how the integration of an environmental mission into a business model may provide a powerful tool that represents a source of competitive advantage. Therefore, far from constituting an exogenous feature of an innovative business model, an environmental perspective may be taken into consideration by social ventures as a viable means to build barriers to entry for less effective institutions in a specific context. Technology also emerges as another key asset easing potential conflicts between commercial and social logics. In particular, by relying on high-technological skills, social ventures can enlarge the scope of their action by enhancing the relevance of social problems.

This chapter acknowledges several limitations. First, the research conclusions have limited validity since they are drawn from the analysis of a single case. Further research on other cases sharing similar characteristics might apply the same framework used here for analysing how organizations pursue a triple-bottom-line strategy in the context of the five criteria for opportunity identification. This could also consider how these affect the business-model design process. Second, at the time as this study, Greentecno was in the start-up phase of organizational growth. This meant that the actual outcomes of strategic planning could not be assessed in terms of opportunity recognition and business model design. A follow-up study could, therefore, focus on how the business-model design process is related to actual social, economic, and environmental performance. Moreover, quantitative research testing of the findings here could contribute to the field as a whole through statistical generalization.

Note

1. Solar irradiation causes the evaporation of water from oceans, lakes, and rivers. In natural conditions, warm air caused by evaporation goes upwards, then cools and condenses in clouds. Water drops forming clouds increase in volume until they reach a weight that makes them fall in the form of rain.

References

Austin, J., Stevenson, H. H. and Wei-Skillern, J. (2006), 'Social and Commercial Entrepreneurship: Same, Different, or Both?', *Entrepreneurship Theory and Practice* 30 (1), pp. 1–22.

Baker, T., Gedajlovic, E. and Lubatkin, M. (2005), 'A Framework for Comparing Entrepreneurship Processes Across Nations', *Journal of International Business Studies*, 36 (5), pp. 492–504.

Bloom, P. (2009), 'Overcoming Consumption Constraints through Social Entrepreneurship', *Journal of Public Policy & Marketing*, 28 (1), pp. 128–34.

Certo, S. T. and Miller, T. (2008), 'Social Entrepreneurship: Key Issues and Concepts', *Business Horizons* 51 (4), pp. 267–71.

Chesbrough, H., Ahern, S., Finn, M. and Guerraz, S. (2006), 'Business Models for Technology in the Developing World: The Role of Non-Governmental Organizations', *California Management Review*, 48 (3), pp. 48–76.

Cohen, B. and Winn, M. I. (2007), 'Market Imperfections, Opportunity and Sustainable Entrepreneurship', *Journal of Business Venturing*, 22 (1), pp. 29–49.

Dean, T. J. and McMullen J. S. (2007), 'Toward a Theory of Sustainable Entrepreneurship: Reducing Environmental Degradation through Entrepreneurial Action', *Journal of Business Venturing*, 22 (1), pp. 50–76.

Dees, J. G. (1998), 'The Meaning of Social Entrepreneurship', Paper, CASE Center for the Advancement of Social Entrepreneurship, Fuqua School of Business, Durham, NC: Duke University.

Dees, J. G., Anderson, B. B. and Wei-Skillern, J. (2004), 'Scaling Social Impact', *Stanford Social Innovation Review*, 1, Spring, pp. 24–32.

Eisenhardt, K. M. (1989), 'Building Theories from Case Study Research', *Academy of Management Review*, 14 (4), pp. 532–50.

Eisenhardt, K. M. and Graebner, M. E. (2007), 'Theory Building from Cases: Opportunities and Challenges', *Academy of Management Journal*, 50 (1), pp. 25–32.

Glaser, Barney G., and Strauss, A. L. (1967), 'Discovery of Grounded Theory. Strategies for Qualitative Research', *Mill Valley*, CA: Sociology Press.

Jick, T. J. (1979), 'Mixing Qualitative and Quantitative Methods: Triangulation in action', *Administrative Science Quarterly*, 24 (4), pp. 602–11.

Leadbeater, C. (2007), 'Social Enterprise and Social Innovation: Strategies for the Next Ten Years', Social enterprise think piece commissioned by the Office of the Third Sector, London.

Mair, J. and Schoen, O. (2005), 'Social Entrepreneurial Business Models: An Exploratory Study', Working paper, Barcelona, SP: IESE Business School.

Mort, G. S., Weerawardena, J. and Carnegie, K. (2003), 'Social Entrepreneurship: Towards Conceptualisation', *International Journal of Nonprofit and Voluntary Sector Marketing*, 8 (1), pp. 76–88.

Moyo, D. (2009), *Dead Aid: Why Aid is not Working and How there is a Better Way for Africa*, New York: Farrar, Straus and Giroux.

Mulgan, G. (2006), 'The Process of Social Innovation', *Innovations*, (Spring) pp. 145–61.

Mulgan, G. (2007), 'Social Innovation: What it is, Why it Matters and How it can be Accelerated', Working paper, Skoll Centre for Social Entrepreneurship, Said Business School – University of Oxford.

Nicholls, A. (2006), *Social Entrepreneurship: New Models of Sustainable Social Change*, Oxford: Oxford University Press.

Patzelt, H. and Shepherd, D. A. (2011). 'Recognizing Opportunities for Sustainable Development', Entrepreneurship Theory & Practice 35 (4), 631–52.

Peredo, A. M. and McLean, M. (2006), 'Social Entrepreneurship: A Critical Review of the Concept', *Journal of World Business*, 41 (1), pp. 56–65.

Phills J. A., Deiglmeier, K. and Miller, D. T. (2008), 'Rediscovering Social Innovation', *Stanford Social Innovation Review* (Fall 2008), pp. 34–43.

Prahalad, C. K. and Hart, S. L. (2002), 'The Fortune at the Bottom of the Pyramid', *Strategy + Business*, 26, pp. 54–67.

Prahalad, C. K. (2004), *The Fortune at the Bottom of the Pyramid*, Upper Saddle River, NJ: Wharton School Publishing.

Seelos, C. and Mair, J. (2005), 'Social Entrepreneurship: Creating New Business Models to Serve the Poor', *Business Horizons*, 48 (3), pp. 241–6.

Simon, H. A. (1979), *Models of Thought*, New Haven, CT: Yale University Press.

Weerawardena, J. and Mort, G. S. (2006), 'Investigating Social Entrepreneurship: A Multidimensional Model', *Journal of World Business*, 41 (1), pp. 21–35.

Westall, A. (2007), 'How can Innovation in Social Enterprise be Understood, Encouraged and Enabled?', *Social Enterprise Think Piece Commissioned by the Office of the Third Sector*, HM Government, London, UK.

Yin, R. K. (1984), *Case Study Research: Design and Methods*, Thousand Oaks, CA: Sage Publication.

Zahra, S. A., Gedajlovic, E., Neubaum, D. O. and Shulman, J. M. (2009), 'A Typology of Social Entrepreneurs: Motives, Search Processes and Ethical Challenges', *Journal of Business Venturing*, 24 (5), pp. 519–32.

Zahra, S. A., Rawhouser, H. N., Bhawe, N., Neubaum, D. O. and Hayton, J. C. (2008), 'Globalization of Social Entrepreneurship Opportunities', *Strategic Entrepreneurship Journal*, 2 (2), pp. 117–31.

11

When David Meets Goliath: Sustainable Entrepreneurship and the Evolution of Markets

Kai Hockerts and Rolf Wüstenhagen

Introduction

Businesses in many industries are increasingly confronted with environmental and social challenges. Rather than just focusing on short-term profits, stakeholders expect firms to meet a triple-bottom line of economic, environmental, and social value creation (Elkington, 1997). The increasing importance of sustainable development creates new risks, but also new opportunities for businesses. Reaping these opportunities requires firms to come up with innovative solutions for tomorrow's markets (Hart and Milstein, 2003; Pacheco et al., 2009). There seems to be an increasing awareness that there is a business case for sustainable entrepreneurial initiatives, and achieving 'green growth' is a popular theme in the political debate (Ki-moon and Gore, 2009). But how does green growth come about? What does it take for sustainable entrepreneurs to blossom? And particularly, is sustainable entrepreneurship something that happens in large firms or small firms?

The aim of this chapter is to provide a conceptual contribution to clarify the role of two different visions of sustainable entrepreneurship, here referred to as 'Greening Goliaths' and 'Emerging Davids'. The objective is to discuss the relative strengths and challenges of large and small firms in embarking on sustainable entrepreneurship, and to develop an evolutionary model of how their compounded impact promotes the sustainable transformation of industries.

The chapter proceeds as follows. First, it clarifies the terminology used and briefly introduces key concepts. Next, it provides a review of existing literature on sustainable entrepreneurship, as well as the two related concepts of environmental and social entrepreneurship. There is also a review of studies at the intersection of firm size and (sustainable) innovation.

Finally, the chapter reinforces its central conceptual proposition by exploring the interplay between 'Davids' and 'Goliaths'.

Conceptual framework

The notion of sustainable entrepreneurship is rather recent and its definition is still emerging. Dean and McMullen's focus is on market failures in their definition of sustainable entrepreneurship as 'the process of discovering, evaluating, and exploiting economic opportunities that are present in market failures which detract from sustainability, including those that are environmentally relevant' (Dean and McMullen, 2007). Cohen and Winn also stress the discovery of opportunity as essential when they posit that sustainable entrepreneurship research examines 'how opportunities to bring into existence future goods and services are discovered, created, and exploited, by whom, and with what economic, psychological, social, and environmental consequences' (Cohen and Winn, 2007: 35).

We explicitly draw on the Schumpeterian (1962 [1934]) notion of entrepreneurship as an innovative process of creating market disequilibria (Shane and Venkataraman, 2000; Eckhard and Shane, 2003) which in turn leads to imitation. Therefore sustainable entrepreneurship is defined here as the discovery and exploitation of economic opportunities through the generation of market disequilibria that initiate the transformation of a sector towards an environmentally and socially more sustainable state.

By linking sustainable entrepreneurship to the transformation of an industry towards sustainable development, we respond to Cohen and Winn's call for going beyond research on 'corporate "greening" initiatives and their impact on firm performance, [which] … is focused on incremental innovation …' (Cohen and Winn, 2007, p. 47). Sustainable entrepreneurship can be linked to both product and process innovation. In industries where key environmental and social aspects occur in the use phase of the product life cycle (e.g. cars or heating systems), sustainable entrepreneurship will more likely be associated with product innovation. In other industries, process innovation may be equally important.

Since sustainable entrepreneurial opportunities are typically linked to market failures or externalities, exploiting these opportunities involves both market- and non-market strategies (Baron, 1995; Hillman and Hitt, 1999). Non-market strategies are defined as the set of activities that firms use to influence social, environmental, and political stakeholders.

We suggest that there are two different types of organizations that engage in sustainable entrepreneurship, namely 'Davids' and 'Goliaths' (see Table 11.1). While inherently metaphorical, these terms will be defined as precisely as possible in this chapter. By Davids, we mean small firms that tend to have been founded recently and have a relatively small market share. In the context of sustainability, we are particularly interested in those firms among the larger population of small firms that explicitly aim at providing not just economic value, but also social and environmental value. By Goliaths, we mean the large incumbent firms that tend to be older and have a relatively high market share.

The emergence of Davids, as well as a process of 'Greening Goliaths', can result in a transformation of an industry towards sustainability. The term 'greening' is used in its colloquial sense. In public discourse, 'greening' is often used as a synonym for sustainable development. It is, however, stressed here that sustainable development should not be restricted to environmental protection alone but needs to include the social and economic dimension as well. Figure 11.1 visualizes the key concepts used in this chapter and how they relate to each other.

Both Davids and Goliaths engage in sustainable entrepreneurship, but not all their activities to improve environmental or social performance can be characterized as sustainable entrepreneurship. In line with the definition of sustainable entrepreneurship provided above, this chapter uses the term 'sustainable entrepreneurship' to describe activities by small or large firms that represent disruptive, rather than incremental innovation. Goliaths routinely engage in incremental environmental or social process innovation; for example, through the introduction of sustainability management systems, eco efficiency, or corporate social responsibility initiatives (Schaltegger, 2002). In the terminology used here, those activities would not qualify for the term (corporate) sustainable entrepreneurship. Equally, Davids who are active in a high-end environmental or social niche, but with no intention to broaden

Table 11.1   Characteristics of Davids and Goliaths

Criteria	Davids	Goliaths
Age	rather new	old, incumbent
Size	small	large
Objective Function	social and/or environmental objectives at least as important as economic objectives	economic objectives dominating, social/ environmental objectives complementary

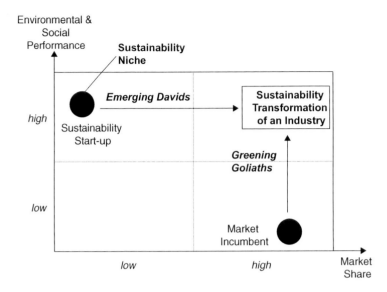

Figure 11.1   'Emerging Davids' and 'Greening Goliaths' (from Wüstenhagen, 1998)

Table 11.2   Delineation of sustainable entrepreneurship

	Davids	Goliaths
Disruptive Innovation	sustainable entrepreneurship	sustainable corporate entrepreneurship
Incremental Innovation	bioneers, social bricoleurs	sustainability management systems, CSR, eco-efficiency

their impact on a wider market, would be categorized as incrementally innovative and hence not sustainable entrepreneurs. These 'bioneers' (Schaltegger, 2002) or 'social bricoleurs' (Zahra et al., 2009) often come from the voluntary sector and sometimes tend to be opposed to consumerism and growth. They worry that mainstreaming requires them to abandon their ideals.

Theoretical context

The term sustainable development ties together concern for the carrying capacity of natural systems with the social challenges facing humanity (Brundtland Commission, 1987; Keating, 1993). As early as the 1970s, sustainability was employed to describe an economy 'in equilibrium with basic ecological support systems' (Stivers, 1976, p. 187). Traditionally, ecologists have pointed to the 'limits of growth' (Meadows et al., 1971; Meadows, 1977; Meadows et al., 1971) and demanded a 'steady state economy' (Daly, 1973; 1991) in order to address environmental concerns. The sustainable development debate is based on the assumption that societies need to manage three types of capital (economic, social, and natural), which may be non-substitutable and whose consumption might be irreversible (Dyllick and Hockerts, 2002).

Daly (1991) stresses the fact that economic capital cannot necessarily substitute natural capital. Forests, for example, provide raw material for paper (which is easily substitutable), but they also maintain biodiversity and absorb CO_2 (Siebenhüner et al., 2005). Another problem of natural and social capital deterioration lies in their partial irreversibility. Moreover, the depletion of natural and social capital may have non-linear consequences. A lake can, for example, absorb nutrients while increasing its productivity, only to break down all of a sudden once a certain level of algae is reached.

If the degradation of natural and social capital has such important consequences, the question arises of why action is not taken more systematically to alleviate it. Cohen and Winn (2007) point to four types of market failure as possible explanations: first, while the benefits of natural or social capital depletion are privatized, the costs are often externalized. Second, natural capital is also often undervalued by society since there is a lack of awareness of the real cost incurred. Information asymmetry is a third reason identified to cause natural and social capital depletion. Cohen and Winn close with the realization that, contrary to economic theory, many firms are not perfect optimizers.

As awareness of sustainable development grows in society, the market failures discussed by Cohen and Winn are likely to diminish. For example, they expect that society will increasingly realize the value of natural and social resources boosting their economic value. As a result, firms will have to internalize costs that have formerly been borne by society. This change is called the sustainability transformation of an industry (Dyllick et al., 1997; Dyllick, 1999).

From social and environmental entrepreneurship to sustainable entrepreneurship

While social and environmental aspects of sustainable development are inextricably linked, a large part of the academic literature on sustainability entrepreneurship deals with either one or the other.

A first group of authors put environmental innovation at the heart of their work. These contributions have coalesced around the theme of eco-innovation, which more recently has spawned the sub-discipline of clean-technology venturing (Hart and Milstein, 1999; Parker and O'Rourke, 2006; Boehnke and Wüstenhagen, 2007). A second line of publications deals with innovations aiming at social improvements (e.g. health, education, community development). Here, the term social innovation can refer to product or process innovations with a social purpose. A sub-group of these types of innovations concerns the so-called bottom of the pyramid (BOP) thinking (Prahalad and Hart, 1999; Prahalad and Hammond, 2002a). Social innovation is also used to refer to the process of starting and improving social enterprises.

The notion that sustainable development drives disruptive innovation (Christensen, 1997) has come quite naturally to the sustainability debate (Hockerts, 1999, 2003; Cohen et al., 2007; Wüstenhagen et al., 2008; Hall et al., 2010; York and Venkataraman, 2010). Sustainable entrepreneurship has been proposed as a 'breakthrough discipline for innovation' (Fussler, 1996), as a 'source of creative destruction' (Hart et al., 1999: 23), as well as the beginning of the 'next industrial revolution' (Braungart and McDonough, 1998, p. 82; Lovins et al., 1999: p. 1; Senge and Carstedt, 2001, p. 24). From this has emerged a large number of publications advancing tools for furthering the creation of new markets through environmental innovation (Fussler, 1996; McDonough and Braungart, 2002a; 2002b; Kolk and Pinkse, 2004).

In his influential book on eco-innovation, Fussler (1996) states that a majority of today's firms are not actively pursuing sustainability entrepreneurship as a strategy to create market share. However, he does not believe that this 'innovation lethargy' (Fussler, 1996, p. 9) will persist in the years to come. Using a number of anecdotal case studies he shows that innovative firms can succeed in driving ecological innovation profitably, not by following current customer demand but by creating future market space. This notion that firms can actively transform market structures to make them more conducive to ecological innovation is also proposed by Dyllick (1999). Schaltegger and Wagner (2008) even propose that the ambition to transform an industry is a defining element of sustainable entrepreneurship, implying that sustainable entrepreneurial firms not only see sustainability as central to core business activities, but at the same time aim for mass-market transformation beyond the eco-niche (Villiger et al., 2000). On the social side of sustainability entrepreneurship, the term 'corporate social innovation' was first introduced by Rosabeth Moss Kanter (1999, p. 125) who argues that firms should use social issues as a learning laboratory for identifying unmet needs and for developing solutions that create new markets. She describes, for example, BankBoston's effort in setting up a Community Bank, which eventually evolved into a new market for the bank. More recently, Patrick Cescau, CEO of Unilever, has defined corporate social innovation as a way of finding new products and services that meet not only the functional needs of consumers for tasty food or clean clothes but also their wider aspirations as citizens (cited in Webb, 2007).

An important sub-theme of corporate social innovation is the focus on low-income markets. Prahalad and Hart (1999) talk in this context of the potential of the BOP as a source for 'the great leap downward' (Christensen et al., 2001, p. 92). The BOP premise is that by focusing on the unmet needs of low-income populations (i.e. those who are situated at the base of the wealth pyramid), firms can create profitable markets while also helping the poor address some of their most urgent needs (Christensen et al., 2001; Prahalad et al., 2002a; Prahalad and Hart, 2002b). Prahalad's most notable assumption is that BOP markets have to pay a 'poverty premium' (Prahalad et al., 2002a). This means that many poor have to pay more for products and services such as food, water, medication, credit, or telecommunication than their middle or upper-class compatriots. By using BOP thinking, MNCs are believed to better target their design as well as improve the distribution so as to bring down the poverty premium.

In parallel to the corporate version of social entrepreneurship described above, there is also a growing literature on start-up ventures motivated by social innovation. The concept of social entrepreneurship emerged in the late 1990s (Boschee, 1995; Henton et al., 1997; Warwick, 1997; Bornstein, 1998; Dees, 1998a; 1998 b; Brinckerhoff, 2000; Dees et al., 2001a; 2001b; Drayton, 2002). However, it has only recently reached the academic debate (Haugh, 2006; Light, 2006; Mair and Marti, 2006; Mair et al., 2006; Nicholls, 2006; Perrini, 2006; Hockerts, 2007; Peattie and Morley, 2008; Robinson et al., 2009).

Ultimately, sustainable entrepreneurship is about a combination of economic, social, and environmental value creation. Such integrated views of sustainable entrepreneurship are only starting to emerge in the academic literature (Cohen and Winn, 2007; Dean and McMullen, 2007; Schaltegger and Wagner, 2008).

Firm size and the diffusion of sustainable innovation

Whether large or small firms are more likely to pursue sustainable entre-preneurship is a question that has rarely been asked in the academic literature. In terms of entrepreneurship more broadly, however, the influence of firm size on innovation is almost a classic theme. On the one hand, using an economies of scale argument, large firms have been hypothesized to be more innovative because of their broader resource base which allows them to pursue higher levels of research and development (R&D) (e.g. Galbraith, 1956; Schumpeter, 1942; Kamien and Schwartz, 1982). In his meta-analysis of 20 studies, Damanpour (1992) finds that the positive relationship between size and innovation is stronger in manufacturing than service industries and relates more to innovation implementation than initiation. A contrasting but equally popular view in the literature is that small firms are more flexible and therefore avoid some of the organizational inertia that characterizes large firms, leading to a negative correlation between firm size and innovation (Acs and Audretsch, 1987; 1988; Audretsch and Acs, 1991; Stock et al., 2002).

The innovation management literature has highlighted the particular challenges that large incumbent firms face in the light of radical innovation (Christensen, 1997; Leifer, 2000), and suggested ways to overcome those challenges such as the creation of a 'radical innovation hub' (Leifer, 2001) or co-operation with outside venture capitalists (Chesbrough, 2000). Despite specific opportunities to improve innovation management in incumbent firms, Burgelman points out that there are inherent tensions in marrying large corporations with radical innovation, and that organizational attempts to overcome the challenges, such as new venture departments, will remain 'a design for ambiguity' (Burgelman, 1985, p. 52).

One way to resolve the controversy around firm size and innovation is to move from a static to a dynamic perspective. Innovation scholars with an evolutionary economics perspective have highlighted that large and small firms play differing roles in different phases of industry evolution. As Utterback and Suarez (1993) point out, the technological trajectory of an industry is characterized by discontinuities, which lead to the emergence of a technological paradigm change (Nelson and Winter, 1982). When a new technological paradigm emerges, this results in the creative destruction (Schumpeter, 1962 [1934]) of existing competencies, thereby improving the selection environment for small entrepreneurial firms and other industry outsiders who are more flexible to pursue new opportunities without the liabilities of existing assets (Tushman and Anderson, 1986; Utterback, 1994). In terms of industry development, a technological paradigm change is usually characterized by a high degree of variation; that is, a large number of new entrants experimenting with new product designs (Utterback et al., 1993; Metcalfe, 1994). As soon as a dominant design (Utterback and Abernathy, 1975) emerges, there is a shift from variation to selection; that is, industry consolidation and an increasing number of exits.

When it comes to the diffusion of sustainable innovation, firms are faced with additional challenges because of a double externality problem (Rennings, 2000). As in the case of conventional innovation, there is an externality in that technological spill-over prevents the innovator from appropriating the full value of an innovation. In the case of sustainable innovation, however, there is a second externality, namely the lack of internalization of environmental or social cost for incumbent technologies. The presence of external costs has two important effects: first, it reduces the relative (private) benefit of sustainable innovation for customers. Firms which want successfully to commercialize sustainable innovation therefore need to make special efforts in convincing customers that the product they are offering is not just good for society, but also good for them. Second, the flip side of this is that government policy is playing a more important role in commercializing sustainable innovation, because it is the role of government to internalize external cost through taxation or other economic policies. Therefore, innovating firms in the realm of sustainability need to understand government policy more so than their conventional counterparts, pointing to the importance of non-market strategies in the context of sustainable entrepreneurship.

'Emerging Davids', Greening Goliaths, and their interactions

This chapter conceptualizes the notion that starts-ups and market incumbents each have a role to play in the transformation of industries towards sustainable development. It can be observed that more and more sustainable ventures emerge as an industry is increasingly pressured to adopt sustainable development. These 'Emerging Davids' usually display a high level of environmental and/or social performance that is attractive to a select number of consumers who are very concerned about sustainability issues. However, Davids often fail to reach a broader mass market. In some cases they even have no intention to grow being content to remain in their niche.

Market incumbents, on the other hand, tend to focus initially on sustainability communication and accounting systems (e.g. Seuring, 2004; Beske et al., 2006; Burritt and Saka, 2006; Morsing and Schultz, 2006;

Halme and Huse, 1997). While these may lead to gradual improvements, they tend to be not as efficient as hoped for (Hamschmidt and Dyllick, 2001; Schaltegger, 2002). However, faced with growing competition from 'Emerging Davids', incumbents increasingly engage in their own form of corporate sustainable entrepreneurship. These 'Greening Goliaths' promise to achieve a broader impact, since they have the potential to reach out to a mass-market audience (Villiger et al., 2000).

Extant literature on sustainable entrepreneurship has tended to cover either incumbents or new start-ups. There is very little discussion of the interplay between these two players when they engage in sustainable entrepreneurship, with the exception of a few empirical cases that are summarized in Table 11.3. These contributions touching upon the David/Goliath theme tend to discuss anecdotal evidence from four main substantive areas: fair trade, organic food, green electricity, and micro-finance. In subsequent theorizing, this chapter will draw on this body of literature aiming to synthesize from it a more encompassing set of insights.

'Emerging Davids': The emergence of sustainability start-ups

New start-ups are unencumbered by the incumbents' fear of cannibalizing the market share of their prior products or devaluing previous investment in their manufacturing processes (i.e. Campion et al., 1999; Nicholls and Opal, 2005). Being often run by idealists, sustainability start-ups are less likely to be caught in a specific technological mindset and more prone to try out innovative approaches. Furthermore, given their status as newcomers, they are more credible when claiming to be part of the solution rather than the problems caused by the incumbents (Hockerts, 2006a). As a result, new start-ups are initially more likely to engage in sustainable entrepreneurship than market incumbents.

What sets sustainability start-ups apart from normal start-up companies is their pronounced value based approach and their intention to effect social and environmental change in society. They are literally the Davids aiming to slay the giant. Realizing that external costs cause environmental and social harm, they make it their business to change market equilibria so as to internalize these costs, and in the process to change the playing field for everybody (Cohen and Winn, 2007). They do this by asking customers to pay a premium for socially and environmentally superior products.

However, the focus on their mission also has some drawbacks. Being involved with one specific innovation, sustainability start-ups have a tendency towards single issue campaigning. They invest all their

Table 11.3 Extant literature discussing examples of 'Emerging Davids' and/or 'Greening Goliaths'

Author	Sector	Area	Contribution
Davies and Crane (2003)	Fair trade	UK	Documents tensions a fair trade start-up experiences with its grassroot ideals as it competes increasingly with incumbents.
Hockerts (2006a)	Fair trade	UK	Describes how fair trade emerged from the voluntary sector, followed by social business start-ups; later retailers and food producers launch own-label fair trade products.
Nicholls and Opal (2005)	Fair trade	UK	Compares mainstream retailers and fair trade start-ups and their strategies for increasing the fair trade market share.
Latacz and Foster (1997)	Organic food	Germany and UK	Discusses the short-comings of the niche marketing structures for organic food in Germany and the UK. Speculates about the role of mainstream supermarkets.
Villiger (2000)	Organic food	Switzerland	Organic food initially offered by smaller wholefood stores and grassroots initiatives, large retailers followed at varying speed.
Dimitri and Greene (2006)	Organic food	USA	Organic food previously sold through dedicated natural food stores; since the year 2000, conventional supermarkets have taken over as the primary sales channel.
Jacobsson and Johnson (2000)	Renewable energy	Europe	Examines the diffusion of renewable energy technologies and the role played by 'prime movers'.
Bird et al. (2002)	Renewable energy	International (10 countries)	Green electricity start-ups relatively unsuccessful due to customer inertia, yet growing competitive threat due to market liberalization causing proactiveness of incumbents.
Wüstenhagen et al. (2003)	Renewable energy	Switzerland	Green electricity initially offered by smaller utilities and grassroots new entrants, large utilities followed at varying speeds.

(continued)

Table 11.3 Continued

Author	Sector	Area	Contribution
Stenzel and Frenzel (2008)	Renewable energy	Germany, Spain, UK	Incumbents initially reluctant to adopt renewable energy (except in Spain); co-evolutionary processes between firms, their technological strategies, and the regulatory environment occur.
Baydas et al. (1997)	Micro-finance	Developing countries	Discusses how commercial banks face challenges when they enter the area of micro-finance and its development agenda.
Campion and White (1999)	Micro-finance	Developing countries	Describes how micro-finance NGOs become more and more like incumbents as they are transformed into regulated financial institutions.
Christen and Cook (2001)	Micro-finance	Latin America	Discusses how micro-finance start-ups are transformed by commercialization and the resulting risk of mission drift.
Cull et al. (2007)	Micro-finance	Developing countries	Discusses the trade-offs between profitability and fighting poverty faced by micro-finance banks.

resources and attention in optimizing one particular environmental or social issue at which they try to excel. So, this chapter will, for example, find that fair trade start-ups put price premiums at the top of their sustainability agenda (Hockerts, 2006a); renewable energy producers prioritize the environmental impacts of energy production (Bird et al., 2002); and banks dedicated to micro-finance dedicated aim at providing loans to the poor (Christen et al., 2001). This might be due to the fact that their entrepreneurs are simply obsessed with one issue. It is this obsession that has often driven them to launch the business in the first place. Given their limited resources, sustainability start-ups are, however, less good at addressing a broad range of sustainability issues. The fair trade labels, for example, have been hesitant to require their suppliers to embrace environmental issues (Robins and Roberts, 1997; Equal Exchange, 2002). Similarly, there is little understanding among micro-finance institutions of how their loans impact upon the environment (Lal and Israel, 2006). And some of the entrepreneurial firms in Germany's emerging solar energy industry have faced criticism about paying low wages, which could be seen as a lack of corporate social responsibility (Williamson, 2008). There are multiple reasons for this. On the one hand, start-ups lack the resources for some of the comprehensive process innovation that Goliaths tend to engage in, such as building up sustainability management systems. Moreover, they are keen to keep communications focused on their main innovation. Finally, some sustainability entrepreneurs become caught up in their own propaganda (Hockerts, 2006b).

While sustainability start-ups are keen to see their market grow, they nonetheless often keep that growth restricted. There is a tendency among sustainability start-ups to keep standards undiluted and demanding. Being supported by idealistic stakeholders strongly committed to the sustainability mission, Davids are doubtful of attempts to lower standards even if this might attract more customers (e.g. Lockie, 2008). Apart from idealistic reasons to keep the market niche committed to the highest environmental or social standards, there is also an economic rationale to this. Being aware that incumbents might easily outspend them in R&D and distribution, should they decide to enter the market niche, sustainability start-ups might prefer to keep their niche at a size that is not attracting undue interest from incumbent competitors. Over time, start-ups will try to continue innovating, thus pushing up requirements for sustainability performance. As a result, sustainability start-ups have an inclination to keep their niches small and exclusive.

'Greening Goliaths': The transformation of market incumbents

In the early stages of an industry's sustainability transformation, market incumbents often react to pressure from stakeholders concerned about sustainability through incremental process innovation; for example, by adopting sustainability communication and management systems in an attempt to better understand the issues they are facing as well as to demonstrate to stakeholders that they are sincere about their concerns. However, incumbents are also restricted by their existing assets, which reflect past investments. These often anchor incumbents in a business-as-usual way of thinking, making it less likely for them to engage in sustainability entrepreneurship. This is particularly the case when sustainability-related product innovation might compete with extant products of the incumbent.

Market incumbents are initially challenged by newcomers where it concerns the primary innovation dimension of the sustainability start-up. Adapting all their product range to the highest sustainability standards is rarely an option. However, given their superior market power, financial resources, and process-innovation capabilities, market incumbents can play catch-up quickly once they decide to become fast followers (e.g. Dimitri et al., 2006; Hockerts, 2006a). Incumbents may, for example, find it opportune to launch copy-cat products that resemble those of the start-ups in order to reap part of the premiums that dedicated consumers are willing to pay. All major electricity utilities have, for example, launched some kind of tariff that promises their clients electricity from environmentally preferable sources (Bird et al., 2002; Delmas et al., 2007). Incumbents may also decide to launch corporate venture capital (CVC) funds to keep an eye on innovating Davids (Teppo and Wüstenhagen, 2009). This provides them with an option to integrate sustainability innovation when it turns out to be disruptive.

While market incumbents tend to lag behind start-ups concerning the primary sustainability innovation, their strength lies in process innovation. For example, they have a tendency to invest in more encompassing sustainability management systems (Hamschmidt et al., 2001). Thus, they will be addressing multiple environmental and social issues where sustainability start-ups focus on one or two issues only. Employing tools such as environmental and social management and reporting systems, market incumbents will find it easier to develop a broad sustainability performance.

In some cases, market incumbents may be interested in less ambitious sustainability standards compared to sustainability start-ups. As an example, in the debate about Switzerland's 'agricultural policy 2002' in the early 1990s, the country's leading retailer Migros actively lobbied for Integrated Pest Management rather than the stricter guidelines of organic agriculture as the standard that would be the base for environmental subsidies to farmers (Villiger, 2000). However, Goliaths are if anything even more interested than Davids in codifying these standards explicitly since they lack the reputation for environmental or social leadership that some sustainability start-ups have (Truffer et al., 2001; Giovannucci and Ponte, 2005). The existence of a broadly accepted product standard or label creates a level playing field between incumbents and start-ups. Research indicates that such standards are not contributing much to the overall performance (Seuring and Müller, 2008). They rather form a minimum requirement that has to be met in order to avoid related problems. Incumbents will tend to attempt to keep standards fixed rather than encouraging continued innovation. The embrace of the Rainforest Alliance label by multinational Kraft can be seen as an example of a multinational trying to enter the fair trade niche without having to be subject to the stricter requirements (i.e. minimum price,

price premiums, pre-financing, long-term contracts) of the Fair Trade Labelling Organisation (FLO) (McAllister, 2004).

Co-evolution of Davids and Goliaths

Both Davids and Goliaths have a role to play in the sustainability transformation of an industry. In fact the interaction between the two resembles a co-evolution, whereby each side moves the transformation further. Co-evolution is a term from biology describing the simultaneous evolution of species who mutually depend on each other (Ehrlich and Raven, 1964). The term has been used to describe the interaction of natural and social systems by ecological economists such as Norgaard (1994). One can distinguish several phases of transformation (see Figure 11.2). In a first stage, sustainability start-ups launch the sustainability innovation to the market. Often these start-ups are run by highly motivated idealists who work in close cooperation with

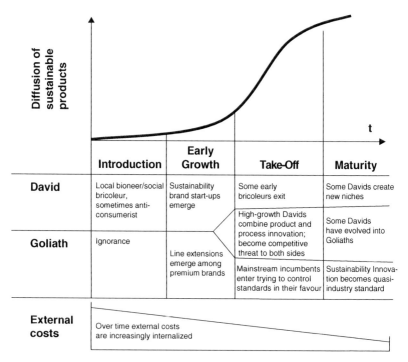

Figure 11.2   Co-evolution of sustainability start-ups and market incumbents towards the sustainability transformation of an industry

NGOs and charities (Meijkamp, 2000; Hockerts, 2006a). Being placed in-between the third sector and the formal economy these alternative players do have profit motives although they are usually more driven by a desire to achieve environmental and social change. In his typology of ecopreneurs, linking the terms 'bio' and 'pioneer', Schaltegger (2002) calls these actors 'bioneers', while Zahra et al. (2009) refer to them as 'social bricoleurs' in the context of social entrepreneurship. Often these bioneers/bricoleurs never grow beyond a small niche, thus actually not effecting disruptive change. However, in a few cases they can change into sustainable entrepreneurs. Both the organic food and the fair trade markets, for example, have seen many specialized producers (e.g. Demeter, CaféDirect) and retailers (e.g. One World Shops; Organic food shops) pop up in the early days of the movement (Dimitri et al., 2006; Hockerts, 2006a). Similarly, local grassroots initiatives engaged in producing their own solar collectors decades before the word 'cleantech' became fashionable in Silicon Valley (Wüstenhagen 2000), and idealist bricoleurs preceded the current quest for lighter, more efficient cars by a long time (Truffer and Dürrenberger, 1997).

While bioneers or social bricoleurs kick off sustainability transformation, they are usually followed quite quickly by some market incumbents once early growth picks up. These would usually be leading premium brands who offer line extensions to capitalize on the growing trend. Since the late 1990s, food producers and retailers have discovered the organic and fair trade niches for themselves (Villiger, 2000). Around the same time, incumbent electric utilities started experimenting with green electricity offerings (Bird et al., 2002), and car manufacturers have launched cleaner cars (Canzler and Knie, 1995). Their offers usually make up only small line extensions. Retailers such, as for example, Sainsbury and the Co-op have been early adopters of both organic and fair trade products.

As the sustainability transformation of a market continues, a different type of sustainability start-up company begins to emerge. The high-growth Davids in this third phase are much more business-like and often backed by more professional investors. They combine the best of both worlds by orchestrating the product innovation of the early Davids with the process innovation that Goliaths are typically good at. Having observed the development of the bioneers, they have a good understanding of the market niche and now aim to extend it through more professional management. These start-up firms do not share the implicit motto of many bioneers that to stay 'small is beautiful' (Schumacher, 1974). Instead they have also a clearer expectation to achieve profitable growth and to extend market share, while defending it against incumbents. Examples for these types of start-ups include the organic retailer WholeFoods market in the US, the British Fair Trade Brand CaféDirect (Hockerts, 2006a), green power marketers such as Green Mountain Energy in the US and Lichtblick in Germany (Wüstenhagen, 2000), and solar cell producers such as Q-Cells or Solarworld in Germany (Schönwandt, 2004).

The final and fourth stage of maturity of sustainability entrepreneurship tends to extend to the mass-market brands that begin to see both a growing competitive threat from the start-ups and a market potential for themselves. Typical examples for this include WalMart's decision to enter the organic market (Gunther, 2006; Warner, 2006), Kraft's adoption of the Rainforest Alliance Label (McAllister, 2004) and the decision of energy incumbent Siemens to follow the lead of their competitor GE and enter the growing wind turbine manufacturing business in 2004 (Lewis and Wiser, 2007). Being more cost-driven than premium incumbents, these late entrants into the sustainability niche often bring process innovation along the supply chain to the table. WalMart, for example, explicitly aims to bring down the cost of organic food so that it no longer remains just a luxury item for the upper middle classes but also becomes accessible for typical WalMart clients (Gunther, 2006). On the one hand, this clearly contributes positively to the sustainability transformation of an industry, because it improves access to products of higher social and environmental quality to a wider part of the market, and is likely to reduce other sustainability impacts through process innovation along the way. On the other hand, the entrance of cost-conscious Goliaths increases the pressure to somewhat lower sustainability criteria and to give up some of the ideals cherished by the first generation bioneers (Lockie, 2008). The Fair Trade Labelling Organization (FLO), for example, has begun to relax some of its standards in response to the pressure from competing schemes such as the Rainforest Alliance label. So to some extent, the price of gaining more breadth may be to lose depth in terms of sustainability quality. At this stage of development, then, it may be expected that there will be a re-emergence of Davids to create new high-end market niches, eventually starting the transformation cycle over again. A typical example is Swiss entrepreneur Nicolas Hayek who, more than a decade after exiting from a joint venture with Daimler that aimed at revolutionizing personal mobility but then resulted in the fairly traditional Smart car, has set up Belenos Clean Power, a new firm to pursue the commercialization of hydrogen-powered electric vehicles.

Conclusion

Sustainable entrepreneurship research so far has neglected the differential roles of large and small firms in transforming industries towards sustainable development. The theme has not been adequately addressed in the corporate sustainability literature either. While sustainable entrepreneurship scholars tend to focus predominantly on the role of start-ups, corporate sustainability scholars tend to focus their attention towards what happens in large firms. This article has aimed at advancing the academic discussion on sustainable entrepreneurship by: (a) highlighting the differential roles of 'Davids' and 'Goliaths' in the sustainable transformation of industries; (b) discussing the specific opportunities and challenges of 'Emerging Davids' and 'Greening Goliaths' as pathways towards sustainable development; and (c) exploring the interaction of entrepreneurial initiatives in small and large companies in bringing about this development. The analysis here has resulted in a dynamic view of industry transformation, where the initial phase is characterized by sustainability initiatives of idealistic 'Davids'. In a second phase, some pioneering 'Goliaths', for example retailers with a higher-quality positioning, mimic some of the David initiatives and try to bring them into their mainstream distribution channels. In isolation, none of these two developments would necessarily lead to sustainable transformation of mainstream markets, because as this chapter has argued above Davids tend to get stuck in their high-quality, low-market penetration niche, while Goliaths have an inherent tendency to react to cost pressures by lowering the sustainability quality of their offerings. However, there is increasing evidence for a next stage of development on both paths. As for 'Emerging Davids', firms such as Wholefoods, Green Mountain Energy, Vestas or Ben & Jerry's have found ways to scale up their sustainable innovations without unduly compromising their sustainability ambitions. However, in the 'Greening Goliaths' camp, there are examples of large firms such as Walmart, GE, Kraft or Toyota which have taken on the challenge of building sustainability into their mainstream business. Arguably, the success of Emerging Davids, which can also be seen as a potential competitive threat, has been instrumental for some of these Goliaths to embark on the level of sustainable entrepreneurship that they did. Therefore, this research would argue that the sustainable transformation of industries is not going to be brought about by either Davids or Goliaths alone, but instead that their interaction is essential.

The conceptual model here points to interesting avenues for further research. It has been suggested that social entrepreneurship research should move beyond the single case study designs in the early days of the discipline and towards larger samples (Hockerts, 2006b). This is certainly true for sustainable entrepreneurship research as well, but this chapter would suggest that additional insights can be gained from comparative studies of sustainable entrepreneurial initiatives in both small and large firms. In such studies, it would be particularly interesting to watch out for the specific challenges encountered by 'Davids' and 'Goliaths' in their attempts to broaden and deepen the level of their impact. This could be done retrospectively by doing in-depth case studies on some of the cases of successful 'Emerging Davids' and 'Greening Goliaths' mentioned above. Even more insightful would be longitudinal case studies of a set of small and large companies moving towards sustainability, whereby the focus could be on either market or non-market strategies of Davids and Goliaths. There is also scope for empirically testing this model in other industries such as the water sector or the greening of information technology (IT) services. A further area of interest would be to specifically investigate arenas where Davids and Goliaths interact. Looking at external corporate venturing programmes in sustainability-related industries such as energy, water, or transport might be a good focus for that. Further research could also take an investor perspective and ask for the optimal portfolio allocation between Davids and Goliaths for simultaneously achieving high economic, social, and environmental performance. Finally, an important fundamental research question is whether there are indeed successful examples of the sustainability transformation of industries; that is, the move towards the upper right corner of Figure 11.1. While there is evidence that the interaction of Davids and Goliaths does make a positive contribution towards this objective, there are also listed numerous limitations and challenges that Davids and Goliaths are each facing on their respective transformation paths. Against the background of some of the sobering trends in global environmental and social impacts (WWF, 2006), it is worth critically examining – although this lies well beyond the scope of this chapter – whether the final outcome of this co-evolution is indeed in line with the requirements of sustainable development.

The model developed here may have important policy implications. The findings discussed in this chapter suggest that what is needed could be referred to as an ambidextrous innovation policy for sustainability. O'Reilly and Tushman (2004) refer to ambidextrous organizations as those that master the art of simultaneously pursuing incremental and disruptive innovation. Similarly, achieving the sustainable transformation of an industry requires a finely tuned mix of disruptive and incremental innovation, which can be promoted if policymakers understand the nuanced interplay of emerging Davids and greening Goliaths, rather than single-mindedly focusing on only one of these paths while neglecting the other. Arguably, policymakers have a tendency to favour incumbents over entrepreneurial start-ups, so designing sustainability policies with an entrepreneurial perspective in mind is a good start, but this chapter would suggest that smart innovation policies should try to leverage cooperation and competition between Davids and Goliaths.

Note

This chapter is based upon Hockerts and Wüstenhagen (2010), 'Greening Goliaths Versus Emerging Davids – Theorizing about the Role of Incumbents and New Entrants in Sustainable Entrepreneurship', *Journal of Business Venturing*, 25 (5), pp. 481–92.

References

Acs, Z. J. and Audretsch, D. B. (1987), 'Innovation, Market Structure and Firm Size', *The Review of Economics and Statistics*, pp. 567–74.

Acs, Z. J. and Audretsch, D. B. (1988), 'Innovation in Large and Small Firms: An Empirical Analysis', *The American Economic Review*, pp. 678–90.

Audretsch, D. B. and Acs, Z. J. (1991), 'Innovation and Size at the Firm Level', *Southern Economic Journal*, pp. 739–44.

Baron, D. (1995), 'Integrated Strategy: Market and Nonmarket Components', *California Management Review*, 37 (2), pp. 47–65.

Baydas, M. M., Graham, D. H. and Valenzuela, L. (1997), Commercial Banks in Microfinance: New Actors in the Microfinance World: Microenterprise Best Practices.

Beske, P., Koplin, J. and Seuring, S. (2006), The Use of Environmental and Social Standards by German First-tier Suppliers of the Volkswagen AG. Corporate Social Responsibility and Environmental Management.

Bird, L. A., Wüstenhagen, R. and Aabakken, J. (2002), 'A Review of International Green Power Markets: Recent Experience, Trends, and Market Drivers', *Renewable and Sustainable Energy Reviews*, 6 (6), pp. 513–36.

Boehnke, J. and Wüstenhagen, R. (2007), Business Models for Distributed Energy Technologies, Evidence from German Cleantech Firms, Academy of Management Conference. Philadelphia, August 2007.

Bornstein, D. (1998), 'Changing the World on a Shoestring', *The Atlantic Monthly*, 281 (1), pp. 34–39.

Boschee, J. (1995), 'Social Entrepreneurship', *Across the Board*, 32 (3), pp. 20–4.

Braungart, M. and McDonough, W. (1998), 'The Next Industrial Revolution', *The Atlantic Monthly*, pp. 82–92.

Brinckerhoff, P. C. (2000), *Social Entrepreneurship : The Art of Mission-Based Venture Development*, New York: John Wiley & Sons.

Brundtland Commission (1987), *Our Common Future* Brussels: World Commission on Environment and Development.

Burgelman, R. A. (1985), 'Managing the New Venture Division: Research Findings and Implications for Strategic Management', *Strategic Management Journal*, 6 (1).

Burritt, R. and Saka, C. (2006), 'Environmental Management Accounting Applications and Eco-efficiency: Case Studies from Japan', *Journal of Cleaner Production*, 14 (14), pp. 1262–75.

Campion, A. and White, V. (1999), Institutional Metamorphosis: Transformation of Microfinance NGOs Into Regulated Financial Institutions: MicroFinance Network.

Chesbrough, H. (2000), 'Designing Corporate Ventures in the Shadow of Private Venture Capital', *California Management Review*, 42 (3), pp. 31–49.

Christen, R. and Cook, T. (2001), Commercialization and Mission Drift: The Transformation of Microfinance in Latin America: CGAP.

Christensen, C. M. (1997), *The Innovators Dilemma, When New Technologies Cause Great Firms to Fail*, Boston: Harvard Business Press.

Christensen, C. M., Craig, T. and Hart, S. L. (2001), 'The Great Disruption', *Foreign Affairs*, 80 (2), pp. 80–95.

Cohen, B. and Winn, M. I. (2007), 'Market Imperfections, Opportunity and Sustainable Entrepreneurship', *Journal of Business Venturing*, 22 (1), pp. 29–49.

Cull, R., Demirguc-Kunt, A. and Morduch, J. (2007), 'Financial Performance and Outreach: A Global Analysis of Leading Microbanks',*. *The Economic Journal*, 117 (517), pp. F107–F133.

Daly, H. E. (1973), *Towards a Steady State Economy*, San Francisco: Freeman.

Daly, H. E. (1991), *Steady-State Economics* (2nd edn), Washington, DC: Island Press.

Damanpour, F. (1992), 'Organizational Size and Innovation', *Organization Studies*, 13 (3), p. 375.

Davies, I. A. and Crane, A. (2003), 'Ethical Decision Making in Fair Trade Companies', *Journal of Business Ethics*, 45 (1), pp. 79–92.

Dean, T. J. and McMullen, J. S. (2007), 'Toward a Theory of Sustainable Entrepreneurship: Reducing Environmental Degradation Through Entrepreneurial Action', *Journal of Business Venturing*, 22 (1), pp. 50–76.

Dees, J. G. (1998a), 'Enterprising Nonprofits', *Harvard Business Review*, 76 (1), pp. 54–66.

Dees, J. G. (1998b), The Meaning of Social Entrepreneurship.

Dees, J. G., Emerson, J. and Economy, P. (2001a), *Enterprising Nonprofits: A Toolkit for Social Entrepreneurs* New York: John Wiley & Sons.

Dees, J. G., Emerson, J. and Economy, P. (2001b), *Strategic Tools for Social Entrepreneurs: Enhancing the Performance of Your Enterprising Nonprofit*, New York: John Wiley & Sons.

Delmas, M., Russo, M. V. and Montes-Sancho, M. J. (2007), 'Deregulation and Environmental Differentiation in the Electric Utility Industry', *Strategic Management Journal*, 28 (2), pp. 189–209.

Dimitri, C. and Greene, C. (2006), 'Recent Growth Patterns in the US Organic Foods Market', *Organic Agriculture in the US*, 129.

Drayton, W. (2002), 'The Citizen Sector: Becoming as Entrepreneurial and Competitive as Business', *California Management Review*, 44 (3), pp. 120–32.

Dyllick, T. (1999), 'Environment and Competitiveness of Companies', in D. Hitchens, J. Clausen, and K. Fichter (Eds) *International Environmental Management Benchmarks*, Berlin: Springer.

Dyllick, T., Belz, F. and Schneidewind, U. (1997), *Ökologie und Wettbewerbsfähigkeit*, Munich: Hanser.

Dyllick, T. and Hockerts, K. (2002), 'Beyond the Business Case for Corporate Sustainability', *Business Strategy and the Environment*, 11 (2), pp. 130–41.

Eckhard, J. and Shane, S. A. (2003), 'The Importance of Opportunities to Entrepreneurship', *Journal of Management*, 29 (3), pp. 333–49.

Ehrlich, P. R. and Raven, P. H. (1964), 'Butterflies and Plants: A Study of Coevolution', *Evolution*, 18, pp. 586–608.

Elkington, J. (1997), *Cannibals With Forks: The Triple Bottom Line of 21st Century Business*, Oxford: Capstone.

Equal Exchange (2002), *Are All Fair Trade Products Organic?*

Fussler, C. (1996), *Driving Eco-Innovation, A Breakthrough Discipline for Innovation and Sustainability*, London: Pitman.

Galbraith, J. K. (1956), *American Capitalism: The Concept of Countervailing Power*, Boston: Hougton Mifflin.

Giovannucci, D. and Ponte, S. (2005), 'Standards as a New Form of Social Contract? Sustainability Initiatives in the Coffee Industry', *Food Policy*, 30 (3) pp. 284–301.

Gunther, M. (2006), 'The Green Machine', *Fortune Magazine*, 7 August 2006: pp. 42–46.

Hall, J., Daneke, G. and Lenox, M. (2010), 'Sustainable Development and Entrepreneurship: Past Contributions and Future Directions', *Journal of Business Venturing*.

Halme, M. and Huse, M. (1997), 'The Influence of Corporate Governance, Industry and Country Factors on Environmental Reporting', *Scandinavian Journal of Management*, 13 (2), pp. 137–57.

Hamschmidt, J. and Dyllick, T. (2001), 'ISO 14001: Profitable? Yes! But is it Eco-effective?', *Greener Management International*, 2001 (34), pp. 43–54.

Hart, S. L. and Milstein, M. B. (1999), 'Global Sustainability and the Creative Destruction of Industries', *Sloan Management Review*, 41 (1), pp. 23–33.

Hart, S. L. and Milstein, M. B. (2003), 'Creating Sustainable Value', *Academy of Management Executive*, 17 (2), pp. 56–67.

Haugh, H. (2006), 'Social Enterprise: Beyond Economic Outcomes and Individual Returns', in J. Mair, J. Robinson, and K. N. Hockerts (Eds) *Social Entrepreneurship*, New York: Palgrave Macmillan.

Henton, D., Melville, J. and Walesh, K. (1997), 'Grassroots Leaders for a New Economy: How Civic Entrepreneurs Are Building Prosperous Communities', *National Civic Review*, 86 (2), pp. 149–56.

Hillman, A. and Hitt, M. (1999), 'Corporate Political Strategy Formation: A Model of Approach, Participation and Strategy Decisions', *Academy of Management Review*, 24, pp. 825–842.

Hockerts, K. (1999), 'The Sustainability Radar – A Tool for the Innovation of Sustainable Products and Services', *Greener Management International*, 1999 (25), pp. 29–49.

Hockerts, K. (2003), 'Sustainability Innovations, Ecological and Social Entrepreneurship and the Management of Antagonistic Assets', Ph.D. Thesis, University St Gallen, Bamberg: Difo-Druck.

Hockerts, K. (2006a), 'CaféDirect: A Social Entrepreneurial Fair Trade Success', in F. Perrini (ed.) *The New Social Entrepreneurship, What Awaits Social Entrepreneurial Ventures*, Edward Elgar.

Hockerts, K. (2006b), 'Entrepreneurial Opportunity in Social Purpose Business Ventures', in J. Mair, J. Robertson and K. N. Hockerts (Eds) *Social Entrepreneurship*, Vol. 1: Palgrave Macmillan.

Hockerts, K. (2007), 'Social Entrepreneurship', in W. Visser, D. Matten, M. Pohl, & N. Tolhurst (Eds) *The A to Z of Corporate Social Responsibility: A Complete Guide to Concepts, Codes and Organisations: 422* Hoboken: John Wiley.

Jacobsson, S. and Johnson, A. (2000), 'The Diffusion of Renewable Energy Technology: An Analytical Framework and Key Issues for Research', *Energy Policy*, 28 (9), pp. 625–40.

Kamien, M. I. and Schwartz, N. L. (1982), *Market Structure and Innovation*, Cambridge University Press.

Kanter, R. M. (1999), 'From Spare Change to Real Change: The Social Sector as a Beta Site for Business Innovation', *Harvard Business Review*, 77 (3), pp. 123–32.

Keating, M. (1993), *The Earth Summit's Agenda for Change* Geneva: Centre for Our Common Future.

Ki-moon, B. and Gore, A. (2009), 'Green Growth is Essential to any Stimulus', *Financial Times*, 17 February 2009, p. 9.

Kolk, A. and Pinkse, J. (2004), 'Market Strategies for Climate Change', *European Management Journal*, 22 (3), pp. 304–14.

Kuckertz, A. and Wagner, M. (2010), 'The Influence of Sustainability Orientation on Entrepreneurial Intentions – Investigating the Role of Business Experience', *Journal of Business Venturing*, 25 (5), pp. 524–39.

Lal, A. and Israel, E. (2006), 'An Overview of Microfinance and the Environmental Sustainability of Smallholder Agriculture', *International Journal of Agricultural Resources, Governance and Ecology*, 5 (4), pp. 356–76.

Latacz-Lohmann, U. and Foster, C. (1997), 'From "Niche" to "Mainstream" – Strategies for Marketing Organic Food in Germany and the UK', *British Food Journal*, 99 (8), pp. 275–82.

Leifer, R. (2000), *Radical Innovation: How Mature Companies can Outsmart Upstarts* Harvard Business School Press.

Leifer, R. (2001), 'Implementing Radical Innovation in Mature Firms: The Role of Hubs', *The Academy of Management Executive* (1993–2005), pp. 102–13.

Lewis, J. I. and Wiser, R. H. (2007), 'Fostering a Renewable Energy Technology Industry: An International Comparison of Wind Industry Policy Support Mechanisms', *Energy Policy*, 35 (3), pp. 1844–57.

Light, P. (2006), 'Searching for Social Entrepreneurs: Who They Might be, Where They Might be Found, What They Do', Research on Social Entrepreneurship: Understanding and Contributing to an Emerging Field.

Lockie, S. (2008), 'Conversion or Co-option? The Implications of "Mainstreaming" for Producer and Consumer Agency within Fair Trade Networks', *Creating Food Futures: Trade, Ethics and the Environment*, 215.

Lovins, A. B., Lovins, L. H. and Hawken, P. (1999), *Natural Capitalism: Creating the Next Industrial Revolution*, Little Brown.

Mair, J. and Marti, I. (2006), 'Social Entrepreneurship Research: A Source of Explanation, Prediction and Delight', *Journal of World Business*, 41 (1), pp. 36–44.

Mair, J., Robinson, J. and Hockerts, K. (eds) (2006), *Social Entrepreneurship* (Vol. 1), New York: Palgrave Macmillan.

McAllister, S. (2004). 'Who is the Fairest of Them All?', *The Guardian*, 24.

McDonough, W. and Braungart, M. (2002a), *Cradle to Cradle: Remaking the Way We Make Things*, New York: North Point Press.

McDonough, W. and Braungart, M. (2002b), 'Design for the Triple Top Line: New Tools for Sustainable Commerce', *Corporate Environmental Strategy*, 9 (3), pp. 251–8.

Meadows, D., Meadows, D. L., Randers, J. and Behrens, W. (1971), *The Limits to Growth* New York: Universe Books.

Meadows, D. L. (1977), 'Alternatives to Growth – In Search for Sustainable Futures', Paper presented at the Proceedings of the 1975 Alternatives to Growth Conference, Woodlands, TX.

Meadows, D. L., Meadows, D. and Randers, J. (1991), *Beyond the Limits*, Post Mills: Chelsea Green Publishing.

Meijkamp, R. G. (2000), 'Changing Consumer Needs by Eco-efficient Services: An Empirical Study on Car-sharing', Unpublished Ph.D. Thesis, DfS Publication No. 3, Delft University of Technology, Delft.

Metcalfe, J. S. (1994), 'Evolutionary Economics and Technology Policy', *The Economic Journal*, pp. 931–44.

Morsing, M. and Schultz, M. (2006), 'Corporate Social Responsibility Communication: Stakeholder Information, Response and Involvement Strategies', *Business Ethics: A European Review*, 15 (4), pp. 323–38.

Nelson, R. R. and Winter, S. G. (1982), *An Evolutionary Theory of Economic Change* Belknap Press of Harvard University Press.

Nicholls, A. (2006), *Social Entrepreneurship: New Models of Sustainable Social Change*, Oxford University Press, USA.

Nicholls, A. and Opal, C. (2005), *Fair Trade: Market-Driven Ethical Consumption* Sage.

Norgaard, R. B. (1994), *Development Betrayed: The End of Progress and a Coevolutionary Revisioning of the Future*, London, New York: Routledge.

O'Reilly, C. A. I. and Tushman, M. (2004), 'The Ambidextrous Organization', *Harvard Business Review*, (April), pp. 74–81.

Pacheco, D., Dean, T. and Payne, D. (2009), 'Escaping the Green Prison: Entrepreneurship and the Creation of Opportunities for Sustainable Development', *Journal of Business Venturing*.

Parker, N. and O'Rourke, A. (2006), 'The Cleantech Venture Capital Report–2006', *Cleantech Venture Network LLC*.

Peattie, K. and Morley, A. (2008), 'Eight Paradoxes of the Social Enterprise Research Agenda', *Social Enterprise Journal*, 4 (2), pp. 91–107.

Perrini, F. (2006), *The New Social Entrepreneurship, What Awaits Social Entrepreneurial Ventures* Edward Elgar.

Prahalad, C. K. and Hammond, A. (2002a), 'Serving the World's Poor, Profitably', *Harvard Business Review*, 80 (9), pp. 48–57.

Prahalad, C. K. and Hart, S. L. (1999), *Strategies for the Bottom of the Pyramid: Creating Sustainable Development*.

Prahalad, C. K. and Hart, S. L. (2002b), 'The Fortune at the Bottom of the Pyramid', *Business and Strategy* (1st Quarter).

Rennings, K. (2000), 'Redefining Innovation – Eco-innovation Research and the Contribution from Ecological Economics', *Ecological Economics*, 32 (2), pp. 319–32.

Robins, N. and Roberts, S. (1997), 'Reaping the Benefits: Trade Opportunities for Developing Producers from Sustainable Consumption and Production', *Greener Management International*, Autumn 1997, 19, pp. 53–67.

Robinson, J., Mair, J. and Hockerts, K. (Eds) (2009), *International Perspectives on Social Entrepreneurship* (Vol. 1). New York: Palgrave Macmillan.

Russo, M. V. (2003), 'The Emergence of Sustainable Industries: Building on Natural Capital', *Strategic Management Journal*, pp. 317–31.

Schaltegger, S. (2002), 'A Framework for Ecopreneurship: Leading Bioneers and Environmental Managers to Ecopreneurship', *Greener Management International*, 2002 (38), pp. 45–58.

Schaltegger, S. and Wagner, M. (2008), 'Types of Sustainable Entrepreneurship and Conditions Sustainability Innovation: From Administration of a Technical Challenge to the Management Entrepreneurial Opportunity', in R. Wüstenhagen, J. Hamschmidt, S. Sharma and M. Starik (eds) *Sustainable Innovation and Entrepreneurship*, Cheltenham, UK: Edward Elgar.

Schumacher, E. F. (1974), *Small is Beautiful*, London: Abacus.

Schumpeter, J. A. (1942), *Capitalism, Socialism and Democracy*, Harper and Brothers.

Schumpeter, J. A. 1962 [1934], *The Theory of Economic Development*, New York: Oxford University Press.

Schönwandt, C. (2004), *Sustainable Entrepreneurship im Sektor erneuerbare, Energien*: Hampp.

Senge, P. and Carstedt, G. (2001), 'Innovating our Way to the Next Industrial Revolution', *Sloan Management Review*, 42 (2), pp. 24–39.

Seuring, S. (2004), 'Industrial Ecology, Life Cycles, Supply Chains: Differences and Interrelations', *Business Strategy and the Environment*, 13 (5), pp. 306–19.

Seuring, S. and Müller, M. (2008), 'From a Literature Review to a Conceptual Framework for Sustainable Supply Chain Management', *Journal of Cleaner Production*, 16, pp. 1699–1710.

Shane, S. and Venkataraman, S. (2000), 'The Promise of Entrepreneurship as a Field of Research', *Academy of Management Review*, 25 (1), pp. 217–27.

Siebenhüner, B., Dedeurwaerdere, T. and Brousseau, E. (2005), Introduction and Overview to the Special Issue on Biodiversity Conservation, Access and Benefit-sharing and Traditional Knowledge', *Ecological Economics*, 53(4), pp. 439–44.

Stenzel, T. and Frenzel, A. (2008), 'Regulating Technological change: The Strategic Reactions of Utility Companies towards Subsidy Policies in the German, Spanish and UK Electricity Markets', *Energy Policy*, 36, pp. 2645–57.

Stivers, R. (1976), *The Sustainable Society: Ethics and Economic Growth*, Philadelphia: Westminster Press.

Stock, G. N., Greis, N. P. and Fischer, W. A. (2002), Firm Size and Dynamic Technological Innovation', *Technovation*, 22 (9), pp. 537–49.

Teppo, T. and Wüstenhagen, R. (2009), 'Why Corporate Venture Capital Funds Fail – Evidence from the European Energy Industry', *Int. J. Entrepreneurship and Innovation Management*, forthcoming.

Truffer, B. and Dürrenberger, G. (1997), 'Outsider Initiatives in the Reconstruction of the Car: The Case of Light Weight Vehicle Milieus in Switzerland', *Science, Technology, & Human Values*, 22 (2), pp. 207–34.

Truffer, B., Markard, J. and Wüstenhagen, R. (2001), 'Eco-labeling of Electricity – Strategies and Tradeoffs in the Definition of Environmental Standards', *Energy Policy*, 29 (11), pp. 885–97.

Tushman, M. L. and Anderson, P. (1986), 'Technological Discontinuities and Organizational Environments', *Administrative Science Quarterly*, 31, pp. 439–65.

Utterback, J. M. (1994), *Mastering the Dynamics of Innovation. How Companies Can Seize Opportunities in the Face of Technological Change* Boston/MA: HBS Press.

Utterback, J. M. and Abernathy, W. J. (1975), 'A Dynamic Model of Product and Process Innovation', *Omega*, 3 (6), pp. 639–56.

Utterback, J. M. and Suárez, F. F. (1993), 'Innovation, Competition, and Industry Structure', *Research Policy*, 22, pp. 1–21.

Villiger, A. (2000), Von der Nische zum Massenmarkt, Strategien und Perspektiven für den Lebensmittelsektor. Wiesbaden: Deutscher Universitäts-Verlag.

Villiger, A., Wüstenhagen, R. and Meyer, A. (2000), Jenseits der Öko-Nische. Basel: Birkhäuser.

Warner, M. (2006), *Wal-Mart Eyes Organic Foods* New York Times (12 May 2006).

Warwick, D. (1997), 'Will Social Entrepreneurs Blossom or Hit Bottom?', *People Management*, 3 (20), p. 56.

Waters, R. (2008), 'Silicon Valley Warns Detroit Rescue Could Pull the Plug on Electric Cars', *Financial Times*, 15, 8 December 2008.

Webb, T. (2007), 'Strategy & Management: Unilever's CEO: Social Innovation and Sustainability the Only Game in Town', *Ethical Corporation*, No. 5 (2007).

Williamson, H. (2008), 'Not Everyone Happy in Germany's Solar Valley', *Financial Times*, 11 March 2008.

WWF (2006), *Living Planet Report 2006* Gland, Switzerland WWF.

Wüstenhagen, R. (1998), Greening Goliaths vs. Multiplying Davids, Pfade einer Coevolution ökologischer Massenmärkte und nachhaltiger Nischen. St Gallen: IWÖ-HSG.

Wüstenhagen, R. (2000), Ökostrom – Von der Nische zum Massenmarkt, Entwicklungsperspektiven und Marketingstrategien für eine zukunftsfähige Elektrizitätsbranche. Zürich: vdf.

Wüstenhagen, R., Hamschmidt, J., Sharma, S. and Starik, M. (Eds) (2008) *Sustainable Innovation and Entrepreneurship*, Cheltenham, UK; Northampton, MA, USA: Edward Elgar.

Wüstenhagen, R., Markard, J. and Truffer, B. (2003), 'Diffusion of Green Power Products in Switzerland', *Energy Policy*, 31, pp. 621–32.

York, J. and Venkataraman, S. (2010), 'The Entrepreneur-environment Nexus: Uncertainty, innovation, and Allocation', *Journal of Business Venturing*, 25 (5), pp. 449–63.

Zahra, S. A., Gedajlovic, E., Neubaum, D. O. and Shulman, J. M. (2009), 'A Typology of Social Entrepreneurs: Motives, Search Processes and Ethical Challenges', *Journal of Business Venturing*, doi:10.1016/j.jbusvent.2008.04.007 (in press).

Index